STUDIES IN CHRISTIAN HISTORY AND THOUGHT

Jerome and his Modern Interpreters

T0385271

Jerome and his Modern Interpreters

Perspectives on the Modern Critical Reception-History of St. Jerome's Corpus

Christopher Knight

Foreword by A.N.S. Lane

Copyright © Christopher Knight 2016

First published 2016 by Paternoster

Paternoster is an imprint of Authentic Media
PO Box 6326, Bletchley, Milton Keynes, MK1 9GG

www.authenticmedia.co.uk

The right of Michael Parsons to be identified as the Editor of this Work
has been asserted by him in accordance with the Copyright, Designs
and Patents Act 1988.

British Library Cataloguing in Publication Data A catalogue record for this
book is available from the British Library

ISBN 978-1-84227-969-6
978-1-78078-270-6 (e-book)

Printed and bound in Great Britain for Paternoster
by Print on Demand Worldwide

For Cherry

*As you were during my life you now live on
forever in my heart as my guide and my inspiration*

STUDIES IN CHRISTIAN HISTORY AND THOUGHT

Series Preface

This series complements the specialist series of Studies in Evangelical History and Thought and Studies in Baptist History and Thought for which Paternoster is becoming increasingly well known by offering works that cover the wider field of Christian history and thought. It encompasses accounts of Christian witness at various periods, studies of individual Christians and movements, and works which concern the relations of church and society through history, and the history of Christian thought.

The series includes monographs, revised dissertations and theses, and collections **of papers by individuals and groups. As well as 'free standing' volumes, works** on particular running themes are being commissioned; authors will be engaged for these from around the world and from a variety of Christian traditions.

A high academic standard combined with lively writing will commend the volumes in this series both to scholars and to a wider readership

Series Editors

Alan P.F. Sell	Visiting Professor at Acadia University Divinity College, Nova Scotia
D.W. Bebbington	University of Stirling, Stirling, Scotland
Clyde Binfield	Professor Associate in History, University of Sheffield, UK
Gerald Bray	Anglican Professor of Divinity, Beeson Divinity School, Samford University, Birmingham, Alabama, USA
Grayson Carter	Associate Professor of Church History, Fuller Theological Seminary SW, Phoenix, Arizona, USA
Dennis Ngien	Professor of Theology, Tyndale University College and Seminary, Founder of the Centre for Mentorship and Theological Reflection, Toronto, Canada

CONTENTS

Acknowledgements   ix
Foreword   xi
Abbreviations   xiii
Note on terminology   xv

Introduction   1
    The Debate   1
    Purpose of the Study   2
    Study Outline   5

Chapter 1   Studying Jerome   5
    Jerome as a Subject of Study   5
    Some Issues of Jerome Interpretation   6
    Central Focus/Methodology/Key Research Questions   8

Chapter 2   Jerome and Biblical Interpretation in
                the Early Church   11
    Introduction   11
    Union with Origen   14
    Divergence from Origen   18
    Augustine and Jerome   27

Chapter 3   Modern Jerome Scholarship (1880-1965)   39
    Introduction   39
    The Landscape of Modern Jerome Study   39
    1880-1914   44
    1915-1939   46
    1940-1955   48
    1956-1965   53

Chapter 4   Modern Jerome Scholarship (1966-1990)   69
    Introduction   69
    1966-1974   69
    1975-1990   88

Chapter 5   Modern Jerome Scholarship (1991-2009)   106
   Introduction   106
   1991-2001   106
   2002-2006   115
   2007-2009   129

Chapter 6   Modern Jerome Scholarship (2010-2014)   151
   Introduction   151
   2010-2011   151
   2012-2013   173
   2014   198

Chapter 7   Conclusion   202

Bibliography   208
   Secondary Sources   209

Indexes
   Author Index   209
   Names Index   234
   Jerome Index   237
   Scripture Index   239
   Subject Index   240

ACKNOWLEDGEMENTS

This book is a substantial revision and updated version of my Master of Theology (MTh) dissertation which was successfully submitted and defended at the London School of Theology in April 2014. During my graduate studies at LST (2012-2014), I was fortunate enough to have been supervised by Professor Tony Lane (Professor of Historical Theology) and Dr. Matthew Knell (Lecturer in Church History and Historical Theology). Both taught me how to achieve clarity and precision in patristic enquiry and how to come to better understand Jerome's world. Professor Richard Price (Professor of the History of Christianity, Heythrop College, London) and Dr. Graham McFarlane (Vice-Principal, Academic, LST) examined the thesis and offered much helpful criticism as well as encouragement to publish it as a monograph.

For my early introduction to the study of theology I wish to acknowledge the Rev. Graham Shaw (sometime Rector of St. Giles—the-Abbot, Farnborough, Kent), who kindly invited me into his homes, both in Walton-on-the-Hill, Surrey and in Isleworth, Middlesex to discuss the finer points of Christian doctrine and the philosophy of religion. Graham's two SCM books, God in our Hands and Power and Authority in the Early Church, were the catalyst for my desire to go on and to research further, the various developments and trajectories of the early Church, whilst also teaching me how the best of theological enquiry can be achieved.

For assisting me in the location and retrieval of key journal articles and patristic texts I should like to thank Alan Linfield (LST Librarian until September 2013) and his successor, Graham Massey. I also wish to acknowledge the guidance and support given to me by Robert Greenhalgh (Portman Rare Books), Christopher Zealley (St. Philip's books), and Nicholas Polkingthorne (Sevenoaks Bookshop), all of whom searched for me both important out-of-print and new Jerome publications. For typing my work so diligently and suffering my constant corrections so bravely, I should like to express my thanks to Clara Badu Amoah. Without Clara's help the final manuscript for publication would never have reached completion. Thanks are also due to the Rev. Canon Michael Insley (my one-time colleague in the Rochester Theological Society) for allowing me the loan of his unpublished MPhil dissertation, 'Aspects of Pagan/Christian Relations in the First Four Centuries of the Christian Era, with Special Reference to Origen.' Michael retired to Dorset in 2013 where Origen has now been safely restored to Michael's new library in Dorchester.

From a very early stage in my research Dr. Michael Parsons (previously Paternoster Commissioning Editor) expressed a keen interest in adding my Jerome work to **Paternoster's** *Studies in Christian History and Thought* monograph series, and throughout the subsequent revision of my thesis he offered encouragement and wise counsel to make the study suitable for publication. I am indebted to Michael for agreeing to typeset my work and for compiling the indexes. I shall always remember our meetings at London's Paddington Station, sharing lunch at Starbucks to discuss the progress of my Jerome project.

Finally, I wish to record the love and support given to me throughout my teaching academic career by my late beloved wife, Cherry, who tragically died from breast cancer in 2008. They say that God moves in mysterious ways and that surely explains why my thesis examiners came to choose 2nd April, 2014, for my viva at LST. For it was on 2nd April, 1977, that I married Cherry at Camberwell Registry Office, South-East London; and thus, my thesis was examined and successfully defended on what would have been our thirty-seventh wedding anniversary (truly miraculous). Before her death, Cherry told me to go on and continue with my research career in Theology and it was entirely due to her that I pursued postgraduate studies at LST. Thus, it is in loving memory of her that I dedicate my Jerome study to Cherry.

Christopher Knight, 2016

FOREWORD

Jerome is an enigmatic figure. He is one of the four great doctors of the Western Church and his translation of the Bible reigned for over a millennium. Yet at the same time his personal flaws are evident to all. His letters are more revealing of his character than was prudent. In his polemics he could be coarse, vulgar and malicious, as well as petty and personal. He was constantly falling out with people and engaging them in controversy. 'Apart from a small circle of friendly woman ascetics and blindly devoted adherents, hardly anyone succeeded in living continuously at peace with Jerome.'[1] Yet despite all of this his achievements were such that he could not be forgotten. He has certainly not been forgotten by modern patristic scholarship, as can be seen by a cursory glance at the bibliography of this book.

One of the first tasks for those who wish to make a thorough study of a historical figure is, of course, to familiarise oneself with what has been written about them. Those wishing to study Jerome now have available to them a thorough survey of all that has been written in English or translated into English since 1880. As well as expounding the literature, Chris Knight does not hesitate to point to the defects that he sees in past studies, though, of course, without descending to the coarseness, vulgarity or malice of Jerome, who was once described as having a rare gift for invective.

Jerome famously encouraged the mother of a celibate virgin with these words: 'Why, mother, do you grudge your daughter her virginity? . . . Are you angry with her because she has chosen to be married to a king [Christ] rather than to a soldier? She has conferred on you a high privilege: you are now the mother-in-law of God!'[2] I cannot offer such an exalted title to Chris Knight but through this book he has perhaps earned himself the more modest accolade of 'midwife to the reception of Jerome studies'.

Tony Lane
London School of Theology

---

[1] Hans von Campenhausen, *The Fathers of the Latin Church* (London: A. & C. Black, 1964), 169-70.
[2] *Letter* 22:20 (NPNF[2] 6:30).

ABBREVIATIONS

AAR	American Academy of Religion Series
ACC	Ancient Christian Commentary on Scripture Series (Ed. T.C. Oden. Downers Grove, InterVarsity Press)
Adv. Jov.	*Adversus Iovinianum* (Jerome)
AV	Authorised Version
BJRL	*Bulletin of the John Rylands Library*
CBQ	*Catholic Biblical Quarterly*
CCSL	*Corpus Christianorum Series Latina*
CJ	*Classical Journal*
CSEL	*Corpus Scriptorum Ecclesiasticorum Latinorum* (Vienna, 1866-)
C.V.	*Contra Vigilantium* (Jerome)
CWE	*Collected Works of Erasmus* (Toronto: University of Toronto Press, 1974-)
DCB	*A Dictionary of Christian Biography* (Ed. W. Smith and H. Wace; London: William Clowes and Sons, 1887, 1880)
De vir.ill.	*De viris illustribus* (Jerome)
EH	*Ecclesiastical History* (Eusebius)
ExpT	*Expository Times*
FOTC	Fathers of the Church Series (CUA Press, 1947-)
Heb. Quest.	*Hebrew Questions* (Jerome)
HSCP	*Harvard Studies in Classical Philology*
HTR	*Harvard Theological Review*
IBS	*Irish Biblical Studies*
ITQ	*Irish Theological Quarterly*
JBL	*Journal of Biblical Literature*
JECS	*Journal of Early Christian Studies*
JMEMS	*Journal of Medieval and Early Modern Studies*
JTS	*Journal of Theological Studies*
LXX	Septuagint (Greek OT)
MSS	Manuscripts
NPNF	*Nicene and Post-Nicene Fathers*, Series 2 (Ed. P. Schaff and H. Wace, Grand Rapids: Eerdmans, vol 3 and vol 6)
NT	New Testament
OCM	Oxford Classical Monographs
OECS	Oxford Early Christian Studies
OECT	Oxford Early Christian Texts
OHM	Oxford Historical Monographs
OL	Old Latin Version
OT	Old Testament
OTM	Oxford Theological Monographs
PIBA	*Proceedings of the Irish Biblical Association*

PL	*Patrologia Latina of J.G. Migne, Patrologine cursus complete* (Paris, 1844-1864)
PRR	*Presbyterian and Reformed Review*
PStud	*Patristic Studies*
Rec Th	*Recherches De Theologie Ancienna Et Medievale*
StP	*Studia Patristica* (Papers presented at the Oxford Patristic Conferences. Formerly Berlin: Akademie — Verlag; Oxford: Pergamon; Kalamazoo: Cistercian Publications; Leuven: Peeters)
TCJ	*The Classical Journal*
ThS	*Theological Studies*
VC	*Vigiliae Christianae*

For the purpose of this study a particular definition of the term 'Late Antiquity' is used as stated below:

The focus of attention for religion in Late Antiquity remains the fourth century C.E. until the seventh century, but the religious practices themselves reach back further into the religious traditions of the Hellenistic and Roman periods... Religious practice and religious affiliation formed an important part of Late Antique life. Late Antiquity witnessed the growth and development of major religious movements while at the same time witnessing the transformation of ancient religious traditions under the influence of a plethora of multi-cultural social and political changes.

R. Valantasis, 'Introduction', in R. Valantasis (ed.), *Religions of Late Antiquity in Practice* (Princeton: Princeton University Press, 2000), 4-5.

....

Jerome was a great scholar and linguist but also a tortured personality, seeing enemies in even the slightest criticism, tart toward his friends and savage toward his supposed enemies; his grovelling acceptance of ecclesiastical authority and his fear of being tainted with even the slightest suspicion of heterodoxy led him to deny his own debt to Origen and to engage in machinations against Bishop John of Jerusalem and to break off an almost lifelong friendship with Rufinus of Aquilaia during the Origenist controversies. He was and remains a controversial figure.

J.F. Kelly, *The Concise Dictionary of Early Christianity* (Collegeville: Liturgical Press, 1993), 85.

Jerome is chief among the theologians of the Latin world and he is in fact almost the only writer we have who deserves the name of theologian.

Letter (Ep. 335) from Erasmus to Pope Leo X; P.S. Allen (ed.); *Erasmi Epiostolae* II (Oxford, 1910), 86.

Throughout the patristic period and most of the medieval period, theology was the study of the Sacred Page. To comment on Scripture was to do theology, and to do theology was to comment on the Sacred Page.

F.J. Matera., *God's Saving Grace* (Grand Rapids: Eerdmans, 2012), xiii.

Introduction

This study examines the critical reception given by some modern scholars (writing in English or whose scholarship is available in English language translation) working between 1880 and 2014 to selected texts/writings drawn from Jerome's corpus. The investigation attempts to shed light on the origins and development of Jerome's exegetical principles and practice (including his hermeneutic), the composition of his commentaries, homilies, letters and polemics as well as how these affected his relations with his associates and contemporaries. By looking at these aspects of Jerome's work through the lens of modern Jerome scholarship the study also illuminates the changing directions and perspectives of Jerome studies and offers a fresh interpretation and understanding of secondary judgements on selected features of the canon of this early Doctor of the Church. In asking whether or not modern scholars have read Jerome's ancient works anew, more critically and with greater empathy than previous, the various secondary reassessments are, for the most part, critiqued using a particular theoretical model constructed by the present author, namely, the 'McGuckin-Freeman' thesis. This model argues (in part) that Jerome's reputation as an exegete is over-stressed (at least, if we look for originality) and that his writings display a failure to think creatively beyond Nicene orthodoxy. The study will argue that Jerome's exegesis is a prime example of patristic commentating both at its best and at its most problematic. It will show how his over-reliance on tradition—especially his theological formula, *Hebraica Veritas*, as well as his sometimes dubious interpretative tactics—caused much opposition, but that despite these faults Jerome's *oeuvre* holds many important insights into the development of the nascent early Christian Church, the formation of Christian identity and the development of Christian orthodoxy (e.g., the debate over the small 's' nature of sin, the fall of humanity, the Trinity and transfiguration).

The Debate

Much has been written about St. Jerome (c. 347-420). To say the least, his reputation as a biblical scholar and exegete has had a divided history, such are the vicissitudes of scholarly fashion. The last twenty years have witnessed an increasing interest in the study of the modern critical reception history of Jerome. This has led historians and theologians to reassess not only Jerome's life and legacy but also his patristic corpus (i.e., his writings and translations produced from the early 370s to 420). Here scholars have offered sometimes quite trenchant arguments about Jerome's *oeuvre* arguing on the one hand that his celebrity as an exegete has been over-stressed (at least if we look for originality)[1] or that

---

[1] See J. McGuckin, *A-Z of Patristic Theology* (London: SCM, 2005), 188.

1

his corpus displays a lack of creativity.[2] Meanwhile others have simply followed convention acknowledging Jerome as the 'founder of the tradition of biblical scholarship and translation in the Western church'[3] and the 'prince of Christian biblical scholars' whose 'works became a fertile ground for the labours of subsequent exegetes'.[4] It has been against this background that both Jerome's character and scholarship have continued to be disputed by modern scholars.

There has been a growing dynamic within modern Jerome scholarship to evaluate Jerome's pioneering attempts to articulate the nature and the sources of authority of the scriptures alongside and against the Jewish and Graeco-Roman world-views. It should be stressed that the steady growth in Jerome scholarship has been due predominantly to the increasing engagement by scholars researching in the field of the history of the early Church.[5] This has resulted in a greater focus upon studying Jerome's corpus from the point of view of its place and worth (or otherwise) in the context of the new Christian literacy, the new biblical scholarship, and the emerging ascetic movement of the fourth and fifth centuries.

Purpose of the Study

By critiquing scholars on their handling of aspects of Jerome's works, this study seeks to examine and elucidate many of the views and claims that have been made by members of the academy critical of certain features of Jerome's canon. The study will chart the changing scholarly directions made and perspectives offered by historians and theologians on selected texts/writings of Jerome both before and after J.N.D. Kelly's seminal study *Jerome* (1975),[6] which provided the first modern, comprehensive treatment in English of the saint. These old and new directions and perspectives in modern Jerome scholarship will be identified, described and examined in as far as Jerome's exegesis (Vulgate Bible and OT/NT commentaries) and other writings (homilies, letters, translations and polemics)

---

[2] See C. Freeman, *A New History of Early Christianity* (New Haven: Yale University Press, 2009), 276.

[3] See A. Grafton and M. Williams, *Christianity and the Transformation of the Book: Origen, Eusebius, and the Library of Caesarea* (Cambridge: Belknap Press, Harvard University Press, 2006), xv.

[4] D. Brown, *Vir Trilinguis: A Study in the Biblical Exegesis of Saint Jerome* (Kampen: Kok Pharos, 1992), 200. One scholar who has gone beyond convention is Christopher Rengers, *The 33 Doctors of The Church* (Rockford: Tan, 2000), 83, who has labelled Jerome 'The Father of Biblical Science'.

[5] For example, see M. Vessey, 'Literature, Patristics, Early Christian Writing', in S.A. Harvey and D.G. Hunter (eds), *The Oxford Handbook of Early Christian Studies* (Oxford: OUP, 2008), 42-65; J. Lossi, *The Early Church: History and Memory* (London: T&T. Clark, 2010); R. Letham, *Through Western Eyes – Eastern Orthodoxy: A Reformed Perspective* (Fearn: Mentor/Christian Focus, 2007); J.H. Lynch, *Early Christianity: A Brief History* (New York: OUP, 2010); Pope Benedict XVI, *The Fathers of the Church: From Clement to Augustine of Hippo* (ed. J.T. Leenhard; Grand Rapids: Eerdmans, 2009); M. Ludlow, *The Early Church* (London: Tauris, 2009).

[6] J.N.D. Kelly, *Jerome* (London: Duckworth, 1975).

cannot be understood apart from a sense of the relative continuity of development of exegesis in the patristic period.[7]

Jerome's modern interpreters (see chapters 2-6 below) have adopted numerous styles of approach to studying the many different aspects to his works, highlighting in particular Jerome's monastic ideals and scholasticism; his innovatory exegesis, translation and biblical interpretation; his unification of philological and theological traditions; his transformation of the literary form of commentary into an authoritative genre; Jerome's asceticism; his personal and theological conflicts with his associates and contemporaries; and, Jerome's role in patronage in late antiquity. This scholarship reflects both past and current concerns over Jerome's *oeuvre*. Whilst scholars have sought to contextualize Jerome's corpus for many years in an attempt to understand the nature of the interpretative hermeneutic at the heart of Jerome's exegesis, it is only very recently that they have undertaken closer critical examination of Jerome's works.[8]

Study Outline

The study is divided into seven chapters. Chapter 1 examines Jerome as a subject of study and seeks to ascertain just how far scholars have attempted to develop a balanced approach to studying Jerome. There then follows a description of some issues of Jerome interpretation looking at particular problems and perspectives that have characterized modern Jerome studies. Finally, the study's research methodology and the key research questions to be addressed are outlined.

Chapter 2 focuses upon Jerome's role and place in biblical interpretation during the period of the early Church, looking in particular at how scholars have viewed Jerome against the background of the conflict between Paganism and Christianity in the fourth century, and Jerome's translation work in relation to classical, Christian and Jewish traditions of interpretation as influenced by the socio-historical structure of Roman society. Attention is also drawn to how early modern scholars have concentrated on the figure of Jerome as an ascetic writer. How Jerome was first influenced by Origen but then diverged from Origen's exegetical principles and methods forms a key part of this chapter, as does Jerome's relation to Augustine.

Chapter 3 investigates the way in which modern Jerome scholarship (1880-1965) advanced as a result of the changing 'revolution in theological method' of

---

[7] I.e., the era of the Fathers of the Church from Clement of Rome to John of Damascus. For a fuller discussion of patristic exegetical practice, see: H.O. Old, *The Reading and Preaching of the Scriptures in the Worship of the Christian Church*. vol. 2. *The Patristic Age* (Grand Rapids: Eerdmans, 1998), chapters 1, 3, 5; and A.J. Hauser and D.F. Watson (eds), *A History of Biblical Interpretation*. vol. 1. *The Ancient Period* (Grand Rapids: Eerdmans, 2003), chapters 1, 3, 4, 12, 13 and 14.

[8] See, for example, S. Rebenich, *Jerome* (Abingdon: Routledge, 2002); M.H. Williams, *The Monk and the Book: Jerome and the Making of Christian Scholarship* (Chicago: University of Chicago Press, 2006); A. Cain and J. Lössl (eds), *Jerome of Stridon: His Life, Writings and Legacy* (Farnham: Ashgate 2009).

the late nineteenth century in Britain, itself occasioned by developments in German historical scholarship which started in the field of secular ancient history. Here scholars made their advances by offering new directions and perspectives on Jerome's exegesis, hermeneutic and theology, and his relations with contemporary associates and opponents. From these developments we gain a clearer insight into Jerome's place in the Latin patristic tradition.

Chapters 4-6 examine the period between 1966-2014 and illumine the gradual renaissance in Jerome scholarship that appeared during these years, emphasizing a number of revisionist secondary reassessments of particular features of Jerome's corpus.

Chapter 7 brings together the information from the previous sections to form a conclusion about the state of the modern critical reception-history of selected texts/writings drawn from Jerome's corpus as it is now seen by scholars of the early twenty-first century.

Chapter 1

Studying Jerome

Jerome as a Subject of Study

Mark Vessey, one of the leading Jerome scholars of his generation, has written:

> Released from the theological discipline of patristics, the writings of the Church Fathers have in recent decades become the common property of students of early Christianity, late antiquity and the classical tradition. In principle, they are now no more (nor less) than sources, documents and literary texts like any others from their time and milieu. Yet even now, when considered in relation to the longer history of Western 'textual' and 'literary' practices and institutions, the collective *oeuvre* of Latin-writing clerics, monks and freelance ascetics of the Later Roman Empire may seem to occupy a place of special, if not canonical importance.[9]

Part of that 'collective *oeuvre* of Latin-writing clerics, monks and freelance ascetics of the Later Roman Empire' belongs, of course, to St. Jerome.

According to Maurice Wiles, 'Jerome's rightful claim to a place among the most distinguished figures in the history of the early church depends primarily on his outstanding achievement as a biblical scholar.'[10] Here, Wiles contextualizes both Jerome's high ranking in, and contribution to, patristic Christian theology. However, whilst Jerome has enjoyed some considerable attention from scholars there have also been certain limitations to this coverage from the academy.[11]

Generally regarded to have been one of the great figures of patristic exegesis, Jerome's life was long and has been well documented. Rebenich has been especially helpful in synthesizing the product of our knowledge on Jerome which modern scholarship has revealed.[12] Thus, scholars have gradually searched for the minutiae of Jerome so that every conceivable aspect of Jerome's writings and

---

[9] M. Vessey, *Latin Christian Writers in Late Antiquity and their Texts* (Aldershot: Ashgate, 2005), vii.

[10] M. Wiles, 'Church Fathers' in J. Bowden (ed.), *Christianity: The Complete Guide* (London: Continuum, 2005), 243-65 (257).

[11] For example, whilst there have been several specialist journal essay case-studies of Jerome published since the mid-twentieth century only six comprehensive books devoted to Jerome's life and works written in English have so far appeared. See F.X. Murphy (ed.), *A Monument to St. Jerome* (New York: Sheed and Ward, 1952); Kelly, *Jerome*; P. Rousseau, *Ascetics, Authority and the Church in the Age of Jerome and Cassian* (OHM, OUP, 1978). Rebenich, *Jerome*; E.J. Hahnenberg, *Bible Maker: Jerome – The Fascinating Story of the Author of the Latin Vulgate* (Bloomington: Author House, 2005); Williams, *The Monk and the Book*.

[12] See Rebenich, *Jerome*, ix-x. For a complete listing and description of which works of Jerome are/are not translated into English, see Rebenich, *Jerome*, 139-44.

interactions can be examined and discussed. However, the problem for scholars has been not only the sheer volume of material available but also rather the problem of interpretation.

Against this background, Jerome's critics have had to be cautious in their attempts to assess Jerome's *oeuvre* balancing good judgement with a clear insight into a complex individual.[13] González, at least, seems to strike the right balance, commenting, 'At first glance, Jerome appeared to be an extremely insensitive person whose only concern was his own prestige. But in truth he was very different from what he appeared, and his rigid façade hid a sensitive spirit.'[14]

The search for the minutiae of Jerome has led scholars to attempt to reveal Jerome's theological project in all of its diversity: biblical exegesis, Catholic theology and the ascetic-ideal. Jerome's theological and exegetical work has been seen by one Catholic theologian as being 'rooted in a kind of resourcement; that is, a historical retrieval of the original structure of God's revelation in the Church';[15] whilst for another, 'the ascetic Jerome is to be found in those of his writings characterized by a strong fear of human sexuality, which clearly echoed the vivid accounts of the Egyptian desert fathers' Temptations in the Wilderness'.[16] So these three pervasive recurring elements (biblical exegesis, Catholic theology, the ascetic-ideal), which helped shape Jerome's corpus have to be seen and understood as acting in convergence.

Some Issues of Jerome Interpretation

Whilst there is some clarity about the chronological sequence of the Jerome corpus,[17] one of the main issues of Jerome interpretation centres upon how its importance (or otherwise) rests upon its relation to the Church's traditional canonical understanding of its sacred Scriptures. So, did Jerome's works offer a distinct interpretation of the Church's Scripture? Pivotal to this argument is Jerome's locus within the Christian West. Burnett believes 'it was Jerome's Latin biblical

---

[13] See J.L. González, *The Story of Christianity* (New York: Harper One, 2010), 1.233.

[14] González, *The Story of Christianity*, 1.238.

[15] This is to be seen in the solemn truth expressed memorably by Jerome, 'Ignorance of the Scriptures is ignorance of Christ,' Jerome, *Commentary on Isaiah 1:1*, quoted in Second Vatican Council, *Dei Verbum, Dogmatic Constitution on Divine Revelation* (Nov. 18, 1965) 25, in D.P. Béchard, SJ (ed.), *The Scripture Documents: An Anthology of Official Catholic Teachings* (Collegeville: Liturgical, 2002) 30, as cited by S. Hahn, *Covenant and Communion: The Biblical Theology of Pope Benedict XVI* (London: DLT, 2010), note 23, 20.

[16] M. Ludlow, *The Early Church*, 160. For a discussion of Jerome's sexual awkwardness and his insistence that his women disciples all had to adopt a life of extreme asceticism (strict self-denial as a spiritual discipline), so as to 'become a man (vir)', see L. Swidler, *Jesus was a Feminist* (Lanham: Sheed and Ward, 2007), 264.

[17] See Rebenich, *Jerome*, 3-59.

translation (the Vulgate) that introduced a new genre of biblical commentary to Western Europe which soon superseded earlier exegetical formats'.[18]

Here it is important to understand that 'Jewish and Christian approaches to biblical exegesis (the careful analysis and interpretation of texts) share a common ancestry: the self-interpretation evident within the Hebrew Bible/Old Testament itself.'[19] What Jerome may have achieved was that bridge between what Burnett has described as 'ancient Christian exegesis (early apologetic and polemical uses of Scripture) and Origen's (c. 186–255) allegorical exegesis which had led to scriptural and theological controversy in late antiquity', and Augustine of Hippo's (354–430) exegesis which had 'set forth exegetical guidelines that included the concept of multiple meanings in Scripture, the authority of the Church's Rule of Faith and the use of lucid scriptural passages in wrestling the meaning from obscure ones'.[20] Just how Jerome may have achieved this has been explained by Brown who cites Jerome's skill as an eclectic scholar in utilizing the best exegetical interpretations available to him from the Antiochene, Alexandrian and Jewish schools.[21] Of all modern Jerome scholars it is perhaps Brown who has been most keen to acknowledge the contributions of Jerome's writings (e.g., to our understanding of the relations between Christians and Jews and to the state of biblical exegesis in the West in the fourth century).[22]

---

[18] C.C. Burnett, 'The Interpretation of the Bible before the Modern Period', in M.J. Gorman (ed.), *Scripture: An Ecumenical Introduction to the Bible and its Interpretation* (Peabody: Hendrickson, 2005), 133-45 (138).

[19] Burnett, 'The Interpretation of the Bible', 133.

[20] Burnett, 'The Interpretation of the Bible', 136-38. For a discussion of the pervasive and decisive role that the 'Rule of Faith' played in the post-New Testament church, see A.J. Kostenberger and Michael J. Kruger (eds), *The Heresy of Orthodoxy* (Nottingham: Apollos, 2010), 54.

[21] Brown, *Vir Trilinguis*, 199. Here it is important to note that the old Antioch versus Alexandria, 'literal' versus 'allegorical', contrast has not been totally abolished in modern scholarship, but made much more subtle. Moreover, Jerome never kept to 'literal-historical' exegesis alone. His exegesis shows just as much typology (interpreting OT texts to relate to Christ or the Church) as other patristic commentators. And his debt to Origen in particular is famous, even if he firmly dissociated himself from Origen's doctrinal 'heresies'. For a full discussion of how the categories 'literal', 'allegorical' and 'typological' may be seen as inadequate (when applied to patristic exegesis), see F.M. Young, *Biblical Exegesis and the Formation of Christian Culture* (Cambridge: CUP, 1997), ch. 9, especially 201-202. Young notes (201): 'To approach patristic exegesis through the "senses" of scripture is not as straightforward or as illuminating as has generally been supposed. Each "sense" is itself multivalent…Besides, this whole approach to describing patristic exegesis overlooks the question of how NT texts were interpreted. Here these categories scarcely apply. It would seem that a more complex approach is needed for describing the process of biblical interpretation in the early church.' For the most recent exposition of the development of Young's understanding of patristic exegesis, see F. Young, *Exegesis and Theology in Early Christianity* (Farnham: Ashgate, 2012), particularly ch. 5.

[22] Brown, *Vir Trilinguis*, 201.

We shall see below in chapters 2–6 that both Burnett and Brown have been challenged by a number of scholars in their interpretations of the value of Jerome's corpus. Here one of the major problems for scholars has been, as Fortin notes, the way in which 'the sacred writers themselves deliberately concealed certain doctrines from the multitude but without ever lying about anything (*nonnulla obtegunt, sed nulla mentiuntur*)'.[23] And that said, as we shall see in chapter 2 below, there is, for example, evidence of a Origen–Jerome–Augustine disjunction over the presentation of divine truth.[24]

One final issue of Jerome interpretation—one which will be fully explored in this study (see chapters 3-6)—relates to the division amongst modern scholars over the question of whether or not Jerome was a 'theologian'. Here particular caution is required when we critique scholars' secondary judgements on this aspect of Jerome's life and work. As Tom Wright has observed:

> By the end of the second century some of the greatest Christian minds were making the study and exposition of Scripture, both the ancient Israelite texts and the more recent Greek ones written by Jesus' followers, a major part of their work in pursuing the mission of the church and strengthening it against persecution without and controversy within. Though we often think of subsequent writers like Origen, Chrysostom, Jerome and Augustine—and, much later, Aquinas, Luther and Calvin—as great 'theologians', they would almost certainly have seen themselves first and foremost as Bible teachers. Indeed, the modern distinction between 'theology' and 'biblical studies' would never have occurred to any of them.[25]

Central Focus/Methodology/Key Research Questions

We have seen how Jerome as a subject of study and certain issues of Jerome interpretation have drawn scholars to debate the place and worth of Jerome's corpus both in the life of the early Church and in the Western culture more generally. We shall see that whilst the early modern study of Jerome from 1880 to

---

[23] E.F. Fortin, 'Augustine and the Problem of Christian Rhetoric (1974)', in R.L. Enos and R. Thompson et al (eds), *The Rhetoric of St. Augustine of Hippo: De Doctrina Christiana and the Search for a Distinctly Christian Rhetoric* (Waco: Baylor University Press, 2008) 219-33 (230-31).

[24] See Fortin, 'Augustine and the Problem', 231-32. Here Fortin cites Augustine's angry reaction to Jerome's commentary on chapter two of the Letter to the Galatians (in which Paul gives an account of his famous altercation with Peter at Antioch, whereby Paul publicly reproached Peter for refusing to eat with the Gentiles) where, 'Following Origen's interpretation, Jerome had attempted to remove any trace of dissension among the apostles by contending that Peter was not guilty of wrong-doing but had merely sought to accommodate himself to the prejudices of the Judaizers,' For two of the best balanced treatments of the patristic interpretation (Jerome versus Augustine) of the Antioch episode in Galatians, see M. Wiles, *The Divine Apostle: The Interpretation of St. Paul's Epistles* in the Early Church (Cambridge: CUP, 1967), 22n.1, 25 and J.B. Lightfoot, *Epistle of St. Paul to the Galatians* (London: Macmillan, 1890), 128-32.

[25] T. Wright, *Scripture and the Authority of God* (London: SPCK, 2005), 2.

1965 (see chapter 3 below) has largely concentrated on examining Jerome's works in their socio-historical context, more recent scholarship post-1965 (see chapters 4-6 below) has contested much of this formative work and has instead looked at Jerome's intellectual powers as one of the principal criterion for judging Jerome's oeuvre.

The central focus of this study sets the modern scholarly reception-history of selected texts/writings drawn from Jerome's corpus against what I have termed the 'McGuckin–Freeman' thesis, namely, that Jerome's reputation as an exegete is exaggerated (at least if we look for originality) and his writings display a failure to think creatively beyond Nicene orthodoxy. McGuckin states:

> Whilst Jerome was one of the most important argumentative *ascetics* of the fourth century and perhaps the most important biblical scholar of the early Western church... his reputation as exegete is over-stressed (at least if we look for originality).[26]

Freeman states:

> He proved too pedantic a thinker ever to engage fully with the intricacies of Greek philosophy. One can see from his writings how he clung to Nicene orthodoxy but failed to think creatively beyond it.[27] ... Jerome never showed any genuine intellectual creativity or had the self-confidence to develop his own theology.[28]

The term 'Nicene orthodoxy' may be understood as encapsulating both the central tenets of the Nicene Creed (as formulated by the Council of Nicaea, 325) and the later Nicene formulation adopted at the Council of Constantinople (381). It was at the Council of Nicaea (325) that the full deity of Christ was affirmed in response to Arius (c. 260-336). Arius had held that the Son is the one through whom the Father created the universe, but nonetheless he is only a creature made out of nothing, not God.[29] At the Council of Nicaea (325) 'significant theological declarations were made regarding the Greek word *ousia* (meaning 'being' or 'essence'): the Son was from the *ousia* of the Father and the Son possessed the same being or essence (*homoousios*) as the Father,' and the Council 'condemned anyone who taught that the Son was "of a different *hypostasis* or *ousia* from the Father".' By the Council of Constantinople (381) 'the Trinity was designated as one in *ousia* (essence) and three in *hypostasis*' (person).' Thus, 'the Father and the Son were "of the same being," and were '"one" almighty, all powerful, good, wise and holy God, who is Father, Son and Holy Spirit.'[30]

[26] McGuckin, *A-Z*, 187-88.
[27] Freeman, *A New History*, 276.
[28] Freeman, *A New History*, 284.
[29] For the full history of the Arian controversy, see R.P.C. Hanson, *The Search for the Christian Doctrine of God: The Arian Controversy 318-381* (Edinburgh: T&T Clark, 1988).
[30] See C. Beckwith, 'Athanasius,' in B.G. Green (ed.), *Shapers of Christian Orthodoxy: Engaging with early and medieval theologians* (Nottingham: Apollos, 2010), 153-89 (159-61, 160n.22).

Whilst the research for this enquiry is largely located within the field of modern Jerome studies (specifically secondary judgements on Jerome) the present study also draws upon the landscape of Graeco-Roman history of the fourth and fifth centuries as well as biblical interpretation in the early Church during the period of the Latin Fathers. Focusing upon selected texts/writings written by Jerome that are available in English, English translation and collected critical editions, and which are covered by modern Jerome scholarship, this study addresses a number of key questions:

(1)   How and why have scholars disagreed on the issue of how this difficult but important writer should be read and interpreted? (e.g., scholars have been divided by implicit but often unquestioned assumptions about the best way to approach Jerome's texts/writings) See chapters 1-6.

(2)   How far can it be agreed that Jerome's linguistic and his scripture hermeneutic lie at the root of his ideas that sometimes scandalized the patristic Church? See chapters 2-6.

(3)   To what extent has modern Jerome scholarship attempted to re-contextualize the way we should read Jerome? See chapters 2-6.

(4)   Have revisionist scholars now succeeded in establishing Jerome as the pre-eminent Doctor of the Church? See chapters 4-7.

(5)   How important a part did Jerome's exegesis play in helping to create, develop and maintain a Christian identity in the pluralistic ancient world? See chapters 2-7.

(6)   Are there any points of continuity/discontinuity between the exegesis of Origen and Jerome, and of the theologies of Origen, Jerome and Augustine, and how have these particularly affected the modern critical reception of Jerome? See chapters 2-6.

(7)   Today, what consensus is there that 'Jerome's significance in the history of Christian exegesis remains tied to the fact that he radically changed direction from Origen?'[31] See chapters 2-6.

(8)   Does modern Jerome scholarship by and large offer a corrective to the 'McGuckin-Freeman' view that Jerome's reputation as an exegete is exaggerated (at least if we look for originality) and his writings lack creativity and, instead, show Jerome's corpus to have been of major importance for the understanding of the Church in the Catholic tradition of the West? See chapters 2-7.

---

[31] C. Kannengiesser, 'Biblical Interpretation in the Early Church,' in D.K. McKim (ed.), *Dictionary of Major Biblical Interpreters* (Downers Grove: IVP, 2007), 1-13 (9).

Chapter 2

Jerome and Biblical Interpretation in the Early Church

Introduction

What was the fundamental theological style (i.e., exegetical principles and practice) that characterized Jerome? What and who were the key influences upon Jerome's particular form of biblical exegesis? Jerome in all of his multiple facets has long been regarded as one of the most puzzling and yet compelling exegetes of the Western tradition writing during the period of the early Church due to the sometimes complex nature of his thought and writings. So, how best can this early biblical scholar be understood?

In this chapter (as well as in chapters 3-4) we shall see how modern scholars came to make their secondary judgements on features of Jerome's *oeuvre* largely upon the basis of examining and contesting Jerome's originality and creativity as an exegete, and Jerome's intellectual abilities as a scriptural theologian. Interestingly, these are the same criteria that modern interpreters of Origen and Augustine have long debated.

Whilst the present enquiry is structured around a critique of secondary judgements about Jerome (i.e., how modern scholars have approached and handled Jerome and what their scholarship has said of his corpus) the purpose of this chapter is to set out the landscape of Jerome's biblical work (i.e., the various areas of Jerome's theological activity), the distinctive features of which modern scholars (1880-2014) have sought engagement with (see chapters 3-6). Thus, this chapter will act as a foundation for all that follows in the subsequent four chapters of our study.

In order to understand the modern critical reception given by scholars to selected tests/writings drawn from Jerome's *oeuvre* it is important to first identify and locate more fully the nature of Jerome's exegetical interests, principles and practice—not only in the historical setting of late antiquity but also, more specifically, in the context of Jerome's principal predecessor (Origen) and principal contemporary (Augustine). By examining the differences and agreements between Jerome, Origen and Augustine we will be able to see how modern scholars have come to judge not only the quality of Jerome's thought and scholarship but also how successful Jerome was in keeping his theology firmly (in those moments where he clearly expressed it) engaged with the times and situations he faced. Furthermore, it is by reading Jerome in conversation with Origen and Augustine, as well as in conversation with important developments in Christian doctrine during the fourth and early fifth centuries, that we can

11

better appreciate why modern scholars have returned to Jerome in order to re-cover and re-articulate his central exegetical insights with renewed vigour.

We will now examine the issue of Jerome and biblical interpretation in the early Church in the context of theology in the patristic era. It was during this period that Jerome and other early theologians (Irenaeus, Tertullian, Origen), as well as the Apostolic Fathers (Clement of Rome, Ignatius of Antioch) and Christian apologists (Athenagoras, Justin Martyr, Clement of Alexandria) 'participated in the path to orthodoxy (the search for Christian identity)'.[1] This triumvirate of early theologians, Apostolic Fathers, and Christian apologists 'would engage in theological debates, which would be of signal importance in the gradual and dialectical path to Christian orthodoxy in the patristic age'.[2] Whilst Jerome's role in these developments would be pivotal (being marked by a large output of theological works) it was, according to Crouzel, probably Origen who was the most prolific author in all of antiquity.[3] Within Jerome's writings, it is important to study his train of thought and to understand perhaps why he argued the way he did—in short, to grasp his logic. First, however, we should establish Jerome's contribution to the path to orthodoxy.

Jerome's contribution to the search for Christian identity included his key influence on 'the debate over the formation of what is now often described as the canon of Scripture where he fought against those attempts to harmonize the Gospels causing the text to move still further from the original.'[4]

Scholars are emphatic that the essence of Jerome's contribution to the path to orthodoxy was his ability to rid the early Church of the confusion that had too long beset it over the question of the canon of Scripture.

If we see the path to orthodoxy to have been the search for Christian identity, it is also important to understand just how the Church Fathers shaped orthodox theology. As Casiday comments:

---

[1] See R.J. Plantinga, T.R. Thompson and M.D. Lundberg, *An Introduction to Christian Theology* (Cambridge: CUP, 2010), 422-35. Plantinga et al strangely omit Augustine from their list of early theologians and Christian apologists who contributed to the path to orthodoxy. For a description of the developing understanding of 'orthodoxy' in the early Church, see H.E.W. Turner, *The Pattern of Christian Truth: A Study in the Relations between Orthodoxy and Heresy in the Early Church* (London: Mowbray, 1954).

[2] Plantinga, *Christian Theology*, 435.

[3] H. Crouzel, *Origen: The Life and Thought of the First Great Theologian* (tr., A.S. Worrall; San Francisco: Harper and Row, 1989), 37. Crouzel's nomination of Origen as probably the most prolific author in all of antiquity might be debatable considering Augustine's prodigious output of writings, generally considered as standing second only to the Apostle Paul in their impact on the Church.

[4] G.R. Evans, 'Jerome', in G.R. Evans (ed.) *The First Christian Theologians* (Oxford: Blackwell, 2004), 234-37 (235). Evans notes (235-36) that 'the new standard version of the Gospels was mainly produced by Jerome from 382-385 in Rome'.

It is a characteristic of Orthodox Christianity that its theological history is conceived of very broadly and valued very highly; in the eyes of many commentators, Orthodoxy quite simply is patristic Christianity.[5]

Here Hall notes:

Jerome's task was to participate in the exposition of patristic doctrine, a task which was necessarily theological and would involve Jerome in controversy, most especially over Origenist heresy, whereby Jerome opposed some of Origen's more provocative speculations such as his denial of the resurrection of the flesh, denial that the Son could see the Father and affirmation that souls exist as rational spirits before being imprisoned in the body.[6]

These two citations may be seen as particularly relevant providing as they do a framework for our understanding of the scholarly debate over Jerome's orthodoxy (see below and chapters 3-6).

Crucially, Jerome's patristic corpus would be produced in the age of Nicene doctrine (re-affirmed by the Council of Constantinople, 381) in which 'the Nicene Creed served as a wise and saving symbol of divine grace which sufficed for the perfect knowledge and confirmation of piety'.[7] Jerome's works therefore took place in the age of the Councils which themselves were charged with defending the faith. It was an age that sought conformity to established, dominant, official religious doctrine. However, it would be many years before Jerome would be described as one of the 'sacred Fathers'[8] or 'masters of the faith'.[9]

---

[5] A. Casiday, 'Church Fathers and the Shaping of Orthodox theology', in M.B. Cunningham and E. Theokritoff (eds), *The Cambridge Companion to Orthodox Christian Theology* (Cambridge: CUP, 2008), 167-87 (167).

[6] S.G. Hall, *Doctrine and Practice in the Early Church* (London: SPCK, 2005), 185-86. For a discussion of how the Church Fathers shaped Eastern Orthodox theology, see A. Schemann, *The Historical Road of Eastern Orthodoxy* (London: Harvill, 1963), 62-197; A. Lossky, *The Mystical Theology of the Eastern Church* (London: James Clarke, 1957), 44-90.

[7] See Casiday, 'Church Fathers', 176. Interestingly, in one of the most recent treatments of the patristic tradition of exegesis, Jerome is not included in Rob Lister's catalogue of Pro-Nicene theologians (Athanasius, Gregory of Nazianzus, Gregory of Nyssa, Augustine and Cyril of Alexandria). See R. Lister, *God is Impassible and Impassioned: Toward a Theology of Divine Emotion* (Nottingham: IVP/Apollos, 2012), 81-90.

[8] Casiday, 'Church Fathers', 179. Here, Casiday tells us that the term 'sacred Fathers' (which, besides Jerome, was also applied to Ambrose and Augustine) was in use during the period of the Carolingian Renaissance of the ninth century and Photius the Great (c. 820-893).

[9] C.A. Hall, *Learning Theology with the Church Fathers* (Downers Grove: IVP, 2002), 9. Hall's 'masters of the faith' are the eight great Doctors of the Church: Athanasius, John Chrysostom, Basil the Great and Gregory of Nazianzus in the East and Ambrose, Augustine, Jerome and Gregory the Great in the West.

Jerome's stature as a 'sacred Father' / 'master of the faith' does not, and should not, obscure the fact that he sometimes veered away from the then dominant tradition of patristic biblical interpretation. As O'Keefe and Reno observe:

> . . .in antiquity, the Septuagint was the dominant form of the Old Testament, both in the Jewish communities throughout the Mediterranean and in the nascent Christian community. In fact, whenever the New Testament writings quote the Old Testament, it is the Septuagint form that is used. What is fascinating, however, is that this dominance, while largely unquestioned (Jerome, who produced the dominant Latin translation of the Old Testament is the exception, for he used the Hebrew rather than the Greek as the basis for his translation), did not foreclose a telling concern about just which words were the right ones.[10]

What is important therefore, is how Jerome viewed the structure and logic of the early Christian interpretations of Scripture in late antiquity, bearing in mind that he had a particular concern about just which words were the right ones, for these interpretations were considered foundational to the path to orthodoxy and the development of Christianity.

Union with Origen

In his early years, Jerome was an ardent admirer of Origen of Alexandria (185-253).[11] Origen was a Christian philosopher-theologian and, like Jerome, was devoted to the scholarly use of Scripture. This was a commonality amongst the Church Fathers. Stylianopoulos notes:

> The Church Fathers were notable scholars of the Bible in their own right. Although the focus of their study of the Bible was the pastoral edification of God's people, the patristic tradition also demonstrates rich intellectual curiosity in pursuing biblical and theological knowledge for the sake of truth. The Fathers used contemporary methodologies derived from the Greek and Jewish traditions, properly qualified by theological criteria, to explore the depths of scripture. Convinced of the universal significance of the truth of scripture and the universal mission of the

---

[10] J.J. O'Keefe and R.R. Reno, *Sanctified Vision: An Introduction to Early Christian Interpretation of the Bible* (Baltimore: John Hopkins University Press, 2005), 50.

[11] As late as 393 Jerome was still seen as the 'Latin Origen'. See Rebenich, *Jerome*, 44. It is significant that in his *Lives of Illustrious Men* (392/393), Jerome devoted the largest entry to Origen, commenting upon his 'immortal genius' as an assiduous student of the Holy Scriptures. See NPNF² 3:373-74. For a discussion of the influence Origen had on later theologians in the Latin West (including Jerome and Augustine), specifically the ways in which theologians often appropriated Origen's exegesis in their own work, see T.P. Scheck, *Origen and the History of Justification: The Legacy of Origen's Commentary on Romans* (Notre Dame: Notre Dame Press, 2008), 64, 86-128; J.W. Trigg, *Origen: The Bible and Philosophy in the Third-Century Church* (London: SCM, 1985), 244-58.

Church, they did not shrink from engaging the contemporary intellectual world philosophically and philologically.[12]

However, some caution is required here. Surely, it should not be assumed or asserted (as Stylianopoulos does) that all of the Church Fathers were adept at engaging the contemporary intellectual world philosophically and philologically. For example, as we have already seen, Freeman (2009) has contested that Jerome proved too pedantic a thinker ever to engage fully with the intricacies of Greek philosophy.

Up until 393, the date from which Jerome opposed Origen's system of beliefs known as Origenism (which included the belief that the repentance of the devil and demons could be predicted, and allegorized Paradise so as to deny its historicity)[13] Jerome strove to absorb Origen's hermeneutical perspective. As Hall observes:

> He (Jerome) left a huge legacy of careful biblical scholarship, in which the influence of the great Origen pervades, not only in erudite learning, but in allegorical interpretation. Jerome himself thus became one of the principal purveyors of the spiritual exegesis of Origen to the West, where his influence as a biblical interpreter came to prevail.[14]

Origen's hermeneutical perspective involved the arrangement of different versions of the Bible in columns across the pages of a Codex. This was a new way of studying the biblical text. Here, Lössl has illustrated Origen's innovating work as a biblical textual critic and translator:

> Sorely aware that early Christians as well as Greek-speaking Jews were working with a Greek translation of the Hebrew scriptures, he compiled a synopsis which listed versions of the text and its main translations at the time. Because of its six columns, this work was called Hexapla.[15]

---

[12] T.G. Stylianopoulos, 'Scripture and tradition in the Church', in *Companion to Orthodox Christian Theology*, 21-34 (28-29). For a more recent account of how the early Christian thinkers developed some of the most important doctrines of Christianity, often by means of a sophisticated method of philosophical thinking that was separate from their emphasis on the inerrancy of Scripture, see G. Karamanolis, *The Philosophy of Early Christianity* (Durham: Acumen, 2013).

[13] Hall, *Doctrine*, 185-86.

[14] Hall, *Doctrine*, 187. Here Hall notes that 'Gregory the Great and Bernard of Clairvaux, who read the Song of Songs as a love affair between the soul and its Saviour, had learnt their spirituality through the commentary of Origen that Jerome made available'. Carol Harrison, *Beauty and Revelation in the Thought of Saint Augustine* (Oxford: Carendon, 1992), 89-90, has commented: 'Allegorical exegesis is...an attempt to seek the spiritual depth of the literal text, to find the significance of the sign, the meaning of the word. Thus, in the Latin tradition...*allegoria* is the usual term for the spiritual sense'—and, for St. Jerome '"*allegoriam, id est intelligentiam spirutalem*"' [Jerome, *In Amos*, 2.4.].

[15] Lössl, *Early Church*, 112.

It would be the *Hexapla* (an elaborate tool for textual criticism of the Hebrew Scriptures in which parallel columns made possible critical comparisons previously unenvisioned) which would prepare the way for Jerome's exegetical work. Jerome would develop his use of the Hexapla in his translations and commentaries having studied the original at Caesarea.[16] And, as an example of Jerome's absorption of Origen's hermeneutical perspective, Grafton and Williams note that 'A passage of Jerome's commentary on Galatians. . . was a virtual paraphrase of Origen's work on the same letter.'[17]

Origen's *Hexalpa*—'the first real critical text of the Old Testament prepared in the 220s[18]—would be of significance since it would later allow Jerome 'to turn to the Hebrew texts to translate the Old Testament into Latin, having concluded that they were superior to the Septuagint'.[19] Thus, the Origen-Jerome nexus is observed through the engagement by both exegetes in biblical textual criticism. Moreover, both Origen and Jerome 'appreciated that manuscripts differed from one another and that some were better than others, because certain texts could be shown to contain more original and thus more authentic readings of the text'.[20] Jerome came to believe that the Septuagint was not only unreliable (by mistranslating the Hebrew) but also incorporated dubious texts that even Jews did not accept as 'sacred'.[21] However, this did not prevent Jerome from using Origen's *Hexapla* (without acknowledgment) in writing his commentaries on the Hebrew prophets.

Whilst Origen and Jerome were united in their belief that for exegesis to take place it was important to have a sound text of scripture, and both shared the aim of establishing and promoting the Bible's literal, historical sense (the original language of scripture), Jerome did not always follow Origen. For example, Brown suggests that whilst Jerome 'adopted a number of Origen's allegorical interpretations in specific instances', he was 'sometimes inconsistent in following Origen's stated principles of exegesis'.[22] Origen's stated principles of exegesis (*On First Principles*) were based upon his belief that biblical texts have three levels of meaning corresponding to the three levels of human existence (spirit, soul and body).[23]

---

[16] A. Grafton and M. Williams, *Christianity and the Transformation of the Book* (Cambridge: Belknap Press, Harvard University Press, 2006), 91.

[17] Grafton and Williams, *Christianity*, 95.

[18] R. Williams, 'Origen', in *First Christian*, 132-42 (133).

[19] R.N. Soulen, *Sacred Scripture* (Louisville: WJKP, 2009), 27.

[20] Soulen, *Sacred Scripture*, 31.

[21] Soulen, *Sacred Scripture*, 32.

[22] D. Brown, 'Vir Trilinguis – A Study in the Biblical Exegesis of St. Jerome' (M. Litt thesis, University of Oxford, 1989), ii.

[23] Williams, '*Origen*', 135. Origen's *On First Principles* was a foundational work—the first attempt in history at a systematic Christian theology, establishing Origen as a figure crucial to the whole development of Christian thought and doctrine. See Origen, *On First Principles* (Foreword by J.C. Cavadini; Notre Dame: Ave Maria, 2013), Brian E. Daley, *Origen's De Principiis*: A Guide to the Principles of Christian

In contrast to Origen, Jerome's work was undertaken in the context of Jerome using a critical historical-grammatical exegesis to find the primary meaning of the text Jerome's pursuit of an honest quest for truth.[24]

Jerome's early assimilation of Origen's hermeneutical perspective occurred between 380 and 392. Both exegetes agreed the Bible to be an inspired text and although the early hermeneutical proximity of Origen and Jerome to the biblical text is important we find that later on in Jerome's career there were to be tensions resulting from some of Origen's ideas being judged by Jerome to be outside the boundaries of orthodoxy. For example, at the end of the fourth century, Origen's exegesis of Isaiah 6 came to be seen as one of his 'most grievous mistakes'.[25] In an early polemic against Origen written in 396, Jerome denounced this exegesis (for questioning the resurrection of the body for his belief that the devil might repent and for declaring that the seraphim mentioned by the prophet are the divine Son and the Holy Ghost) as 'Origen's worst deviation of orthodoxy'.

In the course of the debate about Origen's orthodoxy in the last decade of the fourth century, the latter's exegesis of Isaiah, was a 'central issue' for Jerome.[26] We shall see below how Jerome's initial, early union with Origen, was further fractured by what Jerome saw as Origen's additional deviations from orthodox

---

Scriptural Interpretation,' in J. Petruccione (ed.), *Nova et Vetera: Patristic Studies in Honor of Thomas Patrick Halton* (Washington: Catholic University of America Press, 1998), 3-21, and for a fuller discussion for Origen's hermeneutics of Scripture, see M. Ludlow, 'Anatomy: Investigating the Body of Texts in Origen and Gregory of Nyssa,' in S. Douglas and M. Ludlow (eds), *Reading the Church Fathers* (London: T&T Clark, 2011), 132-53, E.D. Lauro, *The Soul and Spirit of Scripture within Origen's Exegesis* (Boston: Brill, 2005).

[24] For a discussion of the relationship between the Bible and hermeneutics in church Orthodoxy, see T. Sytlianopoulos, *The New Testament—An Orthodox Perspective*, (Brookline: Holy Cross Orthodox, 1997), 1.76; R. Letham, *Through Western Eyes*, 192-93; and A.N.S. Lane, 'Scripture, Tradition and Church: An Historical Survey', *Vox Evangelica* 9 (1975), 37-55. Elsewhere, Matthew Bates has pointed to some of the perils faced by exegetes during the period of the early Church: 'For many ancient expositors, giving attention to the bare letter of scripture alone (i.e., the "literal sense") was brought to lead a hermeneutical death—if not also to a more fearsome eternal demise—whereas unpacking the "spiritual sense" thought life for the expositor and his audience.' Here Bates finds the letter/spirit antithesis is on display in Origen *Princ.* 4.1.6; *Cels* 7.20; Athanasius *First Epistle to Serapion* 8; Didymus the Blind, *The Holy Spirit* 57; Gregory of Nyssa *Against Eunomius* 3.5; and Augustine *Doctr. chr.* 3.5. See M. Bates, *The Hermeneutics of the Apostolic Proclamation* (Waco: Baylor University Press, 2012), 161n.144. For a useful introduction to Scripture as Divine Mystery, see D.H. Williams, *Evangelicals and Tradition: The Formative Influences of the Early Church* (Milton Keynes: Paternoster, 2005), 70-79. For the classic translation of Origen's *Against Celsus*, see H. Chadwick, *Origen: Contra Celsum* (Cambridge: CUP, 1986).

[25] A. Furst, 'Jerome Keeping Silent: Origen and his Exegesis of Isaiah' in Cain and Lossl, (eds.), *Jerome*, 141-52 (151).

[26] Fürst, 'Jerome', 151.

and because of these deviations, 'Origen would fail to be accorded the same Church approval given to Jerome'.[27]

Between 380 and 393, Jerome took a variety of exegetical ideas from Origen. As we have seen, Jerome was initially attracted to the allegorical method of Origen, although later he severely criticised it.[28]

Jerome's early view of Origen is found in one of Jerome's letters where he extols Origen's labours to interpret scriptures through both exegesis and public oration in churches.[29] Jerome's early praise of Origen also extended to Origen's three 'senses of Scripture' (corresponding to the text's body, soul and spirit) as expressed in Origen's *On First Principles* (4.2.4).[30] Significantly, spiritual exegesis is common to both Origen and Jerome, further confirming the early Origen-Jerome union. Both Origen and Jerome believed that the 'body' of Scripture is the literal sense (the historical-grammatical meaning of the text) that is obvious on an initial reading. Both took the Bible itself as the authority for their exegetical method.

Finally, Jerome's early union with Origen was marked by a mutual interest in philology. Origen's *Hexapla* was a philological work and Jerome's corpus would also involve numerous philological exercises.[31] Despite this, it should be noted here that there is no correspondence whatsoever between Origen's three 'Senses of Scripture' (body, soul, and spirit) and Jerome's 'science of Scripture' (philology, exegesis, and translation).

Divergence from Origen

We shall now look at how Jerome's early union with Origen began to break as a result of developments post-Nicaea. Jerome's divergence from Origen would be the product of discord over Arianism and Origenism. The differences of interpretation regarding the origin of Christ between the Arians and Origenists followed on from the Trinitarian controversy sparked by the teachings of Arius (c. 250–c. 336).[32]

---

27 C.A. Hall, *Reading Scripture With The Church Fathers* (Downers Grove: IVP, 1998). Hall notes that Origen did not receive the designation of 'church father' because the consensus of the church judged certain of his ideas to be outside the boundaries of orthodoxy.

28 See G. Bray, *Biblical Interpretation: Past and Present* (Downers Grove: IVP, 1996), 91. For a critique of evangelical criticism of Origen's use of the allegorical method to undercut the Bible's meaning, see B. Litfin, 'Origen', in B.G. Green (ed.), *Shapers of Christian Orthodoxy: Engaging with early and medieval theologians* (Nottingham: Apollos, 2010), 108-52.

29 Jerome, *Letter* 84.8 (Litfin 'Origen', 109).

30 Litfin, 'Origen', 125-26.

31 For a discussion of these philological works, see Cain and Lössl (eds), *Jerome*, Part II.

32 W.H. Frend, *The Early Church: From the beginnings to 461* (London: SCM, 1982), 140. For a full discussion of the origins and development of Arianism, see R.C.

According to Ferguson, doctrinal controversy 'threatened the unity of the church and with it, Constantine's goal of harmony in the empire, since Arianism raised fundamental questions about the definition of the church and of the deity it worshipped'.[33] However, on this point not all scholars are agreed. For example, Ayres has argued that it is misleading to assume that these controversies were about the 'divinity of Christ' if that implies either a priori agreement about the meaning of ascribing divinity to the Son, or if it means that these controversies focused on this specific question.[34]

On 22 May, 359 the Trinitarian debate was concluded by a new creed—the Fourth Creed of Sirmium or 'Dated Creed', 'which respectfully rejected the use of ousia ('being' or 'essence') to refer to God, and said that the Son was 'like the Father who begat him, according to Scriptures', [35] and whilst the 'Dated Creed' 'defined the Son as like (*Homoios*) the Father, it did not add the Origenist 'in all things'.[36]

What effect did this rejection of Origenism have upon Jerome's divergence from Origen? Here our concern is with Jerome's position (360-380) just before the statement of the Council of Constantinople (381), which evoked Nicaea 'as a theological precedent which established its authority as a definitive rule of orthodox identity'.[37] Until 360 church councils had been concerned with 'the nature and redemptive activity of God, Arius had been condemned at Nicaea and Arianism had become the archetypal heresy by denying the saving divinity of Christ, the very essence of Christian identity'.[38]

We can now say of Jerome that before embarking upon his own corpus (from 380) he had witnessed an important codification of Christian orthodoxy (the 'Dated Creed') whilst Origenism had failed to impact in the theological debate over the shaping of trinitarian doctrine and language. As Theokritoff suggests:

Gregg and D.E. Groh, *Early Arianism: A View of Salvation* (London: SCM, 1981); R.C. Gregg (ed.), *Arianism: Historical and Theological Reassessments* (September 5-10, 1983, Oxford) (Philadelphia Patristic Foundation, 1985).

[33] E. Ferguson, *Church History* (Grand Rapids: Zondervan, 2005), 1.187.

[34] L. Ayres, *Nicaea and its Legacy: An Approach to Fourth Century Trinitarian Theology* (Oxford: OUP, 2004), 14.

[35] Hall, *Doctrine*, 146.

[36] Frend, *Early Church*, 157.

[37] J.R. Lyman, 'Arius and Arians', in Harvey and Hunter (eds), *Handbook of Early Christian Studies*, 237-57 (237). However, Ayres has seriously questioned the idea that the Council of Nicaea, 'in one decision and in one pronouncement, identified for the Church a term (*Homoousios*) that secured its Trinitarian and Christological beliefs against heresy and established a foundation for subsequent Christian thought'— Ayres, *Nicaea and its Legacy*, 11.

[38] Lyman, 'Arius and Arians', 237-38.

Origen's failure to distinguish clearly between generation from God the Father and creation by him allowed the Arians to claim that the Son was some sort of superior creature: was not the Father the origin of both? [39]

Whilst the first phase in Jerome's divergence from Origen was the discord over Arianism and Origenism, the second phase would be a growing discord over the question of Christian cosmological doctrine. Here Liftin has noted how 'every aspect of Origen's thought celebrated the cosmic mystery that the Word became flesh to lead the souls of the faithful back to the divine'.[40] Both Origen and Jerome upheld Christian piety but they differed fundamentally in their use and understanding of cosmological doctrine. This would illustrate another example of Jerome's radical change of direction from Origen.

Origen's concern with Christian cosmological doctrine is somewhat ironic as in later life (249-254) he was persecuted and tortured by the pagan Emperor Decius for refusing to deny his Christian faith.[41] But Origen was a Christian Platonist and, according to Platonist philosophy, 'the philosopher's eternal soul (unlike the body in which it is trapped) retains an affinity for the world above, and so naturally gravitates in that direction'.[42] This is well demonstrated by Litfin who has suggested that in Origen's version of Christian life, 'the believer must long for Christ as a deer pants for water, embarking on an intense, lifelong pursuit after the heavenly "logos"'.[43] And, thus, for Origen, the role of the exegesis was to explain the great cosmic drama of fall and return, by showing how salvation is 'the descent of God into our fallen estate through Jesus Christ, and the ascent of our souls back to God through participation in his Son'. [44]

---

[39] E. Theokritoff, '"Creator and Creation', in *Companion to Orthodox Christian Theology*, 63-77 (64). For a wider discussion of Jerome's position during the Origenist controversy, see Williams, *The Monk*, 97-102, 179-80, 238, 244-45, 284-94; E.A. Clark, *The Origenist Controversy: The Cultural Construction of an Early Christian Debate* (Princeton: Princeton University Press, 1992), 11-42, 121-51, 159-93. Clark's judgment on Jerome (he was shrewd and acerbic) reinforces the conventional wisdom regarding Jerome's character.

[40] Litfin, 'Origen', 108.

[41] Litfin, 'Origen'. 118. Origen was also an opponent of the pagan critic Celsus. See Origen, *Against Celsus* 7.44., as cited by Litfin 'Origen', 133n.65.

[42] Litfin, 'Origen', 123. On the nature of Origen's Platonism, see M. Insley, 'Aspects of Pagan/Christian Relations in the First Four Centuries of the Christian Era with Special Reference to Origen: A Study in Church Growth' (MPhil thesis, University of Nottingham, 1985), 127-28.

[43] Litfin, 'Origen', 123-24.

[44] Litfin, 'Origen', 124-25. For a fuller account of Origen's understanding and interpretation of cosmological prinicples, see Karamanolis, *Philosophy*, 62, 69, 89-97, 102, 104, 110-11, 113, 115-16. Karamanolis writes: 'Origen in his *On Principles* speaks of the sensible world but also of souls, angels and spirits. For Origen, God is the creator of both the ineligible (incorporeal) and the sensible (corporeal) realms. This is why in *On Principles*, he proceeds from the intelligible principles (God) to their effects (first intelligible entities, then sensible entities)' (62).

Another insight to Jerome's use and understanding of cosmology is to be found in his private letters. Here Jerome writes as a contemporary of Augustine of Hippo (354-430) who, according to Theokritoff, 'dominated (together with his spiritual heirs) Western cosmology up to modern times'.[45] Jerome's letters 'are a textual source from which we are able to reconstruct his view of pagan-Christian relations'.[46] But, do they display Jerome as the 'brave fighter against Origenist heresy'[47] and an opponent of Origen's Christian cosmological doctrine? Was Origen's view of the unapproachability of God (interestingly pursued and taught by the Cappodocian Father Basil the Great, 330-379, as the 'incomprehensibility of God')[48] anathema to Jerome?

Amongst modern Jerome scholars, Rebenich is especially critical of Jerome's weakness as a theologian and his failure to understand the new theological developments of the East:

> He preferred polemical simplification to subtle distinction, doctrinal conservation to fresh ideas, rhetorical display to substantial argument, learned allusions to discursive ramifications, dogmatic reassurance to intellectual receptivity, and authoritative decision to independent judgement.[49]

We note here how Rebenich's view that Jerome preferred doctrinal conservation to fresh ideas, closely parallels Freeman's (2009) claim that in his writings Jerome clung to Nicene orthodoxy but failed to think creatively beyond it.

Jerome's Letter 15 to Damasus, written during Jerome's stay at Maronia in c. 376/377 (his retreat in the 'desert of Chalcis') is very important, for whilst 'clearly addressing the acrimonious disputes about the triune Godhead which still convulsed the East and divided it from the West, and which were reflected in the tragic schism fragmenting the Christian community at Antioch',[50] it sees Jerome defending his position on the Trinity and well before he had come to fully adhere to Nicene orthodoxy. In addition, the particular Christian cosmological doctrine adhered to by Jerome at this time is clearly evident, with Jerome's use of the metaphorical use of 'sun' and 'stars' to denote the changing

---

[45] Theokritoff, 'Creator', 65.
[46] M.R. Salzman, 'Pagans and Christians' in *Handbook of Early Christian Studies*, 186-202 (197). For the most recent account of the ideas, rituals and beliefs that Christians and pagans shared in Late Antiquity, see C.P. Jones, *Between Pagan And Christian* (Cambridge: Harvard University Press, 2014).
[47] Rebenich, *Jerome*, ix.
[48] R. Letham, 'The Three Cappadocians', in *Shapers*, 190-234 (192). Here Basil made the distinction between the being of God (who God is), which is beyond our capacity to know, and the actions of God, which we can know. On Basil, see also A. Meredith, *The Cappadocians* (London: Geoffrey Chapman, 1995), 19-38; A. Louth, 'The Cappadocians,' in F. Young, L. Ayres and A. Louth (eds), *The Cambridge History Of Early Christian Literature* (Cambridge: CUP, 2004), 289-301, esp. 291-95; S.M. Hildebrand, *Basil of Caesarea* (Grand Rapids: Baker, 2014).
[49] Rebenich, *Jerome*, 71.
[50] Kelly, *Jerome*, 52.

fortunes of Christian belief in the West and East. The following extract from Letter 15 illumines Jerome's early position (post-Nicaea):

> Now the sun of righteousness is rising in the west; in the east, Lucifer, who had fallen, has set his throne above the stars . . . Just now, I am sorry to say, after the Nicene Creed, and the decree of Alexandria, in which the west has joined, the Campenses, that Arian brood, demanded that I, a Roman, accept the novel formula of three *hypostaseis*.... ... There is only one nature of God, and this alone truly exists..... God alone, who is eternal, that is, who has no beginning, truly bears the name of 'essence'. Whoever declares that there are three, that is three *hypostaseis*, tries under the name of piety to allege that there are three natures. And if this is true, why are we severed by walls from Arius, when in faithlessness we are united? . . . Let us be satisfied to speak of one substance and of three subsisting persons: perfect, equal, coeternal.[51]

Here, as Kelly has rightly noted, 'Jerome is perfectly ready to affirm that there are three subsistent persons in the consubstantial Trinity, but he cannot swallow "hypostasis" as synonymous with "person".'[52]

Letter 15 was written before Jerome first learnt of Origen's writings.[53] Whilst Origen's thought celebrated the cosmic mystery that the Word became flesh to lead the souls of the faithful back to the divine we see, in contrast, in Letter 15, how Jerome's metaphorical use of cosmological references (the sun, the stars, the angels, the sky, the earth and the seas) might have been applied specifically in the context of illustrating the bringing of Christian doctrinal enlightenment. However, critics might see it as no more than just one of Jerome's many masterpieces of propaganda,[54] and it is unclear just how far Jerome was writing or wishing to advance, and affirm here, the cause of Nicene orthodoxy. Much later, in 394-397, Jerome would face condemnation from Augustine for failing to define his orthodoxy and 'his relation to the Origenist tradition' more clearly'.[55]

---

[51] Jerome *Ep.* 15 to Damasus, as cited by Rebenich, *Jerome,* 72-74. Elsewhere, Prestige has made a similar observation of *Ep.* 15 noting how Jerome's Letter 'had violently denounced the formula of three hypostaseis and branded it as Arian.' See G.L. Prestige, *God in Patristic Thought* (London: SPCK, 1969), 237.

[52] Kelly, *Jerome,* 53.

[53] Rebenich, *Jerome,* 17.

[54] Rebenich views Letter 15 as such an example: 'At the Councils of Nicaea (325) and Alexandria (362), Arius and Arianism were condemned. However, at Alexandria, the *"homoousios"* formula of Nicaea was reinforced (the Son is of one substance [*ousia*] with the Father), and the Origenist distinction of the *hypostaseis* of the three divine persons was admitted. Although the synod gave rise to new controversies Jerome is exaggerating the novelty of the "three *hypostaseis*" theology to please Damasus'. See Rebenich, *Jerome,* 181n.29.

[55] Rebenich, *Jerome,* 45-46. On Origen's understanding of orthodoxy, see M. Edwards, *Catholicity and Heresy in the Early Church* (Farnham: Ashgate, 2009), ch 4. Edwards writes: 'Both the manhood of Christ and his divinity were more strongly affirmed by Origen than by any theologian before him, but he could make disciples of the majority only when traditional sanctions against the preaching of two gods or two

We shall shortly continue the discussion about Jerome's divergence from Origen but, at this juncture, it is important for us to understand the spirituality of Jerome in the years just before his embarkation upon his patristic corpus, because it is this aspect of Jerome's life, perhaps more than any other, which helps explain his break with Origen in 393.

Whilst it is mostly in his later letters after 380 that we find examples of Jerome's reference to pagan literature,[56] it is in the early letters (372-379) that we find Jerome describing his hermit life[57] with Jerome using much pathos in conveying his departure from worldly things.[58] This period of mental and spiritual turmoil saw Jerome 'uneasily aware of the fascination pagan literature, his beloved library, and the intellectual delights that Antioch had for him'.[59] It is in these early letters (e.g., Letter 4, written at Antioch) that we find Jerome talking of his search for the ascetic life.[60]

There seems some evidence that Jerome may have been inspired in his ascetic-life and living in the desert by the life of John the Baptist. Although asceticism and the hermit-life in the desert are themes that run through the patristic tradition,[61] Jerome's imitation of John the Baptist's asceticism/life in the desert is signalled in several ways. For example, for Jerome—like John the Baptist—asceticism is not for monks alone but for all the faithful.[62] Thus, Jerome reflected on John's trip to the desert:

John the Baptist had a saintly mother and his father was a priest; but neither his mother's love nor his father's wealth could prevail upon him to live in his parents'

---

sons had been obviated. In the interim he had suffered so much obloquy from defenders of these sanctions that, when his doctrines were vindicated, they were not recognised as his' (79). See also P. Widdicombe, *The Fatherhood of God from Origen to Athanasius* (Oxford: OUP, 2004), 7-120.

[56] Rebenich, *Jerome*, 119.
[57] Kelly, *Jerome*, 40.
[58] Kelly, *Jerome*, 40. Jerome's expression for living in the desert was 'following nakedly the naked Christ'. See A. Louth, *The Wilderness of God* (London: DLT, 2003), 22.
[59] Kelly, *Jerome*, 41.
[60] Kelly, *Jerome*, 41.
[61] For example, Augustine's summary view of John the Baptist: 'If you want to know what perfection man can attain to, it is John'. See André Retif, *John the Baptist: Missionary of Christ* (Westminster: Newman, 1953), 27. Other fathers' views of John are found in the writings of Maximus, Chrysostom, Basil, Gregory of Nyssa, Gregory of Nazianzus, Ambrose, Leo and Gregory the Great.
[62] A.J. Burke, Jr, *John the Baptist: Prophet and Disciple* (Cincinnati: St. Anthony Messenger, 2006) 170. For a helpful account of the early Christian interpretation of Scripture and its intersection with religious life, see D. Burton-Christie, *The Word in the Desert* (Oxford: OUP, 1993) and for a useful history of the first Christian solitaries, derived from, amongst others, the writings of Johan Cassian (c. 360-435), Palladius (c. 365-425) and Jerome, see P.F. Anson, *The Call of the Desert: The Solitary Life in the Christian Church* (London: SPCK, 1964). For a full account of early Christian asceticism, see H. von Campenhausen, *Tradition and Life in the Church: Essays and Lectures on Church History* (London: Collins, 1968), 90-122.

house at the risk of his chastity. He took up his abode in the desert, and desiring only to see Christ refused to look at anything else.[63]

Kelhoffer has described in considerable detail the witness of Jerome to a 'plurality of sentiments about John's locust eating',[64] as well as Jerome's 'time spent with monks in the wilderness (375-377) prior to his ordination to the priesthood, when he might himself have dined on grasshoppers with them'.[65]

> Even if some monks of Jerome's day did not still eat the same things that the Baptist ate (so *Adv. Iovin.* 2.15), Jerome does not miss an opportunity in his letters to offer the *type* of food John ate as a model for other believers. As is well known, Jerome advocates asceticism with regard to food, even referring in one of his letters to such arguments in response to the anti-ascetic arguments of the monk Jovinian.[66]

Significantly, it is on the very topic of the diet of John the Baptist that Jerome's interpretation differs from that of Origen. Whilst Jerome leans towards the ascetic/spiritual interpretation of John's diet (eg., 'Jerome lifts up John's diet as a confirmation of the Baptist's Nazarite identity, pursuit of virtue, and a compulsory model for grieving widows'), Origen inclines towards a figurative/allegorical interpretation (e.g., 'hails John's way of life as an example of how to care for one's soul through a simple diet noting how John's eating locusts signifies the Baptist's mission of preaching an exalted word').[67] The one aspect of John where there is evidence of a Jerome-Origen union is their confirmation that 'John was endowed with prenatal grace and thus was freed from original sin before his birth'.[68]

We now return to Jerome's increasing divergence from Origen. The period 372-379 was the period of Jerome (a Christian) in some conflict over the reading of pagan authors.[69] Jerome's first essay in scriptural interpretation (a commentary on Obadiah, now lost) displayed an exegesis 'wholly allegorical and mystical'.[70] Here the early influence of Origen is quite probable but other influences are possible also. Rebenich suggests that:

> In writing his commentaries, Jerome borrowed from virtually all the Christian biblical exegesis available to him. . . . Recent research has rightly stressed that Je-

---

63 Jerome, Ep. 125, *Select Letters of Saint Jerome* (tr. F.A. Wright; Cambridge: Harvard University Press, 1954), 409, as cited by Burke, Jr, *John*, 170. For one of the earliest accounts of Jerome's life in the desert, see P. Monceaux, *St. Jerome: The Early Years* (London: Sheed and Ward, 1933), 111-84.

64 J.A. Kelhoffer, *The Diet of John the Baptist: "Locusts and Wild Honey" in Synoptic and Patristic Interpretation* (Tübingen: Mohr Siebeck, 2005), 78-79.

65 Kelhoffer, *Diet*, 169.

66 Kelhoffer, *Diet*, 169.

67 Kelhoffer, *Diet*, 149-50, 170.

68 Burke, Jr, *John*, 166.

69 Kelly, *Jerome*, 42.

70 Kelly, *Jerome*, 45.

rome as biblical scholar learned from Jewish exegesis at least as much from Origen.[71]

We should note here and be reminded that the sphere of activity and influence of Origen over Jerome continued beyond the start of Jerome's corpus in the early 370s. However, Jerome critics have displayed little agreement over the exact period of trajectory of the Origen-Jerome nexus and the full reasons for Jerome's eventual, radical change of direction from Origen. One possible explanation for this may be the continuing debate over the respective merits of Origen and Jerome as biblical scholars, and exactly how far, and for how long, Jerome absorbed Origen's works. Freeman is of the view that Jerome's use of polemic in his writings negates him from being viewed 'as a great Christian mind like Origen'.[72]

Freeman's enthusiasm for Origen and criticism of Jerome may now be compared with the following assessment of Jerome made by Williams:

> Jerome's life and work, viewed as a cultural programme, impresses upon the observer a sense of coherence… Jerome's scholarly innovations were linked at several points to the imperatives of his monastic vocation… The multiple earlier exegetes he cited became his authorities, displacing the claim to power inherent in the practice of interpretation… Abasing himself, at least rhetorically, before these illustrious predecessors, Jerome could re-emphasize his own monastic humility. And through his juxtaposition of competing traditions of interpretation with texts of differing authority, Jerome could further confuse the issue, wielding his power as commentator convertly.[73]

In contrast, on Origen, Williams declares, 'Jerome's entire literary career was founded on the prestige of Origen.'[74] Here Williams clearly shows how Jerome's monumental legacy was built upon the earlier heritage of Origen. Whilst Freeman and Williams edge in favour of Origen over Jerome, one of Britain's leading Jerome scholars, Dennis Brown, has offered this pro-Jerome judgment:

> It is clear that Jerome had a much more extensive and profound knowledge of Hebrew than did any other Christian scholar, including Origen. Jerome had the same quantitative use of Hebrew as did Origen, but he added to it a qualitative use of Hebrew as a guide to the right *meanings*.[75]

Therefore amongst scholars there is no consensus on Origen's domination over Jerome as a biblical scholar. Interestingly, Williams' view of Jerome denies

---

[71] Rebenich, *Jerome*, 55.
[72] Freeman, *A New History*, 187. Elsewhere, Mark Edwards has been more generous in his judgment on Jerome suggesting that 'far from augmenting the blemishes in Origen's work, he distilled the best of his exegesis and spared the Greekless reader any knowledge of his doctrinal heresies'. See M. Edwards, *Catholicity*, 131.
[73] Williams, *The Monk*, 261-62.
[74] Williams, *The Monk*, 97.
[75] D. Brown, 'Jerome and the Vulgate' in *A History of Biblical Interpretation*, 355-79 (356).

Freeman's charge that Jerome lacked any genuine intellectual creativity and, also, questions McGuckin's suggestion that Jerome's reputation as exegete is overstressed (at least if we look for originality).[76] What can be said is that within Catholic biblical interpretative traditions Jerome had a major and pervasive influence. For example, by the late Middle Ages one of the most influential biblical exegetes, Nicholas of Lyra (c. 1270-1349), a French Franciscan known for his literal approach to biblical interpretation and his extensive use of Jewish interpretation, was 'showing obvious reliance on Jerome'.[77] However, it is generally accepted that it was Jerome who established Origen's influence over most of later Western exegesis.

We have now seen how Jerome initially borrowed from Origen (duality of interpretative biblical method) and how from 393 Jerome steadily broke away from Origen. The question of Jerome's exit from Origen's influence may be explained by Jerome's efforts during the 390s to construct himself as a Christian writer with his own authority.[78] For example, the period 390-393 saw Jerome 'heavily engaged in broadening the sphere of Hebrew learning, extended to materials that had already been naturalised within the Christian tradition by their use among his Greek predecessors',[79] and in 'devoting himself to the Hebrew original or Hebrew verity (*Hebraica veritas*) in his translation works (first version of the Old Testament, prefaces for Proverbs, Ecclesiastes, and the Song of Songs)'.[80]

However, Rebenich is sceptical of Jerome's departure from Origen's influence, claiming that Jerome was not wholly successful (after 393) in breaking free his own corpus from 'the Origenian persona'.[81] In defence of Jerome, Rebenich asserts:

> Jerome was entirely in line with the contemporary practice of both Christian and pagan authors when he extracted the writings of preceding authors. And, in the Latin west, he played an important role as an intermediary of Greek and Hebrew

---

[76] McGuckin, *A-Z*, 188.
[77] C. Patton, 'Selections from Nicholas of Lyra's *Commentary on Exodus* ', in S.E. Fowl (ed.), *The Theological Interpretation of Scripture: Classic and Contemporary Readings* (Oxford: Blackwell, 1997), 114-28 (114).
[78] See Williams, *The Monk*, chapter 1 and chapter 3.
[79] Williams, *The Monk*, 94.
[80] Rebenich, *Jerome*, 53-54. Jerome's developing hermeneutic (i.e., his formulation of, and devotion to, the *Hebraica Veritas*) took place between 382 and 385 and may possibly (although we have no direct evidence) have emanated from Jerome's reading of Paul's letter to the Romans (i.e., the way in which the apostle Paul introduced his message to the Jewish and Gentile believers in Rome—'To The Jew First'—Rom 1:16). For a discussion of the notion of 'To the Jew First,' see D.L. Bock and M. Glaser (eds), *To The Jew First: The Case For Jewish Evangelicalism in Scripture And History* (Grand Rapids: Kregel, 2008); A.X.J. Fritz., *To The Jew First or to the Jew at Last?* (Eugene: Pickwick, 2013).
[81] Rebenich, *Jerome*, 50.

exegesis. Jerome's exegetical importance can properly be compared with the theological importance of Augustine.[82]

Here Rebenich is cautioning students of Jerome against taking too negative an opinion of the *doctor ecclesiae* by giving undue focus to Jerome's plagiarism and concerns over the independent quality of his scholarship. And, of course, Rebenich's assertion that 'Jerome's exegetical importance can properly be compared with the theological importance of Augustine,' challenges (in part) McGuckin's (2005) claim that Jerome's reputation as exegete is over-stressed (at least if we look for originality). It is to the Jerome-Augustine interface that we now turn.

Augustine and Jerome

Augustine and Jerome were contemporaries. Their relationship and the commonality (or otherwise) of the theologies they embraced require close examination. For Augustine and Jerome, the differences, oppositions and boundaries between pagan philosophy and Christian theology were quite distinct. Like Jerome, Augustine had his own particular interests and concerns with scripture. We shall now look at these and see how far they did or did not find agreement with Jerome.

First, Augustine believed that the Rule of Faith (a summary of essential Christian doctrine) both guides scriptural interpretation and arises out of scripture in complex ways. An early example of the Rule of Faith is found in Irenaeus' *Against Heresies* (esp. *Haer* 1.10.1-2 and 2.27.1 – 2.28.1) and was an 'apostolic confession of faith also known as the *regula* (a summary of the apostolic preaching, fixed in outline but flexible in detail and wording)',[83] and the

---

[82] Rebenich, *Jerome*, 55-56. It must be said more recent scholars have not reached the same conclusion as Rebenich regarding the theological importance of Augustine. For example, Matthew Drever has written: 'It is difficult to dispute the widespread influence of Augustine in Western Christianity. His continued legacy, however, is a different question. Augustine has come under fire on various fronts, and his views on *creatio ex nihilo* and the divine image are no exception to this trend.' See M. Drever, *Image, Identity, and the Forming of the Augustinian Soul* (Oxford: OUP, 2013), 3.

[83] E. Ferguson, 'Creeds, Councils and Canons', in *Handbook of Early Christian Studies*, 427-45 (428). Here (427) Ferguson notes that 'the two most widely used and ecumenically acceptable creeds (the confessions of faith) are also historically the most problematic: The Apostle's Creed in western churches and the Nicene Creed, originating in the East and accepted in the West'. Irenaeus' *Against Heresies* was 'an attack on Christian Gnosticism and on Marcion, whom Irenaeus associated with such Gnostics.' See R.A. Norris, 'Irenaeus,' in *Dictionary of Major Biblical Interpreters*, 558-60 (558). The particular rendition of the 'rule of faith' (*regula fidei*), 'the variably worded but thematically consistent epitomes of apostolic teaching used in second- and third- century Christian catechesis,' found in Irenaeus' *Against Heresies*, declares 'the work of the Creator, the Almighty, Maker of heaven and earth, as the foundation of the economy of salvation'. See P. Blowers, 'Doctrine of Creation; in *Oxford Handbook of Early Christian Studies*, 906-31 (907). In the 'Rule of Faith'

regula 'was to be distinguished from the declaratory creeds (confessions of faith) of the fourth century which were not initially liturgical but doctrinal, to safeguard Christian truth from heresy'.[84] What was important for Augustine (as it was for Jerome) was obtaining the correct text and reading of the Scriptures and establishing the canonical books handed down in the Church from the time of the apostles.[85] As Roland Teske has observed:

> In his arguments against thee Manichees, the Donatists, and the Pelagians, Augustine appealed to the tradition of the Church in three different senses: against the Manichees he appealed to the Church as the bearer and custodian of the Scriptures, against the Donatists he appealed to the universality of the Church's tradition against that of a small segment of the Church, and against the Pelagians he

---

Irenaeus found a defining hermeneutic. Irenaeus (*Against Heresies* 2:28.1) states: 'Having the truth itself as our rule and the testimony concerning God set clearly before us...it is appropriate that we investigate the mystery and administration of the living God, and so increase in love for him who has done and still does such great things for us.' See J.R. Payton Jr., *Irenaeus on the Christian Faith: A Condensation of Against Heresies* (Cambridge: James Clarke, 2012). Thus, the 'rule of faith' (*regula fidei*) defines in summary what is to be believed as necessary for salvation and this understanding of the 'rule of faith' is found in Jerome who makes appeals to it in *Ep.* 107 (written c. 400) on the education of a daughter of a pagan: 'I speak thus to you, Laeta, my most devout in Christ, to teach you not to despair of your father's salvation. My hope is that the same faith which has gained you your daughter [Paula] may win your father too, and that so you may be able to rejoice over blessings bestowed upon your entire family' (*Ep.* 107:2). See S.L. Greenslade (ed.), *Early Latin Theology: Selections from Tertullian, Cyprian, Ambrose and Jerome* (Louisville: WJKP, 2006), 333. For a discussion of the primitive 'rule of faith' as understood in the second/third century, see T. George (ed.), *Evangelicals and Nicene Faith* (Grand Rapids: Baker Academic, 2011), 9-13. On the understanding of the inherited 'Rule of Faith' during the fourth century, see Ayres, *Nicaea*, 78-81. For the meaning of tradition and the rule of faith in the early Church, see R. Rombs and A. Hwang (eds), *Tradition and the Rule of Faith in the Early Church* (Washington: Catholic University of America Press, 2010). For an overview of how the results of the doctrinal arguments of the early Church Fathers remain in the classic formulations of Christian doctrine such as the Nicene Creed, see M.F. Wiles, *The Making of Christian Doctrine* (Cambridge: CUP, 1967). For a full account of Irenaeus's argument against the Gnostics (In the second book of *Adversus Haereses* Irenaeus draws attention to the 'logical absurdity of the Gnostic system or systems,' especially 'the Gnostic idea of God,' revealing 'the inconsistencies of a view which proclaims the infinity and supremacy of the ultimate God while at the same time denying his responsibility for the material world'), see R.A. Norris, *God and World in Early Christian Theology: A Study in Justin Martyr, Irenaeus, Tertullian and Origen* (London: Adam & Charles Black 1966), 65-68 (65). For a more recent examination of the Gnostics and Gnosticism which argues that we cannot interpret, or even identify Christian Gnosticism without Platonic evidence, see M. Edwards, *Christians, Gnostics and Philosophers in Late Antiquity* (Farnham: Ashgate, 2012).

84 Ferguson, ''Creeds', 431.

85 See R.J. Teske, 'Augustine's Appeal to Tradition,' in *Tradition and the Rule of Faith in the Early Church*, 153-72.

appealed to the teaching of earlier bishops from the time of the apostles until the present.[86]

This was the historical and Christian doctrinal context in which Augustine's theology was developed.[87]

Augustine's strictures about scriptural interpretation in *De Doctrina Christiana* (*On Christian Doctrine*) 'included the belief that no reading of scripture could be legitimate if it failed to shape the readers into a community that embodies the love of God as shown forth in Christ',[88] and, in like vein, both Augustine and Jerome would grapple with an appropriate way of understanding the discourse of scripture. In this sense, there is an Irenaeus – Augustine – Jerome nexus, in as much as each found in the Rule of Faith (*regula fidei*) a defining hermeneutic. Each were 'defenders of the Rule of Faith'.[89] From Irenaeus, Augustine came to see that with text and interpretation what emerges is 'an unbroken dialogue or discourse between a book and people, between Scripture and tradition, between the letter and the spirit, and between the word and the experience of those hearing it.'[90]

Both Augustine and Jerome were Neoplatonists.[91] Neoplatonism was a modified form of the philosophy of Plato developed in the third century, incorporating Phythagorean and Aristotelian features, along with elements of oriental mysticism. Craig Bartholomew's study of the book of Ecclesiastes gives us insight into how the influence of Neoplatonism on Augustine and Jerome 'priv-

---

[86] R.J. Teske, 'Augustine's Appeal to Tradition,' 172.

[87] For the most recent accounts of Augustine's theological development, see M. Hollingsworth, *Saint Augustine of Hippo – An Intellectual Biography* (London: Bloomsbury, 2013), 11-37, C.C. Pecknold and T. Toom (eds), *T&T Clark Companion to Augustine and Modern Theology* (London: Bloomsbury, 2013), 3-109; D.C. Alexander, *Augustine's Early Theology of the Church: Emergence and Implications, 386-391* (New York: Peter Lang, 2008), 18-21, 90-103, 129-58, 183-216.

[88] S. Fowl, *Engaging Scripture: A Model for Theological Interpretation* (Oxford: Blackwell, 1998), 153n.66. See, also, S.D. Neeley, D.B. Magee in L.M. Thomas, 'Synoptic Outline of Saint Augustine's De Doctrina' in R.L. Enos and R. Thompson et al (eds.), *The Rhetoric of St. Augustine: De Doctrina Christiana and the Search for a Distinctly Christian Rhetoric* (Waco: Baylor University Press, 2008), 11-32; Augustine, *De Doctrina Christiana* (ed. and tr. R.P.H. Green; Oxford: Clarendon, 1995), especially Book Three, 133-95.

[89] M. Holmes, 'The Biblical Canon', in *Handbook of Early Christian Studies*, 406-26 (418).

[90] J. Kugel and R. Greer, *Early Biblical Interpretation* (Philadelphia: Westminster, 1986), 157, as cited by S. Fowl, *Engaging Scripture*, 8n.11. Fowl notes 'for a particularly concise example of the complex interconnectedness of the "Rule" and scripture, see Augustine's 18th tractate on John'.

[91] On Augustinian Neoplatonism, see M.S. Horton, *Covenant and Eschatology: The Divine Drama* (Louisville: WJKP, 2002), 15. For Jerome's Neoplatonic allegorical and Christological reading of books of the Old Testament, see C.B. Bartholomew, *Ecclesiastes* (Grand Rapids: Baker Academic, 2009), 21.

ileged the spiritual reading of the Bible.'[92] And in the case of Jerome's allegorical reading of Ecclesiastes, we see a strong emphasis upon 'spiritual devotion' and the importance of asceticism to the Christian life.[93] However, there remains some disagreement amongst scholars regarding Jerome's ability to assimilate philosophic/theological ideas to the same degree as Augustine. For example, David Wright believes, 'Jerome was no philosopher or theologian, but a giant of scholarship—one in whom Christianity's Hebraic inheritance partly came into its own, in the teeth of dominant Hellenism.'[94] Wright's dismissal of Jerome as a non-philosopher and non-theologian stands in stark contrast to his appraisal of Augustine's philosophical/theological development, which was influenced by 'Manichaeism, [a late Gnostic ascetic religion from Persia] Ambrose's intellectual weight and allegorical exegesis, the challenge of Christian asceticism and Neoplatonism's vision of spiritual reality'.[95]

An example of Augustine's religious development is found in the section of the *Confessions* describing Augustine's search to understand the substance of God in which Augustine admits his error in having earlier thought of God by 'the analogy of the human body' before coming, through the study of philosophy, to understand the spiritual wonder of God's created order—'the body of heaven, air and sea, and even of the earth.'[96]

---

[92] Bartholomew, *Ecclesiastes*, 29.

[93] Bartholomew, *Ecclesiastes*, 27. Jerome's commentary 'became the standard interpretation of Ecclesiastes until it was challenged by the Lutheran reformers', see Bartholomew, *Ecclesiastes*, 26. Very early on in his *Commentary on Ecclesiastes* (ch 1.1:1) Jerome remarks 'according to the spiritual sense, "the preacemaker," the beloved of God, the Father, "and our Preacher," is Christ, who pulled down the dividing wall, "and by his incarnation abolished the hostilities" and made both one, saying: "My peace I give to you, my peace I leave with you." Or him, the Father said to the disciples: "This is my beloved Son, in whom I am well pleased: listen to him."' See Saint Jerome, *Commentary on Ecclesiastes* (tr. and ed. with a Commentary by R.J. Goodrich and D.J.D. Miller; New York: Newman, 2012), 35.

[94] D. Wright, 'The Latin Fathers', in I. Hazlett (ed.), *Early Christianity: Origins and Evolution to AD 600* (London: SPCK, 1991), 148-62 (154).

[95] Wright, 'Latin Fathers', 155-56. For a fuller account of Augustine and his relation to Manichaeism, see Hollingsworth, *Saint Augustine* (London: Bloomsbury, 2013), 7; J.D. BeDuhn, *Augustine's Manichaean Dilemma, 1: Conversion and Apostasy, 373-388 CE* (Pennsylvania: University of Pennsylvania Press. 2010); idem, *Augustine's Manichaean Dilemma, 2: Making a 'Catholic' self, 388-401 C.E.* (Pennsylvania: University of Pennsylvania Press, 2013). For the fullest account of Manichaeism, see idem, *The Manichaean Body* (Baltimore: Johns Hopkins University Press 2000). Augustine's relation to Ambrose is fully discussed in N.B. McLynn., *Ambrose of Milan: Church and Court in a Christian Capital* (Berkeley: University of California Press, 1994), 237-38, 256-60.

[96] St. Augustine, *Confessions* (rev. T. Gill; Alachua: Bridge-Logos, 2003), 159-60. Hollingsworth has noted how Augustine's *Confessions* was written 'to show how the singularities of one life veil over what is common to all—human consciousness, its navigation of time and form the indefatigable impulse to religion.' See Hollingsworth, *Saint Augustine*, 48, and, for Augustine's understanding of God as mys-

And here Hollingsworth has noted Augustine's decision to describe (in the final book of his *Confessions)* 'the exquisite irony of our having to breach the things of eternity in syllables and words that must give up their meaning in time' as simply 'the abyss of this age and the blindness of our flesh'.[97]

There are certain parallels between Augustine and Jerome's lives (e.g., letter writing, composition of homilies/sermons and the search for the truth of Scripture), and enough convergence of thinking between the two to talk of an Augustine-Jerome correspondence. Like Augustine, Jerome was also a Catholic Christian, was drawn to allegorical exegesis,[98] the challenge of Christian asceticism and Neoplatonism's vision of spiritual reality.

We now move on to the relationship between Augustine and Jerome regarding theological issues. Augustine was opposed to the Pelagians[99] and had specific views on the respective roles of God's grace and human freedom, original sin, the nature of salvation and predestination.[100] Jerome, too, was an opponent,

---

tery, see *Saint Augustine: Essential Sermons* (Introduction and notes by D.E. Doyle; tr. by E. Hill and ed. by B. Ramsey; New York: New City, 2007), 195-202.

[97] Augustine, *Confessions* XIII, 23, 34 as cited by Hollingsworth, *Saint Augustine*, 45n.27.

[98] Somewhat ironically Brown has noted that Jerome, in his last commentary on Jeremiah (begun 414 or 415), was critical of Origen's excessive allegorical interpretations, referring to Origen as 'that allegorist'. See Brown *Vir Trilinguis*, 131. Ramsey, *Beginning to Read the Fathers* (London: DLT, 1986), 31, notes that 'Jerome believed the orthodox way was to tread the narrow path between an over-literalism on one side and an over-allegorization on the other'.

[99] See P. Brown, *Augustine of Hippo: A Biography* (London: Faber, 1967), 340-407. Ferguson, *Church History*, 276-77, observes, 'Pelagianism placed an emphasis on human perfectionism instead of divine grace. In the case of Pelagianism, Augustine prepared for the rejection of the old ideals of the autonomy of human ethics and reason in favour of a pessimistic view of human morality without divine aid. Augustine began to oppose Pelagius and his associates about 412.' For Augustine's response to Pelagius and Pelagianism, see J.E. Rotelle, *The Works of Saint Augustine: Answer to the Pelagians* (New York: New City, 1997). Elsewhere, J.F. Kelly notes: 'Disturbed by Augustine's view human s contribute virtually nothing to their salvation he [Pelagius) began to sharpen his own ideas, allowing for the possibility of sinlessness but focusing more on human cooperation with God's grace.' See J.F. Kelly, 'Pelagius', in D. McKim (ed.) *Dictionary of Major Biblical Interpreters* (Downers Gove: IVP, 2007), 808-12 (808).

[100] Letham, *Through Western Eyes*, 78. Many scholars have tried to illuminate the thought of Augustine's *Confessions*. For one ground-breaking study of Augustine's spiritual/religious development as described in the *Confessions*, see R. McMahon, *Augustine's Prayerful Ascent: An Essay on the Literary Form of the "Confessions"* (London: University of Georgia Press, 1989). McMahon's was the first book in English to define a coherent literary form in Augustine's masterpiece. According to the publisher 'In separating Augustine the speaker from Augustine the writer, McMahon identifies the literary form of the *Confessions* as providentially guided prayer—a written record of the speaker's unrehearsed, dynamic encounter with God.' In similar vein Kenneth Steinhauser has examined in some detail the problem of the unity or

writing his own polemic against Pelagius (*Liber adversus Pelagium*) in 415. So, is there any Augustine-Jerome correspondence here?

Augustine's formulation of his doctrine of original sin was provoked in part by his opposition to the views of the British monk, Pelagius.[101] Pelagius believed 'that the commandment "Be perfect, therefore, as your heavenly Father is perfect" (Matt. 5:48) ought to be taken as a real human possibility, one that could actually be achieved'.[102] Pelagius's view 'denied that Adam's primal sin had any inevitable effect on later human beings, other than by setting a bad example by which subsequent generations were tempted and which they overwhelmingly imitated, falling into sin of their own individual accord'.[103] Salvation, accordingly, is 'possible on the basis of a person's works, with no need of grace other than the natural capacities with which God has endowed humanity in creation, especially rational free-will'.[104] Augustine challenged Pelagius's ideas because he saw them as 'nullifying the supernatural grace of Christ that is observed in scripture and, instead, considered that salvation cannot be achieved by human works, but requires the special grace of Christ to be instilled into the human soul'.[105] Inherent in Augustine's doctrine of original sin (as found in his *The Perfection of Human Righteousness*) is the belief that grace is an absolute for salvation because of the inevitability of sin.[106] Pelagius and Julian of Eclan-

lack of unity among the thirteen books of the *Confessions*. For his account of why 'the thirteen books of Augustine's *Confessions* frequently leave scholars perplexed because of apparent inconsistencies among these books and the various disjunct themes treated therein, see K.B. Steinhauser, 'The Literary Unity of the *Confessions*' in *Augustine: From Rhetor to Theologian*, 15-30. For a critique of the strict historicity (or otherwise) of the *Confessions*, see J.J. O'Meara, 'Augustine's *Confessions*: Elements of Fiction,' in *Augustine: Rhetor to Theologian*, 77-95. See also, F.M. Young, 'The *Confessions* of St. Augustine: What is the genre of this work?' *Augustinian Studies* 30 (1999), 1-16. Finally, for a revisionist interpretation of Augustine's *Confessions*, arguing that the way Augustine 'is usually presented through the *Confessions* and through Peter Brown's biography,' is unsatisfactory, see C. Harrison, *Rethinking Augustine's Early Theology: An Argument for Continuity* (Oxford: OUP, 2006), vi, 3-4, 21-22, 56-63, 252-54. For a study of Augustine's view of the human condition, see R. O'Connell, *St. Augustine's Early Theory of Man, A.D. 386-391* (Cambridge: Belknap Press, Harvard University Press, 1968); idem, *St. Augustine's Confessions: The Odyssey of Soul* (Cambridge: Belknap Press, Harvard University Press, 1969); idem, *The Origin of the Soul in St. Augustine's Later Works* (New York: Fordham University Press, 1987); P.R. Kolbet, *Augustine and the Cure of Souls: Revising a Classical Ideal* (Notre Dame: University of Notre Dame Press, 2010); M. Drever, *Image, Identity, and the Forming of the Augustinian Soul* (New York: OUP, 2013).
101 Plantinga, *Christian Theology*, 196.
102 Plantinga, *Christian Theology*, 196-97.
103 Plantinga, *Christian Theology*, 197.
104 Plantinga, *Christian Theology*, 197.
105 Plantinga, *Christian Theology*, 197.
106 See E.L. Watkin, 'The Mysticism of St. Augustine' in M.C. D'Arcu et al *A Monument to Saint Augustine* (London: Sheed & Ward, 1945), 105-19 (108). However,

um opposed Augustine's doctrine of original sin,[107] but did Jerome? It would seem not. Through many of Jerome's letters (especially those written to Augustine) we witness a constant note that 'what Jerome is unfolding is a systematic theory of sexuality and its place, or rather lack of place, in the earnest Christian life'.[108] Like Augustine, Jerome saw sexuality as a source of guilt for sin and inclination toward sin. According to Kelly each also saw 'marriage' to be a 'poor second best to virginity, the original state willed by God.[109]

Here, however, Kelly is surely wrong about Augustine, for he misreads Augustine's understanding of the virtues of marriage which, in fact, Augustine supported (Augustine *Confessions*, Bk 6, 12-15). Kelly also tells us that Augustine was 'profuse in expressions of affection, of yearning for intellectual communion with Jerome',[110] demonstrated by Augustine's willingness to have his own writings criticised by Jerome. If there is sign of a Jerome-Augustine nexus

---

Mary Clark, *Augustine* (Washington: Georgetown University Press, 2007), 52, has raised doubts over Augustine's attempts to fully develop his doctrine of original sin: 'Augustine confessed that he did not know in what way the punishment for Adam's sin was transmitted to the human race, but he was certain that the effects of the sin were experienced by Adam's progeny.' For a full discussion of Augustine's doctrine of original sin, see S. MacDonald, 'Primal Sin', in G.B. Matthews (ed.), *The Augustinian Tradition* (Berkeley: University of California Press, 1999), 110-39.

[107] Letham, *Through Western Eyes*, 78. According to John Piper 'Pelagius denied the doctrine of original sin and asserted that human nature at its core is good and able to do all it is commanded to do'. See, J. Piper, *The Legacy of Sovereign Joy: God's Triumphant Grace in the Lives of Augustine, Luther, and Calvin* (Wheaton: Crossway, 2000), 56. Kenton Sparks, *God's Word in Human Words* (Grand Rapids: Baker Academic, 2008), 240, notes 'Augustine's belief in the mystery of God and how Augustine stressed that God was free to change his commands to human beings as he wished'. For an account of Julian's theology and religious policy, see S.N.C. Lieu, *The Emperor Julian* (Liverpool: Liverpool University Press, 1986), 41-58.

[108] See Kelly, *Jerome*, 102.

[109] See Kelly, *Jerome*, 102. For Jerome's views on virginity, see N. Adkin, *Jerome on Virginity: A Commentary on the Libellus de Virginitate Servanda* (Letter 22) (Cambridge: CUP, 2003). For a description of Augustine's attempts to formulate an orthodox understanding of celibacy (*De sancta virginitate* – on Holy Virginity), see D.G. Hunter, *Marriage, Celibacy and Heresy in Ancient Christianity: The Jovinianist Controversy* (Oxford: OUP, 2007), 269-72. It is important to note here that 'belief in original sin eventually became an indispensable dogmatic constituent of the theology of Baptism in the Western Church'—L.G. Walsh, *The Sacrament of Initiation* (London: Geoffrey Chapman, 1998), 82. For a full account of Jerome's and Augustine's views on marriage, see P.L. Reynolds, *Marriage in the Western Church: The Christianization of Marriage during the Patristic and Early Medieval Periods* (Leiden: Brill, 2001), 148, 207-12, 217, 259-60, 271-309. For examples of Jerome's epistles (nos. 77, 107, 108, 127, 128, 133) relating to women's role in the wider world, see E.A. Clark, *Woman in the Early Church* (Washington: Michael Glazier, 1983). For Jerome's gradation of virginity as a superior way of life to widowhood (*Ep.* 22.15), see J.D. Ernest, *The Bible in Athanasius of Alexandria* (Leiden: Brill, 2004), 286n.19.

[110] Kelly, *Jerome*, 218.

over Augustine's doctrine of original sin there seems also sign of correspondence over Augustine's view of Pelagius, with Jerome describing Pelagius as
having 'wits addled with Scots porridge'.[111] Is there evidence of a Jerome convergence with Augustine's views on the roles of God's grace and human freedom and the nature of salvation and predestination?

When we look for evidence of Jerome's theology of God's grace, human
freedom, and the nature of salvation and predestination we face a particular
difficulty in that Jerome (unlike Augustine)[112] did not always easily clarify his
faith. Jerome rarely wrote as a theologian although, as we have seen, he was
happy to engage in theological controversies when and wherever those arose.
However, as earlier noted, one of Jerome's strengths was in the spiritual interpretation of the Bible and it is here we find Jerome's position on the role of
God's grace, human freedom, and the nature of salvation and predestination
stated in his exegesis [of Isa. 3:7]. Here Jerome's spiritual interpretation is
moral and, in its culmination, Christological.[113]

> Therefore let us not concur immediately in the judgment of the multitude, but
> when we have chosen to lead we shall know our real worth and shall be humbled
> under the mighty hand of God, for God, who resists the proud, gives grace to the
> humble. How many there are who promise others food and clothing and do not
> have bread and clothing because they themselves are hungry and naked, and do
> not have spiritual food and do not keep Christ's tunic whole! Full of wounds they
> boast and they are healers. They do not observe what Moses said: Do not seek to
> become a judge, lest perhaps you be unable to remove iniquities. Jesus alone heals
> all sicknesses and infirmities. About him it stands written: He heals the broken
> hearted and binds up their wounds.[114]

What is clearly evident here is Jerome's belief 'that to be poor was to follow
the naked Christ in one's own nakedness, and that Christ and his cross were the
human race's only hope of salvation'.[115] What unified Augustine and Jerome
was the understanding that it was Christian practice to seek beneath the letter
for the deeper spiritual meaning of the sacred Scriptures.

---

[111] R. Price, *Augustine* (London: Fount, 1996), 45. Here we should note that Augustine
was strongly opposed to Pelagius's doctrine of the sound reason and will, and the belief that human nature could do more than it really can. For the way in which Augustine and Jerome attacked Pelagius's moral interpretation of the Pauline letters (e.g.,
Romans) and his views on sin 'that we are saved or damned by the examples we follow', see Kelly, 'Pelagius', 809-10. For a recent critique of Augustine's rebuke of
Pelagius's theology of moral reform (i.e., Pelagius's denial of 'transmitted and original sin, and Pelagius's view that the will is free, unhindered by a depraved nature so
that an assisting grace lacks necessity'), see M. Barrett, *Salvation by Grace* (Phillipsburg: P&R, 2013), 2-9.
[112] See St. Augustine, *The Trinity* (tr. S. McKenna; Washington: CUAP, 1963).
[113] Ramsey, *Fathers*, 37-38.
[114] Jerome, *Commentary on Isaiah*, as cited by Ramsey, *Fathers*, 37-38.
[115] Ramsey, *Fathers*, 94.

We noted earlier that Augustine and Jerome would wrestle with an appropriate way of understanding the discourse of scripture and it was in this area that they came into conflict. The disagreement would be over Christian pedagogy (Christian teaching) and exegetical practice. Here it should be noted again that during 394-397 Augustine and Jerome were in dispute over the Origenist controversy, and it was from this period that the convergence of thinking between the two ended.

In 395 Augustine was consecrated Bishop of Hippo, and it was 'from 395 that some of Augustine's key texts were written or reworked and concluded during his mature period as a theologian and church leader '.[116] On Christian pedagogy both Augustine and Jerome held similar positions on sex and the superiority of celibacy and a negative evaluation of sexuality is a constant that runs through both their written corpuses. Both believed that all human beings partake in the Fall of Adam and Eve and on the faith that in Jesus Christ God has opened up a way of healing and salvation. Both understood sexual desire as being capable of presenting a drive to disorder towards chaos and evil, since it is linked with the curse of death, the consequence of the Fall. These parallel understandings shaped much of the Christian teachings of Augustine and Jerome. However, Augustine and Jerome eventually came to hold different positions on marriage. Whilst Augustine wrote to rehabilitate the married state (*De bono coniugali* – *On the Good Marriage*), Jerome wrote to denigrate it (*Against Helvidius*).

But what was it that drew Augustine and Jerome further apart between 395-420? During this period what was the precise nature of the discord between Augustine and Jerome over Christian pedagogy and exegetical practice? Crucially, what was the hermeneutical proximity of Augustine and Jerome at this time? As we shall now see on these questions, patristic scholars remain divided.

During 397-426 Augustine completed his *De Doctrina Christiana* (*On Christian Doctrine*) which was the principle work in which Augustine explains his hermeneutical methodology and which formed Christian pedagogy and exegetical practice for many centuries.[117] In this important treatise Augustine stated his belief that 'all doctrine concerns signs and things' and that it is by means of corporal and temporal things that we may comprehend the eternal and spiritual', and that 'the Holy Church exists as God's body and bridge; whereby

---

[116] W.G. Jeanrond, *A Theology of Love* (London, T&T Clark, 2010), 47. Here Jeanrond selects Augustine's *On the Good of Marriage* (401), *The Homilies of St. John* (415), *The Trinity* (417), *The City of God* (418-420), and *On Christian Doctrine* (426). It is worth noting that both Jerome and Augustine's works in this period were being widely published and circulated to a growing, literate, Christian audience. See H.Y. Gamble, *Books and Readers in the Early Church: A History of Early Christian Texts* (New Haven: Yale University Press, 1995), 132-37.

[117] See S.D. Neeley et al, 'Synoptic Outline', 11-32.

Salvation can be considered as healing by that faith and correction'.[118] Augustine's treatise also addressed the manner in which biblical interpretation should proceed ('canons of exegesis') so that objectivity was maintained.[119] Richard Price considers the work as also characterized 'by its illustration of the relation between love of God and love of neighbour.[120] Augustine understood Christ to mean 'that we must love all people equally'.[121] Prices interpretation of Augustine's magisterial work stresses Augustine's call to each Christian:

> ... to build his own circle of friends who love one another as themselves and help one another to grow in the love of God, an ideal of friendship which gave Augustine a special interest in the development of religious community brings into focus the mutual interest of Augustine and Jerome in forging communal Christian discipleship.[122]

However, in the context of their developing estrangement it is perhaps somewhat ironic that *On Christian Doctrine*, as a late Augustinian text, should parallel Jerome's earlier asceticism. Price notes that even before his conversion at Milan in 386 Augustine 'was attracted by the idea of setting up a community where he and his closest friends could devote themselves to study and reflection'.[123]

We do not know how Jerome would have responded to Augustine's *On Christian Doctrine* since the treatise was not completed until 426, six years after Jerome's death. However, it was Jerome's exegesis and desire to give explanations of the biblical books that brought him into hostile encounter with Augustine.[124]

Between 395-430 Augustine was 'engaged in a number of key theological and ecclesiastical struggles: the Donatist controversy; the lengthy conflict with

---

[118] See S.D. Neeley et al, 'Synoptic Outline' *De Doctrina Christiana'* (Bk 1, Bk 2) 12-21. For a detailed critique of Augustine's use of signs/symbols as part of his Christian pedagogy and exegetical practice, see P.J. Leithart, 'Seminars and Social Salvation (mostly) in *De Doctrina Christiana*,' in W. Cristaudo and Heung-Wak Wong (eds.), *Augustine: His Legacy and Relevance* (Hindmarsh: ATF, 2010), 1-36.

[119] H. Chadwick, *Augustine* (OUP, 1986), 35.

[120] Price, *Augustine*, 78. Augustine covers these features in Bk 1, vii-viii, of *De Doctrina Christiana*.

[121] Price, *Augustine*, 79.

[122] Price, *Augustine*, 79.

[123] Price, *Augustine*, 79. For an account of Augustine's arrival in Milan and fatherly welcome by Bishop Ambrose, which opened his eyes to the truths of Christianity and baptized him into the faith, see N.B. Mcynn, *Ambrose of Milan*, xiii-xiv.

[124] The Jerome-Augustine conflict over biblical exegesis had already begun earlier in 394-395, when Augustine entered into a protracted correspondence with Jerome (culminating in 404/405) over the latter's exegesis of Gal. 2:11-14 (Paul's chastisement of Peter at Antioch) and where Jerome denied that there was any real difference of opinion between the two apostles. See Brown, *Vir Trilinguis*, 130. For a detailed record of Jerome's correspondences with Augustine, see J. Trigg, *Biblical Interpretation* (Collegeville: Michael Glazier, 1988).

Pelaganism; lingering Manicheism; and his monumental *The City of God* in which he replied to certain arguments linking the sack of Rome in 410 to the empire's acceptance and adoption of Christianity'.[125] Discord between Augustine and Jerome during this period may have had its roots in Augustine's earlier, initial resistance to the gospel, prior to his conversion, as recounted in his *Confessions*.[126]

> Augustine at first claims to have had intellectual problems with the Christian faith. . . . But the problem for Augustine was deeper — a matter of the will, desire and affections…As he nears his conversion, Augustine continues to reiterate his dilemma: the problem is no longer the truthfulness; the problem is his will, desires and affections.[127]

Augustine's *Confessions* appeared in 400 and 'may have been read by Jerome who, in contrast, had no problems with the gospel, believing that Scripture contained no contradictions and was infallible'.[128] Significantly, the object of Augustine's pre-conversion intellectual position on the Christian faith (trapped in sinful self, infatuated by philosophical pursuit, captured by the Manichaean heresy and conversion to Neoplatonism) sits at variance with Jerome's certainty of the *providentia* of God and Scripture. It is also important to note that when Augustine was writing his *Confessions*, 'Jerome was being tormented by the great divide between Christ and Cicero.'[129] Ironically, during his student days (370-375) Augustine's 'first intellectual turning point' was Cicero's now lost *Hortensius*.[130]

We shall now examine Jerome's hostile encounter with Augustine in 394-395. At this time, Augustine was neither convinced by Jerome's scholarship, nor by Jerome's orthodoxy requesting Jerome to condemn Origen's heresies.[131]

---

[125] B.G. Green, 'Augustine', in Green (ed.), *Shapers*, 235-92 (238).

[126] Augustine, *Confessions*, 187-215. Augustine's conversion to Christianity occurred on 15 August, 386. Augustine had been greatly moved by the conversion of the famous orator and philosopher, Marius Victorinus, as told by Simplicianus. 'You called me saying, "Awake, you who sleep, arise from the dead, and Christ will give you light"' (199).

[127] Green, 'Augustine', 253-55.

[128] Ferguson, *Church History*, 224.

[129] J. Harries, 'Patristic Historiography', in *Early Christianity*, 269-79 (271). Evans, 'The Early Church in The World ', in *First Christian*, 58-64 (59), notes: 'In the days before the sack of Rome (410), *Cicero's Republic* and *On Laws* are both much preoccupied with the importance of the preservation of justice and sound government. In the first century, the link between integrity and satisfactory conduct in high office was already growing more tenuous, and the slide into incompetence and corruption in public office in the State coincided with the emergence of Christianity and the development of an institutional Church. By the fourth and fifth century it was difficult for contemporaries not to be conscious that cultural standards were slipping, as well as standards in public office'.

[130] Ferguson, *Church History*, 269.

[131] Rebenich, *Jerome*, 45-46.

Rebenich has drawn particular attention to Jerome's exegesis in his *Commentary on Galatians*, by suggesting that Paul's confrontation with Peter at Antioch (Gal. 2:11-14) was deliberately set up 'to serve the expectations of both the Gentile and the Jewish Christians and Augustine's annoyance at Jerome's hermeneutic of returning 'to the Hebrew original when translating the Old Testament into Latin'.[132] Here, Rebenich contests that Jerome had been influenced by Origen's scholarship, and that Augustine's required Jerome to 'define his relation to the Origenist tradition'.[133] Rebenich believes that Jerome's critics now had serious concerns about Jerome's 'abandoning the divinely inspired version of the Septuagint thus creating a Judaized Old Testament and his decision for *Hebraica veritus* and the Jewish exegesis led to the accusation that he was deviating from Christian tradition'.[134] For example, Rufinus the Syrian was another critic of Jerome, believing 'the Septuagint to be the only true and legitimate, divinely inspired version of the Old Testament'.[135] Jerome's response to Augustine's criticisms came in 397 and was sweetly sarcastic:

> . . . . .that many might know that when you challenge me, I am afraid, and that when you, a man of learning, write to me, I keep quiet like an ignorant man, now that someone has been found who knew how to stop my garrulous tongue.[136]

So far, we have seen a number of parallels and differences between Jerome and Augustine in their approaches to biblical interpretation in the early Church. Although their relationship during the 390s was strained, they were not, as biblical exegetes, wholly incompatible. We have noted above evidence of some hermeneutical proximity (the *Rule of Faith*) and convergence over the application of allegorical exegesis and the interpretation of the doctrine of original sin. But what truly unites Jerome and Augustine is their understanding of God's triumphant grace. On the one hand we have Jerome's life acting as 'a wondrous example of God's grace working through human ambiguities (he struggled with his jagged personality all his life)'[137] and, on the other, Augustine who believed 'that he is happy who possesses God'.[138]

---

[132] Rebenich, *Jerome*, 45.

[133] Rebenich, *Jerome*, 45. Here, Jerome's emulation of Origen's commentaries on Galatians may be seen as paradoxical considering the comment Jerome made in the Origenist controversy when he referred to Origen's 'detestable exegesis' (cf *Ep.* 84.3). See Brown, *Vir Trilinguis*, 128n.62, 130.

[134] Rebenich, *Jerome*, 58. Rebenich notes that 'Jerome's campaign for the superiority of the Hebrew text threatened his entire programme of *studia scripturarum.*'

[135] Rebenich, *Jerome*, 54.

[136] Rebenich, *Jerome*, 46.

[137] Hall, *Reading Scripture*, 109.

[138] T.A. Hand, *Augustine on Prayer* (New York: Catholic Publishing, 1986), 17.

Chapter 3

Modern Jerome Scholarship (1880-1965)

Introduction

In this chapter (as well as in chapters 4-6) we shall see how modern scholars came to make their secondary judgments on features of Jerome's *oeuvre* largely upon the basis of examining and contesting Jerome's theological style and, in particular, his originality and creativity as an exegete, and his intellectual abilities as a scriptural theologian. It is interesting that these are the same criteria that modern interpreters of Origen and Augustine have long debated.

The Landscape of Modern Jerome Scholarship

Although the beginning of the modern critical study of Jerome is often assigned to the work of J.N.D. Kelly (*Jerome*, 1975) our examination of the modern critical reception of Jerome's corpus can begin much earlier with studies dating from 1880, the period by which the modern literary and textual criticism of Jerome's corpus was becoming more and more sophisticated. These studies have embraced investigations into a variety of topics relating to Jerome's *oeuvre*: the influence of Jerome on the canon of the Western Church; the value of the Vulgate OT for textual criticism; the style of the letters of Jerome; Jerome's work on the Psalter; the figure of Jerome as an ascetic writer; Jerome's Catholic churchmanship; Jerome as a translator; Jerome's heritage and legacy; Jerome's exegetical method; Jerome's treatises in the theological controversies of the West; Jerome and Trinitarian Christological problems; Jerome's violent invective; Jerome and Western biblical philosophy; Jerome's humanism; and, Jerome's Hebrew manuscripts.

We shall now look at a selection of these studies where we need to be conscious of the theological environment against which they were each produced (i.e., the rise and trend of modern biblical scholarship from the late nineteenth to the mid-twentieth century).

Writing in 1963 Alan Richardson suggested that the rise of modern biblical research may be dated to the early nineteenth century, when new methods of historical study (e.g., the development of archaeological, critical, literary, philological and philosophical forms of enquiry) began to be applied to the study of the Bible and Christian origins generally.[1] Central to Richardson's case is how

---

[1] A. Richardson, 'The Rise of Modern Biblical Scholarship and Recent Discussion of the Authority of the Bible', in S.L. Greenslade (ed.), *The Cambridge History of the Bible: The West from the Reformation to the Present Day* (Cambridge: CUP, 1963), 294-338 (294). Here, it is important to note that, despite his wide-ranging analysis,

these radical changes to modern biblical studies caused scholars to review their own theological presumptions.[2]

Thus, when we look at selected modern Jerome scholars and their critical reception of particular texts/writings drawn from Jerome's corpus, we shall see these critics paying close attention to Jerome's style and his historical setting, and analysing what Jerome was talking about in a more objective way, since the interpretation of Jerome's works could now be undertaken using all the resources made available by the nineteenth century revolution in theological method occasioned by the rise of modern historical and critical biblical scholarship. In short, a new historical criticism would see Jerome's *oeuvre* being viewed as historical texts worthy of more than just a literalist form of critical reception.

The changes that were to come over Jerome scholarship in the last two decades of the nineteenth century (new principles of enquiry and modern methods of criticism) meant that literary criticism (the examination of the contents of Jerome's works with a view to determining the date, authorship, integrity and character of the various writings) and textual criticism of Jerome's corpus found a new momentum. As well as the importance of the 'historical Jerome', scholars were now to critically examine the point of view of 'Jerome the writer', to discover, amongst other things, the author's bias, to ascertain what his purpose was in writing and to identify the great issues in which he was involved as a patristic writer and commentator.

From 1880, therefore, Jerome scholars would begin to adopt the tools of enquiry with which modern scholarship had to work as it sought by fresh insights to reveal new facets of the truth enshrined within Jerome's canon.

Sheppard and Thiselton have described the key dynamic of this new modern scholarship in the new modern age of the nineteenth century:

In the modern age of nineteenth-century Europe, beyond the imagination of the classical age, the substance of persons, events, ideas and things became further grounded in the specificity of their time and place and a deeper assessment of circumstance.[3]

Therefore towards the end of the nineteenth century a new prevailing historicism developed which, as Sheppard and Thiselton note, 'often combined aes-

---

Richardson fails to mention how what was decisive in developments in patristic scholarship from the nineteenth century was less the 'revolution in theological method' than developments in German historical scholarship, which started in the field of secular ancient history. For a comprehensive account of how nineteenth century German (Protestant) theology developed, and was influenced by, a growing body of historical and theological criticism, see A.E. McGrath, *The Making of Modern German Christology, 1750-1990* (Leicester: Apollos, 1994).

[2] See A. Richardson, 'Rise of Modern Biblical Scholarship', 296-300.
[3] G.T. Sheppard and A.C. Thiselton, 'Biblical Interpretation in the Eighteenth and Nineteenth Centuries', in D.K. McKim (ed.), *Dictionary of Major Biblical Interpreters* (Downers Grove: IVP, 2007), 45-66 (55).

thetic criticism with social-scientific approaches to refine the understanding of specific genres of literature so that scholars could empathetically interpret the original form and social function of an ancient tradition'.[4] The implications of this for Jerome scholarship are obvious: henceforth critics of Jerome's corpus would need to be more circumspect in their assessment of the origin, locus and interpretation of Jerome's writings.

In their analysis of the background to this changing landscape of historical, biblical criticism, Sheppard and Thiselton argue two key points. First that 'since there was no equivalent to the modern genre of "history" in antiquity, texts from that time now required a fresh critical analysis to determine when and how they can be trusted to report accurately past events and ideas'.[5] Second, 'that English critics in particular, became more interested in knowing the "historical authors" original intent, requiring critics to move from the text…to the mind of its supposed author'.[6]

This shift in perspective (the growing sophistication of literary-historical 'methodologies') would hold a special significance for modern Jerome scholarship since it would encourage both a renewed interest in, and revival of knowledge of, early Christian sources. One such source identified in 1907 by E.A.W. Budge was Palladius (c. 363-431), a travel writer and monk in Egypt and author of the *Lausiac History*, which documented seventy biographies of Egyptian holy men and women, as well as experiments in monastic lifestyle. Palladius had met Jerome in Bethlehem and had described him as a man who 'possessed the vices of envy and evil-eyedness'.[7]

But did this fourth century judgement on Jerome act, in any way, as a barometer for early twentieth century scholarly opinion on the man from Stridon? Clearly, there is some evidence that it did. For example, even in 1918, some modern Jerome scholars were still offering customary, stereotypical, portraits of Jerome. An example of this is found in the work of Williston Walker. Walker's *A History of The Christian Church*[8] documents the intentions of key figures in the story of the Church. On Jerome, Walker states:

> Jerome had a restless desire to know the scholarly and religious world… Jerome himself was one of the most vindictive of disputants… Jerome's best use of his unquestionable learning was as a translator of the Scriptures… He urged by trea-

---

4 Sheppard and Thiselton, 'Biblical Interpretation', 55.
5 Sheppard and Thiselton, 'Biblical Interpretation', 55.
6 Sheppard and Thiselton, 'Biblical Interpretation', 57.
7 Palladius, *The Paradise or Garden of the Holy Fathers* (tr. E.A.W. Budge; London, 1907), 1.173-74, as cited by O.F.A. Meinardus, *Monks and Monasteries of the Egyptian Deserts* (Cairo: American University in Cairo Press, 1992), 31 n.87. Elsewhere, Rebenich, *Jerome*, 45, records that 'There was a certain amount of rivalry between the monasteries in Bethlehem and Jerusalem, and Palladius, in his *Lausiac History*, pointed at the ill will and envy between the groups.'
8 W. Walker, *A History of the Christian Church* (New York: Charles Scribner's Sons, 1918, repr. Edinburgh: T&T Clark, 1949).

tise and by letter... In his controversial writings Jerome's littleness of spirit is often painfully manifest.[9]

This portrait of Jerome is decidedly robust and covers a wide number of characteristics and behaviours we often associate with Jerome's life and work, and yet it fails to probe beneath the surface and explain the man's literary (i.e., exegetical) achievements.

The essential text for such a reading of Jerome, and fundamental to the new historical-critical scholarship, was Frederic Farrar's *History of Interpretation* (1896).[10] For Farrar 'a perfect exegete' would possess 'a genius cognate with that of the sacred writer, so that the interpreter would be thoroughly honest and devoid of any misleading influences due to his own a priori convictions'.[11]

Whatever impact Farrar's discourse on the aim of the interpreter may have had, the early twentieth century focus for modern Jerome scholars would be an ongoing search to judge Jerome's hermeneutic (i.e., the *Hebraica Veritas* relating to the Hebrew original)[12] in terms of its service to Christian theological understanding. Put another way, there would be critical discernment of Jerome's corpus in order to understand its contribution within the community of faith both in antiquity and the modern-age.

In order to judge Jerome's hermeneutic scholars would need to appreciate Jerome's translation-style. Here Jerome faced a particular problem, namely the unliterary style of the Scriptures, which was a 'cultural problem for the educated ecclesiastic of the fourth century'.[13] For Jerome, writing effectively and translating the Bible clearly were imperatives. Significantly, one of Jerome's contemporaries, Basil of Caesarea (330-379), believed the Bible to have been written in 'a barbarian tongue' and whose 'style is unlearned'.[14] For Jerome, there was a cultural issue to be faced, namely, making the Bible intelligible

---

9. Walker, *The Christian Church*, 174-75.
10. F.W. Farrar, *History of Interpretation* (Grand Rapids: Baker, 1961 [1896]).
11. Farrar, *Interpretation*, 4-5, as cited by Sheppard and Thiselton, 'Biblical Interpretation', 59.
12. For one of the earliest of the modern studies of Jerome's hermeneutics, see H.F.D. Sparks, 'Jerome as Biblical Scholar,' in P.R. Ackroyd and C.F. Evans (eds.), *The Cambridge History of the Bible* (Cambridge: CUP, 1970), 1.510-41, especially 523-32. 'Jerome's developing hermeneutic (i.e., the formulation of, and devotion to, the *Hebraica Veritas* took place between 382 and 385 and may possibly (although there is no direct evidence) have emanated from Jerome's reading of Paul's letter to the Romans (i.e., the way in which the apostle Paul introduced his message to the Jewish and Gentile believers in Rome—'To the Jew First'—Rom. 1:16). For a discussion of the notion of 'To the Jew First', see D.L. Bock and M. Glaser (eds.), *To the Jew First: The Case for Jewish Evangelism in Scripture and History* (Grand Rapids: Kregel, 2008); A.X.J. Fritz, *To the Jew First or To the Jew at Last? Romans 1:16c and Jewish Missional Priority in Dialogue with Jews for Jesus* (Eugene: Pickwick, 2013).
13. J.J. Murphy, 'St. Augustine and the Debate about a Christian Rhetoric', in *The Rhetoric of St. Augustine*, 205-18 (210).
14. Murphy, 'St. Augustine', 210.

through clarity of expression and refinement of language in order that readers might better learn and understand the Word of God.

Here it is important to understand that during the fourth century a new Christian culture was emerging. Not only had the Emperor Theodosius (379-395) suppressed paganism by a series of decrees (391-394) but the rest of the fourth century saw significant Christian progression, so much so 'that the converter of St. Augustine, Ambrose of Milan, could refer to his age as Christian times, *Christiana tempora*.'[15]

It was against this background of a marginalised paganism and rising Christianity that Jerome undertook his translation work, and it was because Jerome was 'still concerned that heathen sources were being used to attack the doctrine of the resurrection of the body'[16] that he felt a particular urgency to seek after scriptural truth by adopting a simple, clear style. Jerome states:

> We do not wish for the field of rhetorical eloquence, or the snares of dialecticians, nor do we seek the subtleties for Aristotle, but the very words of Scripture must be set down.[17]

However, as a biblical translator one of Jerome's tasks was to address the question of the relation of the Scriptures to the developing tradition of the Church in the fourth and fifth centuries. Jerome was a Catholic exegete and this fact would hold a special significance for the way in which Jerome conducted his scriptural work. Wallace-Hadrill has opined that the Catholic views the church in a particular way—'as the Body of Christ mediating the Divine life of Christ to people through organs of continuity, ministerial and sacramental, which are of Divine ordinance'.[18] However, during the fourth century the inerrancy of Scripture was not a given absolute.[19] Thus, Jerome's translation work had to be undertaken in the context of a non-consensual view of Scripture.

---

[15] Murphy, 'St. Augustine', 206. Elsewhere Ramsay Macmullen has written: 'Theodosius promulgated harsh anti-pagan laws and ordered the destruction of the huge, the world-famous Sarapis temple in Alexandria.' See R. Macmullen, *Christianity and Paganism in the Fourth to Eighth Centuries* (New Haven and London: Yale Univesity Press, 1997), 2. For one of the most useful accounts of how the way was 'opened up' for Christianity to develop during the fourth century, see M. Edwards, 'Pagan and Christian Monotheism in the age of Constantine,' in S.C.R. Swain and M. Edwards (eds.), *Approaching Late Antiquity* (Oxford: OUP, 2004), 211-34.

[16] Murphy, 'St. Augustine', 212.

[17] Jerome, *Liber contra Helvidium de perpetua virginitate Marie* xii, quoted in M.J. Kelly, 'Life and Times as Revealed in the Writings of St. Jerome Exclusive of his Letters,' *PStud* 52 (Washington: Catholic University of America, 1944), 59, as cited by Murphy, 'St. Augustine', 212n.35.

[18] S. Wallace-Hadrill, 'A Fourth Century View of the Origins of Christianity', *ExpT* 67 (1955-1956), 53-56 (53).

[19] Wallace-Hadrill, 'A Fourth Century View', 53. According to Geisler and Roach, 'Church history is plagued with deviant views on the topic of the inerrancy of Scripture.' See N.L. Geisler and W.C. Roach, *Defending Inerrancy* (Grand Rapids: Baker, 2011), 17. Toom has noted, 'In the fourth century, the designation "Scripture" did not

Having looked at the landscape of modern Jerome scholarship we can now proceed to an examination of how modern scholars have received selected texts/writings drawn from Jerome's corpus.

1880-1914

An important early reassessment of Jerome's exegetical principles and practice, by C.J. Elliott, appeared in 1880.[20] Elliott states:

> Whatever opinion may be formed of the philological accuracy of Jerome's Hebrew scholarship, his superiority in this respect to all the ecclesiastical writers who preceded him, and to all who for many centuries followed him, will be universally allowed. At the same time it is a task of considerable difficulty to determine the precise nature and extent of Jerome's obligations to his Hebrew teachers (Barrabanus and others), and thus to discriminate accurately between those criticisms which were original, and those for which he was indebted to his Jewish instructors.[21]

Here Elliott's judgement on Jerome is balanced but cautious. If there is a criticism it is that in his indebtedness to his Jewish teachers (his habit of borrowing from others) Jerome 'received and transmitted statements without investigation'.[22]

Elliott draws particular attention to the deficiency of Jerome's critical scholarship, which lay principally in etymology (i.e., the history of the origin and development of a word). For example, Elliott notes that in his treatise on proper names, Jerome is 'guilty of perpetuating etymological conceits'.[23] From this, Elliott concludes that 'a lack of critical accuracy and discernment pervades the writings of Jerome'.[24] Ironically, however defective (in Elliott's view) may have been the amount of his *critical* scholarship, Elliott proceeds to acknowledge some of Jerome's major contributions to exegesis in the early Church, principally his commentaries which, despite their imperfections, were 'a distinct improvement upon the work of earlier exegetes.'[25]

In the early twentieth century other Jerome scholars were focusing upon some of the more technical aspects of Jerome's corpus. For example, in 1911 Alexander Souter investigated the Old-Latin authorities for the text of the Gospels in Jerome's translation revision. Souter states:

yet denote a universally agreed upon and closed collection of inspired writings.' See T. Toom, 'Augustine on Scripture,' *Companion to Augustine and Modern Theology*, 75-90 (83-84).

20 C.J. Elliott, 'Hebrew Learning Among the Fathers', *DCB* 2 (1880), 851-72.
21 Elliott, 'Hebrew Learning', 864-65.
22 Elliott, 'Hebrew Learning', 865.
23 Elliott, 'Hebrew Learning', 866. Elliott argues that Jerome's tendency to perpetuating 'exegetical conceits' is 'further illustrated in his epistle to Paulinus, *De studio scripturarum*, in which he assigns *iniquitas* as the meaning of the proper name *Hamman*'.
24 Elliott, 'Hebrew Learning', 866.
25 Elliott, 'Hebrew Learning,' 867-68.

It does not seem to have occurred to any one to examine fully what type or types of Old-Latin text Jerome actually cites in his surviving works... But certainly a new era in the study of St. Jerome has dawned with the publication of the first volume of the Vienna edition of his works, containing Epistles 1 to 70.[26]

From his own reading of Epistle xxi (written by Jerome to Pope Damasus, himself the begetter of the Vulgate) Souter argues a case for Jerome having habitually used in his revision of St. Luke's Gospel an Old-Latin text practically identical with cod. Vercellensis (a) traditionally said to have been written by Eusebius of Vercelli himself (*ob.* 371).[27] Here Souter's claim raises the question of just how far Jerome's Vulgate textual work (from the Greek text) was his own. If Souter's thesis is correct it may well be taken as evidence for the McGuckin (2005) view that Jerome's reputation as an exegete is over-stressed (at least if we look for originality). Whilst Souter's essay is important to our understanding of Jerome's exegetical method when translating the Greek text, it does not illuminate any further our knowledge of Jerome the Jewish exegete.

However, we do get further insights into Jerome's exegetical method from Hugh Pope's critique of Jerome's Latin translation of St. Paul's Epistles.[28] Pope's essay provides us with important information about how Jerome revised rather than translated parts of the NT. The central thrust of Pope's reassessment was 'to call in question the truth of a generally received proposition, viz., that the present Clementine Vulgate text represents St. Jerome's correction of the Latin text of St. Paul's Epistles as it existed in his day'.[29]

Here Pope, like Souter, is in revisionist-mode but, as we shall now see, he is somewhat inconsistent in challenging earlier understandings of Jerome's translation practice. For example, in his evaluation of Jerome's Latin text of St. Paul's Epistles Pope finds Jerome to have used his own "freedom" in rendering certain words (e.g., in Titus) and "correcting" certain Epistles (e.g., 1 Cor.).[30] Despite these findings Pope then concludes that whilst there is certainty that 'St. Jerome revised the Latin text of the Gospels' there is less certainty 'that he revised that of the Epistles or the rest of the NT'.[31] But, surely, upon his own analysis and evidence, Pope might have partly concluded that there is some certainty that Jerome revised some Epistles.

---

[26] A. Souter, 'The Type or Types of Gospel Text used by St. Jerome as the Basis of his Revision, With Special Reference to St. Luke's Gospel And Codex Vercellensis', *JTS* 12 (1911), 583-92.

[27] Souter, 'Type of Types of Gospel Text', 591. For Souter's account of how Jerome 'polished' the earlier Latin translations of the biblical books then known, see A. Souter, *The Text and Canon of the New Testament* (London: Gerald Duckworth; 1913; repr. 1965), 22, 29, 32, 41, 44, 49, 57, 65, 78, 81, 131.

[28] H. Pope, 'St. Jerome's Latin Text of St. Paul's Epistles', *ITQ* 9 (1914), 413-45.

[29] Pope, 'St. Jerome's Latin Text', 413.

[30] Pope, 'St. Jerome's Latin Text ', 420-21.

[31] Pope, 'St. Jerome's Latin Text', 440. For the later modern record of Jerome's translations of the NT, see Rebenich, *Jerome*, 53.

1915-1939

From 1915 Jerome scholars were temporarily moving away from the principles and practice of Jerome towards Jerome's position in, and relation to, the Grae-co-Roman culture within which he worked and from which his corpus was produced. For example, A.S. Pease[32] reassessed the attitude of Jerome to the pagan culture which was 'yielding to the Christian',[33] finding that despite Jerome's lack of literary output aimed at paganism Jerome did receive from the old faith certain influences which would shape his writings (e.g., 'he acquired a sense of literary style, which made him extremely sensitive to works of unrhetorical composition'[34]). Pease notes that Jerome 'remained very sensitive to criticisms against his style, and apologised for its defects on the grounds of absence from Latin associations',[35] whilst 'Jerome's tastes were offended by the stylistic rudeness of the early Christian writings'.[36]

In 1923 John Chapman, following Souter's earlier work on Jerome's Vulgate textual revision (from the Greek text) and the issue of just how far this was Jerome's own, widened the debate still further by investigating the question of whether or not Jerome was the author of the whole Vulgate NT or only of the Gospels.[37] Although deciding in favour of Jerome's sole authorship of the Vulgate NT (in contrast to Souter), Chapman readily acknowledged why doubts had arisen, specifically over the question of why it was that Jerome's commentaries contained interpretations which did not later materialise in the Vulgate.[38]

On the precise issue of the quality of Jerome's biblical scholarship, Chapman's reassessment of Jerome's method of revising sacred texts provided a judgment which might suggest a possible correspondence with the McGuckin (2005) view that Jerome's reputation as exegete is over-stressed (at least if we look for originality).

---

[32] A.S. Pease, 'The Attitude of Jerome towards Pagan Literature', *Proceedings of the American Philological Association* 50 (1919), 150-67.

[33] Pease, 'Attitude of Jerome', 150. Here Pease describes Jerome as 'a Christian of distinction and influence in a period of transition'.

[34] Pease, 'Attitude of Jerome', 152.

[35] Pease, 'Attitude of Jerome', 153.

[36] Pease, 'Attitude of Jerome', 153.

[37] J. Chapman, 'St. Jerome and the Vulgate New Testament ', *JTS* 24 (1923), 33-51; 113-25; 282-99.

[38] Chapman, 'St. Jerome,' 37-38. Chapman notes: 'The date of Jerome's commentaries is about 387 and Jerome did not issue his revision of the whole NT until 391. Thus there will be four years between the text of the commentaries—which is a stage towards the Vulgate—and the Vulgate itself,' 38. Chapman is adamant that 'independence of Vulgate from St. Jerome's commentaries is impossible' (47), and that 'the Vulgate revision of St. Paul was made by St. Jerome some years later than his four commentaries on Pauline epistles' (48). Chapman further asserts, 'I do not see how any serious argument can be made to show that St. Jerome is not the author of the Vulgate' (48).

Timidity in correcting the O.L. and the eventual adoption of readings already to be found in some O.L. codex or other, is characteristic of St. Jerome in the Gospels, and we have seen the same in the Epistles.[39]

During the 1930s, scholars returned to examining the exegetical principles and practice of Jerome. In these exercises, scholars would highlight the historical interest of particular elements of Jerome's corpus, and in so doing would demonstrate a more positive reception of Jerome's work.

Algernon Ward's study of Jerome's work on the Psalter[40] describes how Jerome made several versions of this composition (two were revisions, and the third was a version direct from the Hebrew). Of Jerome's Hebrew Psalter (*Psalterium uxta Hebraeos*) from 392-393, Ward praises the way in which Jerome had held steadfast (despite opposition from Augustine) to his 'abandonment of the Greek text of the OT in favour of "Hebraica Veritas" as the "textus authenticus",' which Jerome considered to be 'the fountain-head itself'.[41] Of particular interest here is Ward's claim that Jerome's 'Hebrew' Psalter is of special historical significance (as well as 'a fine piece of scholarship') for providing 'evidence as to the Hebrew text of the fourth century (i.e., several hundred years before the oldest Hebrew MS known to us'[42] [pre-Dead Sea Scrolls]. For his opinion that Jerome was 'the best biblical scholar of ancient times'.[43] Ward may be seen as one of the more prominent modern Jerome apologists. And, of course, his view of Jerome here goes well beyond McGuckin's (2005) view that Jerome was perhaps the most important biblical scholar of the early Western church.

In 1933 the Loeb Classical Library published a collection of the select letters of Jerome.[44] This invaluable resource gave scholars insight into Jerome's extra-exegetical interests (asceticism, virginity, women, clergy, widows, education, monasticism and the family). Letter writing forms a distinct and important part of Jerome's corpus. In his translation of this selection of letters, F.A. Wright notes that Jerome's letters are one of the four most famous collections of letters in Latin literature.[45]

In his *Introduction* to the letters Wright offers comment on their style and subject, and infers from them evidence of Jerome's attitude, character and personality. Declaring Jerome to have been 'a wonderful master of words'.[46]

---

[39] Chapman, 'St. Jerome', 115.

[40] A. Ward, 'Jerome's Work on the Psalter', *ExpT* 44 (1932), 87-92.

[41] Ward, 'Jerome's Work', 90-91.

[42] Ward, 'Jerome's Work' 91. Ward was writing before the discovery of the Dead Sea Scrolls.

[43] Ward, 'Jerome's Work,' 91.

[44] Jerome, *Select Letters* (tr. F.A. Wright; Cambridge: Loeb Classical Library/Harvard University Press, 1933).

[45] Jerome, *Select Letters*, xiii. The three other collections are those of Cicero, Seneca and Pliny.

[46] Jerome, *Select Letters*, xiii.

Wright briefly compares Jerome with Cicero (who is his closest example in Latin literature), making the distinction between the two men very clear: 'Cicero wished to please everybody; Jerome wished to please no one.'[47] Here Wright may well be pointing to Jerome's reputation (whether deserved or not) for sometimes violent, polemical invective.

From his selection of letters, Wright reads Jerome to have been a student of cosmology, a man critical of those who abandoned asceticism and a supporter of chastity and virginity.[48]

In 1937, Charles Mierow offered an apologetic for Jerome based largely upon Jerome's letters.[49] Mierow speaks of us as being 'emboldened' by Jerome's life and writings.[50] The centrepiece of Mierow's defence of Jerome is his reassessment of what he describes as 'some outstanding traits of Jerome's character and personality as a man, as a teacher, as a scholar'.[51] For example, Mierow highlights how Jerome, despite his life as an 'ascetic, monk and solitary,' desired human contact [evidenced by the large numbers of his extant letters] and how Jerome's letters 'often monographs on theological or exegetical questions made him 'a sort of Christian oracle on matters of faith and conduct'.[52] We shall see later on in this chapter and in chapter 4 and chapter 5 below how a number of modern scholars have similarly viewed Jerome as a theological resource (i.e., as a source of authoritative information on early Christianity).

However, as we shall now see, Mierow's radical view of Jerome as acting as a 'sort of Christian oracle' would come under attack from some of the next generation of Jerome scholars active between 1940 and 1955.

1940-1955

Jerome scholarship during the 1940s would see scholars contesting Jerome's textual criticism and hermeneutic. In 1944, the issue of Jerome's textual criticism became the subject of an article by Karl Hulley.[53] Scholars were now particularly interested in discovering just how far Jerome might have displayed some resistance to the utilization of textual criticism in his use of the Hebrew text for his Vulgate OT. In his opening statement, addressing the writing of Jerome's Vulgate Bible, Hulley remarks, 'It is but natural to presume that among the qualifications which he possessed for his undertaking, knowledge of the principles of textual criticism must have been of prime importance.'[54]

---

47   Jerome, *Select Letters*, xii – xiii.
48   Jerome, *Select Letters*, xiv.
49   C.S. Mierow, 'An Early Christian Scholar', *TCJ* 33.1 (1937), 3-17.
50   Mierow, 'Christian Scholar', 9.
51   Mierow, 'Christian Scholar', 12.
52   Mierow, 'Christian Scholar', 12-14.
53   K. Hulley, 'Principles of Textual Criticism Known to St. Jerome,' *HSCP* 55 (1944), 87-109.
54   Hulley, 'Principles of Textual Criticism,' 87.

Hulley's reassessment of Jerome's critical method and procedure suggested that Jerome's work was born out of his view of three categories of textual error: namely, errors of translation, errors caused by ill-judged attempts at textual emendation, and errors made by careless or incompetent copyists.[55]

The details of textual criticism known to Jerome were *Lower Criticism* (the establishing of the text and textual errors and their causes) and *Higher Criticism* (changes in book—division, rejection of parts of a work, pseudepigrapha [questions of authorship/forgeries] and alteration of texts).[56]

Crucial to how scholars have understood Jerome's critical principles, exegetical procedure and practice has been their understanding of the priority that he gives to the *Hebraica Veritas* / the Hebrew truth. It was this hermeneutic together with Jerome's support of the Rule of Faith which embodied Jerome's defence of the Jewish canon of the OT and his belief that the 'Hebrew verity' was the ultimate and unadulterated source of the Bible, and which he regularly exalted above the Greek.

In 1947, W. Den Boer[57] addressed the issue of how early Christian authors and preachers, in their contact with the Hellenistic world, faced the problem of how to render the Jewish mode of thinking revealed in the Bible intelligible to outsiders.[58] The major point of controversy here focussed upon the allegorical interpretation—which, Den Boer notes, 'the Alexandrian school accepted and applied, whereas the Antiochian school set out from the literal and historic meaning and allowed only such explanation as would bring the text under consideration into relation with Jesus Christ and his mission.'[59]

What, then, of Jerome's hermeneutic? Den Boer makes an important and revealing point when he states, 'Before Origen we hardly come across a definite opinion on the method of interpreting the Holy Scriptures.'[60] Furthermore, Den Boer argues that 'Origen's interpretation of Holy Scripture (whereby Origen made allegory the keystone of his own exegesis and rejected a literal explanation) represents—together with Clement of Alexandria—the earliest opinions

---

[55] Hulley, 'Principles of Textual Criticism,' 88-89.

[56] Hulley, 'Principles of Textual Criticism,' 89-109. For a detailed critique of Jerome's understanding and application of Lower/Higher Criticism, see W.A. Oldfather (ed.), *Studies in the Text Tradition of St. Jerome's 'Vitae Patrum'* (Urban: The University of Illinois Press, 1943).

[57] W. Den Boer, 'Hermeneutic Problems in Early Christian Literature,' *VC* 1.3 (1947), 150-67.

[58] Den Boer, 'Hermeneutic Problems,' 150.

[59] Den Boer, 'Hermeneutic Problems,' 150. Importantly, of the patristic Church Fathers it was Origen and Gregory the Great who were the two practitioners of the four senses of the Bible: the literal-historical sense; typological (or allegorical); tropological (moral meaning) and eschatological (the final outcome of salvation history). See D. Farkasfalvy, *Inspiration and Interpretation: A Theological Introduction to Sacred Scripture* (Washington: Catholic University of America Press, 2010), 120-29.

[60] Den Boer, 'Hermeneutic Problems', 151.

on the interpretation of Biblical tradition.'[61] The implications of this for Jerome's hermeneutic (*Hebraica Veritas / Hebrew truth*) seem to have been two-fold. First, whilst Jerome opposed heretical doctrines that contested the doctrine of the OT, he had also to face up to Jewish polemics against the NT. Second, in following Clement (c. 150-c.215),[62] and understanding that 'the Scriptures have a historical, paradigmatic and allegorical meaning,'[63] Jerome was faced with one of the most important underlying issues in exegesis (one that still dominates biblical debate today), the relationship of the OT to the NT. Whilst Den Boer considers the OT 'points to Christ and represents *types* of the coming Redeemer,' and 'the Jewish biblical tradition held there to be a *moral* meaning to the OT,'[64] Jerome was faced with the question of how Jewish should Christianity be? If Jerome's hermeneutic was fully operational between 382 and 385 when Jerome was in Rome starting his revision of the Bible, then it took place largely against a blank-canvas. As Den Boer comments, 'the possibilities of interpreting the Holy Scriptures were not clearly defined, even in the most sharp-witted mind (the Greek Origen) of pre-Constantine Christianity.'[65]

During the 1950s Jerome scholarship grew apace building upon that foundational heritage of Jerome studies which had developed since 1880. Whilst some early scholars (between 1880 and 1947) had identified certain contradictory elements in Jerome's critical procedure (i.e., certain inconsistencies in translation style and exegetical method), later scholars (between 1952 and 1965) would now begin to contest such criticism, albeit not always in a convincing fashion.

For example, in 1952 a new collection of essays on Jerome appeared which amounted to a *memorial* to the saint providing, as it did, a critique of the various phases of Jerome's career (e.g., hermit, exegete, historian, spiritual director and humanist).[66] Two essays focussed upon Jerome as an exegete (Hartmann)[67]

---

[61] Den Boer, Hermeneutic Problems,' 158. Here Den Boer cites Origen's *De princ.* IV, 3, as evidence for 'Origen's pivotal role in the Christian interpretation of the Scriptures of the Church'.

[62] According to Dennis Brown 'Jerome spoke approvingly of Clement.' See D. Brown, 'Jerome', in *Dictionary of Major Biblical Interpreters*, 565-71 (566). Similarly, Rebenich, *Jerome*, 98, notes how Jerome had a 'fondness for certain theologians' including 'Clement, Tertullian, Hippolytus of Rome and Dionysius of Alexandria.'

[63] Den Boer, 'Hermeneutic Problems,' 159.

[64] Den Boer, 'Hermeneutic Problems,' 159.

[65] Den Boer, 'Hermeneutic Problems,' 166. For a discussion of the state of patristic exegesis prior to Jerome, see Farkasfalvy, *Inspiration and Interpretation*, 120-39. Farkasfalvy notes, 'The theologians of the third century opened a new era in the history of Christian thought...they began to exploit systematically and methodically the riches of the OT and NT by using them as source material both for apologetics (the defence of the faith against Jews and heretics) and for doctrinal systematization' (120).

[66] Murphy, *A Monument*.

[67] L.N. Hartmann, 'St. Jerome as an Exegete,' in *A Monument*, 37-81.

and Jerome and the canon of the Holy Scriptures (Skehan).[68] Hartmann finds Jerome to have been an 'eclectic' scholar utilizing what he saw as the 'best' exegesis of the 'Alexandrian/Antiochian schools' but 'avoiding the excesses of both.'[69] It may well have been this eclectic method which helped progress Jerome's exegetical skill and later achievements as a biblical scholar. This is certainly the implication of Skehan's essay 'St. Jerome and the Canon of the Holy Scriptures' where Skehan speaks of 'a final victory for his [Jerome's] approach to biblical studies.'[70] However, and somewhat ironically, Skehan then claims that despite the later fame of Jerome's Vulgate Bible, the actuality has been that 'Jerome's presentation of the canon of the Holy Scriptures, representing the formal teaching of the Church's greatest Scriptural Doctor has, in fact, not been followed by the Church.'[71]

Clearly, Skehan's claim regarding the Church's negative reception of Jerome's presentation of the canon of the Holy Scriptures would seem to contradict in some way his earlier assertion of 'a final victory for his [Jerome's] approach to biblical studies'. There is certainly some ambivalence here. Equally questionable is Skehan's view (unsubstantiated) that 'in the familiar distinction between his theory and his practice with regard to the canon, there are remarkable instances of his docility toward the voice and practice of the Church,'[72] for as an intransigent controversialist (when the occasion demanded) Jerome can hardly ever be described as having been easily led or tractable.

---

[68] P.W. Skehan, 'St. Jerome and the Canon of the Holy Scriptures,' in *A Monument*, 259-87.
[69] Hartmann, 'Jerome as an Exegete,' 51-52. This view of Jerome would be later endorsed by Dennis Brown who writes 'Jerome was essentially an eclectic scholar.' See Brown, 'Jerome', in *Major Biblical Interpreters*, 565-71 (569).
[70] Skehan, 'Jerome and the Canon,' 259.
[71] Skehan, 'Jerome and the Canon,' 259. Here Skehan is not correct. For example, with regard to the book of Hebrews, the Western church, largely under the influence of Jerome and Augustine, accepted Hebrews as canonical by the fifth century. See B.S. Childs, *The Church's Guide for Reading Paul: The Canonical Shaping of the Pauline Corpus* (Grand Rapids: Eerdmans, 2008), 238. Elsewhere, the authors of *Reinventing Jesus* have entered into this morass to clearly show Jerome's pivotal importance to the canon of the Holy Scriptures followed by the church: 'In the West, a flurry of unofficial canon lists were composed by leading church fathers, and during the fourth century the core books were always included. By 393 the canon was effectively closed when Augustine weighed in on the matter. Jerome added icing on the cake by discussing at some length the disputed books. Further, he included the twenty-seven New Testament books in his translation (known as the Vulgate). Since that time, the Catholic Church (except in rare instances) has never questioned which books were in and which were not.' See, J.E. Komoszewski, M.J. Sawyer and D.B. Wallace, *Reinventing Jesus: How Contemporary Skeptics miss the Real Jesus and Mislead Popular Culture* (Grand Rapids: Kregal, 2006), 130.
[72] Skehan, 'Jerome and the Canon,' 260.

In 1954 an entirely different reading of Jerome was provided by H.E.W. Turner.[73] In this work, one of Turner's interests was to trace the background to episcopal authority. Turner writes:

> In Christian antiquity two theories were held associated with the names of St. Jerome and Theodore of Mopsuestia... The former conceived of the monepiscopate as evolved, as it were, from below through the emergence of a leading member of a collegiate episcopacy into a position of *de jure* authority...The second view traces the emergence of the monepiscopate as a process directed from above, the Apostles acting through lieutenants such as Titus and Timothy forming the connecting link between the Apostle and the local presbyterates. The unofficial role of the Pauline young men becomes converted into a primitive form of metropolitical jurisdiction...Bishop Lightfoot's classical dissertation on the Christian Ministry favoured the view of St. Jerome, the work of Bishop Gore, revised by C.H. Turner, upheld the theory of Theodore...It would be a probable conclusion that both processes contributed to the evolution of the monepiscopate in different parts of the Christian Church and at different speeds.[74]

Here Turner's reading of Jerome is entirely correct but it is presented without any supporting evidence.[75] Elsewhere on Jerome's orthodoxy, Turner is far from generous, claiming that Jerome 'could expound the theory of the threefold sense of Scripture as of unexceptional orthodoxy'.[76] There is a strange irony in Turner's decision to place Jerome (surely well-known to Turner for his occasional usage of allegory and his early admiration of Origen) in the anti-allegorist camp. Thus:

> St. Jerome accuses the allegorists of neglecting the plain meaning of the prophets and apostles, of exalting their own statements into the Law of God, and of forcing a reluctant Scripture to bend to their will; Origen wandered into the open spaces of allegory content to interpret single words and mistaking his own ingenuity for ecclesiastical mysteries.[77]

Here Jerome may well be displaying some inconsistency (if not hypocrisy)— Jerome as a sometime allegorist criticizing Origen *the* allegorist—but equally we can see in Turner's extract citation from Jerome's Letter 53 above, Jerome defending biblical orthodoxy in a completely unashamed way.

---

[73] H.E.W. Turner, *The Pattern of Christian Truth: A Study in the Relations between Orthodoxy and Heresy in the Early Church* (London: Mowbray, 1954).

[74] Turner, *Pattern*, 346-47. Yannis Papadogiannakis notes that at the council of Constantinople (553) 'the writings of Theodore of Mopsuestia were condemned summarily'. See Y. Papadogiannakis, *Christianity and Hellenism in the Fifth-Century Greek East: Theodoret's Apologetics Against the Greeks in Context* (Cambridge: Harvard University Press, 2012), 3.

[75] For such evidence e.g., Jerome's arrangement of clergy into a neat hierarchy of ascending excellence (Jerome, *Comm. in Ep. Ad Titum*, ii, 15), and Jerome's portrayal of the ideal episcopal household (Jerome, *Ep. 52, 7, Adv. Iovinianum*, i. 3), see P. Rousseau, *Asctics*, 125n.1, 126n.7, 128n.17.

[76] Turner, *Pattern*, 291.

[77] Jerome, *Ep. 53, 7, Comm. in Isa.* lib. v, *Praef,* as cited by Turner, *Pattern*, 291n.7.

1956–1965

In 1956 Henry Bettenson's *The Early Christian Fathers*[78] devoted itself to those Fathers of the early Church that preceded Jerome. However, a number of footnote citations given over to Jerome by Bettenson throw important light upon Jerome's exegetical methods and influences.

First, in looking at the writings of Ignatius (Bishop of Antioch) to the Smyrnaeans, Bettenson quotes Ignatius's words on the physical Resurrection:

> For I know and believe that even after his resurrection he was in a physical body, and when he came to Peter and his companions he said, 'Take hold and feel me, and see that I am not a bodiless phantom.'[79]

Here Bettenson observes that 'Jerome ascribes this form of the saying to the *Gospel according to the Hebrews*, though Eusebius, who knew that gospel, was unable to place it, and Origen, who also knew it, ascribes the saying to the Teaching of Peter.'[80] Whether or not Jerome was correct in his attribution is not the real question to ask. Rather what is important is the way in which Jerome decided to act counter to Origen's earlier attribution of the saying. So, is this suggestive of Jerome's originality/creativity? Is it a pointer to Jerome being a greater exegete than Origen? It remains very much an open question.

Next, Bettenson focuses upon Tertullian's comments relating to Montanism and the Holy Spirit, where Tertullian states:

> [At the Transfiguration] Peter 'did not know what he was saying'. How was that? Was it because of mere aberration, or in accordance with the rule (as we have maintained in support of Prophecy) that a state of ecstasy, of being 'out of one's mind' accompanies the operation of grace? For a man who is 'in the spirit,' especially when he beholds the glory of God and when God speaks through him, must inevitably lose consciousness, overshadowed as he is by the Divine Power (*Adversus Marcionem*, iv.2).[81]

Here it is Jerome's capacity to act as a 'theological resource'[82] a key feature of Jerome's work as a biblical scholar—which demonstrates Jerome working to proffer information on earlier unnoticed patristic texts.

Finally, in his discussion of the Latin translations of Origen's works (from the Greek), Bettenson makes a distinction between 'the free, and often theologically "bowdlerized," versions of Rufinus of Aquilea' and 'the more faithful translation of Jerome,'[83] where Rufinus and Jerome have each rendered passages of Origen but which are not directly translated from the Greek. Here Betten-

[78] H. Bettenson (ed. and tr.) *The Early Christian Fathers: A selection from the writings of the Fathers from St. Clement of Rome to St. Athanasius* (Oxford: OUP, 1956).
[79] Bettenson, *Early Christian Fathers*, 48.
[80] Bettenson, *Early Christian Fathers*, 48n.4.
[81] Bettenson, *Early Christian Fathers*, 131.
[82] Bettenson, *Early Christian Fathers*, 131n.6, notes that 'Jerome mentions a lost work of Tertullian "On Ecstasy," in six books.'
[83] Bettenson, *Early Christian Fathers*, 185.

son's more positive reception of Jerome's exegesis of Origen over Rufinus might call into question McGuckin's (2005) claim that Jerome's reputation as exegete is over-stressed (at least if we look for originality). However, some caution is required. Does a more faithful translation (of Origen) equate to a more original translation? No. A faithful translation is simply one that is true to the facts (to the original wording/phrasing). Either way, here Bettenson ranks Jerome a more accurate exegete than Rufinus.

During the period 1956-1965 scholars also increasingly emphasized the critical treasures to be found within in Jerome's biblical exegesis. For example, Raphael Loewe's essay discussing the literary spheres of patristic and scholastic exegesis of the Bible[84] opens with a reference to the writings of a few of the Church Fathers for the study of the rabbinic exegesis of the Bible, noting 'the few rich seams—especially the writings of St. Jerome and Ephraem Syrus'.[85]

Loewe then directly praises Jerome's vocabulary for not only providing insights into 'the origin and development of a Christian vocabulary' but also for providing information 'for the study of the semantics of modern and medieval languages in Europe'.[86] Having highlighted the value of Jerome's vocabulary (unlike Elliott, 1880), Loewe then gives an example of the efficacy of Jerome's exegesis, citing Psalm 1 where he finds Jerome avoiding the figure of Jesus as the main character (i.e., the happy man of the Psalm) in favour of 'the just in general' which Loewe views as 'a fairly obvious explanation, which it is not surprising to find paralleled in the Jewish tradition'.[87]

Whilst we cannot say, on the basis of Loewe's example alone, that Jerome's exegesis made a clear, distinctive contribution from the Christian side to the

---

[84] R. Loewe, 'The Jewish Midrashim and Patristic and Scholastic Exegesis of the Bible,' *StP* 1 (1957), 492-514. Loewe observes, 'The Midrashim are anthologies of the exegetical remarks or sermons of individual rabbis or schools' (510).

[85] Loewe, 'The Jewish Midrashim,' 493. Ephraem Syrus (c. 306-373) 'was the classic writer of the Syriac-speaking church and basically represented a pre-Nicene (but anti-Arian) Semitic Christianity' who 'defended the essential mystery of God'. See Ferguson, *Church History*, 219-20.

[86] Loewe, 'The Jewish Midrashim,' 495. The influence of Jerome's exegesis and vocabulary over some other patristic authors cannot be overstated. For example, Jerome's influence on Gregory the Great's second homily on the book of Ezekiel can be readily seen. John Moorhead has observed: 'In his second homily on the book of Ezekiel, Gregory discusses the circumstances in which the word of the Lord came to the prophet, who was by the river Chebar [Ezek. 1:3], paying particular attention to the significance of the proper nouns used in the text. The meanings of the words in Hebrew had been explained by Jerome, a scholar of that language whose explanations Gregory largely follows.' See J. Moorhead, *Gregory the Great* (New York: Routledge, 2005), 52. For the influence of Donatus (the fourth century grammarian) over Jerome's insistence upon the rules of grammar, see J. Richards, *Consul of God: The Life and Times of Gregory the Great* (London: Routledge, 1980), 29.

[87] Loewe, 'The Jewish Midrashim,' 500.

Jewish,[88] we can look to some other scholars engaged in this and other allied areas to see how far Jerome's critical method may have helped to bring about important changes to the reading of the Bible.

Describing the early Church debate over the origins of the Greek Bible (LXX) Elias Bickerman has observed that Jerome was 'virtually alone in asserting with Aristeas, Josephus "and the whole Jewish school" that "only the Pentateuch was translated by the Seventy".'[89] Here the significance of Jerome's position on the origins of the Greek Bible is that it was contrary to the view of Augustine 'who believed that the whole Bible was translated by the seventy-two interpreters, whose version is customarily called Septuagint (*De civ. Dei* XVIII, 42)'.[90]

In 1959, two biographical studies of Jerome appeared which further made the case for Jerome as a leader of, and giant amongst, the Church Fathers.[91] Steinmann calls Jerome an 'intellectual leader' and the 'patron saint of exegetes'.[92] Significantly, both of these descriptions are at variance with the McGuckin-Freeman thesis on Jerome. Steinmann adds:

> In every sense of the word, Jerome was the Man of the Scriptures, a Christian library in himself...in its majesty and its poetry, the Vulgate far surpasses Augustine's Confessions and Ambrose's hymns, not to speak of Cicero...He outstripped all his rivals. He is the most outstanding of the Latin Fathers.[93]

This is clearly one of the strongest apologias for Jerome that we have so far seen. For Steinmann, examples of the critical treasures to be found within Jerome's biblical exegesis include his Latin translation of the Gospels ('correcting obvious earlier mistranslations to make the new Latin translation more ac-

---

[88] For Jerome's view on Jewish Christians, see J. Stevenson (ed.), *A New Eusebius: Documents illustrative of the history of the Church to A.D. 337* (London: SPCK, 1957), 69. Stevenson notes that at the time of Jerome 'Jewish Christians were regarded as heretical' and 'Jerome writing to Augustine (*Ep.* 112.13), regards them as neither Jews nor Christians.'

[89] E.J. Bickerman, 'The Septuagint as a Translation,' *Proceedings of the American Academy for Jewish Research* 28 (1959), 1-39 (5-6). Bickerman notes: 'From the second century C.E. on, Christian writers began to ascribe the translation of the whole Bible into Greek to the original company of interpreters...Christian writers likened the "Seventy Two" Elders of Aristeas to the Seventy Elders who assisted Moses, and spoke of the "Seventy" translators of the Bible. Therefore, the name of the Septuagint (LXX) given to the Greek Bible' (5-6).

[90] Bickerman, 'The Septuagint,' 6n.10. On the Septuagint controversy between Jerome and Augustine, see W. Schwarz, *Principles and Problems of Biblical Translation: Some Reformation Controversies and their Background* (Cambridge: CUP, 1955), 17-44.

[91] J. Steinmann, *Saint Jerome and his Times* (tr. R. Matthews; Notre Dame: Fides, 1959); C.C. Mierow, *Saint Jerome: The Sage of Bethlehem* (Milwaukee: Bruce, 1959).

[92] Steinmann, *Jerome*, 355.

[93] Steinmann, *Jerome*, 357.

curate, graceful and polished in style')[94] and the epistles of St. Paul ('where his commentaries on Philemon and Galatians in particular, demonstrate his simplicity of style, full of judicious summaries and fine passages, deliberately undertaken by Jerome so that as wide a readership as possible could benefit').[95] All of these may be seen as features of Jerome's 'theological style'.

In similar vein to Steinmann, Charles Mierow finds Jerome's Vulgate to have been 'a monumental scholarly labour',[96] and cites a number of examples of critical treasures to be found within Jerome's biblical exegesis, including Jerome's historical commentary on St. Matthew's Gospel (commissioned by Eusebius of Cremona) in which Jerome made an important translation, interpreting the phrase 'our daily bread' in the Lord's prayer as referring to Christ, the bread of life.[97]

Again, matching Steinmann's critique, Mierow praises Jerome's ability to 'offer clear exposition enabling his readers to grasp the proper meaning of the ancient scriptures.'[98] Here Mierow's comments perfectly capture Jerome's priority to keep his theology firmly engaged with the times and situations he faced. Nothing was more important to Jerome than making the ancient Scriptures intelligible to his readers. Here Mierow's critique of Jerome clearly challenges McGuckin's (2005) proposition that Jerome's reputation as exegete is over-stressed (at least if we look for originality) and seriously questions Freeman's (2009) view that Jerome never showed any genuine intellectual creativity or had the self-confidence to develop his own theology.

In 1960, the renowned patristic scholar and then Lady Margaret Professor of Divinity at Oxford, F.L. Cross, documented Jerome's role in preserving some of Origen's exegetical works.[99] Cross notes,

---

[94] Steinmann, *Jerome*, 138-39. Here it is worth noting that Jerome's translation of the Gospel of John later benefitted St. Thomas Aquinas in his commentary on the Fourth Gospel, by giving Aquinas John's opening words as '*In principio erat Verbum*'. See S.F. Brown, 'The Theological Role of the Fathers,' in M. Dauphinais and M. Levering (eds), *Reading John with St. Thomas Aquinas: Theological Exegesis and Speculative Theology* (Washington: Catholic University of America Press, 2005), 9-20 (16). For the way in which Thomas' exegesis of John drew partly upon Didymus the Blind (via Jerome's Latin translation), most especially on the procession of the Holy Spirit, see G. Emery, *The Trinitarian Theology of St. Thomas Aquinas* (Oxford: OUP, 2007), 276. For how Aquinas was 'deeply immersed in Patristic writings,' especially those of John Chrysostom, Origen, Jerome, Augustine and Pseudo-Dionysius, see D.L. Whidden III, *Christ the Light: The Theology of Light and Illumination in Thomas Aquinas* (Minneapolis: Fortress, 2014), 4.
[95] Steinmann, *Jerome*, 178-80.
[96] Mierow, *Jerome*, vii.
[97] Mierow, *Jerome*, 77.
[98] Mierow, *Jerome*, 68.
[99] F.L. Cross, *The Early Christian Fathers. Studies in Theology* (London: Duckworth, 1960).

Origen's exegetical treatises fall into three groups—Commentaries, Homilies and Scholia. The aim of the Commentaries was scholarly, namely to expound the text scientifically (though this did not preclude their author from allegorising); the Homilies were primarily edificatory; while the Scholia were detached notes on particular passages.

The *Commentaries* (or 'Tomes'), begun at Alexandria, occupied Origen through most of his life. They are the finest part of his exegetical work and won the warm admiration of Jerome…As regards the OT, Origen commented on Genesis, on several of the Psalms, on nearly all the Prophets and on the Song of Songs (twice); but very much has been lost. The second of Origen's Commentaries on the Canticles was praised by Jerome in the highest terms and it is in Jerome's Latin version that it survives.[100]

Cross was one of the earliest modern scholars to chronicle and highlight Jerome's importance as a 'theological resource' for our knowledge and understanding of several of the significant as well as minor patristic figures of the second to fifth-centuries.[101]

Another early study of Jerome appearing in 1960 was that by H.F.D. Sparks, then Oriel Professor of the Interpretation of Holy Scriptures in Oxford.[102] In this work, Sparks presented an account of the life of Jerome, Jerome's work as a Bible translator and as a Bible text critic and Jerome's contribution to the development of the Bible canon. Sparks reads Jerome very much as an apologist, noting 'the vigour of mind, acidity of tongue, and mastery of the telling phrase, that characterised all his work'.[103] In the following observations his admiration for Jerome is clearly stated:

> By his 'indefatigable' study of Hebrew Jerome turned himself into a near unique phenomenon at any period in the history of the early Church—a 'trilingual' (competent in Latin, Greek, and Hebrew). In his youth he had also studied Aramaic (what he calls 'Chaldaic'…as a result of his sojourn in the desert of Chalcis he had become a fluent speaker of Syriac…He writes, too, as if he had more than a nodding acquaintance with 'Arabic.' And in addition to these linguistic attainments, he had acquired, through his early training in the Latin classics, an exceptionally pure and incisive Latin style. He was thus possessed of every qualification that a successful translator could require.[104]

In his critique of Jerome Sparks highlights in particular those aspects of Jerome's *oeuvre* that undoubtedly acted in furthering Jerome's wider fame in late

---

[100] Cross, *The Early Christian Fathers*, 126.

[101] Cross cites Jerome's references to, amongst others, Polycorp, Quadratus Aristo of Pella, Theophilus of Antioch, Melito of Sardis, Pantaenus, Minncius Felix, Hippolytus Sextus Julius Africanus, Pierius, Gregory Thammaturgus, Methodies of Olympus, Novatian, Victorius of Pettau and Commodian.

[102] Sparks, 'Jerome as Biblical Scholar' in *The Cambridge History of the Bible*, 1.510-41.

[103] Sparks, 'Jerome as Biblical Scholar,' 516.

[104] Sparks, 'Jerome as Biblical Scholar,' 517.

antiquity even though it seems that fame was sometimes not always properly earned.

> His ascetic interests are represented by translations of the *Rule* and eleven of the letters of Pachomius, and his antiquarianism by translations into both Greek and Latin of the *Gospel according to the Hebrews*. On several occasions he was asked by highly placed ecclesiastics in the East to provide Latin versions of their official or controversial correspondence. And such was his reputation as a translator in the West that he was often credited with having translated many more authors than in fact he had: there was at one time a rumour current in Spain, for example, that he had translated Josephus, Papias, and Polycorp.[105]

This caveat, as offered by Sparks, acts as a reminder to us that surrounding the reception of Jerome as biblical scholar lies some uncertainty.[106] However, Sparks remains, for the most part, a positive critic, finding that 'What Jerome bequeathed to posterity in the field of translation was made up of a variety of separate elements that differed, not only in character but also in execution.'[107] For Sparks, these separate elements, especially those that made up Jerome's Bible translation of the Vulgate—a process taking more than twenty years—cost Jerome 'much toil and anxiety'.[108]

Does Sparks find Jerome wanting in these areas? First, Sparks notes how Jerome played up the actual amount of NT revision he completed:

> We might suppose that having finished the gospels, Jerome would naturally go on to treat the other books of the NT in the same way; and on more than one occasion he writes as if he had ('The New Testament I have restored in accordance with the Greek').[109] There are good grounds for regarding such a statement as one of Jerome's all-too-common exaggerations... Furthermore, although the Vulgate Acts, epistles and Revelation are traditionally attributed to Jerome, there are serious difficulties in believing that they are in fact his. Certain features, characteristic of Jerome, are lacking in the Vulgate version of these books; the prefaces attached to them in the Vulgate are clearly not his; and the quotations from them in his writings frequently display such a wide divergence from the Vulgate as to make it almost impossible to suppose that they and the Vulgate have a common origin.[110]

Jerome's tendency to overemphasize his achievements was undoubtedly a flaw in his character but cannot be seen as a weakness in his work as a biblical scholar. We have to look at Jerome's actual literary output and measure his accomplishments against the work of his predecessors and contemporaries ac-

---

[105] Sparks, 'Jerome as Biblical Scholar,' 517-18.
[106] Other examples are the extent of Jerome's revision of the OT on the basis of the Septuagint, and the extent of his activities in revising the NT (outside of the Gospels).
[107] Sparks, 'Jerome as Biblical Scholar,' 518-19.
[108] Jerome, *Praef. in Sam. et Reg*, as cited by Sparks, 'Jerome as Biblical Scholar,' 518n.3.
[109] Jerome, *De Vir. Ill.* 135; *Ep.* **71, 5**, as cited by Sparks, 'Jerome as Biblical Scholar,' 519n.2.
[110] Sparks, 'Jerome as Biblical Scholar,' 519.

cordingly. One thing is certain—Jerome's work as a biblical scholar did not meet with the immediate favour of the early Church. Sparks states:

> The acceptance of Jerome's works by the Church took time. Only his revision of the gospels was at all widely accepted during his lifetime. It had been commissioned by the pope, and this conferred on it a certain official status. But his work on the OT was a private venture, undertaken either on his own initiative or at the request of his friends. It had in consequence to make its own way on its merits. Churchmen have always been conservative, and it is likely that not a little of the welcome accorded to his gospels was due to the fact that they were merely a revised version of the familiar Old Latin and not a fresh translation. When he went on to the OT, the majority would doubtless have preferred him to continue along the same lines. Jerome, however, decided otherwise.[111]

Here, Sparks demonstrates, yet again, not only the uncertainty surrounding the reception of Jerome as biblical scholar but also the unpredictability of Jerome the man, a man always ready to turn his back on convention in his search for the correct textual transposition of scripture.[112]

For Sparks 'Jerome was, next to Origen, the greatest biblical scholar of the early Church.'[113] This, of course, closely parallels McGuckin's (2005) claim that Jerome was perhaps the most important biblical scholar of the early Western church. Yet, despite his undoubted exegetical abilities, Jerome found translation to be a skill difficult to achieve.[114]

As for Jerome's originality as an exegete, Sparks is somewhat cautious in his judgments especially on the Vulgate translation:

> His revision of the gospels was inevitably conservative. It was an early work; it was designed as a revision and not a fresh translation; and it was commissioned by the pope and was to receive the official papal *imprimatur*. So Jerome set himself deliberately to keep changes to a minimum and assured Damasus in his preface that he had 'used his pen with restraint.'[115]...But relatively speaking the changes are few. What is remarkable about them is their inconsistency...He always worked in a hurry.[116]

---

[111] Sparks, 'Jerome as Biblical Scholar,' 520. Sparks notes: 'He [Jerome] started on a revision of the Old Latin OT and became increasingly concerned to secure the best Septuagint texts obtainable on which to base it. But in the end he either gave it up before he had finished, or suppressed or lost the greater part of it if ever he did finish it. His interests were now concentrated on his new translation form the Hebrew,' 520-21.

[112] Spark notes how 'Questions of translation technique and details connected with the "mechanics" of translation obviously occupied Jerome's mind continuously,'522.

[113] Sparks, 'Jerome as Biblical Scholar,' 510.

[114] Jerome, *Praef. Chronic. Eus*; as cited by Sparks, 'Jerome as Biblical Scholar,' 522n.2.

[115] Sparks, 'Jerome as Biblical Scholar,' 523.

[116] Jerome, *Praef. in Chronic. Eus.*, *Ep.* 117.12, as cited by Sparks, 'Jerome as Biblical Scholar,' 524n.1.

Whilst this reading of Jerome raises doubts about Jerome's habits (keep changes to a minimum) and characteristics (inconsistency/working in a hurry) as a translator of scripture, we find in the following judgement on Jerome's translation of the OT from the Hebrew some sign of Jerome's capacity for originality:

> Jerome affirms more than once that the principle of 'sense for sense' and not 'word for word' is applicable to the translation of scripture as anything else.[117] This explains the considerable latitude he often allowed himself in the treatment of his original. The simple style of the Hebrew is varied, and its paratactic sentences repeatedly rearranged, in order to conform with more complex Latin idiom: proper names are sometimes translated rather than transliterated...or, if transliterated, perhaps supplied with an interpretative gloss, and the interpretative glosses are not confined to proper names...But what is remarkable is the variety of Jerome's renderings. Time and again he gives the impression that the last thing he would think of doing is to use a word or phrase twice in the same context if he could possibly avoid it.[118]

Of course, for some (Jerome's critics) this will be seen as nothing more than tinkering with the scriptures but for others (Jerome's apologists) it will be seen as a mark of imaginative and independent thought; and Jerome's apologists would say that it challenges McGuckin's thesis that Jerome's reputation as exegete is over-stressed (at least if we look for originality).

With regard to Jerome as a bible text-critic, Sparks notes Jerome's reputation for his 'strictures on the failings of others' before him,[119] and, as to Jerome's own work, Sparks observes further evidence of inconsistency.

> Frequently, no doubt, doctrinal and other considerations, apart from purely textual, determined his choice, so that it is difficult to be certain in the absence of a direct statement, on what grounds in any instance his preference for a particular reading is based. Jerome was always arbitrary.[120]

This judgement on Jerome ('Jerome was always arbitrary') is, indeed, a serious criticism, suggesting that Jerome as Bible text-critic may sometimes have made textual decisions not on reason so much as on whim or random choice. However, we might see this as somewhat harsh. For surely, the only thing that Jerome can be found guilty of here is, as Sparks correctly observes, his assurance that the 'Hebraica veritas...was self-authenticating.'[121]

In the final part of his assessment of Jerome, Sparks focuses upon Jerome as a Bible commentator. Biblical commentaries form a large part of Jerome's corpus. For Jerome the aim of a commentary was 'To explain what has been said

---

[117] Jerome, *Ep.* 106, 29; *Ep.* 112, 19, as cited by Sparks, 'Jerome as Biblical Scholar,' 525n.1.
[118] Sparks, 'Jerome as Biblical Scholar,' 525.
[119] Sparks, 'Jerome as Biblical Scholar,' 526.
[120] Sparks, 'Jerome as Biblical Scholar,' 529.
[121] Sparks, 'Jerome as Biblical Scholar,' 532.

by others and make clear in plain language what has been written obscurely.'[122]
Sparks states:

> Jerome himself does not claim to be in any way a 'master' of scriptural interpreta-
> tion: he is no more than a 'partner' in study with others.[123] But what he does claim
> is he has read as many different authors as possible, that he has plucked from
> them as 'different flowers' as he can, and that he has distilled their essence for the
> benefit of his readers.[124]

Here we see Jerome, not as someone merely muddling through as a Bible
commentator, but as someone regulated by a belief in the necessity of a satisfactory exegesis for the reader being achieved through making clear scripture's
obscurities.[125] However, for Sparks, this statement of Jerome's ideal as a commentator remained largely just that for 'he did not always realise it in practice'.[126] The reason for this may well have been Jerome's tendency to hurry his
commentaries. Sparks observes:

> It was his habit to read all the previous commentaries first and then dictate,[127]
> sometimes so rapidly that his secretaries could not keep up with him[128]—he says
> he frequently got through 1,000 lines a day.[129]

Sparks finds this tendency to rush his commentary work led Jerome to fail to
observe consistency in scriptural interpretation, most especially in his attitude
to and deployment of allegory.[130]

Sparks' critique of Jerome is one of the longest and most detailed in modern
Jerome scholarship. We have seen that his reception of Jerome is mixed. On the
positive side, he praises Jerome's commentaries for their learning (sacred, secular, philological, textual, historical, exegetical)—'They preserve a mass of early
exegetical matter that might otherwise have perished, and which through Jerome found its way into the commentaries of the Middle Ages.'[131] In contrast, it
is only in Jerome's character that Sparks finds real cause for concern and criticism. Spark concludes:

---

[122] Jerome, *Apol.* 1, 16, as cited by Sparks, 'Jerome as Biblical Scholar,' 535n.7.

[123] Jerome, *Ep.* 53, 10, as cited by Sparks, 'Jerome as Biblical Scholar,' 535n.12.

[124] Jerome, *Ep.* 61.1, as cited by Sparks, 'Jerome as Biblical Scholar,' 535n.13.

[125] See Jerome, *Apol.* 1, 16; *Ep.* 105.5; *Ep.* 53,6, as cited by Sparks, 'Jerome as Biblical
Scholar,' 535n.7, n.8, n.9.

[126] Sparks, 'Jerome as Biblical Scholar,' 536.

[127] Jerome, *Comm. In Gal., Lib. III, Prol; Comm. In Amos, Lib. III, Prol.,* as cited by
Sparks, 'Jerome as Biblical Scholar,' 536n.5.

[128] Jerome, *Praef. in Chronic. Eus; Ep.* 117.12, as cited by Sparks, 'Jerome as Biblical
Scholar,' 536n.6.

[129] Jerome, *Comm. In Eph., Lib. II, Prol,* as cited by Sparks, 'Jerome as Biblical Scholar,' 536n.7.

[130] Sparks, 'Jerome as Biblical Scholar,' 538. Here Sparks cites Jerome's commentaries
on Obadiah and Matthew.

[131] Sparks, 'Jerome as Biblical Scholar,' 539.

Undoubtedly, Jerome's major contribution as a biblical commentator was the series of commentaries on the OT prophets who, so far as the Western Church was concerned, provided him with a practically unworked field.[132] Like all his work, these commentaries suffer from the occasional irrelevant incursion into the realms of current ecclesiastical controversy, and they are also disfigured by some nasty exhibitions of petty spite and personal abuse. Nevertheless, they represent an achievement beyond the capacity of any of his contemporaries; they served as both a model and a storehouse for generations of subsequent commentators; and they can be read with profit, even today, especially by a student of the text.[133]

Jerome's work acting as a theological-resource for others is clearly evident. In the same year as the studies by F.L. Cross and H.F.D. Sparks, there also appeared of a major work by Johannes Quasten[134] which brought up to date a number of Jerome attributions and influences, thus increasing our knowledge of Jerome's *oeuvre*. Quasten identifies Didymus the Blind (c. 313-c.397), the head of the catechetical school of Alexandria, as the first exegete—model for Jerome (Jerome having been one of Didymus' pupils) and it is thanks to Jerome that we have in existence a Latin translation of Didymus' treatise *On The Holy Spirit* (written by Jerome for People Damasus between 384 and 392) the Greek original having been lost. [135] The relevance of this to Jerome's corpus becomes clear when Quasten observes that not only Didymus' 'exposition of Galatians (written before 387) served as a source for Jerome's [commentary on the same work],' but that 'Jerome's commentary on Ephesians also relied upon Didymus' interpretation of the same Pauline letter'.[136] It may well be that it was during this period of Jerome's life (i.e., 384-392) that Jerome assimilated the Catholic doctrine of the Holy Spirit (i.e., the Holy Spirit is not a creature – as in Arian doctrine – but consubstantial with the Father and Son) as a consequence of his translation of Didymus' *On the Holy Spirit*. If so, it might be said that Jerome the Catholic scholar-theologian originates from these years.

Elsewhere, Quasten considers Jerome's Latin version of the *Pachomian Rule* (for cenobitism or the monastic life properly so-called for anchorites in S.

---

[132] Jerome, *Comm. In Esa., Lib. I, Prol.*, as cited by Sparks, 'Jerome as Biblical Scholar,' 539n.7.

[133] Sparks, 'Jerome as Biblical Scholar,' 539.

[134] J. Quasten, *Patrology, The Golden Age of Greek Patristic Literature: From the Council of Nicaea to the Council of Chalcedon* (Westminster: Newman / Antwerp: Spectrum, 1960). Quasten was only the editor of *Patrology* (3). The actual author of the section on Jerome was Jean Gribomont, a renowned patristic scholar.

[135] Quasten, *Patrology* (3), 87. Jerome mentions Didymus repeatedly as his *magister* (*Epist.* 50, 1; 84, 3). See Quasten, *Patrology* (3), 85-87.

[136] Quasten, *Patrology* (3), 92. Jerome's commentary on Galatians was written shortly after Jerome's arrival in Bethlehem (c. 386-388). See *St. Jerome's Commentaries on Galatians, Titus and Philemon* (tr. T. Scheck; Notre Dame: University of Notre Dame Press, 2010), 8. Jerome's commentary on Ephesians was written in 386. See Rebenich, *Jerome*, 53. Rebenich also notes (49) the accusation made by Rufinus (*Apology against Jerome*) in 401 that Jerome's Ephesians commentary displayed an over-dependence on Origen.

Egypt) to have been of special importance in providing a model for ascetic/communal living,[137] a model that would later find popularized further in the West.[138] Similarly, Quasten testifies to the historical value of Jerome's Latin version (380) of Eusebius' *Chronicle* (which revised the original text from 325 to 378) and strongly influenced future Western historiography[139] and Jerome's Latin translation of Eusebius' *Onomasticon,* (a dictionary of Holy Land locations and a directory of biblical towns and villages as understood at the time of Eusebius).[140] Here Quasten's descriptions of some of Jerome's non-biblical Latin translation work highlights Jerome's importance in developing our knowledge and understanding of the growth of the early Church from the fourth century to the Middle Ages.

After 1960, some further features of Jerome's corpus came under critical reassessment. According to A. Penna, Jerome was one of the few moralists among the patristic exegetes who engaged in *casuistry* (i.e., the method or doctrine dealing with the cases of conscience and the resolution of conflicting moral obligations).[141] Penna observes that among his many other interests 'Jerome's exegesis displays a concern to carefully examine the ethical aspects of the deeds of the biblical characters.'[142] However, whilst Penna admonishes Jephthah for killing his daughter, a killing which followed from Jephthah's impetus, promise and calling upon God,[143] and Jerome asserts that the killing of the daughter was God's retribution for Jephthah's rashness,[144] it is noteworthy that Jerome's condemnation of Jephthah stands in marked contrast to Ambrose of Milan's praise for Jephthah for his strength and confidence in carrying out his promise.[145]

In 1963, the letters of Jerome again came under scrutiny but this time the focus was to be on their influences upon contemporary and later generations.[146] According to T.C. Lawler Jerome's letters are 'the most competent of his liter-

---

[137] Quasten, *Patrology* (3), 154-55.

[138] Quasten, *Patrology* (3), 155. Quasten notes: 'During the time when anchoritism was in the process of developing in the northern provinces of Egypt, in the south Pachomius the Copt gave shape to its second form, cenobitism'. See Quasten, *Patrology* (3), 154.

[139] Quasten, *Patrology* (3), 312-13.

[140] Quasten, '*Patrology*' (3), 336.

[141] A. Penna, 'The Vow of Jephthah in the Interpretation of St. Jerome,' *StP* 4 (1961), 162-70 (162).

[142] Penna, 'The Vow of Jephthah,' 162.

[143] Penna, 'The Vow of Jephthah,' 164.

[144] Penna, 'The Vow of Jephthah,' 164.

[145] Penna, 'The Vow of Jephthah,' 166. For a more recent discussion of Shielah's sacrifice, see G. Schwab, *Right in Their own Eyes: The Gospel According to Judges* (Phillipsburg: P&R, 2011), 144-47; A. Logan, 'Rehabilitating Jephthah,' *JBL* 128.4 (2009), 665-85.

[146] Jerome, *Letters of St. Jerome*, vol.1, *Letters 1-22* (tr. C.C. Mierow, intro. T.C. Lawler; New York: Newman, 1963).

ary works'.[147] Here Lawler particularly praises Jerome's letters for their sharp criticism of 'contemporary morals' which clearly display Jerome's orthodoxy and support for 'the primacy of the papacy'.[148] As well as demonstrating Jerome's ability to be 'a powerful and devastating polemicist', Lawler finds the extant correspondence to be a 'veritable treasure—trove for the hagiographer, for the theologian, for the scriptural scholar and for the historian of the period'.[149] We can see this as an example of what scholars have come to highlight as Jerome acting as a key patristic theological resource. Beyond their high literary quality and historically valuable content[150] Jerome's letters would also be influential in spreading the monastic ideal and asceticism, both during the fourth and fifth centuries and, later on, into the Middle Ages.[151]

Until 1964 little scholarly interest had been shown in the part directly played by Jerome in the development and history of the hermit-life and the rise of monasticism. Thus, it was with the publication of Peter F. Anson's *The Call of the Desert*[152] that Jerome's call to the solitary life was first properly contextualized. It is perhaps one of the strange ironies of history that one of the earliest travellers, John Cassian, who collected information about the monastic communities and isolated hermits in fourth century Egypt, returned to Palestine about 400 to settle in the monastery at Bethlehem that had been founded by Jerome.

Running almost parallel to the development of cenobite communities in Egypt and Palestine were many different associations of hermits in Syria, from which the solitary life found its way to Asia Minor, Mesopotamia, and Persia.[153] During the period c. 374-379 Jerome led a solitary life in the Desert of Chalcis (Syria), during which time he learnt Hebrew. On this episode in Jerome's life Anson highlights Jerome's 'sexual awakening', prior to his ordination as a priest.

---

[147] Jerome, *Letters*, vol. 1, 3.

[148] Jerome, *Letters*, vol. 1, 3-4.

[149] Jerome, *Letters*, vol. 1, 3-4. On Jerome's importance as a 'theological resource,' see R.C. Hill, Theodoret of Cyrus, *Commentary on the Letters of St. Paul* (tr. with an Introduction by R.C. Hill; Brookline: Holy Cross Orthodox, 2001), 1.8. Hill writes, 'The works of his [Theodoret of Cyrus] illustrious predecessor he regarded, *pace* Jerome, not as grounds for disqualification but as a resource on which to call in his own efforts.'

[150] Jerome, *Letters*, vol. 1, 8.

[151] J. Leclercq, *The Love of Learning and the Desire for God* (tr. C. Misrahi; New York, 1961), 123, as cited by Lawler, *Jerome, Letters*, 1.8n.13.

[152] P.F. Anson, *The Call of the Desert* (London: SPCK, 1964). However, it should be noted that Anson had earlier authored *The Quest of Solitude* (1932).

[153] Anson, *Call of the Desert*, 37. Here it is worth noting that during the later fifth and early sixth centuries the most creative developments in Eastern Christian monasticism occurred not in Egypt or in Syria, but in Palestine, through the work of St. Euthymius and St. Sabas. For the full account of these developments, see Cyril of Scythopolis: *The Lives of the Monks of Palestine* (tr. R.M. Price with an Introduction and Notes by John Binns; Kalamazoo: Cistercian, 1991).

I was fearful to look at, for beneath its covering my body was repulsive…Every day I gave way to tears, every day I emitted groans…often I imagined myself transported into the midst of virginal dances…and my imagination boiled with desires in a frozen body, in which there raged a conflagration of the passions.[154]

Here Anson's citation of an extract from Jerome's *Ep.* 22 (often regarded as Jerome's most famous letter and one drawn upon by countless scholars for its depiction of what Jerome considered to be 'the motives that should inspire those who devote themselves to a life of virginity, and also the rules by which they ought to regulate their daily conduct'[155]) usefully underscores the way in which Jerome felt the need to graphically describe certain autobiographical details. However, Anson might perhaps have included the following citation to more fully emphasize Jerome's mind-set at this early juncture in his ascetic development.

So long as we are held down by this frail body, so long as we have our treasure in earthen vessels, so long as the flesh lusteth against the spirit and the spirit against the flesh, there can be no sure victory. Our adversary the devil goeth about as a roaring lion seeking whom he may devour.[156]

Finally, Anson highlights the importance of Jerome as a spokesperson of the ascetic movement:

St. Jerome, who had lived in Rome from 382 to about 385, helped to familiarize the more devout with the ascetic life in the Near East. It was under his influence that St. Melania (c. 345-410) left Rome for Egypt and Palestine in 372, where she founded a monastery on the Mount of Olives.[157]

On this evidence it would not be too much of an exaggeration to say that Jerome was one of the early "prophets" of asceticism and monasticism.

In 1964, two important studies appeared further shaping our knowledge and understanding of Jerome's corpus.[158] Von Campenhausen's essay on Jerome[159] provides a dual-reassessment of Jerome as a theologian (negative) and Jerome as a literary figure in the history of ideas (positive). Von Campenhausen is certainly no Jerome apologist and his treatment of the exegete is highly critical of Jerome's hermeneutic, von Campenhausen arguing that Jerome's work lacks 'solid methodological and theological principles'.[160]

Von Campenhausen's reassessment of Jerome the theologian corresponds closely to McGuckin's (2005) view that Jerome's reputation as exegete is over-

---

[154] Jerome, *Ep.* 22, 7, as cited by Anson, *Call of the Desert*, 37-38n.1.

[155] Rebenich, *Jerome*, 19.

[156] Jerome, *Ep.* 22, 4 (*St. Jerome: Letters and Select Works*, 1996), NPNF² 6:23.

[157] Anson, *Call of the Desert*, 58.

[158] H. von Campenhausen, *The Fathers of the Latin Church* (London: A&C Black, 1964); D.S. Wiesen, *St. Jerome as a Satirist: A Study in Christian Latin Thought and Letters* (Ithaca: Cornell University Press, 1964).

[159] Campenhausen, 'Jerome ', in Campenhausen, *Fathers*, 129-82.

[160] Campenhausen, 'Jerome', 181.

stressed (at least if we look for originality). Moreover, von Campenhausen finds in Jerome certain personality flaws that marred his progress as a theologian. For example, he finds Jerome to have been a 'man who was never at peace with himself and whose world-view was shaped by the fame of his works'.[161] Here Von Campenhausen's reservations about Jerome's progress as a theologian closely matches Freeman's (2009) claim that Jerome lacked the self-confidence to develop his own theology.

In contrast, von Campenhausen's view of Jerome as a literary figure in the history of ideas is more positive, freely acknowledging Jerome to have been a 'successful scholar' and 'the founder of Western philology'.[162] Like Lawler, von Campenhausen regards Jerome's letters as an important theological resource, displaying, as they do, 'elegance of form hitherto unknown in earlier forms of Christian correspondence.'[163]

We can now look at Wiesen's study of Jerome as a satirist and ask whether his reassessment of Jerome, demonstrates any correspondence to the 'McGuckin-Freeman' thesis. Wiesen's critique illuminates important aspects of the intellectual history of the late fourth century, focussing in particular on Jerome's transformation of a pagan literary genre into a suitable vehicle for Christian propaganda.[164] Whilst finding Jerome not to have been 'the first Christian writer to incorporate satire,'[165] Wiesen believes Jerome's use of satire was 'motivated by the desire to encourage, instruct an improve personal morality amongst people'.[166] Wiesen supports his view by giving two important examples—first, Jerome's use of satire to reveal improper conduct in monasteries and, second, Jerome's use of satire to reform a weak Church and its priesthood.[167] It would appear then that according to Wiesen Jerome was a creative

---

[161] Campenhausen, 'Jerome', 181.

[162] Campenhausen, 'Jerome,' 181-82.

[163] Campenhausen, 'Jerome,' 181-82.

[164] Although Jerome's satire has prompted abundant comment from his own lifetime onwards, few detailed studies of it prior to Wiesen's had appeared. For two earlier attempts to investigate the subject, see M.A. Pence, 'Satire in St. Jerome,' *CJ* 36 (1941), 322-36; A. Weston, 'Latin Satirical Writing Subsequent to Juvenal' (PhD thesis, Yale University, 1915).

[165] Wiesen, *St. Jerome*, 12. Here Wiesen cites Tertullian (c. 160-220) as an early example of the Christian satiric tradition, a writer whose writings 'were much admired by St. Jerome' (14).

[166] Wiesen, *St. Jerome*, 19.

[167] Wiesen, *St. Jerome*, 68. Wiesen notes: 'The monastic movement, which experienced a phenomenal growth in the fourth century, arose in part as a protest against the declining moral standards of the secular clergy. The development of asceticism was a direct challenge to the novel theory of the Church as a *corpus permixtum* including both saint and sinner, a theory which in the fourth century was swiftly replacing the older view of the Church as the community of the holy' (67). For a detailed treatment of the dynamic history of fourth century monasticism, see A.D. Rich, *Discernment in the Desert Fathers: Diakrisis in the Life and Thought of Early Egyptian Monasticism* (Eugene: Wipf & Stock, 2007). There is no scholarly consensus regarding Weisen's

satirist of some considerable skill, and, importantly, there is no evidence within Weisen's critique of any correspondence with the 'McGuckin-Freeman' thesis.

Our final modern Jerome scholar of the 1960s, W.H. Semple, made a reassessment of another key part of Jerome's *oeuvre*—the Latin translation of the canonical books of the OT,[168] confirming that Jerome was a man capable of radical exegesis and of a new scholarly method and principle.[169] In describing the patristic reception given to Jerome's translation work, Semple follows the conventional—wisdom (i.e., NT well received/OT poorly received) but adds more detail on the problems and difficulties that beset Jerome in making his new scholarly method and principle understood by early Church audiences. For example, he finds Jerome's expectation that his readers would be able to cross-reference his Latin translation of the OT against the Hebrew (few Christians knew Hebrew) in order to attest to its accuracy, unrealistic.[170] In addition, Jerome's tendency towards intolerance of those untrained in scholarship who dared to criticize his OT translations—Jerome calling such critics 'sancta rusticitas' (saintly ignorants)—caused increasing public discord.[171]

Semple's critique of Jerome is sometimes contradictory. On the one hand (and, in contrast, to von Campenhausen) he argues that Jerome was a man capable of radical exegesis and of a new scholarly method and principle (thus denying McGuckin's claim that Jerome's reputation as exegete is over-stressed, at least if we look for originality). On the other hand, Semple seriously questions the efficiency of Jerome's OT exegesis for the patristic reader thus partly confirming McGuckin's (2005) view. Certainly it is true that Jerome's patristic critics scorned his use of the Hebrew text instead of the Greek, and the implied slight to the LXX; his seemingly arbitrary omission or inclusion of passages; and, of course, his alteration of the familiar wording. However, Semple argues that any shortcomings in Jerome were far outweighed by his achievements. For example, Semple judges Jerome to have been not just 'a very good scholar' but 'the greatest scholar that the Western Church produced until the Renaissance', thus challenging McGuckin's (2005) claim that Jerome was perhaps the most important biblical scholar of the early Western church.[172] Semple's treatment of Jerome concludes with one final accolade: 'He [Jerome] was far in advance of

---

thesis of a 'phenomenal growth in the fourth century monastic movement'. For example, Andrew Louth has suggested that 'The traditional story of the rise of monasticism as fourth century phenomenon, associated *par excellence* with the Egyptian desert, is a Catholic legend, which, unlike many others, was reinforced, rather than questioned, by Protestant scholarship, happy to regard monasticism as a late, and therefore spurious, development. See A. Louth, 'The literature of the monastic movement,' in *Early Christian Literature*, 373-81 (373).

[168] W.H. Semple, 'St. Jerome as a Biblical Translator,' *BJRL* 48 (1965-66), 227-43.
[169] Semple, 'St. Jerome,' 242-43.
[170] Semple, 'St. Jerome,' 234.
[171] Semple, 'St. Jerome,' 234.
[172] Semple, 'St. Jerome,' 242.

his age in scholarship and critical method' and 'his achievement was the result of an idea carried into effect with labour, courage, and conviction'.[173]

Perhaps the best that can be said of Semple's judgements on Jerome is that they are a mix of an apologia ('He [Jerome] was far in advance of his age in scholarship and critical method') and of conjecture (Jerome's expectation that his readers would be able to cross-reference his Latin translation of the OT against the Hebrew, in order to attest to its accuracy, was unrealistic). Thus, far from us being able to view Semple's essay as an important landmark moment in the critical reception by scholars of selected texts/writings drawn from Jerome's corpus at the end of our first period of modern Jerome scholarship, it stands rather as a cautionary tale in sometimes making secondary judgements on Jerome without consistent argument.

In chapter 3 we have observed some consensus (though by no means unanimous agreement) among scholars on Jerome's stature as one of the most learned of the Latin Church Fathers. Through critical reassessments of selected texts/writings drawn from Jerome's corpus these scholars demonstrated how Jerome mastered nearly the entirety of the antecedent Christian exegetical and theological tradition (both Greek and Latin) largely achieved through his knowledge of Hebrew, Greek and Latin (Jerome as *Vir Trilinguis*) as well as Aramaic. And we have seen how scholars have received the fruit of that knowledge in Jerome's most famous editorial achievement, the Latin Vulgate translation of the Bible, whilst, at the same time, contesting the competency of Jerome's biblical exegesis and theological reflection on Christian Scripture.

---

[173] Semple, 'St. Jerome,' 243.

Chapter 4

Modern Jerome Scholarship (1966-1990)

Introduction

In this chapter we shall examine how scholars (post-1965) have critically received selected parts of Jerome's corpus with some scholars constructing their critiques of Jerome 'in conversation', as it were, with Jerome's earlier predecessor, Origen, and Jerome's contemporary, Augustine. We shall try to measure this late modern Jerome scholarship against the central theoretical model of the present study, namely, the 'McGuckin–Freeman' thesis (i.e., Jerome's reputation as exegete has been over-stressed (at least if we look for originality) and that Jerome failed to think creatively beyond Nicene orthodoxy). Here, however, we might caution for some balance, being reminded that Jerome has long been regarded by the Latin Church as its preeminent scriptural commentator.

Finally, before we begin our examination of post-1965 Jerome scholarship, one more important factor needs to be borne in mind—much of Jerome's prodigious exegetical output was not translated into English before 1965. After 1965 we have more available English translations of Jerome's works in print thus making it easier for scholars who cannot read Latin to follow and critique Jerome's exegetical method. We shall see below how the increase in the publication of English translations of Jerome's exegetical works has been a testimony to the growing interest not only in patristic exegesis but also in Jerome more specifically.

1966-1974

From the mid-1960s scholars began turning their attention to other areas of Jerome's corpus beyond the purely exegetical—though, as we shall see, the exegetical works of Jerome would still command continuing attention.

In 1966 a newly translated volume of the *Homilies of St. Jerome* appeared.[1] Sister Ewald's translation of these homilies provides information on Jerome acting as quite an astute theologian (though perhaps not an entirely original one). For example, in Homily 76 (on Mk 1.13-31) Jerome writes:

> For all of Holy Writ is animated and held together by one Spirit. It is not unlike a necklace held together by the union of its links, so that whichever link you pick up, another suspends from it.[2]

---

[1] Saint Jerome, *The Homilies of St. Jerome*, vol.2 (tr. M.L. Ewald; Washington: Catholic University of American Press, 1966).

[2] Jerome, *Homilies*, 2.132.

Jerome continues:

> Before the advent of the Saviour and the glory of the Gospel, until Christ with the robber opened the door of Paradise, all the souls of the faithful were consigned to the nether world...In the Law Abraham is in hell; in the Gospel, the robber is in heaven. We are not depreciating Abraham in whose bosom we all long to find rest, but we prefer Christ to Abraham, the Gospel to the Law.[3]

Here, of course, any charge of possible anti-Semitism against Jerome (vis-à-vis, 'we prefer...the Gospel to the Law') is countered by Jerome's 'we prefer Christ to Abraham,' for surely Christ was as Jewish as Abraham.

Ewald makes the point that 'there is a question of whether or not the Septuagint was in the hands of Jerome when he wrote or preached his homilies'.[4] Ewald further notes that 'Jerome's homilies are sometimes distinguished by their erudition, sophisticated language, many Greek expressions and variations from the *Hexapla*'.[5] Whilst Ewald's comments do not affirm Jerome writing as a theologian, we do find some further evidence of Jerome's theological abilities in his Homily 75 (Mk 1.1-12).

It is in Homily 75 that Jerome imparts his theology of the Trinity, warning the Arians and the heretics that 'the mystery of the Trinity is in the baptism of Jesus', where 'Jesus is baptized, the Holy Spirit descends under the appearance of a dove, the Father speaks from Heaven.'[6]

Jerome had attacked Arius and Arianism in his Letter 15 to Damasus, written during Jerome's stay at Maronia in the desert of Chalcis (c.376/377). He

---

[3] Jerome, *Homilies*, 2.134.

[4] Jerome, *Homilies*, 2.x.

[5] Jerome, *Homilies*, 2.x.

[6] Jerome, *Homilies*, 2.129. However, scholars are not agreed on Jerome's stature as a homilist. For example, Hendrik Stander in his citation of the great fourth/fifth century homilists on the Ascension of Christ in the West only lists Chromatius (d. 407), bishop of Aquileia, Augustine (354-430), Eusebius of Alexandria and Athanasius of Alexandria (300-373). This seems strange since Jerome did, in fact, write a homily on the Ascension (Jerome, *Homily* 80). See H.F. Stander, 'Fourth- and Fifth-century Homilists on the Ascension of Christ,' in A.J. Malherbe, F.W. Norris and J.W. Thompson, *The Early Church in its Context* (Leiden: Brill, 1998), 268-86 (272); and see, St Jerome, *The Homilies of Saint Jerome* (Homilies 60-96) (tr. M.L. Ewald; Washington: Catholic University of America Press, 1965), 2.159-68. Elsewhere, Raymond notes 'Arianism held that the Logos or Son of God was only a created being made out of nothing, first in the created order true enough but not divine since there was a time when was he was not, thereby denying the Son's unabridged deity.' Arius' view was condemned at the Council of Nicaea. See R. Raymond, 'Classical Christology's Future in Systematic Theology', in A.M. McGowan (ed.) *Always Reforming: Explorations in Systematic Theology* (Leicester: Apollos, 2006), 67-124 (69n.7). For the Arian rejection out of hand of the idea that the Son could eternally coexist with the Father, see J.N.D. Kelly, *Early Christian Creeds* (London: Continuum, 2006), 233. The fullest account of Arius and Arianism is to be found in M. Wiles, *Archetypal Heresy: Arianism through the Centuries* (Oxford: Clarendon, 1996).

had been unwilling to accept the Arian notion of the Son being not eternal or co-eternal with God, believing that there was only one nature of God (one Godhead). Three years later an important event occurred that would restrain Jerome from writing and theologizing beyond Nicene orthodoxy, for it was 'on 27 Feb. 380, that the emperor Theodosius issued an edict that made the Nicene teaching of the bishops Damasus of Rome and Peter of Alexandria compulsory for all his subjects'.[7] However, Jerome's adherence to orthodoxy was, it must be said, not always clear,[8] suggesting that Jerome may sometimes have played an ambivalent role here. For example, whilst Henry Chadwick praises the much excellent material in Jerome's exegesis (especially the translation work), describing Jerome as 'a prodigious scholar from Dalmatia,'[9] he also notes the support Jerome gave to small Jewish churches in Syria by his 'translation into Latin of their *Gospel according to the Hebrews* preserving traditions slightly diverging from canonical Greek gospels, and magnifying the position of James the Lord's brother'.[10]

Significantly, Chadwick remains highly critical of Jerome's intellectual abilities, observing an able scholar but one whose 'immense scholarship could at times be put to the service of passionate resentments and petty jealousies'.[11] (This is a similar finding, of course, to von Campenhausen's view of Jerome as a 'man who was never at peace with himself and whose world-view was shaped by the fame of his works'.) Even more critically, despite the fact that 'Jerome's mental world was Latin' and 'the time was ripe for the emergence of an independent Latin theology'—'Jerome was no thinker.'[12] Here, again, we may note a close correspondence with Freeman's (2009) claim that Jerome never showed any genuine intellectual creativity or had the self-confidence to develop his own theology.

---

[7] Rebenich, *Jerome*, 21. Rebenich comments 'Henceforth the only form of Christianity to be tolerated was the one that acknowledged the full, undivided divinity of Father, Son and Holy Spirit.'

[8] Witness, for example, Jerome's publication (after Jerome's break with Origen from 393) 'of an exact version of the principal passages [from *Origen's On First Principles*] which Rufinus had mitigated and qualified to bring them into conformity with more orthodox opinions expressed in Origen's other writings'. See Chadwick, *Early Church*, 104. Here it should be noted that Jerome's translation of the parts of Origen that he accused Rufinus of suppressing was not because he liked them (which would indeed have made his orthodoxy suspect) but because he thought they proved that Origen was a heretic. For a fuller discussion of how Rufinus made changes to Origen's most famous work at the end of the fourth century, taking out those parts where Origen 'seemed heterodox [contrary to established doctrines] by fourth century (post-Nicene) standards', see J.L. Papandrea, *Reading the Early Church Fathers: From the Didache to Nicaea* (Mahwah: Paulist, 2012), 113.

[9] Chadwick, *Early Church*, 161.

[10] Chadwick, *Early Church*, 22.

[11] Chadwick, *Early Church*, 185.

[12] Chadwick, *Early Church*, 215-16.

Accordingly, it would be Augustine, not Jerome, who would undertake the development of an independent Latin theology—a figure, Chadwick argues, 'who by the range and profundity of his mind came to tower not only over all his immediate contemporaries but over the subsequent development of Western Christendom'.[13]

If we juxtapose Chadwick's claim that Jerome 'was no thinker' with Freeman's (2009) view that Jerome 'proved too pedantic a thinker ever to engage fully with the intricacies of Greek philosophy', we may conclude that there is evidence here of some agreement on Jerome's intellectual capacity. Furthermore, Chadwick's criticism of Jerome ('he was no thinker') is reasonable if we accept (as most scholars today do) that Jerome displayed a general dependence upon Origen for much of his exegetical work. The task of measuring and judging Jerome's intellectual ability must surely be undertaken using other criteria beyond his reliance upon and his borrowings from others. This was clearly recognized by Maurice Wiles, whose book *The Divine Apostle*[14] offered an analysis of the writings of the Greek and Latin commentators of the third, fourth and early fifth centuries on the Pauline Epistles.

> The patristic exegesis of St. Paul is concerned with a wide range of doctrinal issues. These include, in particular, the great issues of grace and faith which were of such importance at the time of the Reformation. Wiles questions whether the Fathers were as insensitive to the Pauline teaching about grace as is often claimed.[15]

The Divine Apostle is of special interest not only because of its clarification of Jerome's place in Pauline interpretation but also due to the way in which Wiles manages to 'trace out the main ways in which St. Paul's writings were expounded in the early centuries'.[16]

So, how does Wiles judge Jerome in this dual-context? First, Wiles makes the following assessment of Jerome's Pauline commentaries:

> He acknowledges his debt particularly to Origen,[17] and there can be no question but that his commentaries are very closely based upon those of Origen.[18] Jerome's work is certainly thorough and erudite, but it has the air of a compilation of Greek learning rather than of a genuinely original Latin composition.[19]

This evaluation of Jerome precisely matches McGuckin's (2005) claim that Jerome's reputation as exegete is over-stressed (at least if we look for originality) and Freeman's (2009) view that Jerome never showed any genuine intellectual creativity or had the self-confidence to develop his own theology. That

---

13 Chadwick, *Early Church*, 215-16.
14 Wiles, *The Divine Apostle* (1967).
15 Wiles, *The Divine Apostle*, dust-jacket.
16 Wiles, *The Divine Apostle*, 2.
17 Jerome, *Comm. in Gal.* Prolog. (308A), as cited by Wiles, *The Divine Apostle*, 12.
18 A. Harnack, *Dear kirchengeschichtliche Ertrag der exegetischen Arbeiten des Origenes* (1919), 141-68, as cited by Wiles, *The Divine Apostle*, 12n.3.
19 Wiles, *The Divine Apostle*, 12.

said, Wiles does affirm, following on from Origen's example,[20] Jerome's important contribution to the exaltation of the Pauline letters to the rank of Christian Scriptures.[21] Here Wiles cites Jerome's dictum that every word of the apostle, every detail about his life, is of great value to the Christian.[22] However, Jerome had some reservations about Paul.[23]

It is worth recording here that Wiles sees Jerome as having been 'the greatest biblical scholar of his age,'[24] thus marginally contesting McGuckin's (2005) view that Jerome was perhaps the most important biblical scholar of the early Western church. Wiles does draw attention to Jerome's occasional tendency towards inconsistency, most notably in his *Commentary on Galatians*.

> In commenting on Gal. iv. 29 (395 B,C) he [Jerome] uses Origen's interpretation of 1. Cor. 9:19 to prove that Paul was free from all sin. A little later on (405 D) he expresses doubt as to the compatibility of Paul's sentiments in Gal. 5:12 with the spirit of Christ and suggests that Paul, being after all only human, may at this point have been led into sin by that other law at work in his members. This doubtless derives from Origen also, although it is tempting to detect a trace of self-knowledge on the part of Jerome when he says that to curse one's enemies is a sin 'in quod frequenter sanctos viros cadere perspicimus'. In typically Origenistic fashion Jerome allows the possibility of an alternative exegesis of the verse, according to which it is a prayer in the spirit of Matt. 18:8-9. Augustine gives a similar interpretation but links it with Matt. 19:12 (*Expos. Gal.* 42 on Gal. 5:4-12).[25]

Perhaps rather than inconsistency (which implies conflicting or contradictory elements) what we can possibly see here is Jerome's indecision over reaching his particular Galatians interpretation. Should not good exegesis allow for the option of variant readings of a text? It should be remembered that other patristic writers found it difficult to agree even on the exact nature and authorship of the Pauline Epistles.[26]

---

[20] Wiles, *The Divine Apostle*, 14. Wiles notes that Origen was 'the first systematic commentator upon the [Pauline] letters,' 14.

[21] Wiles, *The Divine Apostle*, 14.

[22] Jerome, *Comm in Philemon*, Prolog. (599D–602D), as cited by Wiles, *The Divine Apostle*, 14n.4.

[23] Wiles observes that Jerome spoke 'highly of Paul's knowledge of Hebrew and of the law' but admitted 'the imperfection of his Greek' and regarded him as having only 'a moderate knowledge of secular literature,' 17.

[24] Wiles, *The Divine Apostle*, 12. Here Wiles states that 'Augustine was its greatest theologian.'

[25] Wiles, *The Divine Apostle*, 21n.1.

[26] For example, Tertullian and John Chrysostom took entirely different approaches to the Pauline writings. Whereas Tertullian 'clearly regards every word of Paul as fully binding and the Christian unless explicitly revoked by some later revelation of divine authority,' Chrysostom 'is unwilling to compromise in any way his firm belief that Christ is the true author of the epistles in their totality'. See Wiles, *The Divine Apostle*, 15.

Also of interest is Wiles' critique of Jerome's understanding of the nature of human beings (flesh/son/spirit). Here Wiles sets his critique within the following historical context:

> For the great majority of later [patristic] writers the distinction which Irenaeus and Tertullian had drawn between a moral understanding of the concept 'flesh' and a physical or a metaphysical one provided the key which enabled them to give an interpretation of Paul's thought that was wholly free from any Gnostic tendencies. So far from increasing any apparent ambiguity on the subject which there may be in Paul's writings, they tend to eliminate it altogether. The distinction between the different senses of the word 'flesh' was something so vital to them that they tend to apply it not only in the considerable number of instances where it is clearly required by the context but also in a number of other passages of especial interest and importance where its validity is a more open question.[27]

So, what of Jerome's contextualization of the word 'flesh'? Here Wiles again focuses upon Jerome's commentary on Galatians:

> Jerome although he admits that he is in disagreement with the majority of exegetes, refuses to interpret the 'flesh and blood' of Gal. 1:16, with which Paul did not confer, as referring to the apostles, since they were spiritual and therefore could not be designated by such a phrase.[28]

Although this is a somewhat limited example it is still clear that Jerome was most concerned to ensure that any serious misinterpretation of Paul's meaning was avoided, and Jerome's determination here to reject convention in his exegesis surely displays some individualism (if not originality), thus invalidating the 'McGuckin-Freeman' thesis.

We now move on to Jerome's understanding of the 'soul' and 'spirit' which appears, like his understanding of the 'flesh', to have been derived from Origen.[29] Origen had claimed that in 1 Thessalonians, Paul had taught the tripartite division of a human being's nature into body, soul and spirit.[30] For Jerome (like Origen) 'the particular term to be used will be chosen in accordance with the

---

[27] Wiles, *Divine Apostle*, 28-29. For a full account of Irenaeus' opposition to Gnosticism, see R.M. Grant, *Irenaeus of Lyons* (Abingdon: Routledge, 1997), 11-21, P. Foster and S. Parvis (eds), *Irenaeus: Life, Scripture, Legacy* (Minneapolis: Fortress, 2012), 16-17,105-10, 112-17, 133-35, 138-39, 159-64, 166-71,188-89, 203-204; for Tertullian's response to Gnoticism and other heresies, see E. Ferguson, '*Tertullian, Scripture, Rule of Faith, and Paul,*' in T. Still and D.E. Wilhite (eds), *Tertullian and Paul* (London: Bloomsbury, 2013), 22-33. For the most recent examination of the relation of Gnosticism to early Christianity, see M. Edwards, *Christians, Gnostics and Philosophers in Late Antiquity* (Farnham: Ashgate, 2012).

[28] Jerome, *Comm. on Gal. 1:16* (326 c), as cited by Wiles, *The Divine Apostle*, 29n.2. Here there is a distinction to be made between Jerome's scriptural-exegesis on the 'flesh' and Jerome's ascetic usages (i.e., the call to celibacy and virginity) although, of course, there is to some degree, a spiritual element common to both.

[29] Wiles, *Divine Apostle*, 30n.4.

[30] Origen, *Comm. in Rom.* 1:10 (836 A) on Rom. 1:9, as cited by Wiles, *Divine Apostle*, 30n.3.

context—spirit when the reference is to some nobler aspect of man's being, soul when it is to some lower aspect, flesh when it is to some worse aspect still'.[31] Like Origen, Jerome viewed 'spirit' in terms of the human spirit, a key element of our being (incapable of evil),[32] and both considered that it was 'the privilege and destiny of the soul to be joined to the spirit so that it ceases to be soul and becomes what the spirit is'.[33] Of course, Jerome (following Origen) would see a clear distinction to be made between those references to 'spirit' in the scriptures (which referred to the human spirit) and those which alluded to the divine nature of the Holy Spirit.

Here, some concluding remarks need to be made. *The Divine Apostle* is undoubtedly an erudite work of patristic scholarship, adding considerably to our knowledge and understanding of how the early church writers (including Jerome) interpreted St. Paul's Epistles. That said, one scholar in particular, has raised serious questions about the premise that these commentators might have understood the nature of man and the capacity of the mind.

Paul Veyne (Honorary Professor at the Collège de France) and one of France's leading historians, has written:

> As early as the second century AD, some—but not all—Christian authors began to represent God as pure spirit, and Saint Augustine was to argue that the soul was purely spiritual, so did not extend three-dimensionally. Those of us who have been taught in catechism classes that God and the soul are 'pure spirit', or who have heard such words pronounced around us, take them in without difficulty, believing that we understand them and that they are quite simple. But that is far from being the case. They remained incomprehensible and absurd to Saint Jerome, to whom Saint Augustine (who, as we know, was the source of Descartes's *Cogito*) never managed to make them acceptable, despite a lively exchange of letters.[34]

Veyne's depiction here of the 'incomprehensibility' and 'absurdity' of some of the central issues of what we must call 'pneumatology' to Jerome is an assertion made without any proper supportive evidence. But, if true, it must put into doubt some of Jerome's work in this area of biblical interpretation.

Another scholar who also probed much deeper into Jerome's skills as exegete was Benjamin Kedar-Kopfstein whose study of Jerome's *Vulgate*[35] provides a comprehensive critique of Jerome's translation skills and techniques. In

---

[31] Origen, *Comm. in Rom.* 9:25 (1226 A,B) on Rom. 13:1. Cf. Jerome on Gal. 6:18 (438 B) and on Philemon 25 (618B), as cited by Wiles, *Divine Apostle*, 30n.4.

[32] Origen, *Comm. in Rom.* 2:9 (893 B,C) on Rom. 2:1515, and Jerome, on Gal. 3:2 (349D-350 A) and on Eph. 4:4 (495 C), as cited by Wiles, *Divine Apostle*, 31n.1.

[33] Wiles, *Divine Apostle*, 34.

[34] P. Veyne, *When Our World Became Christian, 312-394* (Cambridge, Polity, 2010), 176. Here Veyne argues that it was not until 'the advent of modern thinkers such as Spinoza and Hume' that the nature of man and the capacity of the mind became more fully understood.

[35] B. Kedar-Kopfstein, 'The Vulgate as a Translation: Some Semantic and Syntactical Aspects of Jerome's Version of the Hebrew Bible' (PhD thesis, The Hebrew University, 1968).

this work, Kedar-Kopfstein is more generous in his appraisal of Jerome's critical method and practice than some of the other scholars we reviewed in chapter 3 (e.g., Elliott, 1880; Souter, 1911; Chapman, 1923). On the question of Jerome's intellectual ability, Kedar-Kopfstein prefers to establish the area of expertise held by Jerome and which distinguished him from other early Church biblical scholars (thus the importance for Jerome of a reverence for the Holy Scriptures and the Bible as divinely inspired).[36] This contrasts with Augustine's priority, namely, to promote Christian tenets through writings and sermons.[37]

Kedar-Kopfstein's study of Jerome is of particular significance for whilst it suggests (like Chadwick, 1967) that Jerome may have been an exegete of some importance [38] it raises questions about how far Jerome's classical education prepared him for his exegetical work. Whereas Chadwick (1967) finds Jerome to have had 'limited acquaintance with classical Greek texts'[39] Kedar-Kopfstein finds Jerome to have been a 'proficient classicist'.[40]

Overall Kedar-Kopfstein offers a positive critical reception of the Vulgate, praising Jerome's linguistic proficiencies as a translator.[41] But, somewhat ironically, he acknowledges that 'this work contained inaccurate exegesis'.[42] Here Kedar-Kopfstein cautions that these errors should be viewed in the context of Hebrew knowledge as understood in Jerome's time.[43] If Jerome can be criticized at all, argues Kedar-Kopfstein, it is in respect of his late recognition of his errors/mistranslations.[44] Of his errors, Kedar-Kopfstein believes they were born of a man who knew the Bible and Hebrew well but wrongly translated the Arabic/Jewish 'gutturals.'[45] Kedar-Kopfstein's judgement that Jerome was a man

---

[36] Kedar-Kopfstein, 'Vulgate', 47.

[37] Kedar-Kopfstein, 'Vulgate', 47.

[38] Kedar-Kopfstein, 'Vulgate', 50. Kedar-Kopfstein records, 'On his return to Rome [in 382], he was already considered an authority on the Biblical text.' Likewise, Rebenich, *Jerome*, 30, finds 'The foundation of his [Jerome's] career as an advocate of the ascetic movement and of Nicene orthodoxy, as a translator and commentator of the Bible, and as an intermediary between western and eastern theology was laid in the Eastern Empire, in Antioch, Marionia, and, above all, Constantinople.'

[39] Chadwick, *Early Church*, 215.

[40] Kedar-Kopfstein, 'Vulgate,' 50.

[41] Kedar-Kopfstein, 'Vulgate', 51.

[42] Kedar-Kopfstein, 'Vulgate', 51.

[43] Kedar-Kopfstein, 'Vulgate', 51.

[44] Kedar-Kopfstein, 'Vulgate', 52.

[45] Kedar-Kopfstein, 'Vulgate', 53. 'Gutturals' being a speech sound formed or pronounced in the throat. For two interesting case-studies of Jerome's Hebrew biblical scholarship, see M. Graves, *Jerome's Hebrew Philology: A Study Based on his Commentary on Jeremiah* (Leiden: Brill, 2007). Graves writes: 'Perhaps the most telling sign of Jerome's commitment to Hebrew learning was his choice to dedicate the vast majority of his exegetical works to OT books,' 1; E.L. Gallagher, *Hebrew Scripture in Patristic Biblical Theory: Canon, Language, Text* (Leiden: Brill, 2012), 197-209.

who was well 'equipped for his role as a Bible commentator'[46] has, of course, no bearing on or direct correspondence to McGuckin's (2005) verdict that Jerome's reputation as exegete is over-stressed (at least if we look for originality).

Kedar-Kopfstein's study of Jerome's Vulgate is important for the contribution it makes to our knowledge and understanding of Jerome's twofold objective in his OT translation work: to provide for his readers as reliable a translation of the Bible as possible and to provide a tool in the attack against the 'Jews and heretics'.[47] Of course, according to Kedar-Kopfstein's analysis, Jerome, it would seem, was not wholly successful in meeting the first of these objectives. With regard to Jerome's second objective, scholars remain sceptical of the efficacy of Jerome's polemics against his opponents. Kedar-Kopfstein believes that both of Jerome's objectives depended upon Jerome's belief in the importance of the 'consuetudo scripturarum' (i.e., the traditional Latin wording).[48]

On the question of Jerome's dependence upon the exegesis of others before him, Kedar-Kopfstein is surprisingly uncritical (even generous) seeing Jerome's borrowings from earlier exegetes as Jerome's way of acknowledging their worth rather than acknowledging his own plagiarism of others' translation work.[49] Finally, to illustrate Jerome's ability to be both an astute theologian and exegete when necessary, Kedar-Kopfstein records:

> It is not at all surprising that Jerome would not admit a theological or christological interpretation that contradicted the prevalent situation. Thus, he repeatedly refutes the apparently common notion that 'pascha' was derived from Greek 'paschein' which would establish the link between the feast of Passover, Easter and the Passion.[50]

Here Kedar-Kopfstein's analysis challenges to some degree McGuckin's charge that Jerome's reputation as exegete is over-stressed (at least if we look for originality) whilst it supports that part of Freeman's (2009) view that Jerome held steadfast to Nicene orthodoxy. Far from a criticism (as in the case of Freeman, 2009), Kedar-Kopfstein clearly shows here why Jerome felt it necessary to cling to Nicene orthodoxy.

The publication in 1969 of the second volume of *The Cambridge History of the Bible*[51] offered a study of Jerome by E.F. Sutcliffe,[52] then the Old Testa-

---

[46] Kedar-Kopfstein, 'Vulgate', 53.

[47] Kedar-Kopfstein, 'Vulgate', 55.

[48] Kedar-Kopfstein, 'Vulgate', 56. With regard to Jerome's Vulgate translation it is important to make a clear distinction between Jerome's revision of the Latin New Testament, which can be seen as containing really little more than adjustments to earlier exegesis, and his translation of the OT from Hebrew into Latin, which no one had attempted before and was a far harder exegetical task.

[49] Kedar-Kopfstein, 'Vulgate', 56.

[50] Kedar-Kopfstein, 'Vulgate', 65.

[51] G.W.H. Lampe (ed.), *The Cambridge History of the Bible* vol 2: *The West from the Fathers to the Reformation* (Cambridge: CUP, 1969).

[52] E.F. Sutcliffe, 'Jerome,' in *The Cambridge History of the Bible*, 2.80-101.

ment Professor at Heythrop College. Ranging over Jerome's biography, Jerome's revision of the existing Latin version of the books of the Hebrew Canon, Jerome's exegetical-style and hermeneutic, Jerome's NT commentaries, Jerome's particular interest in the prophetic literature of the OT, Jerome's views on the function of the exegete, Jerome's attitude and treatment of the Septuagint and Jerome's translation skills and his use of the oral assistance of Jewish teachers, Sutcliffe's comprehensive essay incorporates valuable insights as well as some new material.

Of particular interest are Sutcliffe's assessments of Jerome's character and ambitions. He observes Jerome as the scholar with the 'incredible passion for learning, who deplored hindrances to his pursuits,'[53] and how Jerome 'was sensitive and emotional, warm and faithful in affection, quick and vehement in his anger against all that he conceived to be contrary to revealed truth'.[54] It is here that Sutcliffe finds Jerome's ardent temperament to have been a key factor in Jerome's inability to be a conciliator.[55] Yet despite some of these apparent character flaws, Sutcliffe determines Jerome to have been 'passionately devoted to his faith and unwearying in his labours to make the truths of religion better known: the impelling motive of all his biblical study and writing'.[56] The following description of Jerome by Sutcliffe is particularly telling:

> He was an artist in words with a delicate sensitivity for the beauty of language. He refers frequently to the style of his compositions. He knew that it should be adapted to the subject, and his writings exhibit two styles, the one studied and even rhetorical (as in his first *Epistle*, on the woman struck seven times by the sword of the executioner), the other simple and straightforward as in his commentaries. In such works, as he remarks in a letter to Damasus, the meaning is more important than the language, though, even so, he excuses his inability to polish what he had written, as the weakness of his eyes made it necessary for him to dictate.[57]

What Sutcliffe is pointing to here is, again, the astuteness with which Jerome conducted his biblical labours.[58] Throughout his essay on Jerome, Sutcliffe uses the verb 'labours' in respect of Jerome's hard work (sometimes to struggle to do something difficult).[59] Sutcliffe notes with regret that Jerome did not compose a formal treatise on the interpretation of Scripture.[60] Sutcliffe observes:

---

53 Sutcliffe, 'Jerome,' 85.
54 Sutcliffe, 'Jerome,' 87.
55 Sutcliffe, 'Jerome,' 85, 87.
56 Sutcliffe, 'Jerome,' 87-88.
57 Jerome, *Ep.* 21.42, as cited by Sutcliffe, 'Jerome,' 88.
58 Sutcliffe, 'Jerome,' 87-88.
59 For example, Sutcliffe's description of 'the first labours undertaken by Jerome after his settlement in Palestine, was the revision of the existing Latin version of the books of the Hebrew Canon'. See Sutcliffe, '*Jerome*,' 88.
60 Sutcliffe, 'Jerome,' 89.

He has left us only scattered remarks on the subject, though these are numerous. In three places he lays it down that the Scriptures should be understood in three ways, justifying this principle by reference to the Septuagint version of Prov. 22:20 as a command to write the Scriptures in our hearts in a threefold manner. The triple interpretation is explained differently in the three passages, except that in each the literal sense is placed first. In two of them a connection is made with the threefold concept of man as body, soul and spirit, thus showing a dependence on Origen.[61]

Here it must be said that Sutcliffe's analysis, showing a Jerome-Origen linkage on the question of the biblical interpretation of Scripture, is at some odds with what we saw in chapter 2 where a clear distinction was shown to have existed between Origen's and Jerome's understanding of the principles of exegesis.

It is on the issue of Jerome's views on the question of the function of the exegete, and, indeed, on the question of his success or otherwise as an exegete, that Sutcliffe offers some valuable insights. Sutcliffe largely follows convention by stressing Jerome's general exegetical style as being made up of the literal, the spiritual and the allegorical sense.[62]

Before looking at an example of Sutcliffe's critique of Jerome's exegesis, it is important to understand Jerome's view on the function of the exegete. Here Sutcliffe proffers one of the clearest expositions of Jerome's thinking on the subject:

> The function of an exegete, Jerome writes, is 'to discuss what is obscure, to touch on the obvious, to dwell at length on what is doubtful'.[63] Elsewhere he says that the commentator should 'briefly and plainly elucidate what is obscure' and should so write that his own explanations of another's words does not itself need explanation.[64] But in the matter of brevity he is far from attaining his own ideal. But eloquence has no place in a commentary; on the contrary, it should be written in

---

[61] Sutcliffe, 'Jerome,' 89. Origen's rules for the interpretation of the divine inspiration of the Scriptures is found in Book 4.1.2 of *On First Principles*. Here Origen's reference to Prov. 22:20, 21 reads: 'The right way of approaching the scriptures and gathering their meaning, is the following, which is extracted from the writings themselves. We find some such rule as this laid down by Solomon in the Proverbs concerning the divine doctrines written therein: "Do thou portray them threefold in counsel and knowledge, that thou mayest answer words of truth to those who question thee."' See Origen, *On First Principles* (Foreword by J.C. Cavadini and Introduction by H. de Lubac, with translation by G.W. Butterworth; Notre Dame: Ave Maria, 2013), 363. For how Origen tells us, that 'one should inscribe on one's soul the intentions of the holy literature in a threefold manner and how Origen, argues 'just as the human being consists of body, soul and spirit, so does Scripture which God has arranged to be given for the salvation of humankind', See B. Fulford, *Divine Eloquence and Human Transformation: Rethinking Scripture and History through Gregory of Nazianzus and Hans Frei* (Minneapolis: Fortress, 2013), 121.
[62] Sutcliffe, 'Jerome,' 89.
[63] Jerome, PL. 26, 400c, as cited by Sutcliffe, 'Jerome,' 94.
[64] Jerome, PL. 25, 118B, as cited by Sutcliffe, 'Jerome,' 94.

'simple speech'.[65] In composing his work he acknowledges his use of earlier writers, as his purpose is not to give personal views of his own but the treasures of traditional wisdom. Much, however, is inevitably the fruit of his own study. He desired in particular to give the West the benefit of the learning and piety of the Greek writers who were not familiar to those of Latin speech. On difficult matters various opinions are recorded and at times the reader is left to his own judgement to decide which explanation is the best.[66]

Here Sutcliffe's treatment of Jerome the exegete again raises the question of whether or not Jerome was not only expecting too much of his readers but was not himself able (or prepared?) to sometimes complete the task of exegesis fully. Was this perhaps because, as Butterworth has asserted, 'Jerome was a Latin and had little sympathy with the Greek habit of thinking out problems.'[67] Of course, if Butterworth is right then it lends some support to Freeman's (2009) proposition that Jerome proved too pedantic a thinker ever to engage fully with the intricacies of Greek philosophy and never showed any genuine intellectual creativity or had the self-confidence to develop his own theology.[68] This leaves us to consider whether or not Jerome, in his desire 'to give the West the benefit of the learning and piety of the Greek writers who were not familiar to those of Latin speech' (Sutcliffe), may have been guilty of reading the Greek writers in a cursory fashion, with the result that he was unable to exegete 'difficult matters' leaving the reader to decide the true meaning of a text. Again, if this is true, then McGuckin's (2005) view that Jerome's reputation as exegete is overstressed (at least if we look for originality) is upheld.[69]

We need now to consider whether or not any or all of the above is supported by Sutcliffe's critique of Jerome's exegesis? Here, we should be aware that whilst Jerome may have believed that 'eloquence has no place in a commentary,'[70] he appears sometimes to contradict himself. Sutcliffe states:

Skill in translating is fostered by practice, and Jerome was no novice at the art when he commenced the arduous task of translating the OT from the original Hebrew. His previous work of the kind had been from the Greek of Origen and Didymus but it had enabled him to form definite principles. These he set down in the letter 57 to Pammachius which he speaks of as a treatise 'On the best style of translating.' The desired ideal is fidelity to the sense without undue adherence to the words as such, for a translation must be true to the character of the language into which it is made, and this cannot be achieved by slavish reproduction of words. It is true that the principle of 'sense by sense and not word by word' is said not to apply to holy Scripture, 'where even the ordo verborum is a mystery'.[71]

[65] Jerome, PL. 26, 401B, as cited by Sutcliffe, 'Jerome,' 94.
[66] Sutcliffe, 'Jerome,' 94.
[67] G.W. Butterworth, 'Translators' Introduction,' in Origen: *On First Principles*, 33-76 (66).
[68] Freeman, *A New History*, 284.
[69] McGuckin, *A-Z*, 188.
[70] Jerome, PL. 26, 401B, as cited by Sutcliffe, 'Jerome,' 94.
[71] Jerome, *Ep.* 57.5, as cited by Sutcliffe, 'Jerome,' 96.

This does not mean the order of the words, but, by a usage attested elsewhere in Jerome's writings, something like 'the precise character of the words'. In the preface to Job the translation is said to follow at times the words, at times the sense, at times both at once,[72] though this statement is not altogether clear in meaning. Certainly Jerome often neglects the words when they represent mere repetition which would be alien to Latin taste. He even at times inserts words of his own for the sake of clarity, as in Gen. 31:47, 'each according to the propriety of his own language'. ...In places a neat Latin phrase has an ethos quite absent from the simplicity of the Hebrew, as 'if in silent thought thou answer "for" if thou shouldst say in thy heart' (Deut. 18:21).

Having declared that 'eloquence has no place in a commentary,' Jerome then, according to Sutcliffe, 'at times inserts words of his own for the sake of clarity'. With this apparent contradiction in mind, might Jerome here be deemed guilty (yet again) of dishonest exegesis with Jerome sometimes adding words of his own in order to achieve a clearer textual meaning?

Sutcliffe's main criticisms of Jerome's Latin translation style (its occasional lack of clarity, not to mention its sometimes lack of fidelity to Scripture) are directed at Jerome's commentaries on the books of the Pentateuch, as we see in the following example:

> Differences of meaning do not necessarily demonstrate differences in the Hebrew texts. They may merely reflect different ways of vocalizing the same consonants. Thus, in Ps. 2:9, where the Massoretic vocalization gives 'Thou shalt crush them with a rod of iron,' Jerome's version from the Hebrew has *pasces eos*, the verb being read as in Ps. 22 (23):1, 'the Lord is my shepherd': a meaning that harmonizes badly with the 'rod of iron'. Again, the present Hebrew reading of Ps. 71 (72):12 means 'he will rescue the poor man at his entreaty,' whereas Jerome, with the same consonants, renders it 'he will rescue the poor man from the mighty'.[73]

Jerome's defence of his Latin translation style (as found in *Ep.* 57) is somewhat cavalier, as the following extract demonstrates:

> In translating the Chronicle of Eusebius of Caesarea into Latin, I made among others, the following prefatory observations: 'It is difficult in following lines laid down by others not sometimes to diverge from them, and it is hard to preserve in a translation the charm of expressions which in another language are most felicitous. Each particular word conveys a meaning of its own, and possibly I have no equivalent by which to render it, and if I make a circuit to reach my goal, I have to go many miles to cover a short distance (*vix brevis viae spatia consumo*). To these difficulties must be added the windings of hyperbata, differences in the use of cases, divergences of metaphor; and last of all the peculiar and if I may so call it, inbred character of the language. If I render word for word, the result will sound

---

[72] Jerome, PL. 28, 1081A, as cited by Sutcliffe, 'Jerome,' 96. In *Ep.* 57 (*To Pammachius on the Best Method of Translating*) Jerome defended his method of translation ('to give sense for sense and not word for word') by an appeal to classical, ecclesiastical and NT writers. Whilst Sutcliffe is correct in observing that Jerome did not write a formal treatise on the interpretation of Scripture, *Ep.* 57 remains the closest to such a composition.

[73] Sutcliffe, 'Jerome', 97-98.

uncouth, and if compelled by necessity I alter anything in the order or wording, I shall seem to have departed from the function of a translator... If anyone imagines that translation does not impair the charm of style, let him render Homer word for word into Latin, nay I will go farther still and say, let him render it into Latin prose, and the result will be that the order of the words will seem ridiculous and the most eloquent of poets scarcely articulate.'[74]

Here Jerome's defence of his Latin translation style appears almost selfish in seemingly downplaying such important issues as fidelity to the text being translated ('lines laid down by others') and the avoidance of divergence ('it is difficult... not to diverge...'). Jerome seems almost to relish in his argument that it is by translating into another language that 'the charm of expressions' of an earlier translation are more felicitously rendered.

What then, of Sutcliffe's final judgement on Jerome? Sutcliffe believes, without reservation, that 'Jerome was the most successful of the ancient translators,'[75] whose work (e.g., for the history of exegesis) was immensely valuable.[76] Sutcliffe concludes:

The lifelong labours of Jerome all bear witness to his ardent devotion to Holy Scripture. For him, 'knowledge of the Scriptures' means 'the riches of Christ...'[77]

Hence his exhortations to his correspondents: 'I beg you, dear brother, live with them, meditate on them, make them the sole object of your knowledge and inquiries.'[78]

And to a priest: 'Frequently read the divine Scriptures; rather, never let the sacred text out of your hands. Learn what you have to teach...The speech of a priest should be seasoned with the words of Scripture.'[79]

'Make knowledge of the Scriptures your love and you will not love the vices of the flesh' (*ep.* 125.11). And in the explanation of the Scriptures, he reminds his readers, we always stand in need of the Spirit of God.[80]

Thus, it is with Sutcliffe's (1969) assessment that the modern critical reception of Jerome now moved forward with a new momentum.

---

[74] Jerome, *Ep.* 57.5 (*St. Jerome: Select Works and Letters*), NPNF² 6:114.

[75] Sutcliffe, 'Jerome', 99.

[76] Here, Sutcliffe cites the following Jerome works: the Vulgate Bible (as we know it); Jerome's Letters (those incorporating biblical exegesis); *Liber de Nominibus Hebraicis* (a collection of all the proper names of the OT and NT and assigned to each its traditional meaning with their traditional etymological explanations); *Liber de Situ et Nominibus Locorum Hebraicorum* (a gazetter of the towns, mountains, rivers, and other geographical names occurring in the Bible; *Liber Hebraicorum Quaestionum in Genesim* (on selected passages of Genesis, of a character till then completely unknown, whose purpose was to correct erroneous opinions about the Hebrew books, and mistakes in the Latin and Greek codices). See Sutcliffe, 'Jerome,' 99-100.

[77] Jerome, PL. 23, 936A and 24, 17B, as cited by Sutcliffe, 'Jerome,' 100-101.

[78] Jerome, *Ep.* 53.10, as cited by Sutcliffe, 'Jerome,' 101.

[79] Jerome, *Ep.* 52.7f, as cited by Sutcliffe, 'Jerome,' 101.

[80] Jerome, PL. 25, 1159B, as cited by Sutcliffe, 'Jerome,' 101.

The early 1970s now saw scholars reassessing in a more defined manner Jerome's dependence upon Origen and the Latin Classics.[81] Margaret Schatkin, whilst noting the general dependence of Jerome's *Commentary on Galatians* upon Origen's exegetical work, also observed J.B. Lightfoot's judgement that Jerome's Commentary was 'the most important patristic commentary on the Epistle to the Galatians ever and any failures were far outweighed by Jerome's wide knowledge and critical acumen,'[82] Grützmacher's view that Jerome's Commentary (despite some reliance upon earlier Greek exegesis) was 'a far better work than his subsequent translation works'.[83] Such endorsements of Jerome's exegetical powers may balance the often-applied criticism that Jerome was too often the follower of Origen, rather than an original, creative exegete, in his own right.

As regards Jerome and the Latin Classics, Hagendahl records that Jerome's attitude towards profane Latin literature was 'determined by his immersion (from early school education) in the *quadriga* of classical authors (Terence, Sallust, Cicero and Vergil) on whom good Latin was centred in late antiquity.'[84] As well as evidence of classical Latin poetical reminiscences in Jerome's letters,[85] Hagendahl suggests that the influence of the prose-writer Cicero over Jerome the classicist was paramount.[86] Hagendahl comments 'He is to Jerome *rex oratorum et latinae linguae illustrator*, and equally his chief informant in matters of philosophy.'[87] Thus, Jerome may be seen as an important literary resource for our knowledge and understanding of Cicero's varied works.[88] Although Cicero's influence over Jerome's prose style may have been superior to all others it was not over-arching. For example, Hagendahl notes that Jerome showed (unlike Augustine) no concerns for things 'historical and political' and, consequently, 'showed little interest in *De re publica*'.[89] Finally, Jerome's 'ten consolatory writings (in the form of letters) show him to have been the foremost representative in Latin Christian Literature of this genre, much fostered by

---

[81] See for example, M.A. Schatkin, 'The Influence of Origen upon St. Jerome's Commentary on Galatians,' *VC* 24.1 (1970), 49-58; H. Hagendahl, 'St. Jerome and the Latin Classics,' *VC* 28.3 (1974), 216-27.

[82] J.B. Lightfoot, *The Epistle of St. Paul to the Galatians* (Grand Rapids: 1967), 232, as cited by Schatkin, 'Influence of Origen,' 52n.17. For a more recent illustration of the power of Jerome's *Commentary of Galatians*, see M. Edwards (ed.), *Ancient Christian Commentary on Scripture, New Testament VIII, Galatians, Ephesians, Philippians* (Downer's Grove: IVP, 1999), 10-12, 14-15, 22-24.

[83] G. Grützmacher, *Hieronymus, eine biographische Studie zur alten Kirchengeschichte* (Leipzig/Berlin, 1901-08), 2.36f., as cited by Schatkin, 'The Influence of Origen,' 52n.18.

[84] Hagendahl, 'Latin Classics', 217n.4.

[85] Hagendahl, 'Latin Classics', 218-19.

[86] Hagendahl, 'Latin Classics', 220.

[87] Hagendahl, 'Latin Classics', 220.

[88] Hagendahl, 'Latin Classics', 220.

[89] Hagendahl, 'Latin Classics', 222.

the philosophers',[90] whilst 'a detailed comparison [Jerome's *Ep.* 60, 8, 1 and Quintilian's *Institutio oratoria*, 3,7,10] seems to suggest that Jerome was dependent on the great teacher of rhetoric, Quintilian'.[91] Whilst all of this suggests that Jerome was, indeed, a well-informed Latin classicist, the criticisms of Jerome's limited knowledge of classical Greek literature (Chadwick, 1967) and Jerome's limited engagement with Greek philosophy (Freeman, 2009) still remain.

In 1971 the publication of Jaroslav Pelikan's *The Emergence of the Catholic Tradition (100-600)*[92] confirmed Jerome's significant role in shaping the dominance of 'Christian theology over Jewish thought' though it was a triumph that 'came more by default than by conquest'.[93] Pelikan observes how the early theologians saw it as important not to over-criticize the OT and so avoid the danger of assigning to that most substantial part of the Bible 'a sub-Christian status'.[94] What was important was for exegetes and exegesis to respect 'the relation between the covenants' (i.e., agreements between God and the Israelites) as found in the NT and describing 'Israel as the chosen people'.[95] Through their respective writings both Origen and Jerome participated in this dialogue.

The context for Jerome's participation and role in the covenants 'dialogue' is set out by Pelikan, who argues that 'The Old Testament achieved and maintained its status as Christian Scripture with the aid of spiritual exegesis.'[96] Whilst Pelikan finds no evidence for any early Christian exegete who both af-

---

[90] Hagendahl, 'Latin Classics', 224.
[91] Hagendahl, 'Latin Classics', 225.
[92] J. Pelikan, *The Christian Tradition (A History of the Development of Doctrine)* 1: *The Emergence of the Catholic Tradition* (100-600) (Chicago: University of Chicago Press, 1971).
[93] Pelikan, *The Christian Tradition*, 1.22. Pelikan believes the victory resulted from 'the movement of Jewish history rather than the superior force of Christian exegesis or learning' (20); and, 'After the sack of Jerusalem in A.D. 70 and its desecration during the following years, Jewish polemic against Christianity was increasingly on the defensive, while Christian doctrine felt able to go its own way, without engaging the rabbis in a continuing dialogue' (20-21).
[94] Pelikan, *The Christian Tradition*, 1, 23. Here, Pelikan cites 'Marcion in the second century and biblical criticism of the nineteenth century', as being guilty of this trend. For a full discussion of Marcion's religious thought and Marcion's Theological Reform, see R.J. Hoffmann, *Marcion: On the Restitution of Christianity—An Essay on the Development of Radical Paulinist Theology in the Second Century* (Chico: Scholars, 1984).
[95] Pelikan, *The Christian Tradition*, 1.23. For a detailed account of the elements of continuity and discontinuity between the various covenant-types, see P.J. Gräbe, *New Covenant, New Community* (Milton Keynes: Paternoster, 2006), 1-57; S.W. Hahn, *Kinship by Covenant: A Biblical Theological Study of Covenant Types and Texts in the Old and New Testament* (New Haven: Yale University Press, 2005). For a description of the variety of 'covenants of promise', see T.A. Chrisope, *Confessing Jesus as Lord* (Fearn: Christian Focus, 2012), 49-77.
[96] Pelikan, *The Christian Tradition*, I.81.

firmed 'the doctrinal authority of the Old Testament and interpreted it literally,'[97] he is perhaps less than generous to Jerome in favouring Marcion of Sinope (c.70-150 CE) as the most important church figure 'for raising the question of the authority of the OT in the Christian community and for compelling at least some clarification of the question.'[98]

Pelikan's 1971 study also provided a reading of two other important areas of Jerome's theology as found in his polemic and letter corpus (asceticism and catholicity). According to Pelikan the growth of Christian asceticism in the third century reinforced the causal connection between the virgin birth and the holiness of Jesus Christ.[99] In addition, Jerome held to a particular view of marriage, sex and virginity, in relation to human salvation. Here some of Jerome's writings[100] show Jerome to have taken a different position to his predecessor Tertullian (c.160-c.220), who opposed marriage and sex. According to Pelikan, Jerome believed that 'Christ and Mary were the models of true chastity (i.e., virginity)' and Jerome's 'ascetical theology praised marriage because it was the way virgins were brought into the world'.[101] Here Pelikan's reading would suggest that Jerome put a very high value on virginity but its juxtaposition [by Jerome] to marriage may be seen as somewhat incongruous.

Elsewhere Pelikan notes the context within which Jerome's contribution to the doctrine of catholicity was made:

---

[97] Pelikan, *The Christian Tradition*, I.81.

[98] Pelikan, *The Christian Tradition*, I.81. Here Pelikan, in fact, contrasts Augustine with Jerome on this important issue stating 'Augustine lumped Manes with Marcion in his defence of the OT against the Manicheans, and Jerome attacked Marcion as a representative of the hatred and contempt for the works of the creator that, marked many heretics.' Marcionism was an early Christian heresy that saw the God of the OT as a tyrant in contrast to the God of the NT who is all-loving. Whilst it is Marcion who is often seen to be the founder of the 'idea' of the NT canon there has been considerable scholarly debate over the precise nature of his influence. For an account of the debate over Marcion's role in the formulation of the NT canon, see M.J. Kruger, *Canon Revisited: Establishing the Origins and Authority of the New Testament Books* (Wheaton: Crossway, 2012), 31, 68, 136-37, 141, 161, 174, 228, 229; C.E. Hill, *Who Chose the Gospels? Probing the Great Gospel Conspiracy* (New York: OUP, 2010), 176-78. For a detailed discussion of Marcion's importance as a religious reformer and teacher, see Hoffman, *Marcion*, 1-74, D.W. Deakle, 'The Fathers Against Marcionism: A Study of the Methods and Motives in the Developing Patristic Anti-Marcionite Polemic' (PhD thesis, Saint Louis University, 1991), 18-42, E.C. Blackman, *Marcion and his Influence* (London, SPCK, 1948), ix-x, 1-14, B. Green, *Christianity in Ancient Rome: The First Three Centuries* (London: T&T Clark, 2010), 61-73, J.D. BeDuhn, *The First New Testament: Marcion's Scriptural Canon* (Salem: Polebridge, 2013), 11-23.

[99] Pelikan, *The Christian Tradition*, I.288.

[100] For example, *Against Jovinian* 1.39 (PL 23.266), 1.40 (PL 23:269), *Ep.*22.38.3 (CSEL 54:203) as cited by Pelikan, *The Christian Tradition*, 1.298.

[101] Pelikan, *The Christian Tradition*, I.288-89.

Fundamental to the orthodox consensus was an affirmation of the authority of tradition as that which had been believed 'everywhere, always, by all [ubique, sem-
per, ab omnibus]'. The criteria for what had constituted the orthodox tradition
were 'universality, antiquity, and consensus.'[102]

and

The criterion of universality required that a doctrine, to be recognized as the
teaching of the church rather than a private theory of a man or of a school, be
genuinely catholic, that is, be the confession of 'all the churches…one great horde
of people… with one voice re-echoing the praises of Christ' [*Hier. Vigil*.5 (PL 23:
343)].[103]

Thus, it was within this context that Jerome's catholic views on marriage, sex,
virginity, celibacy and monasticism were propagated.

In 1972 Peter Brown's study *Religion and Society in the Age of Saint Augustine*[104] documented the patronage given to Jerome and how this support from
local Roman aristocracies influenced his standing and the quality of his literary
output. Significantly, Jerome's writings, being Christian, may have directly
helped to end paganism in Rome—because Jerome's corpus dates from the
early 370s, some ten years before the disestablishment of the official pagan
cults of Rome by Gratian in 382. However, as Brown observes, even after the
transformation of the Late Roman Empire (from paganism to Christianity) it
was 'a transformation in which much of the Roman secular tradition was preserved'.[105] Moreover, Brown notes that it is 'the correspondence of Jerome
which throws a vivid, but exceedingly erratic, light on the Roman scene'.[106]
Brown also finds an important place for Jerome's writings in the Christianization of the Roman aristocracy.

As revealed in the correspondence, above all of Jerome and, to a lesser extent, in
the works of Paulinus, Augustine, Pelagius and Palladius the history of the conversion of the Roman families is part of the history of the impact of an extreme
'oriental' form of asceticism on the religious life of Rome. This ascetic movement
represented a radical departure from the previous Christian traditions of Rome.[107]

This text citation from Brown, affirms Jerome's important influence over
Rome's evolving Christian life. However, we should also remember that it was
Jerome's asceticism which eventually helped encourage the abandonment of

---

[102] Pelikan, *The Christian Tradition*, I.333.
[103] Pelikan, *The Christian Tradition*, I.333. Jerome wrote his polemic *Against Vigilantius* in 406 blaming Vigilantius 'for repudiating the cult of relics, the observation of
vigils, celibacy and monasticism in south-west Gaul'. See Rebenich, *Jerome*, 50.
[104] P. Brown, *Religion and Society in the Age of Saint Augustine* (London: Faber, 1972).
[105] Brown, *Religion*, 164.
[106] Brown, *Religion*, 169.
[107] Brown, *Religion*, 168-69.

Rome for the centres of the new devotion—the Holy Places and the coenobite settlements in Egypt.[108]

The early 1970s also witnessed a renewed scholarly interest in Jerome's contribution to the shaping of the knowledge and understanding of the Scriptures in the early Church. The major work here was Hans von Campenhausen's *The Formation of the Christian Bible*.[109] This was the classic modern presentation of a very important but strangely neglected subject in historical theology.

Campenhausen finds Jerome to have been a pivotal figure in championing the Apostle Paul and supporting the authentication and authority of the Pauline Epistles against Marcionite forgeries.[110] Whilst Campenhausen finds the real 'New Testament' theologian to have been Irenaeus (with his highly original typology of the Four Gospels as symbols of salvation-history)[111] he considers Jerome to have been central to influencing the restriction of the corpus of normative books of the Bible, including the Pauline epistles and the Apocalyps-

---

[108] Although it is Pachomius (d.346) who has long been regarded as the early founder of monasticism. Philip Rousseau notes 'Jerome was aware of a cenobite tradition in Egypt but wrote of it in only the most general terms.' See P. Rousseau, *Pachomius: The Making of a Community in Fourth Century Egypt* (Berkeley: University of California Press, 1985), 54. Here Rousseau is mistaken for Jerome claimed that 'the monasteries of Nitria were rife with Origenism'. See Jerome, *Ep.* 92, as cited by Rich, *Discernment*, 35n.297. Jerome was also highly critical of the desert theologian Evagrius Ponticus (c. 345-399), calling him a heretic and an Origenist. See Jerome, *Ep.* 133.3, as cited by Rich, *Discernment*, 40n.9. For a full account of the Evagrius/Origen relationship, see A.M. Casiday, *Evagrius Ponticus. The Early Church Fathers* (London: Routledge, 2006), 29-35. It should be noted that Rousseau's observation that 'Jerome was aware of a cenobite tradition in Egypt' is something of an understatement for, of course, it is well-known that in 385 Jerome travelled in company with two Roman ladies (Paula and her daughter Eustochium) to Palestine. As Meinardus has commented: 'They continued heir journey to Egypt where they visited the monasteries of the Desert of Scatis. On returning to Palestine they settled in Bethlehem where Paula founded four monasteries, three for nuns and one for monks. It was the latter monastery over which Jerome presided and where he was engaged in most of his literary work. See Meinardus, *Monks and Monasteries*, 4. For a further discussion of the role of Pachomius in the development of monasticism, see Rousseau, *Ascetics*, 30, 34, 56-58, 63. On Jerome's translation from Greek into Latin of the mature Pachonian Monastic Rule (laying down the dress, food and sleeping arrangements all to be uniformly observed by every monk without distinction) see H. Chadwick, 'Pachomios and the Idea of Sanctity,' in H. Chadwick, *History and Thought of the Early Church* (London: Variorum Reprints, 1982), 11-24 (20).

[109] H. von Campenhausen, *The Formation of the Christian Bible* (London: Adam and Charles Black, 1972).

[110] Campenhausen, *Formation*, 179n.160. Here, Campenhausen makes an interesting observation about Jerome, namely, that Jerome acknowledged Tatian's own edition of the Pauline epistles where Tatian had polished and touched up the style (Jerome, *Comm. Tit.*, prol.).

[111] Campenhausen, *Formation*, 197-99,

es.[112] Of all Pauline writings it was perhaps the Pastoral Epistles which were most problematic for Jerome having, as Campenhausen observes, originally been 'written for the purpose of combating heresy'.[113] That is not to say that Jerome did not accept them, following on from Tertullian's acknowledgement of the early spread of 'vetus et novum testamentum,'[114] (he did) but during Jerome's time there was considerable suspicion that they might have been 'apocryphal' writings.[115] As always, here Jerome's concern was to actively contest the defining limits of the NT canon. It seems that Jerome's Latin translations certainly played an important role in the developing notion of 'testamentary' deposition or instrument ('Instrumentum') denoting the particular documents of the old and new divine covenants.[116]

1975-1990

In the preface to his 1975 book *Jerome*,[117] J.N.D. Kelly observed that J. Steinmann's *St. Jerome* (1959) was 'too light-weight to count'[118] as one of the excellent, though somewhat outdated biographies that had hitherto been published. Thus, Kelly intended that his volume would 'fill the gap'[119] in the literature on Jerome, by offering the first, comprehensive study in English. Kelly states:

> At the same time, since Jerome is one of the most human and fascinating figures of his epoch, I have tried to make the book accessible to the growing number of 'intelligent general readers' who are attracted by the early Christian centuries.[120]

However, if this was his aim Kelly might have been best advised to have included a bibliography with his book. As it stands Kelly's *Jerome* is still considered not only the classic, seminal account of Jerome but also the benchmark against which all other subsequent studies might be judged.

So what of Kelly's critical reception and reassessment of Jerome's corpus as set against the 'McGuckin-Freeman' thesis? Introducing his analysis of Jerome,

---

[112] Campenhausen, *Formation*, 232.

[113] Jerome, *Comm. Tit.*, prolog, as cited by Campenhausen, *Formation*, 234n.130.

[114] Tertullian, *Adv. Marc.* IV, 1,1: *alterius instrumenti vel quod magis usui est dicere testamenti*, as cited by Campenhausen, *Formation*, 267n.362.

[115] Campenhausen, *Formation*, 234. For the most recent modern critique of the 'authentication' and 'authorship' questions surrounding the Pastoral Epistles, see B.D. Ehrman, *Forgery and Counterforgery: The Use of Literary Deceit in Early Christian Polemics* (Oxford: OUP, 2013), 192-17. Ehrman states: 'Taken collectively or as individual letters, the Pastoral epistles thus have appeared to a strong majority of critics to be pseudepigraphic productions of a post-Pauline age' (211), and 'In short, it appears that the same author produced the three pastoral letters. Moreover, there are very good reasons for thinking this author was not Paul' (201).

[116] Campenhausen, *Formation*, 267, 268n.306.

[117] Kelly, *Jerome*, vii.

[118] Kelly, *Jerome*, vii.

[119] Kelly, *Jerome*, vii.

[120] Kelly, *Jerome*, vii.

Kelly observed that the 1970s had seen a considerable advance in Jerome research though the absence of 'properly annotated editions of Jerome's works' was a major concern.[121]

Central to Kelly's study are reassessments of Jerome as translator and commentator. Kelly describes the period 386 to 393 as 'a period of prodigious, sometimes feverish literary activity', in which 'Over and above his other preoccupations, Jerome was pouring out a spate of books—translations, commentaries, scholarly studies and compilations, even an outline history of Christian literature.'[122] Here Kelly, like Quasten (1960), identifies Jerome's translation of Didymus's treatise *On the Holy Spirit* as being of special importance allowing as it did for the work's wider availability in the West.[123]

It is significant that Kelly does note instances where Jerome's translations may have failed to uphold Nicene orthodoxy. For example, on Jerome's rendering of the thirty-nine homilies by Origen on select parts of St. Luke's Gospel, Kelly remarks:

> What in fact astonishes us is the large number of passages in which he has incorporated unaltered either theologically dubious speculations of Origen (e.g., about the ultimate transformation of the blessed into angels, or the pre-existence of souls and their incarceration in bodies as the result of a pre-temporal fall), or opinions (e.g., about the need of Mary, indeed of Jesus, for purification) which he must have known to be offensive to contemporary orthodoxy.[124]

Here Kelly's criticism of Jerome including 'opinions... which he must have known to be offensive to contemporary orthodoxy' is clearly at odds with Kedar-Kopfstein's (1968) belief that 'it is not at all surprising that Jerome would not admit a theological or Christological interpretation that contradicted the prevalent situation'.

On Jerome the biblical commentator, Kelly focuses upon Jerome's commentaries on Philemon, Galatians, Ephesians and Titus (387/388), largely compilations from earlier exegetes, chiefly Origen.[125] These commentaries, Kelly argues, show exegesis which is 'usually derivative'.[126] This, and Kelly's following remarks about Jerome's work on Ephesians, might suggest that McGuckin's (2005) view that Jerome's reputation as exegete is over-stressed (at least if we look for originality) may well hold some credence.

> In *On Ephesians,* where numerous, often lengthy fragments of Origen's original Greek survive and where Rufinus was to pounce on almost a score of passages which slavishly incorporated questionable items of Origenistic theology, the

---

[121] Kelly, *Jerome*, vii.

[122] Kelly, *Jerome*, 141.

[123] Kelly, *Jerome*, 142. Kelly notes, 'In his treatise Didymus had argued for the full divinity of the Spirit against the view that he was a creature', and Kelly commends it 'as a pioneer work of originality and acuteness' (142).

[124] Kelly, *Jerome*, 143.

[125] Kelly, *Jerome*, 145.

[126] Kelly, *Jerome*, 146.

enormous extent of his indebtedness, going far beyond anything his admissions might suggest, is demonstrable.[127]

Again,

By contrast [to *On Galatians*] *On Ephesians* has a more chaotic air, the result partly of its rushed composition, partly of the sheer difficulty of this baffling epistle. Allegorical or spiritual exegesis is slightly more in evidence, but in the main Jerome struggles valiantly to establish the literal sense.[128]

Having earlier noted Jerome's acknowledgement of his own feeble powers in undertaking these commentaries,[129] Kelly then sets out his most damning criticisms of Jerome's commentaries on the Pauline epistles:

What is chiefly disappointing, especially in expounding Galatians and Ephesians, is Jerome's failure to understand, much less present adequately, the profound theological issues with which these letters are concerned.[130]

Here it is clear that Kelly rebukes Jerome for his lack of clarity in his exegesis of the Pauline epistles. However, Kelly is prepared to recognise some independent thought on the part of Jerome (apart from 'the large-scale borrowings from Origen')[131] in Jerome's commentary on Ecclesiastes.[132]

As well as Kelly's biography of Jerome (1975) also saw the publication of three journal essays reassessing aspects of Jerome's exegesis.[133] Metzger's 'The Practice of Textual Criticism Among the Church Fathers,' postulates that far from being 'uncritical' the Church Fathers did engage upon 'direct and conscious criticism, at least so far a lower or textual criticism is concerned'.[134] Metzger's essay provides a positive secondary judgement on Jerome acknowledging Jerome's 'scholarly acumen and circumspection' as well as his 'sustained critical labours... among the most outstanding of any age'.[135]

Though Metzger considers Jerome to have been a patristic writer of some considerable talent,[136] he finds Origen to have been the greater textual scholar

---

[127] Kelly, *Jerome*, 145-146.

[128] Kelly, *Jerome*, 147.

[129] Jerome's acknowledgement is found in his *Comm. on Galatians* prol; *Comm. On Ephesians* prol. (PL 26: 369-70; 543-44). See Kelly, *Jerome*, 145n.33.

[130] Kelly, *Jerome*, 147.

[131] Kelly, *Jerome*, 150.

[132] Kelly, *Jerome*, 150-51.

[133] B.M. Metzger, 'The Practice of Textual Criticism among the Church Fathers', *StP* 12 (1975), 340-49; D.F. Heimann, 'The Polemical Application of Scripture in St. Jerome,' *StP* 12 (1975), 309-16; J.T. Cummings, 'St. Jerome as Translator and as Exegete,' *StP* 12 (1975), 279-82.

[134] Metzger, 'Textual Criticism,' 340.

[135] Metzger, 'Textual Criticism,' 340.

[136] Metzger, 'Textual Criticism,' 340. Here Metzger cites Irenaeus (c.130-c.200) 'as possibly the earliest patristic writer to display critical activity (*Contra Haer. V.xxx.*1.) by referring to the authority of NT manuscripts as well as suggesting the origin of the textual corruption which he had before him (e.g. the Apocalypse)'.

of the early Church.[137] In what sense does Metzger assess Jerome's scholarly acumen? For Metzger, Jerome's scholarly acumen is demonstrated by his willingness/unwillingness to adopt a particular reading of a text, thereby testifying to the authority (or otherwise) of particular biblical manuscripts.[138] However, it is important to note here that scholars have continued to question whether or not *full exegesis*, as opposed to *commentary*, occurred during the age of the patristic writers of the early Church.[139]

Metzger's essay includes one observation of particular relevance to our study of Jerome:

In addition to providing information concerning the existence of variant readings in current copies of the New Testament, occasionally the Fathers conjecture that a scribal error may have occurred earlier in the transmission of the text and that as a result all manuscripts have become corrupt.[140]

Jerome, as we saw earlier in chapter 3, in writing his commentaries, borrowed from virtually all the Christian biblical exegesis available to him (and was not afraid to acknowledge this) but in so doing was aware of the dangers of relying too heavily upon patristic testimony alone and without discrimination. Jerome was certainly one of those patristic writers who made textual comments which testify to the presence of variant readings in the manuscripts of the New Testament. Furthermore, as we also saw earlier in chapter 3,[141] Jerome showed considerable scholarly discernment in evaluating the divergent readings and in accounting for the emergence of the variants.

---

[137] Metzger, 'Textual Criticism,' 343.

[138] Metzger, 'Textual Criticism,' 343. Here, Metzger cites Augustine and Athanasius as being among those other 'patristic writers of a later date' who engaged in textual criticism of the Greek Bible by noting the emergence and existence of variant readings in contemporary copies of the New Testament.

[139] For example, J.F. Kelly has noted that Pelagius (c. 360-425) [a contemporary of Jerome] 'wrote in an era when exegesis did not form a separate discipline from theology'. See Kelly, 'Pelagius', in *Dictionary of Major Biblical Interpreters*, 808-12 (809). Also, see R.C. Hill, *Theodoret of Cyrus: Commentary on the Letters of St. Paul*, vol.1. Hill writes: 'It is perhaps proverbial to apply the term "uncritical" to the great majority of the Fathers—in their approach to the biblical text... This is to make the point that "exegesis" is a term less applicable to their work than "commentary", in dealing with a Greek text from the NT the Fathers (at least those in the East) suffer from fewer exegetical handicaps, obviously' (8), and the various essays in R. Valantasis (ed.), *Religions of Late Antiquity in Practice* (Princeton: Princeton University Press, 2000), especially C. Stewart, 'Evagrius Ponticus on Prayer and Anger,' 65-81, and N.V. Harrison, 'Gregory of Nazianzen Homily on the Nativity of Christ,' 443-53.

[140] Metzger, 'Textual Criticism,' 346.

[141] See, Hulley, 'Principles of Textual Criticism.'

In 'The Polemical Application of Scripture in St. Jerome,' D.F. Heimann[142] investigated Jerome's polemical functions of scriptural quotations in one of Jerome's disputation works, the treatise *Adversus Jovinianum* (*AJ*). Here Heimann found evidence in Jerome's *AJ* of Jerome 'drawing upon the development of literature—both 'classical and Patristic,' especially in the Latin tradition;'[143] and, contrary to general belief, a work 'of congruent arrangement of parts rather than a poorly planned digressive polemic, some harmony and coherence in what too readily appears to be only an undisciplined excursus into the field of Bible quotation on Jerome's part'.[144]

Heimann finds Jerome the polemicist to have been a man whose favourite ploy was 'Scriptural one-upmanship'.[145] Jerome's ploy of 'Scriptural one-upmanship' is clearly demonstrated in the following:

> In establishing the basic framework for his interpretation, Jerome is willing to support either of two positions. If an Old Testament example corroborates his argument, Jerome asserts the radical continuity of Old and New Testament revelation. If it contradicts his position, he then argues the opposition between the two traditions, and emphasizes the superiority of the Gospel mandate.[146]

Is this honest exegesis? Is Jerome here not in danger of being seen to be falsifying the Bible in order to prove and declare his own scriptural views? Critics of Jerome have long been concerned about Jerome's unwillingness to openly state his full theological position and so the search for 'Jerome's theology' has consequently floundered.[147]

It is also worth observing here that Kelly (1975) corroborates with Heimann (1975) regarding Jerome's habit of reading between the lines of Scripture in order to establish his desired position on a particular topic. For example, Kelly claims Jerome (in *AJ*) 'resorts to an unnatural exegesis to distort the scriptural record'.[148] In other words, both Heimann and Kelly are suggesting that Jerome is guilty of subjective exegesis. This is, indeed, a powerful charge against Jerome's exegesis.

Another scholar holding reservations about Jerome's sometimes questionable exegesis (i.e., suspect inclusions/omissions) is J.T. Cummings, who argues that Jerome allowed his 'judgement' to be unduly influenced 'by certain predilections (theological, philosophical, rhetorical) rather than adhering simply to the textual evidence'.[149]

---

[142] D.F. Hiemann, 'The Polemical Application of Scripture in St. Jerome,' *StP* 12 (1975), 309-16.

[143] Heimann, 'Polemical Application,' 309.

[144] Heimann, 'Polemical Application,' 309.

[145] Heimann, 'Polemical Application,' 310.

[146] Heimann, 'Polemical Application,' 311.

[147] Heimann, 'Polemical Application,' 311.

[148] Kelly, *Jerome*, 186.

[149] Cummings, 'St. Jerome,' 279-82. Cummings further observes that 'Jerome's own practice in citing biblical texts in writings certainly or probably post-dating his revi-

So far, we have seen Kelly, Heimann and Cummings (all writing in 1975) casting doubts about Jerome's exegesis. However, other scholars at this time were critically examining other aspects of Jerome's work. For example, the publication of a second revised edition of the first volume of the German scholar Aloys Grillmeier's *Christ in Christian Tradition*[150] offered not only a new account of the theological development between Origen and the Council of Nicaea, a much fuller history of the Logos-sarx Christology and the Christological development between Ephesus and Chalcedon, but also, for our purposes, a reassessment of Jerome's Christological position.

On Jerome's picture of Christ, Grillmeier asserts that Jerome's 'Christological formula' was not as clear as 'the other Latins,'[151] with Grillmeier basing his judgement here on Jerome's failure to reach 'the Latin formula of the "one person of Christ in two natures"'[152] (i.e., Christ Jesus, the Son of God is both God and man).[153] Here Grillmeier is especially critical of Jerome since this Latin formula was 'in the circle of Jerome's acquaintances'.[154] This is a quite remarkable criticism, for it seems to be implying that Jerome was not able to achieve intellectual mastery of the Christological problems. If true, this would, of course, give support to Freeman's (2009) claim that Jerome lacked the self-confidence to fully intellectualize his theology.

Whilst Jerome's Christological formula placed a 'strong stress on the humanity of Christ,' with 'the body of the Lord having its sufferings and desires,'[155] Grillmeier notes, with Jerome (unlike Hilary of Poitiers), 'There is still no consideration of the way in which God and man are one in Christ.'[156] Somewhat contradictorily, whilst arguing that 'Jerome did not treat Christology

---

sion of NT and Psalter was inconsistent, sometimes following the Vulgate and sometimes following an Old Latin version' (279).

[150] A. Grillmeier, *Christ in Christian Tradition*, vol.1: *From the Apostolic Age to Chalcedon (AD 451)* (Oxford: Mowbray, 1975). On the Logos-sarx Christology, whereby the Logos needs the incarnation for perfect Sonship (*sarx-Christi*), see Grillmeier, *Christ*, vol. 1, 238-45.

[151] Grillmeier, *Christ*, 1.400-401. Grillmeier notes: 'Jerome puts forward his Christological formula taking a middle course between Apollinarian—Arian monophysitism and the "rationalistic" Christology of the old adoptionists and Photinus.'

[152] Grillmeier, *Christ*, 1.401.

[153] As expressed, for example, by Augustine in his *Enchiridion* (written in 421/422). In this work Augustine's Christological expression reads, 'when he [Christ Jesus] was the only Son of God, not by grace, but by nature, so that he might be also full of grace, he became also the Son of Man. He has himself both natures, and from these two natures is one Christ (*idemque ipse utrumque ex utroque unus Christus*)'. See R. Rombs, 'Augustine on Christ,' in *Augustine And Modern Theology*, 39-40.

[154] Grillmeier, *Christ*, 1.401. By 'in the circle of Jerome's acquaintances,' Grillmeier is referring here to 'before Augustine in the writing *Fides Isatis ex Iudaeo* (IV), the accuser of Pope Damasus who was converted from Judaism and later returned to it' (401).

[155] Grillmeier, *Christ*, 1.401.

[156] Grillmeier, *Christ*, 1.402.

in such detail and at such a depth as Hilary,'[157] Grillmeier concedes that, with Jerome, 'The picture of Christ's humanity and its activity is truer than that in the writings of the Bishop of Poitiers. Christ means much more for his devotion than for his theology.'[158] Finally, Grillmeier praises Jerome's Christological-soteriological special stress on 'saving the soul' clearly exemplified both in his *Commentary on Matthew* and in his *Commentary on Isaiah.*[159] Jerome in his letters stresses the importance of faith in Christ's divine glory as a means to personal salvation.[160]

The publication in 1977 of J.N.D. Kelly's *Early Christian Doctrines*[161] provided an account of Jerome's contribution to the canon of Scripture, eschatology, Christology and soteriology. Kelly's judgement on Jerome's attitude to canonical scripture is set against a juxtaposition of Origen's and Jerome's positions on the Apocrypha. Thus, whilst Origen 'made much use of the Apocrypha',[162] Jerome's position seems to have been much more cautionary. Kelly states:

> The West, as a whole, was inclined to form a much more favourable estimate of the Apocrypha… Jerome, conscious of the difficulty of arguing with Jews on the basis of books they spurned and anyhow regarding the Hebrew original as authoritative, was adamant that anything not found in it was 'to be classed among the apocrypha,' not in the canon.[163]

It goes without saying that the church fathers envisaged the whole of the Bible as inspired by God. Jerome was in union with the other fathers in believing that 'Scripture was not only exempt from error but contained nothing that was superfluous.'[164] In his commentary on Ephesians, Jerome stated that 'in the divine Scriptures every word, syllable, accent and point is packed with meaning'[165] and, in his commentary on Philemon, he declared 'those who slighted the commonplace contents of Philemon were simply failing, through ignorance, to appreciate the power and wisdom they concealed'.[166] However, it is important to observe some caution here. Whilst Kelly's exposition of Jerome's belief in the inerrancy and value of Scripture is quite clear perhaps it should not be taken at face value—for there was a dispute over the inerrancy of scripture between Jerome and Augustine (Jerome *Ep.* 56, 102, 106, 112, 115; Augustine *Ep.* 28, 40, 67, 71). Despite this it remains the case that the essential disagreement be-

[157] Grillmeier, *Christ*, 1.402.
[158] Grillmeier, *Christ*, 1.402.
[159] Grillmeier, *Christ*, 1.402.
[160] For example, *Ep.* 120, 9, as cited by Grillmeier, *Christ*, 1.401. *Ep.* 120 was written by Jerome in 406.
[161] J.N.D. Kelly, *Early Christian Doctrines* (London: A&C Black, 1977).
[162] Kelly, *Doctrines*, 54-55.
[163] Kelly, *Doctrines*, 55.
[164] Kelly, *Doctrines*, 61.
[165] Jerome, *Commentary on Ephesians* (Eph. 2:3,6), as cited by Kelly, *Doctrines*, 62.
[166] Jerome, *Commentary on Philemon* (Prologue), as cited by Kelly, *Doctrines*, 62.

tween Jerome and Augustine was, as we saw earlier chapter 2, was not over scriptural inerrancy (which neither doubted) but questions of interpretation.

Elsewhere, Kelly gives examples of Jerome's eschatology. Whilst labelling Jerome 'the greatest of Latin exegetes'[167]—thus, raising doubts over McGuckin's (2005) proposition that Jerome's reputation as exegete is overstressed (at least if we look for originality)—Kelly observes that 'It was in the fourth and fifth centuries that the doctrine of human nature became an issue of prime importance in the Church.'[168] Jerome's attitude to fallen humanity and God's grace is summed up in his declaration, 'It is for God to call and for us to believe,'[169] with Jerome showing 'the part of grace is to perfect that which the will has freely determined; yet our will is only ours by God's mercy'.[170] Here Kelly is in agreement with Grillmeier regarding Jerome's emphasis upon 'saving the soul'.[171] For Jerome, human salvation through God's mercy (and faith in Christ's victory) were paramount.

As regards Jerome's Christology, Kelly observes how Jerome's Christology is close to Pelagius, 'who viewed that Christ's life could reasonably be offered in place of ours because, being innocent, He did not already deserve death on His own account'.[172] This is an interesting if perhaps somewhat ironic observation bearing in mind how Jerome and Augustine were later allies in their opposition to Pelagianism (in 407).[173]

On Jerome's soteriology, specifically his conception of baptism, Kelly first describes the three beliefs about the effects of baptism current in the fourth/fifth centuries due largely to Cyril of Jerusalem, for whom baptism was 'the bath of regeneration' in which 'we are washed both with water and with the Holy Spirit'.[174] The three beliefs held about the efficacy of baptism were that it gave 'the remission of sins, the blessing of sanctification/spiritual rebirth and salvation, and impressed a seal on the believer's soul'.[175] Significantly, by the time of

---

[167] Kelly, *Doctrines*, 75.

[168] Kelly, *Doctrines*, 344. Jerome's contribution to the debate over the doctrine of human nature is more fully discussed by Grillmeier. See Grillmeier, *Christ*, 1.401-402. Grillmeier notes 'Jerome's strong stress on the humanity of Christ, with body and soul with 'the body of the Lord having its sufferings and desires' (401).

[169] Jerome, *Commentary on Isaiah* (*In Isa* 49, 4), as cited by Kelly, *Doctrines*, 356.

[170] Jerome, *Ep*. 130, 12, as cited by Kelly, *Doctrines*, 356.

[171] See Grillmeier, *Christ*, 1.402.

[172] Pelagius on Galatians (Gal. 3.13) as cited by Kelly, *Doctrines*, 390. Here, it should be noted that all Kelly does is to cite both Pelagius and Jerome on one uncontroversial point.

[173] Rebenich, *Jerome*, 46. On Jerome and Pelagius, see Kelly, *Jerome*, 309. On Augustine and Pelagius, see Rebenich, *Jerome*, 51-53.

[174] Kelly, *Doctrines*, 428-29.

[175] Kelly, *Doctrines*, 428-29. The Greek and Latin Fathers used many expressions to designate the sacrament of baptism. Clement of Alexandria has explained some of them. Baptism, he says, is a bath because it washes away sin; a grace which remits the punishment due to sin; an illumination, since it enables one to contemplate the

Jerome and Augustine the strict Latin doctrine of original sin had been estab-lished.[176] Jerome acknowledged 'that sins, impurities and blasphemies of every sort are purged in Christ's laver, the effect being the creation of an entirely new man',[177] but Jerome had doubts about the efficacy of baptism as a means of guaranteeing the Christian against future sin, and adduced 'numerous Scriptural passages to show that the baptized are not only exposed to temptation but are quite capable of succumbing to it'.[178] Here, then, Jerome is quite clear in his belief that baptism could not ensure protection against recapitulation into sin.

However, Kelly's critique of Jerome on baptism/sin is not consistent. Having already recorded Jerome's own affirmation of his belief that baptism was not a guarantee against future sin, Kelly then completely misreads Jerome.

> For Augustine any child born into the world was polluted with sin, and baptism was the indispensable means to its abolition. Jerome echoed his ideas, teaching that once children have been baptized they are free from sin, but until then they bear the guilt of Adam.[179]

Here, Kelly misunderstands the phrase 'they are free from sin'. All this means is free from original sin, not incapable of sin in the future. This inconsistency surely puts a serious question mark against Kelly's assessment of Jerome's soteriology.

One of the central issues surrounding Jerome has always been just how far (if at all) Jerome inspired the notion of 'theology' (i.e., 'doing theology') as a discipline during the fourth and fifth centuries. One scholar at least has argued that Jerome was responsible for distinguishing three forms of exegesis: the homily, the commentary, and the *scholia* (or detailed notes on especially diffi-cult passages).[180] More than this Jerome (with Augustine, Hilary and other Fathers) provided *rationes authenticatae*.[181] However, whilst Evans acknowledges these important contributions of Jerome, she does not proffer acceptance of Jerome as either an 'orthodox' or 'polemical' theologian. For Evans, 'academ-ic' theology would not evolve until the later twelfth and thirteenth centuries. It

---

holy and salutary light; a perfection, because it lacks nothing (Cf. *Paedag.* 1.6). Au-gustine calls baptism not only the bath of regeneration but also the sacrament of Christ (*De fide et op.* 12.18), the sacrament of the new life and of eternal salvation (*Cont. Cresc.* 2.13. 16), and the sacrament of the Trinity (*Serm.* 269.2). For a further discussion of Augustine's understanding of the meaning of 'baptism', see St. Augus-tine, *On Faith and Works* (tr. and annotated by G.J. Lombardo; New York: Newman, 1988), 2, 9, 13, 14, 19, 20.

176 Kelly, *Doctrines*, 430.

177 Jerome, *Ep.* 69, 2f, as cited by Kelly, *Doctrines*, 429.

178 Jerome, *Adv. Jov.* 2, 1-4, as cited by Kelly, *Doctrines*, 429-30.

179 Kelly, *Doctrines*, 430.

180 G.R. Evans, *Old Arts and New Theology: The Beginnings of Theology as an Academ-ic Discipline* (Oxford: Clarendon, 1980), 43.

181 Evans, *Old Arts and New Theology*, 143.

would appear that the 'was Jerome a theologian' debate remains very much unresolved.

Elsewhere, Peter Brown's study of the cult of the saints in Latin Christianity,[182] showing how the cult of the saints was 'the dominant form of religion in Christian Europe (though Christianity itself was born without such a cult), demonstrated how this form of religiosity engaged the finest minds of the Church' and drew from members of the educated upper classes 'some of their most splendid achievements in poetry, literature and the patronage of the arts'.[183] On one occasion Jerome challenged a critic of the cult of relics:

> [So you think] therefore, that the bishop of Rome does wrong when, over the dead men Peter and Paul, venerable bones to us, but to you a heap of common dust, he offers up sacrifices to the Lord, and their graves are held to be altars of Christ.[184]

The cult of the saints (i.e., the role of tombs, shrines, relics and pilgrimages connected with the sacred bodies of the saints) involved men and women living in harsh and sometimes barbaric times relying upon the merciful intercession of the holy dead to obtain justice, forgiveness, and to find new ways to accept their fellows. Brown tells us the shrine containing a grave or a fragmentary relic, was very often called quite simply, the 'place' (*Locus sanctorum*).[185] Just how far Jerome honoured and feared such places is testified thus:

> Whenever I have been angry or had some bad thought upon my mind, or some evil fantasy has disturbed my sleep, I do not dare to enter the shrines of the martyrs. I quake with body and soul.[186]

Jerome etched the Christian cult of the saints in Rome in his writings,[187] and Brown records how Jerome described the effect of growing numbers of relic shrines on the geography of the city: in worshipping the saints Jerome said, 'The city has changed address.'[188] In this way 'the bishops of Western Europe came to orchestrate the cult of the saints in such a way as to base their power

---

[182] P. Brown, *The Cult of the Saints: Its Rise and Function in Latin Christianity* (Chicago: University of Chicago Press, 1981). Richard Price considers Brown's text to be 'beyond doubt a literary masterpiece'. See R. Price 'Martyrdom and the Cult of the Saints,' in *Oxford Handbook of Early Christian Studies*, 808-25 (811). Whilst in his essay (815) Price includes Tertullian as an important early source of information for our knowledge and understanding of the witness of martyrs, he does not mention here the role of Jerome.

[183] Brown, *Cult*, 9.

[184] Jerome, *Contra Vigilantium*, 8, *PL* 23.34, as cited by Brown, *Cult*, 9.

[185] Brown, *Cult*, 11. For a discussion of how Jerome became the most eloquent champion of pilgrimage to Jerusalem/Bethlehem for the veneration of the graves of the martyrs, see A.H. Bredero, *Christendom and Christianity in the Middle Ages* (Grand Rapids: Eardmans, 1994), 90-91. See also Jerome, *Ep.* 58.2.

[186] Jerome, *Contra Vigilantium*, 12, *PL* 23, 364 C, as cited by Brown, *Cult*, 11.

[187] Jerome, *Ep.* 22-28, as cited by Brown, *Cult*, 36.

[188] Jerome, *Ep.* 107.1, as cited by Brown, *Cult*, 42.

within the old Roman cities on these new towns outside the town'.[189] Thus, Jerome's accounts are useful in indicating both the levels of patronage given to the cult of the saints and the impact of this particular cult on the social world of Latin Christendom. And Brown's positive reception to Jerome's veneration of the cult of the saints and the cult of relics (as recorded in Jerome's letters) highlights one of Jerome's most distinctive contributions to our knowledge and understanding of Roman religion during the fourth and fifth centuries.[190]

A further perspective on the significance of Jerome regarding the late fourth-century cult of martyr-saints/shrines was offered by Henry Chadwick in his 1982 collected essays *History and Thought of the Early Church*.[191] In his article 'St. Peter and St. Paul in Rome: The Problem of the *Memoria Apostolorum ad Catacumbas*,'[192] Chadwick highlighted the tense climate and controversy which surrounded those (like Jerome) who advocated the preservation of saints' relics/shrines (many clergy were opposed to the practice) and noted:

> Even Jerome conceded to Vigilantius that the cult of the martyrs led to excesses...but consoled him with the reflection that it did no one much harm (*Adv. Vigil.* 7). Jerome clearly saw that by this time the movement had gathered far too much impetus for the clergy to put any brake on it; any serious attempt to do so could only be too little and too late.[193]

In 1983, Dennis Brown published his 'Saint Jerome as a Biblical Exegete,'[194] an attempt 'to set out, in a systematic form, the background and principles of exegesis used by St. Jerome, the greatest biblical scholar of the 4th century'[195] with Brown here directly challenging McGuckin's (2005) view that Jerome was 'perhaps the most important biblical scholar of the early Western church'. Brown's principal justification for his judgement on Jerome is the manner by which Jerome steadfastly worked towards removing 'transmissional errors in the biblical text' in order to 'establish a trustworthy text'.[196] But, of course, as we have already observed earlier in chapter 3, there is no modern scholarly consensus on Jerome's success here—and nor should we forget the considerable opposition Jerome faced from some of his contemporaries (e.g., Augustine) over the orthodoxy of his biblical exegesis. However, Brown considers Jerome's dominance over other exegetes to have been unparalleled: 'Jerome's

---

[189] Brown, *Cult*, 8. According to Brown, 'the cemetery areas in which the graves of the saints lay were pointedly peripheral to the city of the living' (42).

[190] For example, Damasus was known as the great patron of the catacombs. See Brown, *Cult*, 36.

[191] H. Chadwick, *History and Thought of the Early Church* (London: Variorum Reprints, 1982).

[192] Chadwick, 'St. Peter and St. Paul in Rome: The Problem of the *Memoria Apostolorum ad Catacumbas*', *JTS* 8 (1957), 31-52.

[193] Chadwick, '*St. Peter and St. Paul in Rome*,' 48n.3.

[194] D. Brown, 'Saint Jerome as a Biblical Exegete', *IBS* 5 (1983), 138-55.

[195] Brown, 'Saint Jerome,' 138.

[196] Brown, 'Saint Jerome,' 142n.14, citing Jerome, *Ep.* 27.1

excellence as a textual critic was unmatched in the early Church, even by Origen.'[197] Other scholars have begged to disagree.[198] According to Jerome, a commentary ought always to

> Repeat the opinions of the many...so that the judicious reader, when he has perused the different explanations... may judge which is the best, and, like a good banker, reject the money from a spurious mint.[199]

Here, apart from his clever use of metaphor ('like a good banker, reject the money from a spurious mint') Jerome is clearly placing considerable confidence in his readers for them to be able to distinguish the most reliable and truthful biblical interpretation.

As to Jerome's dependence upon others for his exegetical writings, Brown, concurring with Schatkin (1970), states:

> In most of his commentaries, Jerome acknowledges the previous authors from whom he has borrowed, and it could almost be said that Jerome's commentaries are nothing but a compendium of portions culled from the works of others.[200]

Finally, Brown's critique of Jerome bears a close correspondence with Freeman's (2009) view that Jerome displayed a lack of theological creativity. Observing Jerome to have been 'an eclectic scholar, borrowing principles of textual criticism, and specific interpretations of scripture from other scholars both Christian and Jewish,' Brown concludes that 'Jerome was not primarily a creative thinker although his works are not devoid of novelty.'[201]

In 1984 Karlfried Froehlich's study of the sources of early Christian thought,[202] examined patristic writers and their texts, essential to an understanding of Christian theology. Looking at the early Western and North African roots, Froehlich observed that 'Antiochene hermeneutics colored much of Jerome's exegetical work... and an eclectic use of hermeneutical rules remained

---

[197] Brown, 'Saint Jerome,' 142.

[198] Most notably Rebenich (2002), who argues in favour of Origen, claiming Jerome's exegesis was 'strongly dependent on earlier expositors, especially Origen, prompting doubts as regards [Jerome's] theological and exegetical originality'. See Rebenich, *Jerome*, 29.

[199] Brown, 'Saint Jerome,' 143.

[200] Brown, 'Saint Jerome,' 143.

[201] Brown, 'Saint Jerome,' 152. For further discussion of Jerome's borrowings from Jewish interpretations of Scripture, see C.T.R. Hayward, 'Jewish Traditions in Jerome's Commentary on Jeremiah and the Targum of Jeremiah,' *PIBA* 9 (1985), 100-120. Hayward notes: 'His linguistic ability in Aramaic and Syriac meant that he had a wide range of Jewish traditions at his disposal, since he had access to material handed on in languages other than Hebrew. In particular, it is highly probable that he was conversant with traditions now preserved in the Targum, that ancient translation-cum-interpretation of the Hebrew Bible which was transmitted in Aramaic' (101).

[202] K. Froehlich, *Biblical Interpretation in the Early Church* (Philadelphia: Fortress, 1984).

characteristic of the Western development.'[203] This confirms what we saw earlier in chapter 3 where scholars identified Jerome as an eclectic exegete whose attention to the literal-sense preserved the grammatical and historical emphases of the Antiochene School.

The publication in 1986 of the fourth volume of Johannes Quasten's *Patrology*[204] (edited by Angelo Di Berardino) included another reassessment of Jerome's corpus (by Jean Gribomont), and brought up to date the foreign (as opposed to English) bibliography on Jerome.[205] Here our attention will centre upon judging how far Gribomont's reassessment acted as a corrective (or otherwise) to Kelly (1975)[206] and how far Gribomont's critique of Jerome's writings parallels in any way, the 'McGuckin-Freeman' thesis.

Gribomont describes Jerome as 'strong in his Roman faith'[207] and the writer of 'pious, erudite letters, brilliant disputations and satires of the clergy... which presaged an exceptional career'.[208] Of that career (from 386) Gribomont notes how, for Jerome, his move to Bethlehem led him to become a 'meticulous' biblical translator and an adaptor of 'exegetical treasures' whilst 'The Old Testament took precedence over the New, and Hebrew over Greek.'[209]

Here Gribomont's judgment on Jerome is clearly not in agreement with McGuckin (2005). Gribomont's Jerome is a meticulous biblical translator and an adaptor of exegetical treasures—somewhat removed from McGuckin's view that Jerome's reputation as exegete is over-stressed (at least if we look for originality). What of Freeman's (2009) argument that Jerome's work lacks genuine intellectual creativity? Here, Gribomont is quite adamant that whilst Jerome's

---

[203] Froehlich, *Biblical Interpretation*, 23-24. Here Froehlich comments 'Western hermeneutics in the Augustinian tradition finally crystallized its rules into the standard form of a fourfold sense of Scripture—literal, allegorical, tropological (moral/the soul), and anagogical (our heavenly home)'.

[204] J. Quasten, *Patrology* vol. IV: *The Golden Age of Latin Patristic Literature from the Council of Nicaea to the Council of Chalcedon* (ed. A.D. Berardino with an introduction by J. Quasten; Westminster: Christian Classics, 1986). Unlike volumes I, II and III of his *Patrology*, Johannes Quasten did not himself pen any of the essays in vol. IV. Serious illness prevented him from completing the work.

[205] Quasten, *Patrology* IV.212-246. Quasten, 218, records nine foreign studies on Jerome published between 1900 and 1970.

[206] It is noteworthy, and quite surprising, that Gribomont nowhere directly engages textually with Kelly's seminal study of Jerome, merely citing it as an available biography.

[207] Gribomont, '*Jerome*,' in Quasten, *Patrology* IV.214.

[208] Gribomont, '*Jerome*,' in Quasten, *Patrology* IV.215.

[209] Quasten, *Patrology* IV.216. Here, it should be noted that today there is still a general scholarly consensus that Jerome did not revise the Latin text of the NT epistles, a fact already observed by Gribomont, who posits: 'There is a tendency to attribute to him [Rufinus the Syrian] the completion of the revision of the New Testament according to Jerome's principles, in as much as Jerome himself had not proceeded beyond a revision of the gospels during his stay in Rome.' See Gribomont, '*Jerome*,' in Quasten, *Patrology* IV.195-246 (217-18, 222).

doctrinal synthesis was 'neither personal nor comprehensive' he showed 'true originality in the field of both exegesis and ascesis'.[210] Quite obviously, here there is no support for Freeman's (2009) claim that Jerome lacked the power of creative and independent thought in his writings.

Does Gribomont's Jerome, then, offer a corrective to Kelly (1975)? Here no clear conclusion can be made. Whilst Kelly views Jerome's exegesis as sometimes derivative and lacking in originality Gribomont takes the opposite view. Both authors agree upon Jerome's tendency to cull ideas from others (in his use of exegetical sources) but disagree upon the question of Jerome's overall exegetical originality. The Kelly/Gribomont dichotomy here remains one of the more intriguing 'Jerome debates' still worthy of further scholarly investigation.

By the late 1980s scholars were continuing to discuss the origins and originality of Jerome's exegesis. For example, in the view of Elizabeth Clark, Jerome's tendency to derivative exegesis can be traced back to the late 380s with his *Commentary on Ephesians*, 'when he was still mining Origen's exegetical works to compose his own Scriptural commentaries'.[211] Whilst this may be of some interest (Jerome, of course, as we have already seen, readily acknowledged and defended his tendency to derivative exegesis, which he engaged in for the purpose of locating and developing the correct biblical text) the real significance of Clark's essay for our present study is its coverage of a model of salvation history (at the centre of Jerome's corpus) drawn from the settlement made at the Council of Nicaea (325). Clark's acknowledgment of 'Jerome's belief that all sins can be forgiven, a belief implied in the teaching of the *apokatastasis*, and his confession that there will be a graded reward in heaven based largely on one's ascetic fervor or lack of it'[212] perhaps might suggest that Jerome had indeed the ability to think creatively beyond Nicene orthodoxy thus contesting Freeman's (2009) view.

The model of salvation history drawn from the settlement at Nicaea encompassed the notion that 'salvation is by divine intervention and human representation' and man 'can be adopted by identifying with Christ, the only "natural" Son of God'.[213] Clearly Jerome's confession that 'there will be a graded reward in heaven based largely on one's ascetic fervor or lack of it' was Jerome's own

[210] Quasten, *Patrology* IV.242-43. Here Gerald Bray takes a different position to Quasten on Jerome's 'Greek' dependence, arguing: '[Jerome] was motivated by a certain Roman chauvinism which made him somewhat antipathetic to things Greek.' See G. Bray, *Creeds, Councils and Christ* (Fearn: Christian Focus, 2009), 41-42.
[211] E.A. Clark, 'The Place of Jerome's Commentary on Ephesians in the Origenist Controversy: The Apokatastasis and Ascetic Ideals', *VC* 41.2 (1987), 154-71.
[212] Clark, 'Jerome's Commentary on Ephesians,' 164. The *apokatastasis* being that important element of the doctrine of creation (i.e., the providential rehabilitation of free, spiritual beings and their eventual universal restoration to original unity and beatitude). For a full explanation and applied meaning of the term 'Apokatastasis' in the third to sixth century, see M. Ludlow, *Universal Salvation: Eschatology in the Thought of Gregory of Nyssa and Karl Rahner* (Oxford: OUP, 2009), 38-44.
[213] Papandrea, *Early Church Fathers*, 239.

supplement to the Nicene understanding of salvation and one that did not embody a commonly accepted observation. And so, here at least, we see Jerome wiling and capable of thinking creatively beyond Nicene orthodoxy, thus denying Freeman's (2009) charge against him.

On Jerome's attitude to the body and soul, Peter Brown believes Jerome was strongly influenced by Tertullian (c.200), 'the master of Latin rhetoric,' whom Jerome read 'with delight' and 'with all too great profit'.[214] Like Tertullian, 'Jerome believed abstinence from sex was the most effective technique with which to achieve clarity of soul.'[215]

We saw earlier in chapter 3 how Jerome viewed celibacy and virginity as pathways to the holy life. Widowhood was also seen by Jerome to have 'been a noble state'.[216] Earlier during his stay in Rome Jerome made it his practice to give 'spiritual direction to devoted women, most of whom would have been virgins or widows'.[217]

Brown's study, *The Body and Society*, devotes a whole chapter to Jerome under the heading 'Learn of me a Holy Arrogance'.[218] There Brown describes Jerome as a 'Dalmatian priest of pronounced ascetic views'[219] who had 'a reputation for unusual erudition'.[220] Brown is quite sardonic in criticising one particular aspect of Jerome's *oeuvre*—the writings on the ascetic life.

> Jerome, in fact, knew little of the desert about which he wrote and next to nothing of the particular disciplines on which the Desert Fathers based their certainty that even the sexual urge might be transcended. It was his contemporaries who had explored the life of the Egyptian desert most thoroughly, bringing back news of its exciting possibilities to the monastic settlements of the Holy Land.[221]

This seems very strange considering Brown readily acknowledges that 'Between 375 and 377, he [Jerome] had spent two years of boredom and mounting irritation in a hermit's cell in the Syrian desert, at Chalcis.'[222] Brown's questionable assessment of Jerome as a poor, unreliable witness to the desert life is

---

[214] P. Brown, *The Body and Society: Men, Women and Sexual Renunciation in Early Christianity* (London: Faber, 1989), 78. Brown adds, 'Jerome had always lived close enough to the thought of Tertullian, which he savored as a Latin stylist and frequently consulted as a theological dictionary, to tend to take for granted Tertullian's grippingly physical view of the body and its resurrection' (382).

[215] Brown, *Body*, 100-101.

[216] Jerome, *Letter* 123.1, as cited by Brown, *Body*, 148. In this letter, Jerome speaks of three ladies in Gaul, who had already spent widowhood of forty, twenty and twelve years.

[217] Jerome, *Letter* 45.2, as cited by Brown, *Body*, 266.

[218] Brown, *Body*, 366-86. In Letter 22 (to Paula's daughter Eustochium) Jerome wrote, 'Learn of me a holy arrogance; know that you are better than them all.' Brown, *Body*, 367.

[219] Brown, *Body*, 366.

[220] Brown, *Body*, 366.

[221] Brown, *Body*, 373.

[222] Brown, *Body*, 366.

further compounded by his remark 'Jerome, the Latin, was a man in a hurry, writing to a generation in a hurry. All that he had allowed his readers to know of his experience in Chalcis had been deliberately calculated to heighten their anxiety.'[223] Here Brown's verdict on Jerome is surely false for *Letter 22* gives a very detailed description of the hermit's life which Jerome had experienced and can, in no way, be seen as propaganda—though Brown cites *Letter 22* as evidence of Jerome's haste and deliberate exaggeration of his desert encounter.[224] But we must beware of Brown's statement, 'All that he had allowed his readers to know of his experience in Chalcis had been deliberately calculated to heighten their anxiety,' for this is nothing more than conjecture.

Of Jerome's *Against Jovinian* (Jerome's violent polemic and assault against one of his personal enemies) Brown is somewhat ambivalent arguing it 'acted as an inspiration and as an irritant throughout the Latin World',[225] whilst Brown's chief criticism of Jerome's sexual code for the priesthood (calling for post-marital celibacy of the clergy) is of 'Jerome's invidious exaltation of a purity better left to nuns'.[226] Brown's choice of language here ('invidious exaltation') is, of course, subjective. Jerome was an unwavering advocate of sexual abstinence which was wholly in keeping with his concept of ascetic life. However, Brown's language of criticism in respect of Jerome's promotion of post-marital celibacy of the clergy seems unduly severe.

In his long reassessment of Jerome's corpus, Brown finds the 'Jerome-Origen' question the most challenging to determine.[227] We saw earlier in chapter 2 the nature of Jerome's union with and eventual break from Origen. Brown adds interesting details to this important episode in Jerome's career. For example, whilst Jerome 'remained loyal to Origen as an exegete and textual scholar,'[228] he only realized after 393 'that the works of Origen harbored a view of the person deeply alien to his deepest prejudices and to those of his Latin readers'.[229] Brown finds a significant example of one of Jerome's condemnations of Origen in his *Commentary on Ephesians*, where, 'in rounding on what he took to be the views of Origen, he declared that an ancient Christian image of transformation, by which male and female became one in Jesus Christ, was irrevocably inapplicable to his own times'.[230] Here Jerome's position may be seen as,

---

[223] Brown, *Body*, 375.
[224] Brown, *Body*, 375.
[225] Brown, *Body*, 377. Rebenich notes how this particular work 'caused some annoyance at Rome, not only among Jovinian adherents but also in the ascetic circles that were shocked by the violence of Jerome's polemic'. See Rebenich, *Jerome*, 42 n.9.
[226] Brown, *Body*, 378.
[227] Brown, *Body*, 377-79.
[228] Brown, *Body*, 380.
[229] Brown, *Body*, 380.
[230] Jerome, in *Eph* 3.5.29, as cited by Brown, *Body*, 382-83. Here Brown adds, 'It was important for Jerome's readers in the West that men should remain men, and women should remain women' (383).

to say the least, surprising, bearing in mind Jerome's dependence on Origen (which he tried to disguise) in his Ephesians commentary.[231]

Jerome's view of the eventual fate of the human body (female and male) in the afterlife is found in Letter 75. As Brown describes it 'She would be rewarded, in heaven, by a bond to a recognizable man, in a love that was finally shorn of the taint of physical desire.'[232] Brown concludes his critique of Jerome with two telling descriptors: 'his fashionable misogyny,' and 'his sharp sense of sexual danger'.[233] Again, Brown's judgements surely display labelling ('misogyny' and 'sexual danger') which is open to question. Accusing Jerome of 'fashionable misogyny' is not borne out by the evidence we have of Jerome's life — indeed, he welcomed the patronage of wealthy Roman women and supported women who devoted themselves to the ascetic life—and describing Jerome as a man of a 'sharp sense of sexual danger' is not clarified and is nothing more than a case of subjective guesswork.

Continuing the examination of Jerome's derivative biblical exegesis, scholarly interest in Jerome's use of Jewish Bible exposition was marked in 1990 by an essay by Robert Hayward.[234] Hayward argues that 'St. Jerome stands superior as the most knowledgeable Hebrew biblical scholar, fully aware of the likely impact of his exegesis.'[235] This positive judgement on Jerome is given by Hayward on the basis that Jerome was 'the most outstanding of the Church Fathers in giving us important writings in the period before that of our earliest surviving manuscripts'.[236] Hayward finds a number of problems with Jerome's *Hebrew Questions (Heb. Quest)* (c.392), mostly notably its lack of an 'obvious discernible over-arching plan or theme, no regularly recurring theological concepts, nor, remarkably, any consistent presentation of Jewish tradition...'[237] Hayward finds this particular work of Jerome's lacking in both substance and reliability, and not at all a helpful guide to the state of Jewish Bible exegesis in the late fourth century. It is a criticism offering support for Freeman's (2009) proposition that Jerome lacked the intellectual ability to analyse theologically.

That said, like some other scholars we have already examined (e.g., Kelly, 1975; D. Brown, 1983) Hayward's critique of Jerome appears somewhat ambivalent. First, he affirms Jerome's superiority amongst the Church Fathers as

---

[231] See Rebenich, *Jerome*, 49.

[232] Jerome, *Letter* 75.2: 686, as cited by Brown, *Body*, 384.

[233] Brown, *Body*, 385.

[234] R. Hayward, 'Some Observations on St. Jerome's *Hebrew Questions on Genesis*, and the Rabbinic Tradition,' *PIBA* 13 (1990), 58-76.

[235] Hayward, 'Some Observations,' 58.

[236] Hayward, 'Some Observations,' 58.

[237] Hayward, 'Some Observations,' 59. See St. Jerome's *Hebrew Questions on Genesis* (Tr. with an Introduction and Commentary by C.T.R. Hayward; Oxford: Clarendon, 1995). It is disconcerting to find that Hayward contradicts what he has previously said about Jerome's *HQG* in his 1990 *PIBA* essay by noting: *HQG* represents the most ordered and sustained attempt by any Christian writer, up to Jerome's time, to transmit to the Church Jewish scholarship in its own terms' (1).

'the most knowledgeable Hebrew biblical scholar' and then he criticizes Jerome's lack of 'any consistent presentation of Jewish tradition'. In the following citation Hayward is not prepared to grant Jerome any credit for originality in his *Hebrew Questions* exegesis (Jerome is derivative).

> The Hebrew commentary which he [Jerome] produces derives on the one hand directly from his Jewish sources, some of which may, in a slightly altered form, be extant in known writings, and on the other hand, from his own efforts to ape and imitate Jewish scholarly procedures and methods which he had learned.[238]

Therefore whilst Hayward's analysis does not provide clear evidence of Jerome's pre-eminence amongst the Church Fathers on the criteria of being 'the most knowledgeable Hebrew biblical scholar,' it does offer some interest in as much as it shows how particular methods of 'exegetical procedure' were already well-established in Judaism by his [Jerome's] time.[239]

---

[238] Hayward, 'Some Observations,' 62.

[239] Hayward, 'Some Observations,' 71. See R. Hayward, 'Saint Jerome, Jewish Learning and the Symbolism of the Number Eight,' in A. Andreopoulous, A. Casiday and C. Harrison (eds), *Meditations of the Heart: The Psalms in Early Christian Thought and Practice* (Brepols: 2011), 141-59.

Chapter 5

Modern Jerome Scholarship (1991-2009)

Introduction

So far we have seen modern scholars making a number of secondary judgements on selected texts/writings drawn from Jerome's corpus often 'in conversation,' as it were, with Jerome's relation to his predecessor Origen and with his contemporary, Augustine. In this chapter we shall witness this same scholarly dialogue being not only continued but also extended to include the way in which modern Jerome scholars have received Jerome from the perspective of what they have perceived to be Jerome's later importance and relation to Erasmus and Luther.

1991-2001

In Peter Brown's published Curt lectures for 1988[1] we gain an insight into the value of parts of Jerome's corpus for our understanding of the political culture of the late Roman Empire. First, on the importance of rhetoric training and learning amongst the noble upper classes, Brown notes 'Rhetoric was seen as a preparation for public life',[2] and 'Christian writers of the fourth and fifth centuries wielded rhetoric with dazzling effect.'[3] These Christian writers were highly educated men and a result of their writings was to spread 'a Christian populism, that flouted the culture of the governing classes and claimed to have brought, instead, simple words, endowed with divine authority, to the masses of the empire'.[4] This confirms what we saw earlier in chapters 2 and 3 regarding Jerome's contribution to the development of a Christian identity (the people amongst people).

During the 1990s scholars continued their quest for evidence of the extent of Jerome's dependence on earlier authors for his biblical exegesis. For example, Rebenich found that accusations of plagiarism against Jerome could now be confidently stated, announcing, 'It is now widely accepted that his [Jerome] contemporary critics were not mistaken in accusing Jerome of compilation.'[5]

---

[1] P. Brown, *Power and Persuasion in Late Antiquity: Towards a Christian Empire* (Madison: University of Wisconsin Press, 1992).

[2] Brown, *Power*, 43.

[3] Brown, *Power*, 74.

[4] Brown, *Power*, 74.

[5] S. Rebenich, 'Jerome: The "Vir Trilinguis" and the "Hebraic Veritas",' *VC* 47.1 (1993), 50-77 (53). Rebenich notes the following Greek/Latin theologians (besides Origen) upon whom Jerome was sometimes dependent: Hippolytus, Didymus, Euse-

Of the wide range of Jerome's borrowings and exegetical influences, Rebenich further records:

Recognition of the extent of Jerome's carefully disguised plagiarism has naturally prompted doubt about his theological and exegetical originality. Many students of Jerome in this century have thus formed a negative opinion on the *doctor ecclesiae* which came so more easy since Jerome made ostentatious show of his exegetical qualities and wide reading.[6]

However, Rebenich cautions against this trend amongst scholars to question Jerome's intellectual powers as theologian and exegete and defends Jerome's inclination towards self-promotion.[7] Moreover, Rebenich considers that Jerome's 'exegetical importance can properly be compared with the theological importance of Augustine'.[8]

Here whilst Rebenich's defence of Jerome (the exegete) and his borrowings puts into question McGuckin's (2005) judgement that Jerome's reputation as exegete is over-stressed (at least if we look for originality), it should be remembered that it was not uncommon for the works of patristic exegetes to be derivative of others.

The wide extent of Jerome's borrowings and exegetical influences was similarly identified in an essay by Neil Adkin.[9] On Jerome's tendency to copy from other Greek and Latin theologians, Adkin believes Jerome was not heavily dependent upon Gregory Nazianzus because 'Gregory (unlike Jerome himself) did not have the Hebrew.'[10] This is not to say that Jerome was not, in some aspects, influenced by Gregory. For example, Adkin notes that whilst 'Jerome had never heard Ambrose preach in Milan... Jerome will often have listened to Gregory's sermons in Constantinople.'[11] Moreover, Adkin argues 'Jerome's

---

bius of Caesarea, Theodorus of Heraclea, Appollinaris of Laodicea, Eusebius of Emesa, Epiphanius of Salamis, Tertullian and Victorinus of Pettau.

[6] Rebenich, 'Jerome,' 55.

[7] Rebenich, 'Jerome,' 55-56.

[8] Rebenich, 'Jerome,' 55-56.

[9] N. Adkin, 'Jerome, Ambrose and Gregory Nazianzen (Jerome, *Epist.* 52, 7-8),' *Vichiana*, 4 (1993), 294-300.

[10] Adkin, 'Jerome', 296. Adkin's view of the 'Jerome-Gregory' relationship is not upheld either by John McGuckin or Christopher Beeley. McGuckin observes: 'Jerome travelled to hear Gregory preach, and was probably there for the *Theological Orations*. On the basis of that encounter he ever afterwards called Gregory "my teacher in exegesis"'(*Ep.* 50.1; *Ep.* 52.8). See J. McGuckin, *Saint Gregory of Nazianzus* (Crestwood, St. Vladimir's Seminary Press, 2001), 264-65. Elsewhere, Jerome describes Gregory as 'my instructor in the Scriptures'. See NPNF[2] 3:382. Beeley comments that in 380 Gregory may have 'collaborated with colleagues such as Maximus the Cynic, Gregory of Nyssa, Jerome, or Evagrius in their composition [*Theological Orations*].' See C. Beeley, *Gregory of Nazianzus on the Trinity and the Knowledge of God* (New York: OUP, 2008), 40.

[11] Adkin, 'Jerome', 297. Beeley accords Gregory of Nazianzus the label 'the premier "spiritual theologian" in the Greek patristic tradition,' and further notes: 'His impact

choice of language [*Epist* 52, 7-8] exactly matches his description of Gregory's rhetorical style in *De viris illustribus* (ch. 117),' and 'the letter to Nepotian (*Epist.* 52, 7-8) shows Jerome to have employed striking second-hand formulations to which Jerome was so partial'.[12]

In a second essay, Adkin looked at the personal relations between Jerome and Ambrose, with special reference to Jerome's accusations of plagiarism against Ambrose.[13] Was Jerome favourable or hostile to Ambrose? In 384 and 387 Jerome made two charges of plagiarism against Ambrose.[14] Adkin notes that 'the charges of plagiarism are found in Jerome's *Epist.* 22 (*Libellus de virginitate servanda*, 384) where Jerome accuses Ambrose (in his *De Virginibus*, 380) of plagiarism of content with elegance of form'.[15] Earlier relations between the two had been favourable as both were opposed to Arianism.[16]

Whatever the causes of the later breakdown in relations between Jerome and Ambrose, Adkin is highly critical of Jerome on a number of points, chiefly his hypocrisy in accusing Ambrose of plagiarism and for being himself derivative. Whilst Ambrose was able to write 'theological works which developed a coherent and largely independent line of argument,' Jerome had little aptitude for such abstract reasoning.[17] Adkin's criticism of Jerome is in line with Hayward's (1990) view of Jerome's lack of exegetical/theological coherence, with both Adkin and Hayward closely corresponding with the 'McGuckin-Freeman' thesis that Jerome's reputation as exegete is over-stressed (at least if we look for originality) and that Jerome lacked the capacity to theologize in a creative way.

The critiques of Rebenich (1993) and Adkin (1993) above are illustrative of the way in which scholars during the early 1990s were unable to reach a consensus on Jerome's intellectual powers as a theologian (as found in his biblical exegesis and treatise composition). The criticism that Jerome may have lacked the ability to write creative works of theology still remained open to debate. However, what was not contested was Jerome's stamina to learn Hebrew (unlike Ambrose and Gregory of Nazianzus). It was this advantage that allowed Jerome to excel in scriptural scholarship.

---

on his contemporaries alone was considerable: in addition to Basil [of Caesarea], Gregory of Nyssa, and Amphilochius, we can name Jerome and Evagrius among those who learned from him.' See Beeley, *Gregory of Nazianzus*, 321.

12 Adkin, 'Jerome', 297

13 N. Adkin, 'Ambrose and Jerome: The Opening Shot,' *Mnemosyne* 46 (1993), 364-76.

14 Adkin, 'Ambrose,' 366.

15 Adkin, 'Ambrose,' 367.

16 Adkin, 'Ambrose,' 365.

17 Adkin, 'Ambrose, 374.

During 1993 and 1994 two scholars reassessed Jerome's corpus from the point of view of its value (or otherwise) as a patristic model of literary activity and its influence as a model of Christian humanism and theological method.[18]

Lisa Jardine's *Erasmus, Man of Letters* (1993) compared Jerome with Erasmus, claiming 'Jerome stood for the dissemination of true scripture throughout the Western world' whilst 'Erasmus would stand for the dissemination of humane learning across Europe.'[19] According to Vessey 'no other scholar but Jardine has ever cast the humanist's relationship with his early Christian predecessor so strongly or exclusively in terms of *appropriation* and *secularization*.'[20] This is indeed high praise for Jerome's influence over Erasmus. But does Vessey substantiate his argument?

Vessey's essay 'Erasmus' Jerome' highlights in particular the importance of Jerome's *On Famous Men* (*De viris illustribus*),[21] and Vessey writes 'variously titled, this work of Jerome's was to be enormously influential, both as model of Christian biobibliography and as a source of information on figures from the early Christian period'.[22]

Vessey draws attention to the influence of *Erasmus' Jerome* (*Life and Letters*) (*1516* and *1524*)[23] upon modern Jerome scholarship:

> Erasmus circumvented the traditional pseudo-editorial construction of Jerome in his letters, even while retaining vestiges of it in his own edition, in order to construct a relation of author and work which suited his purposes, and which still affects the way we see this church father. Erasmus' Jerome is substantially the Jerome of modern patristics, not only because Erasmus established the canon of his writings and wrote the first 'historical' biography of the saint but also because twentieth-century interpreters of Jerome continue to rely on a textual narrative (that of the edited *Letters*) that is itself constructed on Erasmian lines.[24]

Here Vessey's conclusion affirms that modern Jerome scholarship may be said to have begun with *Erasmus' Jerome*, and that subsequent scholarship devoted to interpreting Jerome has been largely dependent upon an Erasmian textual narrative of the edited *Letters*.

We saw earlier in chapter 3 how some scholars had been critical of certain deficiencies in Jerome's exegetical scholarship. This theme returned again in

---

[18] See L. Jardine, *Erasmus, Man of Letters* (Princeton: Princeton University Press, 1993); M. Vessey, 'Erasmus' Jerome: The Publishing of a Christian Author,' *Erasmus of Rotterdam Society Yearbook* 14 (1994), 62-99.

[19] Jardine, *Erasmus*, 4:5; 59, as cited by Vessey, 'Erasmus' Jerome,' 65.

[20] Vessey, 'Erasmus' Jerome,' 66.

[21] Jerome properly called this work *On Ecclesiastical Writers* (*De scriporibus ecclesiasticis*).

[22] Vessey, 'Erasmus' Jerome,' 72-73. Vessey adds, 'Like most of the church fathers, but to an exceptional degree, Jerome was his own editor and publisher' (74).

[23] See Erasmus, *Erasmus' Jerome: Life and Letters* (*1516* and *1524*) *The Collected Works of Erasmus*, vol. 61 (ed. R.D. Sider; Toronto: Toronto University Press, 1974).

[24] Vessey, 'Erasmus' Jerome,' 82.

1994 with an allegation that Jerome had employed 'exegetical gymnastics' in his commentary on Isaiah.[25] The following citation demonstrates how Jerome approached his interpretation of the metaphor of the vineyard in his commentary on Isaiah (5:1-7), a metaphor already paraphrased in the Gospels (Matt. 21:33-43 and the parallels):[26]

> Jerome considered Matthew's interpretation of the metaphor so important that he wanted to see it already predicted in Isaiah's passage. This required some exegetical gymnastics, but the allegorical approach to Scripture provided a solution. The key was found in the last word of Isaiah's passage: cry or clamor. Jerome saw a connection here with the cries of the Jews mentioned in the passion story in John's Gospel: 'They cried out "Away with Him! Away with Him! Crucify Him!"' (19:15). And in his comments Jerome then links this text with Ephesians 4:31: 'Put away from you all bitterness and wrath and anger and wrangling (i.e., cries) and slander, together with all malice.' And he continues: 'Because the righteous have shed blood, the blood of the Lord's Passion cried to the Lord, since they answered righteousness with cries, as we read in Genesis (4:10), "Your brother's blood is crying out to me from the ground."' Thus, Isaiah's metaphor could also be interpreted as a rejection of the Jews.[27]

Here might Jerome be charged not only with exegetical dishonesty but also with an undisguised theological attack upon Judaism?[28]

Having spent some considerable time reassessing Jerome's intellectual power as displayed in selected texts/writings in parts of his oeuvre, Jerome scholarship after 1994 returned to studies of Jerome's non-exegetical work; again, largely Jerome's letters and asceticism.

In 1995 Steven Driver examined the development of Jerome's views on the ascetic life.[29] Driver especially praised Jerome's corpus for being one of the foundation stones for the progression of asceticism in the Latin West.[30] However, Driver makes the important point that regarding asceticism and Jerome's life as a Christian hermit/recluse, 'he was not a pioneer'.[31] Moreover, in this area, Driver suggests Jerome showed no innovation/originality.[32] In passing, Driver also comments on Jerome's exegetical powers, noting 'as in the case of his biblical commentaries, his ascetic writings do not reveal an innovative or pro-

---

[25] A.H. Bredero, *Christendom and Christianity in the Middle Ages*, 315.
[26] Bredero, *Christendom and Christianity in the Middle Ages*, 314.
[27] Bredero, *Christendom and Christianity in the Middle Ages*, 315.
[28] Significantly Bredero notes (314): 'The Jewish religion was recognized in the Roman Empire, and its status changed hardly at all when the church received its privileged position. Therefore, Judaism could only be attacked in writing.'
[29] S. Driver, 'The Development of Jerome's Views on the Ascetic Life,' *Rec Th*. 62 (1995), 44-70.
[30] Driver, 'Jerome's Views,' 44.
[31] Driver, 'Jerome's Views,' 45. Driver notes: 'Others had preceded him into the desert, the city and the *coenobium* (monastery). Instead, he might be better termed a barometer' (45).
[32] Driver, 'Jerome's Views,' 45.

foundly original thinker'.[33] Driver's judgements here seriously question McGuckin's (2005) view that Jerome was one of the most important argumentative 'ascetics' of the fourth century, and perhaps the most important biblical scholar of the early Western church, whilst they concur with Freeman's (2009) view that Jerome was not a creative thinker. The scholarly ebb and flow between Jerome critics and Jerome apologists, which is a clear feature of modern Jerome scholarship, would now continue to the end of our period of study in 2014 (see chapter 6 below).

Scholars were also now beginning to identify the important transition Jerome made (between 373 and 380) from the ascetic life to biblical study, commentary and translation. As Driver states:

> Unable to endure the rigors of a harsh ascetic routine, Jerome had at least partly abandoned them in favour of learning the language of the Jewish scriptures. Thus study ...had rescued Jerome from the prison of his desires.[34]

Driver is indicating here that it was the study of Hebrew that brought Jerome relief from his ascetic life.

The publication in 1997 of Boniface Ramsey's study of *Ambrose* drew attention once more to the style and influence of Jerome's asceticism, and Jerome's views on the monastic vocation and on virginity.[35] Here, Ramsey wrote somewhat critical descriptions of Jerome's 'romantic portrayals of the monastic vocation'[36] and Jerome's 'ardent defense' [of virginity] which was 'sometimes embarrassingly one-sided'.[37] On these topics at least it would seem that Ramsey is unwilling to acknowledge both Jerome's sincerity and conviction. And Ramsey's critical questioning of Jerome's attitude towards features of the ascetic life is clearly seen in the following condemnation: 'although Ambrose followed the ancient Christian tradition in seeing virginity as superior to marriage, he did not fall into the temptation of deprecating marriage, which his contemporary Jerome so egregiously did'.[38]

Elsewhere, in 1998, Paul Harvey had further advanced our understanding of Jerome's mental-universe and the chronology of Jerome's move away from the desert, eremitic life to his literary career as a polemicist and biblical scholar.[39] So, when, where and in what format did Jerome develop from an ascetic and into a scriptural scholar? Harvey believes this transition to have been influenced first by the Latin translation of Athanasius' *Life of Antony by Evagrius of Antioch*, 'in circulation, at the latest by 374' (and known to Jerome) whose

---

[33] Driver, 'Jerome's Views' 61.
[34] Driver, 'Jerome's Views,' 61.
[35] B. Ramsey, *Ambrose*, (Abingdon: Routledge, 1997), 8-9.
[36] Ramsey, *Ambrose*, 8.
[37] Ramsey, *Ambrose*, 50.
[38] Ramsey, *Ambrose*, 50.
[39] P. Harvey, 'Saints and Satyrs: Jerome the Scholar at Work,' *Athenaeum* 86 (1998), 35-56.

'language and structure' he then 'imitated in his *Paul*.'[40] Following this development Jerome began to gain 'access to a substantial range of literature, including biblical texts',[41] Finally, Jerome began his career as a scriptural scholar after his arrival in Constantinople (in 380) whereupon he began his study and translation of Origen's thirty-seven homilies on Isaiah, Jeremiah and Ezekiel.[42]

Of Jerome the biblical scholar, Harvey describes Jerome as 'this learned and clever author,'[43] and disagreeing with McGuckin's (2005) view on Jerome's reputation as exegete being over-stressed (at least if we look for originality) argues that in his commentary on Isaiah (completed 410) Jerome 'exhibits seemingly impeccable scholarship'.[44]

Harvey's chronology of Jerome's transition from his desert, eremitic life to his literary career as a polemicist and biblical scholar has not been without its

---

[40] Harvey, 'Saints,' 50-51. Jerome's *Life of Paul the First Hermit* was one of his earliest writings (though the exact date is unknown) possibly written during Jerome's desert period and composed before his stay in Constantinople (379-381). Jerome's *Life of Paul* was originally entitled *Life of Paul of Thebes* and in this work Jerome claimed Paul of Thebes to be the originator of the practice of the solitary (desert) life. See 'Life of Paul of Thebes,' in C. White, *Early Christian Lives* (London: Penguin, 1998), 71-84. Harvey observes 'that at the time he composed his *Life of Paul* (between 375 and 380), Jerome had been introduced to Origen's great instrument of biblical scholarship, the *Hexapla*... Conceivably, this all took place in Syria in the period between ca. 375 to 379' (52-53). With regard to the Jerome-Evagrius relationship and possible lines of influence, there exists some uncertainty. Both were contemporaries (c. 345-c.398?) and friends from an early date (sometime from the early 370s) when they had met in Aquileia. Jerome was Evagrius' protégé, and Evagrius was Jerome's patron (first in N. Italy and then, later, in Antioch). Both were to become pro-Nicene in their theology. Evagrius would become an Antiochene grandee whose own library and treatises Jerome would come to know. That Evagrius influenced Jerome's early asceticism (with Evagrius supporting Jerome during his brief period in the desert of Chalcis in nearly Maronia) there is general scholarly consensus. However, in later life, the Jerome-Evagrius relationship may have become soured though again there is some doubt as to whether or not a breakdown in their friendship (as found in written evidence) was substantive. For example, Casiday suggests that the criticism of Evagrius found in Jerome's *Ep.* 133, written to Ctesiphon in 415, 'is merely suggestive and not at all conclusive'. See A. Casiday, *Reconstructing the Theology of Evagrius Ponticus: Beyond Heresy* (Cambridge: CUP, 2013) 54-55. In *Ep.* 133 Jerome complains about Evagrius' preface to his book on John of Lycopolis (an Egyptian hermit of the latter half of the fourth century, whose reputation for sanctity was only second to Antony): 'who can adequately characterize the rashness or madness which has led him to ascribe a book of the Pythagorean philosopher Xystus, a heathen who knew nothing of Christ, to Sixtus a martyr, a bishop of the Roman church?...Thus many not knowing that its author was a philosopher and supposing that they are reading the words of a martyr, drink of the golden cup of Babylon.' See Jerome, *Ep.* 133, as cited in NPNF[2] 6:274.

[41] Harvey, 'Saints,' 52.

[42] Harvey, 'Saints,' 51.

[43] Harvey, 'Saints,' 35.

[44] Harvey, 'Saints,' 47.

critics. For example, there has been some scholarly disagreement over the dating/composition of Jerome's *Life of Paul the First Hermit*. Here, Rebenich has suggested that 'a reasonable case can be made for dating the work later,'[45] although he does not proffer an actual date.

In 1998 R.A. Markus documented the contribution made by Jerome's corpus to the changes that transformed the intellectual and spiritual horizons of the Christian world from its establishment in the fourth century.[46] According to Markus, it was Jerome's works which helped to enable a Christian identity to be shaped amongst the Roman elite,[47] and it was the time of Jerome and Augustine (c. 380-430) which acted as a landmark in the transition between paganism and Christianity.[48]

The dating of this development of Christian identity by Markus almost coincides, of course, with the dating of Jerome's corpus (early 370s-420). Markus identifies Jerome's earliest contribution to the transition of the intellectual and spiritual horizons of the Christian world from its establishment in the fourth century,[49] suggesting that 'the generation of Jerome and Augustine' were, in the 380s and 390s, 'becoming uneasy about pagan society and secular culture'.[50]

The extent to which Jerome (and Augustine) may have made their own mark in this transition is testified by the following account:

> About the time of Jerome's death in 420 and Augustine's ten years later, the confrontations of the late fourth century between Christians and pagans were receding into the mists. In reality the struggle was over, the battle lines breaking up. Paganism was dying out fast in the senatorial families, and the Church's view of mixed marriages was softening.[51]

Looking more specifically at Jerome's corpus, Markus finds Jerome's writings in praise of the ascetic life especially important for influencing people's conversion to Christianity.[52] However, Markus is critical of Jerome's sometimes provocative behaviour here, considering Jerome to 'have been not the most tactful advocate of the ascetic life',[53] and that it was 'in Jerome's time that op-

45 Rebenich, *Jerome*, 14n.15, citing G. Grutzmachar, *Hieronymus. Eine biographische Studie zur alten Kirchengeschichte* (Leipzig, 1901-8), 1.54-55.
46 R.A. Markus, *The End of Ancient Christianity* (Cambridge: CUP, 1998), 19.
47 Markus, *Ancient Christianity*, 19.
48 Markus, *Ancient Christianity*, 19.
49 Markus, *Ancient Christianity*, 30.
50 Jerome, *Ep.* 21.13.4 and Augustine, *Ep.* 101.2, as cited by Markus, *Ancient Christianity*, 30.
51 Markus, *Ancient Christianity*, 30-31. For a discussion of how this transition occurred partly as a result of Jerome and Augustine's compelling visions of human potential for transformation and spiritual perfectibility, see P. Johnson, *A History of Christianity* (New York: Simon and Schuster, 1995), 110-22.
52 Markus, *Ancient Christianity*, 36. Here, of course, Jerome's influence over Paulinus immediately comes to mind.
53 Markus, *Ancient Christianity*, 38.

position swelled into protest against the growing divide between the religion of the ordinary Christian and that of the ascetic elite'.[54] This analysis by Markus is important identifying as it does the way in which Jerome's manner and posturings may have sometimes divided his friends and supporters of the ascetic life as well as his opponents.

The reassessment of Jerome by Markus show how Jerome's ascetic writings contribute to our understanding of the early Church by revealing and addressing the uncertainties about the meaning of authentic Christianity (i.e., the true Christian faith) in the decades around AD 400. And yet, since the clash between Jovinian and Jerome, there still remained a question mark hanging over the ascetic ideal.[55] Also left unresolved was the continuing dispute over marriage versus virginity. It was left to Augustine to rehabilitate Christian marriage against Jerome.[56] In a final judgement on Jerome, Markus states:

> [Jerome], like Cassian, saw Christian history in terms of a decline from Apostolic perfection to corruption brought by wealth and respectability. It was only a short step to a vision of the monastic life as institutionalised protest, as a 'lived utopia'.[57]

What exactly did Jerome mean by this? An answer is to be found in Jerome's Letter 46 in which he records that all that was wrong with Rome 'was the piquant misbehaviour of Christians in fashionable society'.[58] Clearly, then, Jerome had no time for those Christians who allowed their savoury tastes to rule their lives.

---

[54] Markus, *Ancient Christianity*, 38-39. Markus notes: 'Jerome's advocacy of virginity and asceticism had alienated public opinion in Rome; even some of his friends had been embarrassed' (40).

[55] Markus, *Ancient Christianity*, 158-59. For a discussion on how the Christians Jovinian and Helvidius had called for the parity of married and celibate lifestyles, see A. Jensen, 'Women in the Christianization of the West,' in A. Kreider (ed.), *The Origins of Christendom in the West* (Edinburgh: T&T Clark, 2001), 205-26 (218).

[56] Markus, *Ancient Christianity*, 159. Elsewhere, Jensen comments: 'It is doubtlessly one of the most conspicuous trends in women's history during late antiquity, that such a great number of Christian women turned away from marriage and tried out various forms of celibate existence.' See Jensen, 'Women,' 217. For a more recent discussion of Jerome's attitude to marriage (he levelled 'ascetic admonitions' to 'those noblewomen of Rome who might have wanted to attend dinner parties' which 'were places where heiresses were put on show and where the "Senate House of Ladies" met to discuss the merits of potential brides.') and marriage strategies in the circles of Jerome, see P. Brown, *Through the Eye of a Needle: Wealth, the Fall of Rome, and the Making of Christianity in the West, 350-550 AD* (Princeton: Princeton University Press, 2012), 268-70 (268).

[57] Jerome, *De Vir. ill.* 8,11, as cited by Markus, *Ancient Christianity*, 166. Cassian (c.360-435) was a contemporary of Jerome, a monk and ascetic. For a discussion of Cassian's possible settlement at Jerome's monastic community in Bethlehem in c. 405/406, see C. Stewart, *Cassian the Monk* (Oxford: OUP 1998), 14.

[58] Jerome, *Letter 46.11.2*, as cited by Brown, *Through the Eye*, 268n.45.

In 2001 a monumental study of the ancient Church by Henry Chadwick[59] concluded:

> Jerome was not a thinker or in the stricter sense a theologian. He applied his secular education to the philological interpretation of scripture, and affirmed such an education to be an indispensable equipment (*ep.* 130.17). But he was the most learned scholar of his time, and his revised Latin Bible eventually, not at once, earned him the lasting admiration and gratitude of the western churches.[60]

Here Chadwick's assessment of Jerome (interestingly matching Wright's view), not only closely parallels the 'McGuckin-Freeman' thesis but it also illumines what some scholars see as the 'Jerome paradox'—namely, that whilst Jerome was a talented scholar, his intellectual powers were somewhat limited.

Elsewhere in her 2001 essay 'Christianization and Conversion in Northern Italy,'[61] Rita Lizzi Testa documented the Jerome-Ambrose of Milan axis of influence over the hesitant and uneven spread of Christianity in the fourth century.[62] Recording 'the commonality of anti-Arianism to both Jerome and Ambrose,'[63] Testa believes that there was a direct link between the work of Jerome's early monastic group in the Egyptian desert (c. 370-373) which prepared 'men well along the road of a church career,' and the later decision by Ambrose to establish 'a clerical ascetic group linked to the church in Milan'.[64]

Testa's testimony here to a clear Jerome-Ambrose axis of mutual influence which worked towards the Christianization of northern Italy had hitherto been largely passed over by scholars. However, one might ask whether she has given sufficient weight to the fact that Jerome personally hated Ambrose[65] and accused Ambrose of 'having plagiarized Didymus' treatise *On the Holy Spirit* for his own work on the subject'.[66]

2002-2006

We now turn to a relatively neglected area in the modern reception—history of Jerome, namely, Jerome's role in describing the centrality of the emotions to

[59] H. Chadwick, *The Church in Ancient Society: From Galilee to Gregory the Great* (New York: OUP, 2001).
[60] Chadwick, *The Church in Ancient Society*, 445.
[61] R.L. Testa, 'Christianization and Conversion in Northern Italy,' in *Origins of Christendom*, 47-95.
[62] Testa, 'Christianization,' 67-69.
[63] Testa, 'Christianization,' 68. There were, in addition, two other commonalities linking Jerome and Ambrose—asceticism and the wider struggle against heresy in its various manifestations.
[64] Testa, 'Christianization,' 68.
[65] See Rebenich, *Jerome*, 98.
[66] Rebenich, *Jerome*, 39.

Christian understandings of human identity and fulfilment.[67] Richard Layton states:

> Writers as diverse as Maximus and Augustine placed emotional attachments at the center of a theory of religious knowledge. Desire could bind the seeker for knowledge with the God who was sought, and the satisfaction of desire simultaneously enlarged the capacity for knowledge... His [Jerome's] introduction into Latin exegesis of a doctrine concerning incipient stirrings of affective response, labeled *propassio*, reverberated with distant echoes in medieval thought. Through Jerome's offices, the concept of *propassio* became a memento of a distortion in human emotional experience embedded in the core of the self.[68]

If Layton is right about Jerome then we need to find evidence in Jerome's writings of *propassio* in action as it were. Once located we need to ask how Jerome treats such 'incipient stirrings of affective response'—such as anger, desire, fury, grief, lust, revenge and sin. Layton notes that 'The *propassio* does not consist of an unfocused affective response, but a "thought"—an incipient, yet practical mental state directed toward some action.'[69]

We shall now look at two selected Jerome texts to ascertain Jerome's understanding of the *propassio* and to see how he contextualized it in order to provide guidance to his Christian readers in their faith. First, we shall examine Jerome's *Ep.* 122 (to Rusticus), one of many of Jerome's advisory letters.

Rusticus and Artemia his wife having made a vow of self-restraint broke it. Artemia proceeded to Palestine to do penance for her sin and Rusticus promised to follow her. However, he failed to do so; and Jerome was asked to write this letter in the hope that it might induce him to fulfil his promise. The date is about 408. Jerome writes:

> The Lord judges every man according as he finds him. It is not the past that He looks upon but the present. Bygone sins there may be, but renewal and conversion remove them... For we do not what we would but what we would not; the soul desires to do one thing, the flesh is compelled to do another... Your former wife, who is now your sister and fellow-servant, has told me that, you and she lived apart by consent that you might give yourselves to prayer; but that after a time your feet sank beneath you as if resting on water and indeed—to speak plainly—gave way altogether... But your house—she went on—having no sure foundation of faith fell before a whirlwind of the devil. Hers however still stands in the Lord, and does not refuse its shelter to you; you can still be joined in spirit to her whom you were once joined in body... Moreover, when the fury of the barbarians and the risk of captivity separated you again, you promised with a solemn oath that, if she made her way to the places, you would follow her either immediately or later, and that you would try to save your soul now that by your carelessness

---

[67] See R.A. Layton, 'From "Holy Passion" to Sinful Emotion: Jerome and the Doctrine of *Propassio*,' in P.M. Blowers, A.R. Christman, D.G. Hunter and R.D. Young (eds), *In Dominico Eloquio—In Lordly Eloquence* (Grand Rapids: Eerdmans, 2002), 280-93.

[68] Layton, 'From "Holy Passion",' 280.

[69] Layton, 'From "Holy Passion",' 287.

you had seemed to lose it. Perform now, the vow which you then made in the presence of God. Human life is uncertain. Therefore, lest you may be snatched away before you have fulfilled your promise, imitate her whose teacher you ought to have been.[70]

What we can clearly see in this extract from *Ep.* 122 is how Jerome is continually steering Rusticus towards an understanding of the need for the whole repentance of the sinner which can only come about by holding fast to the plank of penitence. Jerome's advice to Rusticus also highlights the accident of fortune ('Human life is uncertain') faced by all who strive for salvation through faith.

In *Ep.* 123 we find a second example of Jerome's understanding and contextualization of the *propassio*. In this advisory letter Jerome made an appeal to Ageruchia, a high born lady of Gaul, not to marry again. *Ep.* 123 dates from 409 and it is in this epistle that Jerome considers widowhood to be a noble state. Jerome opens his letter in typical *Jeromean* style.

I have several times written letters to widows in which for their instruction I have sought out examples from scripture, weaving its varied flowers into a single garland of chastity... I make these brief remarks to show my young friend that in resolving not to marry again she does but perform a duty to her family... For the devil inflames men to vie with one another in proving the chastity of our beloved widow; and rank and beauty, youth and riches cause her to be sought after by all. But the greater the assaults that are made upon her continence, the greater will be the rewards that will follow her victory.[71]

Here Jerome's advice to Ageruchia (who was seeking the church's protection against the many suitors she was meeting in the palace) stresses the importance of self-restraint in order for a widow not to overstep the bounds of chastity. Moreover, Jerome is appealing to those who have been once married to lives of continence.

In his advisory letters to widows Jerome's understanding and contextualization of the *propassio* is always found and set within a moral framework that points to the central importance of the emotions to the Christian view of the meaning of right and wrong in human behaviour.

You set before me the joys of wedlock. I will remind you of Dido's sword and pyre and funeral flames. In marriage there is not so much good to be hoped for as there is evil which may happen and must be feared. Passion when indulged always brings repentance with it; it is never satisfied, and once quenched it is soon kindled anew. Its growth or decay is a matter of habit; led like a captive by impulse it refuses to obey reason.[72]

Here Jerome is setting out how human desire (passion) can lead to human misery if unrestrained.

---

[70] Jerome, *Ep.* 122, NPNF² 6:225-29.
[71] Jerome, *Ep.* 123, NPNF² 6:230.
[72] Jerome, *Ep.* 123 NPNF² 6:235.

Ep. 123 was Jerome's appeal to one widow (Ageruchia) to preserve her widowhood in order that she could henceforth devote her soul to the Lord. What she might forfeit and what she might gain by doing so is revealed by Jerome:

> It is better to lose a portion of one's substance than to imperil the salvation of one's soul. It is better to lose that which some day, whether we like it or not, must be lost to us and to give it up freely, than to lose that for which we should sacrifice all that we have.[73]

Elsewhere in 2002 Charles Freeman published his book *The Closing of the Western Mind*[74] offered a critique of Jerome in the context of his influence upon the emergence of Catholic Christianity in the West (395-640). Freeman's study is a work of history not theology.[75] Here his critique of Jerome may be seen as the precursor of his later (2009) work.[76] However, it must be said that despite its ambitious objectives, *The Closing of the Western Mind* is somewhat limited in scope and detail on Jerome.

In the book's *Introduction* Freeman sets out the framework for his study:

> This book is a study of a revolution that took place within the Roman empire of the fourth and fifth centuries AD. It involved the victory of what can be termed 'faith' over a tradition of rational thought that had evolved over some centuries in the Ancient Greek world, but it was as much a revolution within Christianity itself as between Christianity and the pagan world... The assumption that the evolution of doctrine was as much a political as a religious matter underlies the central thesis of this book that state and religious authority combined to destroy the tradition of rational thought that had been among the major achievements of the classical world... It was only with the adoption of Aristotle's thought into the Christian tradition by Thomas Aquinas in the thirteenth century that it was restored and it is this restoration that concludes this book.[77]

These are lofty aims indeed but unfortunately Freeman does not grant Jerome sufficient space in his book to show how Jerome's role might have played a part in resolving that conflict over doctrine which had beset the churches during the fourth and fifth centuries.

Where he does critique Jerome, Freeman veers between stereotype and surmise, never really offering either new evidence or a new interpretation. His tendency to generalize is clearly apparent in the following:

> Jerome seems to have been an isolated and troubled individual, tormented by his sexuality, vulnerable to any hint of personal betrayal (and vituperative in response) and obsessive about the necessity for asceticism...yet his mastery of Latin... which he wrote with great elegance, Greek and Hebrew and his meticulous

---

[73] Jerome, *Ep.* 123 NPNF[2] 6:236.

[74] C. Freeman, *The Closing of the Western Mind: The Rise of Faith and the Fall of Reason* (London: Heinemann, 2002).

[75] The publisher's dust-jacket describes Freeman's book as 'a major and highly original work of history'.

[76] Freeman, *A New History*.

[77] Freeman, *Closing of the Western Mind*, xv-xvii.

knowledge of the scriptures gave him the reputation as the leading scholar of the day. His monument remains the Latin translation of the Old and New Testaments, the Vulgate, which reigned as the official Latin translation of the Bible for the Roman Catholic Church until the 1960s.[78]

And again:

> Translation seems to have been Jerome's forte, he was notably less at ease with original and creative work. Many of his commentaries on the OT are drawn almost entirely from earlier commentators (despite his abuse of Ambrose for doing the same).[79]

Freeman is too indecisive in his judgement on Jerome—for, surely, translation either was Jerome's forte or it was not. As for his comment that Jerome 'was notably less at ease with original and creative work' (here paralleling his own later (2009) view that Jerome never showed any genuine intellectual creativity or had the self-confidence to develop his own theology) Freeman gives few examples to justify his claim beyond his rather over critical judgement that in his OT commentaries Jerome was derivative (a fact which, of course, we know Jerome to have himself acknowledged as having been sometimes necessary in order to utilize the best of earlier exegesis).[80]

Perhaps the most surprising of Freeman's claims is that Jerome was profoundly anti-Jewish.[81] Notwithstanding his lack of evidence for such a proposition, Freeman is, of course, wholly incorrect. Jerome's hermeneutic ('Hebraica veritas') confirmed his allegiance to the Jewish scriptures. For Freeman to have overlooked this fact seems very strange indeed.

In 2003 the American scholar Steven Harmon highlighted some interesting points regarding Jerome's eschatology.[82] Placing Jerome amongst those 'ancient Christian theologians' and 'patristic universalists' who believed in 'a wideness in God's mercy,' primarily because they believed this hope was the most coherent reading of the biblical story.'[83] Harmon observes:

> Although Hellenistic thought might also have suggested an eschatology in which the end corresponds to the beginning, the eschatologies of these ancient Christian

---

[78] Freeman, *Closing of the Western Mind*, 280.

[79] Freeman, *Closing of the Western Mind*, 281.

[80] Freeman writes with some relish on Jerome's 'plagiarism': 'He was thoroughly caught out as late as 1941 when the discovery in the Egyptian desert of a voluminous five-book commentary on the prophet Zachariah by Didymus the Blind showed how heavily Jerome had relied on Didymus in his own commentary on the prophet' (281).

[81] Freeman, *Closing of the Western Mind*, 228.

[82] See, S.R. Harmon, *Every Knee Should Bow: Biblical Rationales for Universal Salvation in Early Christian Thought* (Lanham: University Press of America, 2003), 2, 3.

[83] Harmon, *Every Knee*, 2. For Harmon, as well as Jerome, the 'patristic universalists' (who displayed 'the concept of a universal "restoration" (*apokatastasis*) as a distinctive feature of their eschatology)' included Clement of Alexandria, Origen, Gregory of Nyssa, Gregory of Nazianzus, Didymus the Blind, Evagrius of Pontus, and Ambrose (1-2).

theologians were shaped mainly by the Hebrew story of creation, fall, redemption, and consummation, read through the lenses of the church's experience of God's saving work in the person of Jesus Christ.[84]

On Jerome as a 'patristic universalist,' Harmon comments, 'In a commentary on Isaiah, the post-Origenist Jerome noted that the proponents of a universal restoration following an end to the torments of hell "employ those testimonies"—Romans 11:25-26a and other similar texts.'[85] However, there remains a problem with regard to evaluating more precisely Jerome's contribution to the development and influence of patristic universalism. As Harmon writes: 'Traces of a universal eschatological hope appeared in Ambrose and the early Jerome, but the paucity of relevant material in their corpora does not allow us to explore sufficiently the place of the Bible in this aspect of their thought.'[86]

In 2003 another reading of Jerome's asceticism and associated correspondence was provided by David G. Hunter.[87] Jerome had long believed that celibacy was a higher or better life than marriage, and was 'opposed to Jovinian's teaching that marriage and celibacy were equally meritorious'.[88] Hunter suggests that it is 'to Jerome we owe most of what remains of Jovinian's writings, quoted in copious fragments in his two books, *Adversus Jovinianum*'.[89] Of course, this claim by Hunter might be debated bearing in mind that there appears no scholarly consensus on Jerome's rescue of Jovinian's writings.[90]

As a strong Jerome apologist, Hunter particularly praises Jerome's 'defence of Christian celibacy, the ascetical Letter 22 to Eustochium, the polemical *Contra Helvidium*, and numerous ascetical *vitae*.'[91] Hunter also stresses the importance of Jerome as an antiheretical writer, finding Jerome's *Adversus Jovinianum* to have had a dual purpose: first, to 'portray Jovinian as a "heretic"' and second, 'to reinforce Jerome's own identity as an authoritative teacher of ascetic practice and interpreter of Scripture'.[92] However, Hunter's judgement

---

84 Harmon, *Every Knee*, 2.

85 Jerome, *Comm. In Isa.* 18.66.24, as cited by Harmon, *Every Knee*, 2n.14.

86 Harmon, *Every Knee*, 3.

87 D.G. Hunter, 'Rereading the Jovinianist Controversy: Asceticism and Clerical Authority in Late Ancient Christianity,' *JMEMS* 33.3 (2003), 453-70.

88 Jerome, *Epist.* 49.2, as cited by Hunter, 'Rereading,' 454n.4. Hunter observes that, 'as well as Jerome, Jovinian's view that marriage and celibacy were equally meritorious was opposed by Augustine, Siricius and Ambrose'.

89 Hunter, 'Rereading,' 462.

90 For example, Rosenberg records, 'He [Jovinian] wrote a book, now lost,' and of *Against Jovinian* 'The preeminent polemicist and satirist among the western fathers, Jerome appears to have been guilty of overkill in his polemic.' See H. Rosenberg, 'Jovinian,' in E. Ferguson (ed.), *Encyclopedia of Early Christianity* (London: St. James, 1990), 503.

91 Hunter, 'Rereading,' 462.

92 Hunter, 'Rereading,' 462-63. Elsewhere, Vessey notes that 'in the mid-380s, Jerome has self-consciously fashioned for himself the literary *persona* of a Christian writer in the image of Origen, that is, as a master of biblical interpretation and ascetic prac-

that Jerome's polemical treatise was an appropriate 'choice of genre'[93] has been contested by other scholars.[94]

Whilst Henry Chadwick's 2003 study, *East and West: The Making of a Rift in the Church*[95] makes references to Jerome (largely relating to Ambrose, Jerome, and Augustine's support for the filioque (and from the Son of the procession of the Holy Spirit) clause addition and modification to the Constantinople Creed)[96] it does describe Jerome's contribution to our understanding of how a particular social curiosity (the wearing of a beard, cited by Jerome in his commentary on Isaiah 37:21-22) would happen 'to provide abrasions between the Greek and Latin churches'.[97]

In contrast to Chadwick's (2003) study, the second edition of Peter Brown's *The Rise of Western Christendom*[98] contained much more information about Jerome's influence during, what Brown terms, 'Empire and Aftermath (A.D. 200-500), "and the End of Ancient Christianity (A.D. 600-750)".'[99]

For example, Brown notes the way in which Jerome's sheltered piety/asceticism influenced Gregory the Great's early life when 'Gregory took for granted a Mediterranean-wide ascetic sensibility, which was common to both the Latin and the Greek worlds.'[100] A further feature of Jerome which Brown finds worthy of comment, is the apparent contradiction in Jerome's attitude and practice towards 'worldly wisdom'.[101] According to Brown, worldly wisdom

---

tice'. See M. Vessey, 'Jerome's Origen: The Making of a Christian literary persona,' *StP* 28 (1993), 135-45.

[93] Hunter, 'Rereading,' 463.

[94] For example, Rosenberg notes how *Adversus Jovinianus* upset some of Jerome's friends, one of whom 'tried to recall all copies of the treatise'. See Rosenberg, 'Jovinian,' 503.

[95] H. Chadwick, *East and West: The Making of a Rift in the Church: From Apostolic Times until the Council of Florence* (Oxford: OUP, 2003).

[96] Chadwick, *East and West*, 153-54, 219, 230, 242. For a summary account of the conflict over whether the Holy Spirit proceeds from the Father and the Son (*ex Patre Filioque*) or from the Father only, and how it was Tertullian (*Adversus Praxean*) who not only gave the term *Trinitas* to the theological vocabulary of the West, but also the doctrine of 'spiritus a Deo et Filio,' see J. Pelikan 'The Two Sees of Peter,' in E.P. Sanders (ed.) *Jewish and Christian Self-Definition* (London: SCM, 1980), 57-73 (58).

[97] Chadwick, *East and West*, 12: 'Jerome attack on Jovinian, a monk and priest, declared that the only difference between Jovinian and a goat was that he shaved off his beard: Chadwick further notes: 'By the tenth century the custom [for clergy and monks to be bearded] had become a painful issue in disputes between the Greek and Latin churches.'

[98] P. Brown, *The Rise of Western Christendom: Triumph and Diversity, A.D. 200-1000* (Oxford: Blackwell, 2003).

[99] Brown, *Rise of Western Christendom*, 37-141, 219-379.

[100] Brown, *The Rise of Western Christendom*, 199.

[101] Brown, *The Rise of Western Christendom*, 235.

(formed by the classical tradition but tainted by its undoubted pagan past) had a decidedly chequered history during the rise of Western Christendom.[102]

> The great generation of converts of the late fourth century—Jerome, Augustine, Paulius of Nola—had argued vociferously for and against the relevance of 'worldly wisdom' to the Christian. They often took up extreme poses against the pagan classics. These extreme statements were belied by their practice, which often showed them to be men steeped in the ancient tradition. But the invectives of Jerome and others still echoed loudly in the sixth and seventh centuries.[103]

Here Jerome (as well as others) is clearly portrayed in a negative manner suggesting a tendency on the part of Jerome towards inconsistency in his reaction to developments in the 'classical' Latin world.

On a more positive note, Brown observes that in Ireland, during the sixth century, a few letters of Jerome which were available at the ascetic settlement of Bangor, inspired the monks there to meditate and 'to write verses on the birth of Christ whose exultant solemnity echoed similar verses, inspired by the same passages in Jerome, written, in distant Poitiers, by the Italian Venantius Fortunctus'.[104] For Jerome's influence to have reached such a settled community (in the latter part of the sixth century) in such a way is quite remarkable.

In 2005 Edward Hahnenberg drew attention again to the self-representation/self-promotional side of Jerome[105] and, like Hunter (2003), concurred on its significance in establishing Jerome's importance in Christianity.[106]

Up until 2005 few scholars had made any direct links between Jerome's exegesis and its contribution to our understanding of particular 'Orthodox' Jewish-Christian groups within early Christianity. Michael Kruger's study of the manuscript fragment (P. oxy 840) consisting of one vellum leaf from a miniature codex that contains the remains of a discourse between Jesus and his disciples and also a confrontation between Jesus and a Pharisee in the temple,[107] brought forth some new information of particular interest to students of Jerome. In his study, Kruger identifies the possible community of P. Oxy 840 with the Nazarenes, an 'Orthodox' Jewish Christian group,[108] and makes a significant extrapolation regarding Jerome.[109]

Several items suggest that the Nazarenes would have had an intimate knowledge of the temple cult: (a) They were Jewish Christians who remained immersed in the OT law and prophets; (b) Their origins can be traced back to

---

[102] J. Fontaine, *Isidore de Saville* (Paris, 1983), 786-88, as cited by Brown, *The Rise of Western Christendom*, 235n.10.

[103] Brown, *The Rise of Western Christendom*, 235.

[104] Brown, *The Rise of Western Christendom*, 246-47.

[105] E.J. Hahnenberg, *Bible Maker: Jerome* (Bloomington: Author House, 2005).

[106] Hahnenberg, *Bible Maker*, xv.

[107] M. Kruger, *The Gospel of the Savior: An Analysis of P. Oxy. 840 and its Place in the Gospel Traditions of Early Christianity* (Leiden: Brill, 2005).

[108] Kruger, *The Gospel of the Savior*, 229-35.

[109] Kruger, *The Gospel of the Savior*, 231-32.

the original Jerusalem congregation before the flight to Pella; and (c) They demonstrate an impressive awareness of the teaching of rabbinic Judaism in their 'commentary' on Isaiah 8:14 which Jerome records in his own commentary on the book.[110]

Here, whilst Kruger is only identifying Jerome as a source he goes on to qualify Jerome's importance for our understanding of the Nazarenes:

> Jerome's record of the Nazarene commentary on Isaiah reveals that the Nazarenes saw the destruction and judgment of Isaiah 8:14 as applicable to the rabbinic houses of 'Shammai and Hillel, from whom originated the scribes and the Pharisees" because of their rejection of Jesus as the Messiah'...In their commentary on Isaiah 9:14, the Nazarenes describe the teachings of the Pharisees as 'the very heavy yoke of the Jewish traditions'. Also, Jerome notes that the Nazarenes compare the Pharisees (rabbis) to 'the devil and his angels' and describes them as those 'who earlier deceived the people with very vicious traditions'.[111]

Although Kruger's contextualization of particular parts of Jerome's exegesis of Isaiah (demonstrating its relationship to the early second/third century Nazarene 'Orthodox' Jewish-Christian community) does not show Jerome's interpretation to be in itself original thus perhaps giving some support to McGuckin's claim that Jerome's reputation as exegete is over-stressed (at least if we look for originality) it certainly indicates an exegete capable of identifying and comparing OT material in such a way as to highlight how the Nazarenes were in conflict with Pharisaic (rabbinic) Judaism.

Claudia Rapp's study *Holy Bishops in Late Antiquity* (2005) offered a number of readings of Jerome, most notably on Jerome's commentaries on the Pauline epistles, Jerome's views on desert asceticism and Jerome's complaints about ecclesiastical appointments. In her assessment of Jerome's exegesis of the Pauline epistles, Rapp, somewhat strangely, restricts herself solely to Jerome's treatment of Paul's Letter to Titus (written by Jerome in 386).[112] Noting how Jerome failed to also provide a commentary on Paul's First Letter to Timothy, Rapp states:

> However, his [Jerome's] remarks on the passage in Titus 1:5-9 that deals with the moral character of priests draw heavily on the relevant verses of 1 Timothy 3. The catalog of episcopal virtues in both these epistles is eagerly repeated by Jerome, who seizes this opportunity to make pointed jabs against unworthy clergy who indulge in gluttony and excessive drinking, who are given to filthy lucre, who show favouritism in their appointments to the priesthood, and who do not manage to keep their own household in order. The ideal, Jerome insists, is the bishop who embodies all the virtues. The reasoning he gives for the importance of episcopal virtues is not so much the preaching and teaching authority of the bishop, but ra-

---

[110] Kruger, *The Gospel of the Savior*, 231.
[111] Kruger, *The Gospel of the Savior*, 232, citing Jerome *Comm. Isa.* 9.1-4 and 29:20-21.
[112] C. Rapp, *Holy Bishops in Late Antiquity: The Nature of Christian Leadership in an Age of Transition* (Berkeley: University of California Press, 2005), 37-38.

ther his penitential and judicial authority, where personal detachment and impar-
tiality are paramount.[113]

Although Rapp, in her reading of Jerome on the Letter to Titus, claims that Jerome's interpretation of *Church Orders* (qualifications for overseers/elders), with its emphasis upon the bishop's penitential and judicial authority rather than preaching and teaching authority, differed from some other patristic figures[114] (e.g., Tertullian, Clement of Alexandria, John Chrysostom), the examples she cites show Jerome to have been well within that patristic tradition which had long called for episcopal/clerical virtue.[115]

Rapp's treatment of Jerome on the desert is perhaps more considered than her reading of Jerome on Titus. Rapp illustrates how Jerome's rhetoric was deployed in his letters to raise the profile of desert asceticism in the fourth and fifth centuries.

The transformation of the desert or wilderness into a city was always an occasion for a great rhetorical display of marvel. Jerome described the desert as a 'city more pleasant than all others' (*omni amuniorem civitatem*). During his retreat to the desert of Chalcis near Antioch, Jerome extolled his abode with great flourish in his Letter 14 to his friend Heliodorus, whom he tried—in vain—to cajole into joining him. Jerome played on the contrast between the barrenness of the desert and the flowering of spiritual benefits that only life in the desert could bring. The person who exposed his body to the harshness and deprivation of the desert could, he said, stroll through paradise in his mind.[116]

---

[113] Rapp, *Holy Bishops*, 37-38.
[114] Rapp, *Holy Bishops*, 38.
[115] As Rapp notes: 'Late antique reflection on the ideal bishop developed in step with the historical development of the episcopate. In the first centuries, while there were several *episkopoi* whose duties were largely administrative, all that was expected of them was that they be respected and upright members of the community. Beginning in the fourth century, the enhanced visibility of the representatives of the church and the increased array of their responsibilities in a largely pagan world were not without consequence: on the one hand, they triggered new reflections on the relative worth of the public activities of the bishop versus the private pursuit of asceticism, and on the other, they made it more imperative than ever that the bishop lead an exemplary life' (33). Tertullian believed (as Paul demanded) that the bishop should be married only once (*Exhortation to Chastity and On Monogamy*); Clement of Alexandria believed that the bishop should not be avaricious or litigious and should hold to a virtuous living (*On virginity*); Origen believed that the episkopos should enjoy a good reputation (*Homily on Leviticus*) where the bishop will fulfil his ministry by practicing the virtues listed in 1 Timothy 3 (*Commentary on the Letter to the Romans*); John Chrysostom also argued for bishops to be held in good repute (*On the Priesthood*) as did Ambrose (*Letters*); and Basil of Caesarea called for a high quality of clergy (*Ep.* 54). See Rapp, *Holy Bishops*, 34-36.
[116] Jerome, *Ep.* 14.10, as cited by Rapp, *Holy Bishops*, 118. According to Guy Stroumsa 'Paradise' soon became associated with the blissful state of the elect, which would eventually be graphically reconstituted in the monastic cloister: already for Jerome, the monastery was identified with a paradise. See Jerome, *Ep.* 125, as cited by G.G.

Jerome's actual description of the benefits that life in the desert could bring, and his understanding of 'paradise' as found in *Ep.* 14, shows the Jeromean rhetoric at full flight. He tells Heliodorus:

> O desert, bright with flowers of Christ!... O wilderness, gladdened with God's special presence! What keeps you in the world, my brother, you who are above the world? How long shall gloomy roofs oppress you? How long shall smoky cities immure you? Believe me, I have more light than you. Sweet it is to lay aside the weight of the body and to soar into the pure bright ether. Do you dread poverty? Christ calls the poor blessed. Does toil frighten you? No athlete is crowned but in the sweat of his brow. Are you anxious as regards food? Faith fears no famine. Do you dread the bare ground for limbs wasted with fasting? The Lord lies there beside you. Do you recoil from an unwashed head and uncombed hair? Christ is your true head. Does the boundless solitude of the desert terrify you? In the spirit you may walk always in paradise. Do but turn your thoughts thither and you will be no more in the desert.[117]

Here we can clearly see Jerome deploying highly coloured language—a style of rhetoric which seems to have produced a great impression in the West.[118]

As well as illustrating how Jerome viewed the desert landscape and the significance of the retreat to a barren setting for the promotion of spiritual growth, Rapp's interpretation of Jerome's desert asceticism also extends to coverage of Jerome's understanding of the desert as a state of mind.[119] Like John Chrysostom, Clement and Origen, Jerome considered the desert landscape to be important but not vital to achieving the desert state of mind (i.e., inner tranquillity allowing for communion with God).[120]

Noting how Jerome understood that the desert state of mind was also achievable in other environments besides the desert landscape,[121] Rapp observes:

> Jerome was able to distinguish between the desert as a geographical space and the desert as a metaphor for complete solitude of the individual with God, which is equal to paradise[122]: 'As long as you are at home, make your cell your paradise, gather there the varied fruits of Scripture, let this be your favourite companion, and take its precepts to your heart...But to me a town is a prison and a solitude

---

Stroumsa, 'Introduction: the paradise chronotype,' in M. Bockmuehl and G.G. Stroumsa (ed.), *Paradise in Antiquity: Jewish and Christian Views* (Cambridge: CUP, 2010) 1-14 (9).

[117] Jerome, *Ep.* 14 NPNF[2] 6:17. Heliodorus, originally a soldier, but now a presbyter of the Church, had accompanied Jerome to the East, but, not feeling called to the solitary life of the desert, had returned to Aquileia. Here he resumed his clerical duties and in course of time was raised to the episcopate as bishop of Altinum. The letter was written in the first bitterness of separation and reproaches Heliodorus for having gone back from the perfect way of the ascetic life. The date is 373 or 374.

[118] For example, Fabiola, a Roman aristocrat, was so much enchanted by it that she learned the letter by heart (Jerome, *Ep.* 77, 9).

[119] Rapp, *Holy Bishops*, 119-20.

[120] Rapp, *Holy Bishops*, 119-20.

[121] Rapp, *Holy Bishops*, 120.

[122] Rapp, *Holy Bishops*, 120.

paradise. Why do we long for the bustle of cities, we whose name (*monachus*) speaks of loneliness?'[123]

Significantly, amongst the other environments favoured by Jerome for facilitating the desert state of mind was the monastic cell.[124]

In her final assessment of Jerome, Rapp examines Jerome's complaints about ecclesiastical appointments. Nepotism, which had seen episcopal sees being passed from father to son, had earlier been criticised by Origen.[125] Rapp notes:

> A century later, Jerome complained about personal favouritism of this kind in the appointment of clergymen: 'As though they [the bishops] were distributing the offices of an earthly service, they give posts to their kindred and relations; or they listen to the dictates of wealth. And, worse than all, they give promotion to the clergy who besmear them with flattery.'[126]

This practice of nepotism was common throughout the Roman Empire[127] and Jerome's opposition to it was based on his view that 'leadership of people should not be passed on through the qualification of blood ties, but of conduct,' and that 'many bishops treat ecclesiastical office as a *beneficium*, appointing not the most capable but those whom they love'.[128]

Again, Jerome, ever the colourful polemicist, vented his anger at the way in which men with limited (if any) experience of ecclesiastical affairs were too easily given church office:

> Yesterday a catechumen, today a priest. Yesterday at the theatre, today in the church. In the evening at the chariot-races, the next morning at the altar. Recently a fan of actors, now a consecrator of holy virgins.[129]

Elsewhere, Jerome condemned the avarice of the clergy, something that Tertullian, Cyprian and Origen had earlier complained of.[130]

> Jerome had some choice phrases of condemnation for adversaries whom he accused of greed. He rallied against John of Jerusalem for making a profit from 'the

---

[123] Jerome, *Ep.* 125, as cited by Rapp, *Holy Bishop*, 120n.89.

[124] Jerome, *Ep.* 24.3 and 4, as cited by Rapp, *Holy Bishops*, 120n.90. For an account of Jerome's introduction to and development of the monastic ideal, see Rebenich, *Jerome*, 10-11, 16-18, 23-26, 130-31.

[125] Origen, *Homilies on Numbers* 22.4, as cited by Rapp, *Holy Bishops*, 196n.122.

[126] Jerome, *Commentary on the Letter to Titus 1*, as cited by Rapp, *Holy Bishops*, 196n.123.

[127] Rapp, *Holy Bishops*, 196.

[128] Jerome, *Commentary on the Letter to Titus 1*, as cited by Rapp, *Holy Bishops*, 196n.123.

[129] Jerome, *Ep.* 69.9 to Oceanus, as cited by Rapp, *Holy Bishops*, 203n.157.

[130] Rapp, *Holy Bishop*, 218.

piety of the whole world,' insinuating that John was exploiting the pilgrims who came to the Holy City.[131]

In all, Rapp's illumination of some areas of Jerome's work (as exegete, ascetic and polemicist), is informative if at times limited. We now turn to some other scholars who have sought to examine Jerome, a man who perhaps too often felt himself, and showed himself, to be a writer/scholar in possession of the whole truth on the difficult questions of his day.

First, let us consider the view of Jerome as put forward by the American classicist, Professor James O'Donnell:

> Jerome was a tough case…There had never been a town in which Jerome couldn't make himself unwelcome…his record of publications, his trumpeted knowledge of Hebrew, and his reputed access to Origen's own manuscripts gave him the authority to set himself up as judge and jury in all matters of Christian Latin biblical scholarship.[132]

We saw earlier in chapter 2 how Jerome's persona (described by O'Donnell as Jerome acting as 'judge and jury in all matters of Christian biblical scholarship') did not find favour with Augustine. Re-calling the famous incident at Antioch (Gal. 2:11-14), O'Donnell observes:

> He [Augustine] questioned the advisability of Jerome's translation enterprise and disputed him on a critical point of scriptural exegesis. Were Peter and Paul, when they quarrel in Galatians over the mission to the gentiles, really arguing or was it all a didactic show? Jerome needed both men to be on the right side, but Augustine needed the written text to be truthful, and neither was willing to compromise on the question.[133]

Here O'Donnell, like a number of scholars before him, is again raising the question of whether or not Jerome saw his primary theological task as exegetical truth (unfortunately, Jerome would not have read Augustine's '*De Doctrina Christiana*,' with its advice on how to read scripture and what the scriptural exegete needs to know, since it was not completed until 427). If not, then, Jerome might be seen as having deliberately set out to falsify scripture. But, surely, Jerome would never have risked his reputation for holiness and learning by constructing and inserting such a deliberate and mischievous mistake into his Galatians commentary. Yet he might just well have done so. The evidence?

---

[131] Jerome, *Against John of Jerusalem* 14, as cited by Rapp, *Holy Bishops*, 218n.35. Rapp, in fact, slightly misquotes Jerome here. Jerome actually criticizes John of Jerusalem from 'making a profit out of the religion of the whole world' NPNF[2] 6:431). Jerome's *Letter to Pammachius Against John of Jerusalem* (written about 398/399), was a product of the Origenist controversy and was written with much animosity against John. The letter was a treatise to Pammachius, who had been disturbed by the complaints of Bishop John to Siricius, Bishop of Rome, against Jerome. The letter is, throughout, arrogant, violent and contemptuous in its tone.
[132] J.J. O'Donnell, *Augustine: A New Biography* (New York: Harper Collins, 2005), 92.
[133] O'Donnell, *Augustine*, 92-93.

Perhaps the following description of Jerome by O'Donnell gives us a possible answer. O'Donnell tells us that Jerome was a man (like Ambrose and Augustine) 'who built structures, propagated doctrines, and exercised control at a distance,' and a man (again like Ambrose and Augustine) who was successful in 'imposing his views of Christianity on contemporaries and successors'.[134]

O'Donnell's assessment of Jerome clearly gives some support to Freeman's (2009) judgement that Jerome never showed any genuine intellectual creativity or had the self-confidence to develop his own theology. Equally, Augustine himself might be similarly charged with a lack of original thought in his use and interpretation of scripture. It is perhaps telling, not to say somewhat ironic, that O'Donnell writes of Augustine:

> Even his reading in Jerome, whom he knew he had to respect, was always limited and sporadic, even though he could have learned a lot form the Bethlehem obsessive.[135]

> Instead of writing scholarly commentary, Augustine was always much more comfortable taking up individual issues and hammering at them exegetically, and so many of his treatises on doctrinal or moral issues turnout to be extended meditations on scriptural passages. But his style means that he habitually takes his scriptural text out of the context of the original creation (whatever book of scripture that happens to be) and reads it instead against he whole of scripture and against the doctrinal and polemical needs of his time. Much of what he says in that mode is brilliant, even memorable, but little of it stands up as a serious engagement with the text in any way that patristic, medieval, or modern readers would call scholarly.[136]

Thus, with regard to scriptural interpretation, it would seem that Augustine (like Jerome) was also prone to certain shortcomings. Just why and how Jerome and Augustine might have come to alter scriptural passages is clearly explained by O'Donnell:

> What sets him [Augustine] apart...is his preference for the nonliteral sense of scripture as the truest sense. But if every page of scripture is scriptural and Christian, then the Jewish scriptures get largely rewritten in ways that would have surprised the patriarchs of old. Augustine learned this technique of inscribing the new doctrine in the old scriptures from Ambrose and Jerome and passed it on to the Latin west, where it had a long run, until it was challenged by the Reformation. It came to the Latins from Alexandria, where Origen in particular had developed the technique with ingenious mastery.[137]

It is interesting that whilst the relationship between Jerome and Augustine was sometimes fractious[138] (towards the end of his life) Jerome spoke of Augustine

---

[134] O'Donnell, *Augustine*, 111-12.
[135] O'Donnell, *Augustine*, 125.
[136] O'Donnell, *Augustine*, 133.
[137] O'Donnell, *Augustine*, 133-34.
[138] For example, Augustine was disturbed when Jerome suggested to him 'let's play together in the fields of scriptures without offending each other,' replying to Jerome

as 'the restorer of the ancient faith'.[139] However, the Jerome-Augustine nexus remains a paradox.

What is O'Donnell's overall judgement on Jerome? Though he finds the 'chronicle' of Eusebius as Latinized by Jerome, to have been 'dry and sketchy,'[140] he praises Jerome's vast literary enterprise (almost as ambitious and successful as that of Augustine),[141] which made a major contribution to 'the emergence in the Latin West of a distinctively Christian body of religious literature'.[142] O'Donnell states:

> Histories regularly focus on the producers of a high literature, and so too emphasize what can only be called a golden age: the few decades in which Hilary, Marius Victorinus, Ambrose, Prudentius, Ambrosiaster, Jerome and Cassian, to name only the leading lights along with Augustine, created a body of Latin Christian literature that far outshone all that had come before and that would loom large over all that came after.[143]

O'Donnell's labelling of Jerome as 'the master of Christian textual self-promotion,'[144] presenting himself to the world 'as the Latin reincarnation of the Greek polymath exegete Origen of 150 years earlier,'[145] returns us yet again to the debate over Jerome's originality as Bible scholar.

2007-2009

In 2007 Michael Graves offered a strong defence of the integrity[146] of Jerome's biblical scholarship. However, Graves acknowledges:

> Jerome's scholarship [also] suffered at certain points from the limitations of his environment, both in terms of the presuppositions that he held and the tools that were available to him. For example, despite Jerome's zeal to get back to the original reading [of the Hebrew text of Jeremiah], he was hampered by his belief that the Hebrew text in his possession in the fourth century was at all times the original text of Jeremiah. The Greek and Latin texts of the Bible known to Jerome var-

---

that for him scripture study was not a matter of play but a breathless struggle up a mountainside, all serious business. See O'Donnell, *Augustine*, 96n.172, n.173. Moreover, Augustine disliked Jerome's project of translating the Hebrew scripture freshly into Latin. See O'Donnell, *Augustine*, 353n.223.

[139] Jerome, *Ep.* 141, NPNF² 6:282. *Ep.* 141 was written about 418.

[140] O'Donnell, *Augustine*, 251. Elsewhere, David Dungan has inferred criticism of Jerome's tendency to sometimes rush certain of his literary projects. Of Jerome's *Vulgate* translation, Dungan writes: 'Jerome seems to have not spent much effort on deciding which books to include in the New Testament, beyond translating Eusebius' *Ecclesiastical History* into Latin.' See D.L. Dungan, *Constantine's Bible: Politics and the Making of the New Testament* (Minneapolis: Fortress, 2007), 127.

[141] O'Donnell, *Augustine*, 136.

[142] O'Donnell, *Augustine*, 311.

[143] O'Donnell, *Augustine*, 311.

[144] O'Donnell, *Augustine*, 92.

[145] Vessey, 'Jerome's Origen,' 135-45, as cited by O'Donnell, *Augustine*, 92n.166.

[146] Graves, *Jerome's Hebrew Philology* (Leiden: Brill, 2007).

ied greatly one from another, whereas the Hebrew text was essentially uniform, all of which makes Jerome's assumption not unreasonable in his day. But we now see that his evaluations of the fourth century Hebrew text was too high, forcing him at times to offer awkward explanations of the Hebrew (e.g., 27:1).[147]

These reservations aside Graves gives a positive reception to Jerome's Hebrew scholarship:

> As to the quality of Jerome's Hebrew philology in comparison with modern scholarship, the monk of Bethlehem overall receives high marks. With surprising frequency, Jerome engages the Hebrew text in a manner plausible even by today's standards. He certainly approaches the text critically, with a remarkable aptitude for untangling complicated problems... Many of Jerome's comments on the Hebrew are well in line with modern scholarship... In other cases, Jerome's analysis is suggestive for later solutions... or else... he transmits information used by subsequent interpreters to clarify the text. On the whole, the impression left by Jerome is that of a competent Hebrew scholar whose literary and critical sensibilities are quite similar to our own.[148]

Here Graves is a strident Jerome apologist and his award of 'high marks' to Jerome's Hebrew biblical exegesis and, in particular, his observation that in certain instances 'Jerome's analysis is suggestive for later solutions', again raises doubts about McGuckin's (2009) suggestion that Jerome's reputation as exegete is over-stressed (at least if we look for originality).

We have already observed how one of the main concerns of scholars trying to judge Jerome's *oeuvre* has been the apparent inconsistencies in Jerome's work as a biblical scholar. But what was the cause of Jerome's inconsistency? Understanding Jerome's inconsistencies and their causes is an area of modern Jerome scholarship few scholars have embarked upon, apart, perhaps, from Wiles (1967a). In the main scholars have preferred to identify Jerome's inconsistencies per se without a full analysis of their origin. However, in 2007, an essay by Ann Mohr,[149] illuminated a number of problems faced by Jerome which may well have contributed to the sometimes conflicting or contradictory elements in his work.

Mohr opens her essay with a clear statement: 'St. Jerome's difficulties in reconciling his attachment to his classical heritage with his Christian convictions are well known and yet surprisingly hard to chart with precision.'[150]

---

[147] Graves, *Jerome's Hebrew Philology*, 189.

[148] Graves, *Jerome's Hebrew Philology*, 188-89.

[149] A. Mohr, 'Jerome, Virgil, and the Captive Maiden: The Attitude of Jerome to Classical Literature,' in J.H.D. Scourfield (ed.), *Texts and Culture in Late Antiquity: Inheritance, Authority, and Change* (Swansea: Classical Press of Wales, 2007), 299-322.

[150] Mohr, 'Jerome, Virgil, and the Captive Maiden,' 299. See, also, R.A. Markus, *Christianity in the Roman World* (London: Thames and Hudson, 1974), 129, 131. Markus writes, 'It was Julian... who thought that the classics and the Gospels could not go together... Most Christians of Julian's generation appreciated the value of a classical education and rejected the antithesis which Julian tried to foist upon them... In the generation after Julian, and especially around the turn of the century, there is a per-

Might this, then, have been the main cause of Jerome's inconsistencies as a biblical scholar? Mohr continues:

> Harold Hagendahl, in his massively erudite study of Jerome's quotation of the classical authors, concluded that Jerome's attitude 'cannot be defined in a plain and unequivocal formula. It is inconsequent, inconsistent, reflecting opposite tendencies, fluctuating like the currents of the tide.'[151]

It is interesting that Mohr draws this particular citation from a book by Hagendahl that deals directly with (among others) Jerome as a Christian apologist. But what inner-conflicts might Jerome have experienced whist he endeavoured to successfully perform such a role? Did these inner-conflicts in any way contribute to Jerome's sometimes inconsistent work as a biblical scholar? Mohr's essay attempts to provide us with some answers. First, still drawing upon Hagendahl, Mohr sets the framework for such an investigation:

> The two poles of his [Jerome's] attitude towards classical literature are taken to be the account of his celebrated dream in *Letter* 22, written in 384, where he renounced the classics, and the change to 'a more unprejudiced and liberal-minded understanding'[152] of classical literature seen thirteen years later, in *Letter* 70. Between these attitudes he is seen to swing, torn by conflicting feelings of love for the old writers and loyalty to his Christian principles, never able to achieve stability.[153] Such ambivalence is territory which invites a revisit.[154]

Here Hagendahl's (1958) interpretation of Jerome's 'swing' (oscillation), as highlighted by Mohr, is certainly evident in *Letter* 22. As Charles Freeman finds:

> Jerome... had written, in a highly publicized letter to a young girl Julia Eustochium,... that pietas in the home, in the sense of her loyalties to her father, should take second place to her own desires to preserve her virginity by not marrying[155]... The vituperative Jerome is also on record as saying that Praetextatus'

---

ceptible hardening of attitude among Western Christians towards culture...Symptoms of an uneasy conscience about the classics abound among Christians at this time. It was the most learned among them, the men who owed most to classical education like Jerome...or Augustine...who turned most sharply aside from the literature they had loved.'

[151] H. Hagendahl, *Latin Fathers and the Classics: A study on the apologists, Jerome, and other Christian writers* (Goteborgs universitets arsskrift 64, Goteborg, 1958), 309, as cited by Mohr, 'Jerome, Virgil, and the Captive Maiden,' **299**n.1.

[152] Hagendahl, *Latin Fathers*, 208, as cited by Mohr, 'Jerome, Virgil, and the Captive Maiden,' **299**n.2.

[153] Mohr is referring here to Hagendahl's proposition that 'oscillating between aversion and adhesion to the classics Jerome never succeeded in getting over the internal conflict or in reaching a stable equilibrium'. See Hagendahl, *Latin Fathers*, 92, as cited by Mohr, 'Jerome, Virgil, and the Captive Maiden,' **299**n.3, 318.

[154] Mohr, 'Jerome, Virgil, and the Captive Maiden,' **299**.

[155] Jerome, *Ep.* 22, as cited by Freeman, *Closing of the Western Mind*, 236n.9.

[prominent Roman senator who died in late 384] zeal for his pagan religious duties was such that he had certainly gone straight to hell on his death.[156]

We can clearly see here the way in which Jerome begins his early (384) oscillation from paganism towards his support for Christian virtue. However, Freeman asks us to be prudent here in our judgment of Jerome's changing attitude.

> Christians...tended to dramatize desires, particularly those of sexual desire (and here they followed Paul), as if they were cosmic forces, inspired by demons with whom deadly battles had to be fought. Jerome is an excellent example.[157]

Where Freeman is at odds with Mohr is over the question of whether or not Jerome successfully rid himself of that inner-conflict he may have felt whenever he was drawn to his classical heritage whilst interpreting the scriptures. Of Jerome's early stay in the Syrian desert, Freeman asserts:

> Here he was tortured by his sexual desire but he also later recorded a terrible dream in which he was flogged for preferring Cicero to the scriptures. He was warned that if he ever read non-Christian writers again he would suffer worse torments. He seems to have resolved his guilt and continued his reading (or at least he continued to fill his writings with classical illusions).[158]

In contrast to Freeman, Mohr believes Jerome's 'crisis of conscience'[159] (evidenced by his account of his dream at *Letter* 22.30) over classical literature may have been much more prolonged.

> In his dream, Jerome was condemned before the court of heaven as 'Ciceronianus...non Christianus,' and swore never again to read the classical authors: 'domine si umquam habuero codices saeculares, si legero, te negavi' ('Lord, if ever I possess worldly books or read them, I have denied you,' *Ep.* 22.30.5). He seems to have abstained from reading, though not from quoting, pagan authors for more than a decade, perhaps as long as fifteen years, and it is generally agreed that at some point afterwards he began to read the classical writers again.[160]

Whilst Freeman is of the opinion that Jerome 'seems to have resolved his guilt and continued his reading' [of non-Christian writers], Mohr's understanding is that Jerome seems to have abstained from reading [of pagan authors]. There is an obvious contradiction here. Perhaps the best that can be said is that both

---

[156] Kelly, *Jerome*, 96n.23, citing Jerome, *Ep.* 24, as cited by Freeman, *Closing of The Western Mind*, 236n.10.

[157] Freeman, *Closing of the Western Mind*, 241.

[158] Freeman, *Closing of the Western Mind*, 280.

[159] Mohr, 'Jerome, Virgil, and the Captive Maiden,' 299.

[160] Mohr, 'Jerome, Virgil, and the Captive Maiden,' 299-300. Mohr observes: 'The gap between the principle, so well publicized in the account of the dream, and Jerome's literary practice, his use of material form the works of the classical authors in the form of quotations, paraphrases, and illusions, has been noted by both contemporary (e.g., Rufinus, *Apol. Adv. Hier*, 2.6-7) and modern critics (e.g., Rebenich, *Jerome*, 9, 300n.9, n.10).'

Freeman and Mohr, in their own way, point to Jerome's inconsistency in obeying his declared oath to renounce the classics.

Taking up a theme earlier identified by Vessey (1993)—Jerome fashioning for himself a literary *persona* of a Christian writer in the image of Origen—Andrew Cain's paper, 'Origen, Jerome, and the *Senatus Pharisaeorum*,'[161] reassessed Jerome's infatuation with Origen, tracing how Jerome had, during his stay in Rome (382-385), been 'busily making Origen's biblical exegesis available to western readers through a translation of two of his homilies on the Song of Songs'.[162]

In 2006 Andrew Cain, in similar vein to Hunter (2003) and Hahnenberg (2005), again focused upon Jerome's inclination to self-representation/self-promotion:

> It has been suggested that Jerome, eager to jumpstart his career in biblical scholarship, circulated his collected letters to Marcella, perhaps while still in Rome, to promote himself to the Latin-speaking West as the next Origen.[163]

Cain further observed that from being 'under Origen's mesmerizing spell,' Jerome's infatuation with Origen had 'turned into blatant imitatio'.[164] Again, this observation of Jerome's self-representation/self-promotion via imitation of Origen's work, might be seen as evidence of McGuckin's (2005) belief that Jerome's reputation as exegete is too heavily emphasized (at least if we look for originality). Yet, equally, Cain's account of Jerome's hopes for his own recognition as a biblical exegete of distinction (a hope which Jerome saw successfully realized in his own lifetime when he was seen to be Christendom's 'greatest living biblical sage')[165] corresponds closely, and somewhat ironically, to the other side of McGuckin's (2005) thesis, namely, that Jerome was perhaps the most important biblical scholar of the Western Church.

With all of this in mind can we now ask if any recent scholars have provided evidence of serious shortcomings in Jerome's biblical scholarship? One such scholar is Will Rutherford whose work has raised questions about just how far we should regard Jerome as a biblical scholar of distinction.[166] Rutherford's 2007 essay charts the early Christian witnesses for a Christological interpreta-

---

[161] A. Cain, 'Origen, Jerome, and the *Senatus Pharisaeorum*,' *Latomus*, 65 (2006), 727-34.

[162] Vessey, 'Jerome's Origen,' 135-45, as cited by Cain, 'Origen,' 727.

[163] Cain 'Origen,' 727.

[164] Cain, 'Origen,' 727.

[165] Cain, 'Origen,' 732. Cain comments that Origen 'founded and headed a theological school [in Palestinian Caesarea], from 234-253,' and 'when he [Jerome] established his Bethlehem monastery complex he [Jerome] entertained ambitions that in time it would become a seat of learning comparable to Origen's school'.

[166] W. Rutherford, '*Altercatio Jasonis et Papisci* as a Testimony Source for Justin's "Second God" Argument' in S. Parvis and P. Foster (eds), *Justin Martyr and his Worlds* (Minneapolis: Fortress, 2007), 137-44.

tion of OT theophany (a visible manifestation of God).[167] Rutherford believes that Justin Martyr's *Dialogue* 56-62 (Genesis/Exodus/Proverbs) in which Justin offers the most detailed descriptions of a 'second God' who pre-existed alongside the Father of the Universe was partly aided (esp. chapters 61-62) by the lost *Disputation between Jason and Papiscus* (*JP*).[168] Rutherford states:

> What we know of *JP* comes from only a few fragments and descriptions, among which Jerome tells us that it contained a reading (*Scriptum est*) of Genesis 1:1 in which the son is regarded as 'the Beginning': 'In the son God made heaven and earth' (*In filio facit Deus Caelum at terram*).[169] Jerome is mistaken in assigning this same textual reading to both Tertullian and Hilary,[170] and it is not at all certain he 'remembered the precise wording of *JP* correctly'.[171]

Here Rutherford is clearly critical of Jerome's exegetical and intellectual powers in mis-attributing a particular textual interpretation to other church fathers. However, some caution is required since *JP* is a reconstruction from a limited number of fragments and Jerome might at least be congratulated on handing down to us some (albeit questionable) descriptions of what the lost *Disputation between Jason and Papiscus* may have contained.

One feature of Jerome's corpus—his writings on the Transfiguration (hitherto largely neglected by scholars) became a focus of Kenneth Stevenson's 2007 study, *Rooted in Detachment: Living the Transfiguration*.[172] Stevenson acknowledges:

> Of all the writers in antiquity who have written on the Transfiguration, perhaps one of the most influential was Jerome... His homily on the Transfiguration uniquely is on the Marcan narrative... Jerome immediately turns to the spiritual reality of the Transfiguration, which is about ascent and transformation... Jerome's spiritual (i.e., allegorical) treatment of the narrative identifies the shining garments with Holy Scripture—hence the importance of Jesus as the enlivening force for using the Bible.[173]

Here Stevenson is obviously keen to demonstrate Jerome's special contribution to Marcan exegesis.

Stevenson later considers the way in which Jerome identifies (in Mk 4:30-43), the 'inner-cabinet' (i.e., Jesus' choice of his three main disciples—Peter,

---

[167] Rutherford, '*Altercatio Jasonis et Papisci*,' 137.

[168] Rutherford, '*Altercatio Jasonis et Papisci*, 138.

[169] Jerome, *Qu. hebr. Gen.*, as cited by Rutherford, '*Altercatio Jasonis et Papisci*,' 143n.44.

[170] Tertullian, *Adv. Prax* 5.1; Hilary, *Comm. Ps.*2 as cited by Rutherford, '*Altercatio Jasonis et Papisci*, 143n.45.

[171] Jerome, *Comm. Gal.* 3.13: *Memini me*, as cited by Rutherford, '*Altercatio Jasonis et Papisci*, 143n.46.

[172] K. Stevenson, *Rooted in Detachment: Living the Transfiguration* (London: DLT, 2007).

[173] Jerome, *Homily 80* in *Saint Jerome, the Homilies of St. Jerome* (*Homilies 60-96*) (tr. Sister M.L. Ewald), 2.159-68, as cited by Stevenson, *Rooted*, 25-27.

James, John) as 'representing the Trinity'[174] as especially innovative. And Jerome's particular eschatological treatment of the Transfiguration (firmly based upon his belief that 'the Transfiguration is about Jesus being revealed for what he is, and about discipleship being illuminated for what it might lead to'[175]) would be an exegetical-model from whom others would learn (e.g. Bede c. 673-735).[176] Here we see, yet again, Jerome's work acting as a 'theological—resource for later biblical interpreters.

In sum, then, it can be said that Stevenson's critique of Jerome's writing on the Transfiguration challenges McGuckin's (2005) view that Jerome's reputation as exegete is over-stressed (at least if we look for originality) and Freeman's (2009) claim that Jerome never showed any intellectual creativity.

Having just examined how some scholars have tried to understand Jerome's inconsistencies and their possible causes, we can now look at one recent scholars' attempt to give exposition to Jerome's exegetical practice and method.[177] In this work does Thomas Scheck provide any evidence of Jeromean inconsistency or of material that might suggest a correspondence to the 'McGuckin-Freeman' thesis (namely, that Jerome's reputation as exegete has been over-stressed and that Jerome failed to show any genuine intellectual creativity)?

In his introduction to his translation of Jerome's *Commentary on Matthew*, Scheck makes quite clear how he sees Jerome's position in late antiquity (and beyond):

> Jerome was certainly one of the most learned of the Latin Fathers, but he was not a bishop, nor did he take a synthetic view of theological questions, as did his contemporary Augustine, and for these reasons Augustine's theological legacy was far greater.[178] In contrast with Augustine, however, Jerome had mastered both the Greek and the Latin theological traditions, and he was deeply influenced by the

---

[174] Stevenson, *Rooted*, 27.

[175] Stevenson, *Rooted*, 28.

[176] For Bede, see *Homily* 1.24 (on the Matthew narrative) in L.T. Martin and D. Hurst (tr.), *Bede the Venerable: Homilies on the Gospels* (Kalamazoo: Cistercian, 1990), 1.233-44, as cited by Stevenson, *Rooted*, 28n.15. Elsewhere, Andrew Louth has noted, 'Bede's exegetical works seem to be guided by two principles: first, making accessible to his contemporaries the learning of the earlier patristic period (Ambrose, Jerome, Augustine, Gregory the Great) and, secondly, filling in the gaps in the tradition of Latin biblical commentaries.' See A. Louth, *St. John Damascene: Tradition and Originality in Byzantine Theology* (Oxford: OUP, 2002) 286.

[177] St. Jerome, *Commentary on Matthew* (tr. T.P. Scheck; Washington: Catholic University of America Press, 2008).

[178] J.P. O'Connell, *The Eschatology of St. Jerome* (Mundelein: Pontificia Facultas Theologica Sanctae Mariae ad Lacum, 1948) 1, as cited by Scheck, St. Jerome, *Commentary on Matthew*, 3-4. O'Connell states '[Jerome] was not a theologian but an exegete and polemicist. He has left us no methodical and comprehensive studies of theological questions.' Here O'Connell's view must be challenged for Jerome's works, especially his letters and homilies are full of discussions about theological questions of the day and the NPNF[2] 6, *St. Jerome: Letters and Select Works* can be seen as Jerome's well-stocked library of theology.

literature from both streams. Among the Latin Church's scriptural commentators, Jerome is pre-eminent. His outstanding ecclesiastical learning led the Council of Trent to speak of him as 'the greatest doctor in explaining the Sacred Scriptures'. In the seventeenth century, the learned Scripture scholar Richard Simon expressed the opinion that Jerome's commentaries were the most thorough and instructive of his works.[179]

Here Scheck's ranking of Jerome in late antiquity (and beyond) embodies both negative and positive elements. On the one hand, Scheck asserts that Jerome did not take a coherent view of theological questions (as did his contemporary Augustine) and then, on the other hand, considers Jerome (as did the Council of Trent) to have been the superior scriptural commentator of the Latin Church. Certainly, both Scheck's and the Council of Trent's view of acknowledging and applauding Jerome's pre-eminence as a scriptural commentator challenges McGuckin's (2005) claim that Jerome's reputation as exegete is over-stressed (at least if we look for originality), whilst Scheck's criticism of Jerome (his lack of a coherent approach to theological questions) corresponds quite closely to Freeman's (2009) proposition that Jerome failed to show any genuine intellectual creativity.

Jerome's *Commentary on Matthew* was written in Bethlehem in March 398 and Jerome's dedicatee was Eusebius of Cremona, a priest-friend of Jerome to whom he also dedicated his Commentary on Jeremiah.[180] The precise context of Jerome's writing of his *Commentary on Matthew* was significant.[181] It was a hurried work (two weeks) and Scheck is particularly critical of its 'hasty composition,' of its (at times) 'extreme brevity,' and 'numerous inaccurate citations from the Bible and Josephus'.[182] These criticisms might point to Jeromean inconsistency in the exegesis of the commentary as Scheck (drawing upon A. Souter) seems to suggest.

> Jerome's commentary is not very extensive. He translates the text of Matthew's Gospel in the lemma and then paraphrases or explains the words with brief glosses and commentary notes. Souter has made a study of the use of the text of Matthew's Gospel in Jerome's commentary. The most interesting result is the observation that this text is not identical with the Vulgate revision made by Jerome himself... Souter draws the following conclusion: 'From all this it is clear that Jerome had no particular respect for his own revision...even when he was writing a commentary on a Gospel.'[183]

---

[179] Scheck, St. *Jerome's Commentary* on *Matthew*, 3-4.

[180] Scheck, *Jerome's Commentary* on *Matthew*, 15-16.

[181] Scheck notes that Eusebius 'had requested from Jerome an historical commentary on the Gospel of Matthew to provide him reading material and spiritual sustenance' for his voyage to Italy (16).

[182] Scheck, *Jerome's Commentary* on *Matthew*, 16.

[183] A. Souter, 'Notes on Incidental Gospel Quotations,' *JTS* 42 (1941), 12-18 (13), as cited by Scheck, *Jerome's Commentary* on *Matthew*, 16-17.

However, Scheck finds much that is original in Jerome's Matthew translation. Whilst being partly dependent upon 'Josephus, Origen and Eusebius for geographical or historical details,'[184] Scheck notes how Jerome 'shows evidence of a personal knowledge of the biblical sources, of the topography of Palestine, and of current traditions, Jewish and Christian'.[185] But more than this, Scheck finds Jerome's use of Jewish interpretation to have been more than just creative, observing 'the way Jerome adds important details to the Jewish traditions presented by Origen, which suggests that he had independent access to the Jewish materials'.[186] Additionally, Scheck argues 'Kamesar's recent study confirms that Jerome's very real knowledge of Jewish textual and historical scholarship formed the backbone of his own Scripture scholarship.'[187] Again, these observations on Jerome's biblical philology surely challenge Freeman's (2009) claim that Jerome never showed any genuine intellectual creativity.

By its very nature (composed over a short two week period) Jerome's *Commentary on Matthew*, contains some shortcomings. Scheck states:

> Jerome examines the details in the text that seem interesting to him, or for what he read about them in his sources, or for what he knew about them from personal experience or hearsay. He passes over many other details and sometimes expresses regret that he does not have time to develop his interpretations further.[188]

These concerns are clearly expressed by Jerome in the Preface to his commentary. Writing to Eusebius of Cremona, Jerome declares:

> But you urge me to finish the composition in a fortnight, when Easter is now rapidly approaching, and the spring breezes are blowing; you do not consider when the shorthand writers are to take notes, when the sheets are to be written, when corrected, how long it takes to make a really accurate copy; and this is the more surprising, since you know that for the last three months I have been so ill that I am now hardly beginning to walk; and I could not adequately perform so great a task in so short a time. Therefore, neglecting the authority of ancient writers, since I have no opportunity of reading or following them, I have confined myself to the brief exposition and translation of the narrative which you particularly requested; and I have sometimes thrown in a few of the flowers of the spiritual interpretation, while I reserve the perfect work for a future day.[189]

Here, Jerome's ready admittance to throwing in 'a few of the flowers of the spiritual interpretation' (i.e., the allegorical or mystical sense) should be seen as

---

[184] Scheck, *Jerome's Commentary on Matthew*, 17.

[185] Scheck, *Jerome's Commentary on Matthew*, 17.

[186] Williams, *The Monk*, 227-28, as cited by Scheck, *Jerome's Commentary on Matthew*, 17n.58.

[187] A. Kamesar, *Jerome, Greek Scholarship, and the Hebrew Bible: A Study of the Quaestiones hebraicae in Genesim* (Oxford: Clarendon, 1993), 193-95, as cited by Scheck, *Jerome's Commentary on Matthew*, 17n.59.

[188] Scheck, *Jerome's Commentary on Matthew*, 17.

[189] Jerome, *Pref.* to the *Commentary on Matthew* NPNF² 6:495-96.

an example of that important characteristic of Jerome's exegesis, namely, to equalize the demands of both literal and spiritual interpretation.[190]

Overall, Scheck determines Jerome's *Commentary on Matthew* to have been a successful work.

> Jerome's commentary contains some memorable glosses, such as his paraphrase of the response of Jesus to John at the Lord's baptism: 'You baptize me in water, in order that I might baptize you for my sake in your blood' (3:15)…While it is to be regretted that Jerome did not write at greater length on Matthew's Gospel, what he has set down is dense, Spirit-filled exegesis that draws on all canonical Scripture and is governed by the Church's Trinitarian Rule of Faith.[191]

So far, we have seen that for much of the period of modern Jerome scholarship aspects of Jerome's corpus had simply been viewed as a body of work produced within a circumscribed period of time (early 370s-420). Studying particular features of, and selected texts/writings from, Jerome's corpus in isolation had led to a somewhat narrow, traditional/literalist 'reading' of Jerome (i.e., as ascetic, exegete and scholar). This approach would now change with the publication of two major, radical, landmark studies in the field of modern Jerome scholarship.

The edited collection of essays on Jerome by Andrew Cain and Josef Lössl, *Jerome of Stridon: His Life, Writings and Legacy* (2009),[192] sought to provide a 'new' understanding of Jerome's corpus which might be termed 'historical reality', with the focus upon reassessing Jerome's works not only in terms of Jerome's commitment to seeking scriptural truth (via exegesis) and to the reader, by providing a clearer understanding of that truth (vis-a-vis Jerome's provision of biblical commentaries) but also Jerome's commitment to the patristic writer's task as it would have been understood within a growing Christian worldview. Thus, unlike earlier conventional 'readings' of Jerome which had sought to reveal from Jerome's writings historical facts, or religious and intellectual attitudes, we find in Cain and Lössl's edited collection of essays scholars widening the 'Jerome debate' to include (amongst others) discussions of Jerome's invention of the 'Ascetic Hero;' rethinking Jerome's portraits of holy women; new evidence for measuring Jerome's Hebrew competence; and new evidence for a changing attitude to Jerome. In sum, *Jerome of Stridon* (a collection of case-studies) presents completely 'new', reassessments of much of Jerome's corpus. Perhaps the most interesting essays for our appreciation and understanding of the modern critical reception by scholars of selected texts/writings

---

[190] M. Simonetti, *Matthew* 1a (ACC; Downer's Grove: IVP, 2001), xiv.
[191] Scheck, Jerome's *Commentary on Matthew*, 18.
[192] Cain and Lössl, *Jerome*.

drawn from Jerome's corpus are those by Andrew Cain,[193] John Cameron,[194] Giacomo Raspanti,[195] Ralph Mathisen,[196] Mark Vessey[197] and Josef Lössl.[198]

Cain's essay on rethinking Jerome's portraits of holy women begins with a catalogue of attributes and legacies associated with the saint, which is worth citing as it gives us an insight into the problems Jerome himself faced in his attempts to secure a favourable reception of himself and his body of work, described by Cain as 'his vast and varied literary *oeuvre*'.[199]

Of particular note is Cain's observation that 'Jerome's quest for respectability was further frustrated by the fact that his ecclesiastical status was ambiguous at best and scandalous at worst.'[200] Cain surely has in mind Jerome's exit from Rome in August 385 as a fallen priest following upon accusations of alleged sexual impropriety and for inciting, what was then considered to be, a too extreme Christian ascetic way of life amongst wealthy Roman women.[201]

Despite these problems, Cain believes Jerome managed to achieve for himself partial respectability through his heroicizing of holy women (e.g., Asella, in *Ep.* 24, and Marcella, in *Ep.* 127).[202] Here, Cain's argument must be treated with some caution for, as we have already seen, Jerome was ever the master of self-invention and self-promotion, nowhere else more so than in his letter-writings. And whilst Cain reports the way by which Jerome—through his heroicizing of holy women—'was positioning himself with marvellous subtlety as a figure of virtually apostolic proportions, as the pre-eminent advocate of the true Christian faith in all of its ethical and doctrinal dimensions,'[203] it is a judgement on Jerome that is not supported by all scholars.[204]

Cameron's essay 'The Rabbinic Vulgate?' addressed the question of whether or not Jerome may have sought by means of his biblical translations to replace

---

[193] A. Cain, 'Rethinking Jerome's Portraits of Holy Women,' in *Jerome*, 47-57.

[194] J. Cameron, 'The Rabbinic Vulgate?' in *Jerome*, 117-29.

[195] G. Raspanti, 'The Significance of Jerome's *Commentary on Galatians* in his Exegetical Production,' in *Jerome*, 163-71.

[196] R. Mathisen, 'The Use and Misuse of Jerome in Gaul during Late Antiquity,' in *Jerome*, 191-208.

[197] M. Vessey, 'Jerome and the Jeromanesque,' in *Jerome*, 225-35.

[198] J. Lössl, 'Martin Luther's Jerome: New Evidence for a Changing Attitude,' in *Jerome*, 237-51.

[199] Cain, 'Rethinking', 48.

[200] Cain, 'Rethinking,' 48.

[201] This episode in Jerome's life is not at all clear, with the alleged accusations against Jerome having remained not proven at the time of Jerome's exile and eventual resettlement to Bethlehem in 386. For a useful summary of the events surrounding Jerome's fall from grace, see Rebenich, *Jerome*, 39.

[202] Cain, 'Rethinking,' 56. Asella and Marcella were part of Jerome's ascetic circle in Rome.

[203] Cain, 'Rethinking,' 57.

[204] See, for example, Rebenich, who argues that Jerome's 'tactless pen and his ascetic zeal outraged many of the Roman clergy,' one of the many factors contributing to Jerome's exit from Rome in 385. See Rebenich, *Jerome*, 38.

the OT of the Church with the Bible of the rabbis.[205] Arguing that Jerome did not have such an intention and refuting the charge made by some other scholars that Jerome's Latin translation of the Hebrew Bible is predominantly 'Jewish in spirit,'[206] Cameron contests that Jerome's translation-style (translating the Hebrew text correctly/utilizing Jewish philological expertise), 'does not make the *IH* translations "Jewish," it simply (ideally) makes them (philologically) "correct."'[207] This is an interesting reading by Cameron and closely corresponds to Kedar-Kopfstein's (1968) earlier findings regarding Jerome's two-fold objective in his OT translation work, namely, that 'he wished to furnish for his church an accurate version of the Scriptures for the satisfaction of theological needs and to provide an implement in the polemics against the Jews and heretics'.[208] Cameron's defence of Jerome is a reflection of our other selected essayists each of whom offer generally positive critiques of those areas of Jerome's work they individually examine.

Raspanti's essay on the significance of Jerome's *Commentary on Galatians* in his exegetical production considers the contribution of this particular work to the flourishing of Pauline exegesis in the late antique Latin Church, especially in Rome.[209] *Galatians* is a work of the younger Jerome, composed in 386, which Jerome undertook 'because no earlier writers (writing in Hebrew, Latin or Greek) had interpreted this particular NT letter with the dignity the subject required'.[210]

Raspanti's verdict on Jerome's *Galatians* commentary is that Jerome was possibly inspired to undertake the work in order to match and compete with those biblical exegetes whose reputations were already established in Rome.[211] However, there were to be repercussions. As Raspanti states:

> Jerome's work on Galatians, in which Jerome felt it paramount to turn to the original sources, namely, the Hebrew version of the Bible rather than the Greek of the Septuagint (LXX) or the Old Latin Bible (*Vetus Latini*), led to a number of serious consequences.[212]

---

[205] Cameron, 'Rabbinic,' 117.

[206] For example, H.M. Orlinsky, *Essays in Biblical Culture and Bible Translation* (New York, 1974), as cited by Cameron, 'Rabbinic,' 120n.21.

[207] Cameron, 'Rabbinic,' 120.

[208] Kedar-Kopfstein, 'Vulgate,' 55.

[209] Raspanti, 'Jerome's *Commentary on Galatians*,' 163.

[210] Jerome, *In Gal.* Praef. 6 23-6, as cited by Raspanti, 'Jerome's *Commentary on Galatians*,' 164n.7. Jerome was being somewhat disingenuous since the letter to the Galatians had been interpreted elsewhere by Victorinus, Ambrosiaster, Origen, Didymus, Apollinaris of Laodicea and Eusebius of Emesa. See, Raspanti, 'Jerome's *Commentary on Galatians*,' 164.

[211] Raspanti, 'Jerome's *Commentary on Galatians*,' 165.

[212] Raspanti, 'Jerome's *Commentary on Galatians*,' 165. Again, perhaps the most serious opposition to Jerome's commentary came from Augustine who 'questioned Jerome's exegesis that Paul's confrontation with Peter in Antioch (Gal. 2:11-14) was

Raspanti identifies a major opposition force to Jerome's exegesis of Galatians, namely, 'the Western ecclesiastical communities that considered the Septuagint and the Latin translations based on them to be divinely inspired texts'.[213] It was this body of churchmen who feared that Jerome's commentary, 'By not using a text that was shared across the Western Church,'[214] would encourage further heresies. Here Raspanti's description of opposition forces to Jerome clearly shows the manner in which Jerome's career as a biblical scholar was fraught with difficulties and danger. However, Raspanti argues that by some subtle balance of hermeneutic Jerome was able to appease some of his critics.

Thus Jerome found a defence for his exegesis of Galatians in Paul's own hermeneutic of the Bible, drawing attention to Galatians 3:13b-14, where Paul 'might have made certain textual choices when quoting Deuteronomy 21:23 by resorting to an LXX or an original Hebrew version of the text'.[215] By this means Jerome found an 'opportunity to emphasize the authoritative status of the LXX but also stresses the Apostles deference to the Hebrew original'.[216]

According to Raspanti, what this meant was that 'while Jerome reasserts the ecclesiastical authority of the LXX and its divine inspiration, it is possible for interpreters to work on the Hebrew original because this had been done by the model exegete himself, Paul'.[217]

Jerome's defence of his Galatians exegesis shows some evidence of his intellectual powers. What Jerome was evidently seeking to demonstrate was the legitimacy (however Jerome constructed it) 'to use the Hebrew version of the OT as a reference for making systematic changes to the ancient Latin translations (based on the LXX) known as Vetus Latina'.[218]

In his essay, 'The Use and Misuse of Jerome in Gaul during Late Antiquity,' Mathisen draws out other examples of Jerome's self-promotion, as found in his letter correspondences with the peoples of Gaul.[219] In these correspondences Jerome discussed 'theological questions, biblical exegesis, the Christian lifestyle, and accusations of heresy'.[220] Whether or not Jerome's self-promotional

---

staged to serve the expectations of both Gentile and Jewish Christians.' See Rebenich, *Jerome*, 45.

[213] Raspanti, 'Jerome's *Commentary on Galatians*,' 166.
[214] Raspanti, 'Jerome's *Commentary on Galatians*,' 166.
[215] Raspanti, 'Jerome's *Commentary on Galatians*,' 170.
[216] Raspanti, 'Jerome's *Commentary on Galatians*,' 170.
[217] Raspanti, 'Jerome's *Commentary on Galatians*,' 170.
[218] Raspanti, 'Jerome's *Commentary on Galatians*,' 170. Raspanti notes that 'whilst Jerome's position—the work of those who turn to the Hebrew text to improve the Latin translation of the Bible is legitimate—did not amount to a dismissal of the LXX as a valid basis for theological exegesis, it was perceived as provocative and dangerous (e.g., by Augustine),' 170n.20.
[219] Mathisen, 'Use and Misuse,' 196. Mathisen observes that of the extant correspondence with Gauls, 'The twelve letters that were replies to letters from Gauls were addressed to only eight Gallic addressees' (196).
[220] Mathisen, 'Use and Misuse,'193.

strategy here was successful is in some doubt. For example, on the one hand, Mathisen informs us that 'Jerome and his writings had a wide following in Gaul in the fifth/sixth centuries,'[221] and then he tells us, 'Even though he had more Gallic correspondents than Augustine, he had surprisingly little impact in the fifth and sixth centuries.'[222] Thus Jerome's success or failure in Gaul is yet another question in need of further scholarly examination. Where Mathisen may perhaps be more reliable is in his discussion of the relative standings of Jerome and Augustine in Gaul during late antiquity. Mathisen states:

> Unlike Augustine, whom Gauls debated and cited in the context of several issues, hardly anyone cited Jerome as an authority in any of the fifth and sixth century Gallic theological debates. Jerome was directly cited only once as an authority in a Gallic theological controversy.[223]

It is not as though Mathisen is trying to prove here Jerome's possible failure to effectively theologize as Mathisen's later comments testify:

> As for his genuine works...multitudes of them survived as well as contributed to Jerome being cited later in the Middle Ages as an authority on a multitude of different topics. Jerome therefore recovered from the Gallic failure to appreciate him as much as he would have liked in the fourth and fifth century, and went on to become, in AD 1295, one of the four great doctors of the Western church.[224]

In his 'Jerome and the Jeromeanesque,' Vessey makes the important observation that 'The real history of Jerome... is one of continuous *production*—a history that begins... with Jerome the self-producer.'[225] This 'self-fashioning', argues Vessey, has 'fundamentally influenced the modern reception of Jerome'.[226] In Vessey's view there has been a danger of scholars placing upon the person of Jerome images that are purely speculative and without proper formulation.[227]

---

[221] Mathisen, 'Use and Misuse,' 192.

[222] Mathisen, 'Use and Misuse,' 199.

[223] Mathisen, 'Use and Misuse,' 201. Mathisen cites the debate over the nature of the soul between the Gallic theologians Faustus and Claudianus which took place in the late 460s, where both Faustus (a corporealist believing that the soul had a physical material body) and Claudianus (a incorporealist believing that the soul had no material body or form) claimed support for their respective positions from the writings of Jerome (201-202).

[224] Mathisen, 'Use and Misuse,' 208. For a possible explanation of Jerome's 'Gallic failure' (Jerome's lack of success in advertising his scholarly services to the Gallic Christian community' and in attracting a 'continually growing nucleus of patrons and followers to facilitate the circulation of his writings in their own locales within Gaul)' see A. Cain, *The Letters of Jerome: Asceticism, Biblical Exegesis, and the Construction of Christian Authority in Late Antiquity* (Oxford: OUP, 2009), 195-96.

[225] Vessey, 'Jerome,' 226.

[226] Vessey, 'Jerome,' 226.

[227] Vessey, 'Jerome,' 226.

Vessey goes further to say that 'the "jeromanesque" is what modern historical accounts of Jerome seek to avoid relapsing into... it is the name of ...the vast hinterland of myth, legend and pious invention from which our modern historiography of late antiquity is every day more completely detaching itself'.[228] Vessey suggests:

> Erasmus' repristinated 'Jerome' makes a convenient terminus a quo for all that we may now think of as the scholarship on our subject. With Erasmus' edition we hail the Jerome of philology, history and biography—and the end of the 'jeromanesque'... As we acknowledge Erasmus to be a pioneer of modern philology, so we have him partly to thank for the belief that the posthumous history of literary works and figures like Jerome's is best conceived in terms of 'reception'.[229]

Here, it must be said the Vessey is surely being somewhat optimistic about Erasmus' edition marking the end of the 'jeromanesque' for he has clearly overlooked Williston Walkers' (1918) judgement on Jerome (see chapter 3).

Nevertheless, Vessey's tribute to Erasmus' reception-oriented approach and its impact on the modern historiography of late antiquity (of course, including Jerome) underlines the caution that needs to be taken by scholars in avoiding 'jeromanesque' textual monuments to Jerome.

Finally, Lössl's essay 'Martin Luther's Jerome,' parallels Vessey's contribution in a number of ways. Thus, whilst Vessey's model for the modern reception of Jerome was Erasmus, for Lössl it is Luther. Whilst Lössl accepts that 'one of the major patristic influences on Luther and the development of his thought was Augustine and his reception,'[230] he suggests that with Jerome, 'Luther's relationship was complex.'[231] Nevertheless, Lössl stresses, 'It has long been known that Jerome is one of the authors most referred to by Luther.'[232]

According to Lössl, Luther's admiration of Jerome's 'Hebrew scholarship' was profound yet this did not stop him from amending Jerome's exegesis when he found it wanting; and, whilst critical of some aspects of Jerome's 'dogmatic teaching' he found that on 'the doctrine of grace against the Pelagians, he saw Jerome in agreement with himself and Augustine, against his contemporary Erasmus'.[233]

---

[228] Vessey, 'Jerome.' 229. Vessey suggests the date of 1516—when Erasmus published his edition of the works of Jerome—as being the beginning of that process of detachment from the 'jeromanesque' (229).

[229] Vessey, 'Jerome.' 229-30. Vessey adds, 'He [Erasmus] missed no opportunity to build up Jerome's reputation as the promulgator of sound Biblical learning' (231).

[230] Lössl, 'Luther's Jerome,' 238.

[231] Lössl, 'Luther's Jerome,' 239.

[232] Lössl, 'Luther's Jerome,' 239.

[233] Lössl, 'Luther's Jerome,' 239. Lössl notes: 'It is true... that Luther did not rate Jerome the theologian as highly as Augustine, because in his view he had no understanding of Pauline theology in the way Augustine had and therefore had comparatively little to say about Christ and the faith' (239n.17).

In the light of this Lössl concludes that Luther 'seems to have been a keen student of Jerome the Bible translator, exegete, and interpreter'.[234] Lössl argues that looking at Luther's life as a 'biblical scholar' it seems that Luther may have modelled himself on Jerome, and although not wholly in agreement with Jerome on some 'text-critical points' and on 'Jerome's Hebrew,' Luther's 'regular markings of Jerome's comments (from vol. 2 of Erasmus' *Jerome*) suggests that he agreed with them and learnt from them'.[235]

The second radical, landmark study was the publication of a major monograph on Jerome's letters.[236] For this work Andrew Cain proposed a completely 'new' approach to Jerome's correspondence:

> In this book I take a different but complementary approach to the letters than scholars hitherto have taken. Rather than view them exclusively as either textual artefacts or passive historical document, I steer an interdisciplinary course and draw occasionally from both approaches while calling attention to the letters' often underappreciated but fundamentally propagandistic nature. In particular, I examine Jerome's sophisticated use of literary artistry to construct spiritual and intellectual authority for himself through idealized epistolary self-presentation. Now it is a given that Jerome 'self-presented,' and very self-consciously so, in his correspondence. What needs to be explained is why he presented himself in the way that he did in various circumstances and what the answer can tell us about the driving forces behind not only Jerome the epistolographer but also Jerome the man. Previous scholarship has identified instances of autobiographical manipulation in some of the letters. This book, however, is the first systematic investigation of Jerome's strategies for manufacturing authority across the whole range of his extant correspondence.[237]

The real value of Cain's study is his concentration upon those letters (e.g., the two different collections of Jerome's personal correspondence prior to 393) which scholars have hitherto given little scholarly focus to but which can still provide important information on the apologetic and propagandistic features of Jerome's epistolography.[238] Also of interest to Jerome scholars are Cain's three attached appendices. Cain writes:

> In the first, I propose a new system of classifying Jerome's extant letters that is less anachronistic, and truer to the rhetorical norms of late antique epistolography, than all of the existing taxonomies devised by modern scholars. The second appendix takes inventory of letters by Jerome that are known to be lost. In the third and final appendix, I discuss the medieval manuscript tradition of the letters and conclude that Jerome did not release his complete (or even near-complete) correspondence during his lifetime, as other imperial and post-classical Latin prose epistolographers had done.[239]

---

[234] Lössl, 'Luther's Jerome,' 249.
[235] Lössl, 'Luther's Jerome,' 249.
[236] A. Cain, *The Letters of Jerome.*
[237] Cain, *The Letters of Jerome,* 6.
[238] Cain, *The Letters of Jerome,* 7.
[239] Cain, *The Letters of Jerome,* 12.

What, then, is the nature of the critical reception given by Cain to Jerome's lesser-known letters? First, Cain argues that the letters to miscellaneous people (*Epistularum ad diversos liber – Epp.* 2-13, 15-17) written by Jerome prior to his arrival in Rome in the summer of 382, should be regarded as 'a tightly knit bundle of interlocking propagandistic pieces' and not, as previous scholars have seen, as 'passive documentary sources useful mainly for plotting the chronological, prosopographical, and theological coordinates of the first stages of Jerome's career as a monk-scholar'.[240]

Here Cain's interpretation of the motivation behind some of Jerome's earliest letters corresponds closely with that of Megan Hale Williams who has opined:

> Already Jerome's world was one of elective affinities, held together by common ascetic ideals that linked men and women of varying social statuses across a broad swath of the Mediterranean world. In such a milieu, letters took on an intense symbolic significance. They were tokens of affiliation, not merely vehicles for information.[241]

Williams's contextualization of Jerome's early pre-Rome letters ('tokens of affiliation') is demonstrated in Cain's treatment of *Ep.* 2 (written around 374 from Antioch), a letter in which Jerome asks the [Syrian] monk Theodosius if he might allow Jerome to return and resume his monastic life in Syria. Cain observes:

> Jerome's presentation of himself in *Ep.* 2 as an exemplary sinner, like his description of eremitic topography, is roundly conventional. He invokes familiar biblical imagery to cast himself as the prodigal son and as a lost sheep. This sets the stage for a request for Theodosius' intercessory prayers to free him 'from the darkness of this world'. It is telling that in seeking a remedy for his spiritual malaise Jerome turned not to a figure of the church's institutional hierarchy but to a monastic authority. In doing so, he was configuring his epistolary relationship with Theodosius as that of a disciple and his *abba*.[242]

Whilst Cain's suggestion that Jerome's collection of early pre-Rome letters to various people 'sustained its own explicit propagandistic agenda,'[243] (Cain citing *Ep.* 2 as the first clear example) enabling Jerome to position himself according to the value system of desert Christianity ('encapsulating himself as a model of eremitic holiness')[244] does Cain's subsequent treatment of the Rome correspondence (384-385) and post-Rome letters also show Jerome retaining a

---

[240] Cain, *The Letters of Jerome*, 17.

[241] Williams, 32.

[242] Cain, *The Letters of Jerome*, 19. Cain adds: 'After all, we could expect no less from someone who of all the Fathers was certainly one of the most self-conscious about his contemporary and posthumous reception.'

[243] Cain, *The Letters of Jerome*, 19.

[244] Cain, *The Letters of Jerome*, 21-25.

propagandistic approach or is Jerome seen to adapt other letter-writing strategies?

Significantly, Cain finds in the later Rome letters (384-385) evidence of Jerome campaigning to 'manufacture personal authority for himself early on his career'.[245] In other words, in Rome, Jerome was aiming to achieve 'specific propagandistic goals,'[246] and, as we have already noted earlier, Vessey (1993)[247] has proposed that one of Jerome's aims at this time was to present himself to the Latin-speaking west as the next Origen.[248] According to Cain, there were two other propagandistic goals for Jerome during his residence in Rome: to use letter-writing as 'a convenient literary venue, distinct from but complimentary to his biblical commentaries, for communicating *in absentia* his expert knowledge of the Bible';[249] and, in Jerome's sixteen Roman letters (384-385) to Marcella 'sealing a spiritual and scholarly legacy'.[250] These twin propagandistic objectives during his stay in Rome resulted in Jerome's 'first major successes as a biblical scholar and teacher of asceticism'.[251]

Whereas Cain's critique of Jerome's Rome residency and related letter-correspondence emphasizes Jerome the rising scholar and ascetic, Megan Hale Williams believes that there was a third imperative for Jerome at this particular time. Williams states:

> As his Roman letters reveal, until his flight in 385, Jerome thought of himself as a priest, albeit one dedicated to a strictly ascetic life. His literary activities and his relations with female ascetics took place in the context of his role as a member of the clergy of Damasus, bishop of Rome... Jerome's writings were the only currency he had to spend in his exchanges with persons of greater wealth and influence. Once bishops and aristocrats accepted his writings and publicized their interest in his studies, Jerome's work became valuable.[252]

Finally, Cain's assessment of the post-Rome (non-exegetical letters) letters is considered under the heading of 'The Embattled Ascetic Sage.'[253] After leaving Rome in 385 Jerome finally settled in Bethlehem in 386, where over a period of three years Jerome established a monastery, a convent and a hospice for pious travellers.[254] The intellectual world now influencing Jerome's letter-writing is clearly framed by Cain. Thus:

> The landscape of Christian Latin literature in late antiquity was densely populated by theologians—Ambrose, Jovinian, Jerome, Augustine, and Pelagius, to name

---

[245] Cain, *The Letters of Jerome*, 68.
[246] Cain, *The Letters of Jerome*, 70.
[247] Vessey, 'Jerome's Origen'
[248] Vessey, 'Jerome's Origen,' 135-45.
[249] Cain, *The Letters of Jerome*, 83.
[250] Cain, *The Letters of Jerome*, 89-98.
[251] Cain, *The Letters of Jerome*, 127.
[252] Williams, *The Monk*, 53-54.
[253] Cain, *The Letters of Jerome*, 129.
[254] Rebenich, *Jerome*, 41.

but a few—who were driven by a sense of responsibility to educate fellow Christians about how they could best live their faith. In the course of propagating their ideas in writing, all of them constantly engaged to one degree or another in self-justification in order to explain on what authority they taught. Because none of them was writing in a vacuum for himself alone, each inevitably had to clarify to readers in his own (polemical or non-polemical) way why his approach was to be embraced to exclusion of other approaches. Jerome was no different. In fact, he went to greater lengths than most to make the case for why his teachings were intrinsically more beneficial than the ones promulgated by writers with whom he competed for a sympathetic audience.[255]

Cain then examines a selection of Jerome's epistolography from the Bethlehem fears (386-c.419). Of special interest here is Cain's consideration of how Jerome's 'ambiguous ecclesiastical status affected his reception as an authority figure'.[256] Jerome was by now a shamed priest living in exile and, as Cain highlights, 'because Jerome was not a bishop his writings, like those of fellow freelancing monks Pelagius and Rufinus, did not come with the sanction of episcopal authority, as did those of other contemporary writers such as Ambrose and Augustine'.[257]

So, what of these Bethlehem years and Jerome's associated correspondence? Is there any evidence here for Cain's assertion that one of Jerome's fundamental concerns now was 'the unsettling realization that he was but one of many spiritual authorities attempting to make his voice distinctly audible, and attractive-sounding, in an already noisy room'.[258] First, citing *Ep.* 54 (395) to Paula's cousin Furia, on the question of chaste widowhood, and *Ep.* 65 (397) sent to Principia, where Jerome explains why he gave preferential treatment to his female Scriptural students, Cain argues the case for Jerome's use of 'personal exhortation'—a device by which Jerome offers wise counsel.[259] This device is observed at work again in *Ep.* 79 (399) where he writes to a widow (Salvina) offering her advice on ways to uphold her widowhood.[260] Such consolatory letters as these (there were ten in total) were often composed to offer words of comfort to persons afflicted by grief. And yet they also contained an undercurrent of propaganda (e.g., encouraging the bereaved to live a virtuous Christian life of renunciation and poverty).[261] Cain's judgement upon the probable efficacy of Jerome's spiritual advice as contained in his Bethlehem consolatory epistles is unequivocal:

Key facets of Jerome's profile seriously impaired his efforts to establish himself in the eyes of contemporary Christians as a credible figure of spiritual authority.

---

255 Cain, *The Letters of Jerome*, 129.
256 Cain, *The Letters of Jerome*, 143.
257 Cain, *The Letters of Jerome*, 143.
258 Cain, *The Letters of Jerome*, 129-30.
259 Cain, *The Letters of Jerome*, 132-34.
260 Cain, *The Letters of Jerome*, 134.
261 See Rebenich, *Jerome*, 119-20.

In the light of this, two pertinent questions arise. What did Jerome claim was his right to speak on spiritual matters in the first place and then to set himself up as a guide for others? Along these same lines: how did he attempt to distinguish himself from rival spiritual writers with whom he competed for a following?[262]

Among the 'key facets of Jerome's profile' hampering Jerome's ability to make himself a credible figure of spiritual authority were, of course, his reputation as a disgraced priest and lack of episcopal rank. Cain describes these 'key facets' in some detail.[263] But, again, what of Cain's thesis that the 'Bethlehem years' were largely occupied by the urgency for Jerome to get 'his voice distinctly audible, and attractive-sounding, in an already noisy room?'[264] Cain's proposition is given some credence by Megan Hale Williams's treatment of the 'Bethlehem years', years in which she identifies Jerome's 'productive tensions' (symbolized by the question of Jerome's readership being inextricably linked to his relations with his patrons).[265] Thus, Jerome's pressing need to make his writings attractive to readers and patrons alike is stated by Williams:

> Numerous passages of Jerome's writings, especially his letters, show that texts circulated in his day, and among his peers and correspondents, in ways their authors did not anticipate and could not regulate... In his relations with readers and patrons—and in particular, with readers who were also patrons—Jerome had no choice but to cede control over his works... During almost the whole of his productive career, Jerome's relations with readers and patrons played out in the midst of intense theological controversy... These disputes, furthermore, largely took place within the same close-knit network of elite, ascetic Christians in which Jerome's works had their primary currency, so that they intersected at crucial junctures with Jerome's efforts to draw upon that network to reach readers and to secure patronage.[266]

It is significant that Jerome's last surviving letter of spiritual exhortation, *Ep.* 130 (written in 414 to the virgin Demetrias) shows Jerome still dependent upon this 'close-knit network of elite, ascetic Christians,' which was so essential for the promulgation of Jerome's ideas.[267]

Cain's critique of *Ep.* 130 provides clear evidence of this dependence. Noting that Demetrias was 'a teenage virgin from the *gens Anicia*, which next to

---

[262] Cain, *The Letters of Jerome*, 144-45.

[263] Cain, *The Letters of Jerome*, 132-34, 142-44.

[264] Cain, *The Letters of Jerome*, 129-30.

[265] Williams, *The Monk*, 233-60.

[266] Williams, *The Monk*, 234-35. Williams adds: 'The relations between Jerome in Bethlehem, and a circle of monks, priests and bishops in southwestern Gaul, carried on over a period of several decades and lasting until Jerome's death, exemplify the complex patterns by which letters, literary works, and financial patronage circulated between Jerome and his correspondents' (245).

[267] According to Megan Hale Williams, Jerome's 'lifelong argument was for a hierarchy of salvation based on a hierarchy of ascetic renunciation'. See Williams, *The Monk*, 235.

the *gens Ceionia* was the most prestigious family in the late Roman west,'[268] Cain establishes how in *Ep.* 130 Jerome acts as ever the 'self-referential' mentor of virgins and 'spiritual advisor—by-correspondence,'[269] strongly exhorting Demetrias (who had taken the virgin's veil) to remain a life-long virgin and to remain faithful to her religious vocation. Thus, Jerome opens his letter to Demetrias:

> I am to write to Demetrias, a virgin of Christ, who ranks first in the Roman world in nobility and wealth... Her grandmother and mother are both women of distinction, and they have the authority to command, faithfulness to seek out and perseverance to obtain what they ask for. They do not indeed request from me anything new or special, I whose talents have often been exercised upon subjects of this sort.[270]

However, it is precisely this self-referential tone (common to much of Jerome's Bethlehem correspondence) which Cain believes ultimately damaged Jerome's legitimacy as a spiritual and ascetic authority.[271] As Cain concludes:

> Jerome was but one of many Christian spiritual writers in the late fourth and early fifth centuries who competed for a sympathetic audience. Various problematic aspects of his profile... overshadowed his efforts to legitimize himself and his fringe cause among the wider Christian community. To make matters worse for him, the open field of composition, of which he was uneasily aware... virtually guaranteed that his ascetic authority could never be taken for granted as being absolute and undisputed—and indeed it was not, even (sometimes) by those in his inner circle, as the Jovinianist affair made abundantly clear. Jerome accordingly went to great lengths to convince prospective followers why he was a more competent spiritual director than his many rivals and why his teachings were intrinsically superior to theirs.[272]

This final judgement by Cain on Jerome's Bethlehem years (386-c. 419), though clear and robust, has one major weakness. To imply, as Cain does above, that Jerome's asceticism/spirituality was a 'fringe cause among the wider Christian community' is questionable. There is certainly no scholarly consensus on the subject. For example, the strongest argument against Cain's tendentious claim against Jerome can be found in Rebenich (2002), whose study of the saint's role in the public discourse on asceticism shows Jerome to have been an ascetic and an often irascible mentor to many Christian men and women, and one who shaped the ideals of Christian chastity and poverty for generations. Rebenich certainly does not find Jerome's asceticism/spirituality to have been of marginal interest amongst the wider Christian body.

---

[268] Cain, *The Letters of Jerome*, 160, citing M.T.W. Arnheim, *The Senatorial Aristocracy in the Later Roman Empire* (Oxford, 1972) 50.

[269] Cain, *The Letters of Jerome*, 158-66.

[270] Jerome, *Ep.* 130.1, as cited by Cain, *The Letters of Jerome*, 161.

[271] Cain, *The Letters of Jerome*, 166.

[272] Cain, *The Letters of Jerome*, 166.

His [Jerome's] forced departure from Rome was in no way followed by the collapse of the ascetic network carefully constructed by Jerome during his stay in Rome. Letters, treatises, commentaries, and handbooks were addressed to influential Italian patrons like Marcella and Pammachius, who paid for the copyists and secured the **distribution of Jerome's work.** Messengers were sent on special missions delivering orders and inquiries and keeping Jerome in touch with the Christian circles of the western world. Their main task was to maintain communication between Palestine and Italy. His Roman friends were also in contact with ascetic groups in northern Italy, Gaul and Spain whom Jerome approached after he had taken up residence in Bethlehem.

His works of this period responded to the intellectual needs and literary interests of a constantly increasing number of Christians of birth, eloquence, and wealth; that is, of ecclesiastical ad secular dignitaries, who advocated the theological tenets of *fides catholica* and supported the ascetic movement. From among such people—men and women whose prestige and influence, according to Paulinus of Nola, rested on honour, education and possession—the supporters of the ambitious author were recruited. The bond of ascetic and orthodox friendship was now strengthened by an exchange of letters.[273]

---

[273] Rebenich, Jerome, 41-42.

Chapter 6

Modern Jerome Scholarship (2010-2014)

Introduction

Of all the periods of modern Jerome scholarship covered by this study it is during this most recent phase that we witness scholars delving ever more deeply into Jerome's canon to understand and assess Jerome's work as a biblical scholar. Scholars were now tackling a variety of themes which included (amongst others): Jerome's success (or otherwise) in looking to the original language of the OT to discover the literary quality of Scripture; Jerome's early learning environment; Jerome's Latin tradition of Pauline exegesis; Jerome's opinion of women (the female weakness in Jerome's letters); Jerome's contribution to the construction of Christian authority in late antiquity; Jerome's divine-inspired dreams and their relation to the doctrine of God and Christology; parallels between the exegetical works of Cyril of Alexandria and Jerome; biblical interpretation in Jerome's *Vita Hilarionis*; analysis of Jerome and Augustine on the 'Antioch Incident' (Gal. 2:11-14); comedy in Jerome's *Vita Malachi*; Jerome's use of biblical models; Jerome's *Prologus Galeatus* and the OT canon of N. Africa; and Jerome's recent increased reputation within international and ecumenical circles for spiritual and intellectual greatness.

2010-2011

Before proceeding further, it is important to appreciate just how far patristic research had developed by the first decade of the twenty-first century. Brian Daley, S.J. has written:

> Every academic discipline has its growth points, even though it may not always be obvious to people practising the discipline just what those growth points are. In the field of Patristic studies, one of those areas of new interest and development today is clearly early Christian exegesis: how the writers of the early Church, whose works have survived, interpreted and applied to their lives the Hebrew and Greek writings that came to be recognized, over the first three centuries or so of the Church's life, as the Christian canon of Scripture.[1]

Daley then adds a telling rider: 'modern Christian students of the Bible, since the time of the Enlightenment, have tended to be dismissive, if not contemptuous, of the Fathers' attempts to find and express Scripture's meaning'.[2] Interestingly, we

---

[1] B.E. Daley, S.J., 'Christ, The Church, and the Shape of Scripture: What we can Learn from Patristic Exegesis,' in P. Walters (ed.), *From Judaism to Christianity: Tradition and Transition* (Leiden and Boston: 2010), 267-88 (267).

[2] Daley, 'Christ, the Church, and the Shape of Scripture', 267.

certainly found elements of this criticism in some of the early modern scholars' secondary judgements on Jerome as found in chapter 3 of this study. However, what is surprising about Daley's essay is the complete omission of Jerome from his selection of those 'influential and representative fathers, stretching from the late second to the early fifth centuries' who took Christ 'as the unifying center of Patristic biblical interpretation'.[3] Daley's essay can be juxtaposed with Michael Graves' 'The Literary Quality of Scripture as Seen by the Early Church,'[4] where Jerome's 'stream of thought' (Jerome looking to the original language of the OT to discover the literary quality of Scripture) is compared to Augustine's 'stream of thought' (Augustine exploring the literary quality of Scripture by reflecting on the relationship between human conventions and divine inspiration).[5] For Graves both Jerome and Augustine are defined by their 'reaching beyond standard Graeco-Roman cultural conventions in their assessment of biblical texts'.[6]

In his critical reception of Jerome, Graves treads a prudent path between criticism and praise. According to Graves, Jerome's 'initial reaction to the Old Testament as literature was not positive,'[7] with Jerome declaring 'his early assessment of the prophets was that "their style seemed rude and repellent".'[8] Yet, Jerome later came to like the OT as literature. How? Graves offers the following explanation:

> [O]nce he acquired some proficiency in Hebrew, he realised that Hebrew has its own kind of literary quality, which naturally does not come through in translation. Early in his serious study, while discussing the basic difficulty that a translator faces in trying to render the literary beauty of any work into a second language, Jerome explained that the Old Testament only seemed like bad literature to learned men because it was not actually written in Greek or Latin, but in Hebrew: 'Thus it has come about that the sacred writings appear less adorned and lyrical, because the aforementioned men are unaware that they have been translated from Hebrew …What is more melodious than the Psalter? What is more beautiful than the songs of Deuteronomy or Isaiah? What is more elevated than Solomon? What is more polished than Job?'[9]

---

3 Daley, 'Christ, the Church, and the Shape of Scripture,' 272. Here, Daley overlooks Jerome in favour of Irenaeus, Origen, Athanasius and Augustine, though he does admit that his four selected early Christian biblical interpreters were 'chosen almost randomly'.

4 M. Graves, 'The Literary Quality of Scripture as Seen by the Early Church,' *Tyndale Bulletin* 61.2 (Jan 1, 2010), 161-82.

5 Graves, 'The Literary Quality of Scripture,' 161.

6 Graves, 'The Literary Quality of Scripture,' 162.

7 Graves, 'The Literary Quality of Scripture,' 170.

8 Jerome, *Ep.* 22:30, as cited by Graves, 'The Literary Quality of Scripture,' 170.

9 R. Helm (ed.), *Eusebius Werke, Siebenter Band: Die Chronik des Hieronymus* (Berlin: Verlag, 1956), 3-4, as cited by Graves, 'The Literary Quality of Scripture,' 170n.28.

Elsewhere, Graves commends Jerome's 'belief in the artistic quality of the Old Testament in Hebrew'[10] (Isa. 23:4; Jer. 6:2-3) as well as Jerome's 'solid grasp of the artistic capabilities of the Hebrew language'.[11]

> Jerome's manner of appreciating the Hebrew Bible can be summed up in his comment on Isaiah 22:6: 'elegantly it resounds in Hebrew, and also the sense is most beautiful'. Jerome's commentaries never lose their focus on the content of the biblical text, but they also show his awareness and appreciation of the artistic qualities of the Hebrew.[12]

Following these observations, Graves ventures to assert, 'Jerome represents the high point in the first line of argument in defence of Scripture (specifically, the OT) as artistic literature.'[13] Here, Jerome's innovative exegesis in bringing late fourth and early fifth century readers the 'beauty' and 'elegance' of Scripture was especially important. As Denis Farkasfalvy has observed:

> Certainly, the members of the early Church with a Jewish background simply retained their Jewish ideas about the Bible, but, because of their faith in Christ's messianic identity and divinity, they also began to read the Hebrew Bible with a new outlook and gave it a new interpretation.[14]

Thus, Jerome's important contribution to helping the early Jewish readers of the Hebrew Bible to view its text anew cannot be underestimated. Graves concludes:

> Jerome's major contribution to appreciating the literary quality of Scripture is the recognition that it must in some sense be taken on its own terms. Of course, his efforts in this direction were primarily limited to the Old Testament. But Jerome successfully demonstrated that the Old Testament in the original Hebrew did in fact possess artistic merit as literature, and that it only appeared to have a low style because it was being read in translation...Thus, while the monocultural Greeks were content to work with their Greek translations of the Old Testament, the Roman Jerome, who was already accustomed to reaching into a second culture (Greek), was intellectually ready to venture into a third (Hebrew). Once Jerome entered into the thought world of Hebrew, he could see that the Hebrew Old Testament has its own way of being artistic.[15]

This important secondary judgment on Jerome seriously challenges Freeman's (2009) assertion that Jerome 'never showed any genuine intellectual creativity'.

---

10 Graves, 'The Literary Quality of Scripture,' 171.
11 Graves, 'The Literary Quality of Scripture,' 172. Graves comments 'Following tracks laid by Origen and Eusebius, Jerome demonstrated more than any other that the Old Testament was artistic when read in the original Hebrew?'
12 Graves, 'The Literary Quality of Scripture,' 172.
13 Graves, 'The Literary Quality of Scripture,' 172
14 Farkasfalvy, *Inspiration and Interpretation*, 23.
15 Graves, 'The Literary Quality of Scripture,' 179-80.

Like Graves, Pauline Nugent has compared Jerome with Augustine, but this time focusing upon the influences of their early education upon their later development.[16] Nugent considers both Jerome and Augustine to have been 'patristic literary figures and effective practitioners of pedagogy'.[17]

With regard to Jerome, Nugent makes some telling points. For example, she cites evidence from Jerome's *Adv. Rufinus* (I 4.30) as proof of Jerome's 'wondrously tenacious memory while defending himself against the charge that he had broken a vow he had taken while ill never again to read secular literature'.[18] Drawing upon Jerome's *Ep.* 128, Nugent highlights the importance Jerome attached to the understanding and value of the proper use of language, a skill he would apply in his own work as a biblical scholar.

> Let her [Gaudentius' little daughter Pacatula] learn the alphabet, spelling, grammar and syntax. To induce her to repeat her lessons with her little shrill voice, hold out to her as rewards cakes and meads and sweetmeats... Reward her for singing psalms that she may love what she has to learn. Her task will then become a pleasure for her, and no compulsion will be necessary.[19]

Jerome's experience of a generally happy early learning environment (a liberal education) stood him in good stead for his life as a polemicist, well able to reply to any accuser with aplomb, verve and eloquence.

Elsewhere in 2010 a growing interest in Jerome's *Commentary on Galatians* was occupying a number of scholars, in particular Andrew Cain[20] and Thomas P. Scheck.[21] We will start by considering Cain's *JTS* essay, 'An Unidentified Patristic Quotation in Jerome's Commentary on Galatians (3.6.11).' First, Cain's essay begins with a minor discrepancy. Cain states that Jerome's Galatians commentary was drafted 'during the summer of 386'.[22] This is clearly at variance with the ascription of '387' given in *The Principal works of St. Jerome*.[23] And

---

[16] P. Nugent, 'Patristics and Pedagogy: Jerome and Augustine,' *StP* 49 (2010), 3-7.

[17] Nugent, 'Patristics and Pedagogy', 4.

[18] Nugent, 'Patristics and Pedagogy', 4.

[19] Jerome, *Ep.* 128.1, as cited by Nugent, 'Patristics and Pedagogy,' 6n.14.

[20] A. Cain, 'An Unidentified Patristic Quotation in Jerome's *Commentary on Galatians* (3.6.11),' *JTS.* 61.1 (April 2010), 216-25. See, also, St. Jerome, *Commentary on Galatians* (tr. A. Cain; FOTC, 121; Washington: Catholic University of America Press, 2010).

[21] *St. Jerome's Commentaries on Galatians, Titus, and Philemon* (tr. T.P. Scheck; Notre Dame: University of Notre Dame Press, 2010).

[22] Cain, 'An Unidentified Patristic Quotation,' 216. Cain writes: 'In composing his *Commentary on Galatians* he [Jerome] drew from an impressive array of Greek exegetical sources including Galatians commentaries by Didymus the Blind, Apollinaris of Laodicea, Eusebius of Emesa, Theorus of Heraclea, and, most of all, Origen,' 216-217. Of his dependence upon these great Greek writers Jerome stated that he had 'plucked flowers out of their gardens, so that the Commentary was more theirs than his'. See Jerome, *Pref. to Commentary on Galatians*, NPNF[2] 6:497.

[23] NPNF[2] 6:495.

whilst the focus of Cain's article is the identification of the 'anonymous author'[24] of an interpretation of Galatians 6:11 (itself quoted and criticized by Jerome in his Galatians commentary) which reads the verse as showing that Paul was unable to write Greek, Cain does not take issue here with Jerome's claim that he was the first to provide a Latin translation of Galatians.[25] Jerome's self-promotion (which we have already seen to have been a key feature of Jerome's character and working-style) is much in evidence in his *Preface* to his *Commentary on Galatians.*

> I will approach a work [Galatians] unattempted by any writers in our language before me, and which scarcely any of the Greeks themselves have handled in a manner worthy of the dignity of the subject.[26]

For Jerome students the value of Cain's essay is Cain's argument for Eusebius of Emesa being the 'anonymous author' of the unidentified Patristic quotation in Jerome's *Commentary on Galatians* (3.6.11) and his demonstration of Jerome's critical engagement with Eusebius and, in particular, with his commentary on Galatians.[27] Here, Cain's use of the phrase 'critical engagement' is surely a plus for Jerome and decidedly more generous than 'derivative'—a term which perhaps some Jerome critics might have applied. Equally, of course, it partly challenges Freeman's (2009) claim that Jerome proved too pedantic a thinker ever to engage fully with the intricacies of Greek philosophy, and that Jerome never showed any genuine intellectual creativity. So how does Cain judge Jerome's Latin interpretation of Paul's epistle?

We will now compare Cain's *JTS* essay with his FOTC translation of Jerome's *Commentary on Galatians* to see whether or not Cain gives a positive critical reception to Jerome's exegesis. First, Cain makes some preliminary observations about Jerome. Thus:

> In his own lifetime Jerome was an extremely marginalized figure. He was not a bishop but a non-practicing priest who... found himself outlawed by the institutional church. All but a tiny minority of like-minded Christians found his hard-line ascetic philosophy even remotely appealing. He was no Augustine; technical scholarship was his strong suit, not theological synthesis.[28]

On this last point, of course, if Cain is right in this judgment of Jerome, then it gives support to the Freeman (2009) claim that Jerome never had the self-confi-

---

[24] Identified by Cain as being Eusebius of Emesa, 216.

[25] However, elsewhere, Cain does show that the 'Latin Exegetical Tradition' did pre-date Jerome. In Cain's FOTC translation of Jerome's *Commentary on Galatians*, he points to Marius Victorinus (who produced a Galatians commentary in the 360s) and Ambrosiaster (who produced two Galatian editions between 378 and 384). See St. Jerome's *Commentary on Galatians* (tr. A. Cain), 30-31.

[26] NPNF[2] 6:496.

[27] Cain, 'An Unidentified patristic Quotation,' 225.

[28] A. Cain, 'Introduction' in St. Jerome, *Commentary on Galatians* (tr. A. Cain), 15.

dence to develop his own theology. How well does Cain's assessment of Jerome—'technical scholarship was his strong suit, not theological synthesis'—fit into his critique of Jerome's Galatians commentary?

Acknowledging that Jerome hurried his Galatians commentary, and that it was framed by Jerome 'as a piece of consolatory exegesis offered up in her [Marcella's] honor'.[29] Cain suggests that 'The credibility of the *Commentary* itself is... significantly reinforced in as much as it is implied to be the fruit of Jerome's close spiritual and intellectual bond with a circle of exemplary women.'[30]

Overall, Cain is inclined to offer Jerome's Galatians commentary an ambivalent critical reception. First, he praises Jerome.

> Jerome's *Commentary on Galatians* is an extraordinary learned work... The Latin classics surface at every turn in the form of direct quotations, paraphrases, or allusions. Sometimes Jerome borrows others' phraseology in order to enhance his own prose... On a few occasions Jerome uses classical literature as a polemical counterpoint to Christian literature... he cites Terence's famous line, 'Flattery attracts friends, and truth, hatred,' in conjunction with Paul's remark, 'Have I now become your enemy by telling you the truth?' He proceeds to show how inferior Terence is to Paul: 'The Apostle has tempered his statement to those he had called fools and infants and has personalized it, targeting individual people and the Galatian Christians. The poet, however, went perilously astray by making a generalized statement about universal behaviour.'[31]

But, what of Jerome's technical scholarship? Whilst acknowledging that Jerome's Galatian commentary owes most to Origen's work on the same subject, Cain rejects Simonetti's claim that Jerome's Pauline commentaries 'are little more than paraphrases of Origen'.[32] However, Jerome's technical scholarship is put into question by Jerome's own self-admission of failing to carefully structure his work: 'I summoned my secretary and dictated either my own or others' ideas, all the while paying no attention to the method, the words, or the opinions belonging to each.'[33] Such a way of working was hardly conducive either to technical accuracy (of the correct attribution and utilization of his own and others' ideas) or proper theological synthesis (of the biblical text).

Cain then becomes critical of Jerome and is quick to make clear the unsatisfactory nature of Jerome's 'compositional technique':

> Jerome remains vague and does not so much as hint at the proportional make-up of this mixture. This ambiguity and the fact that for individual interpretations he almost never names his Greek sources (virtually none of which survive anyway) make it next to impossible, in most instances, to pinpoint what truly original contributions Jerome may have made to the exegesis of Galatians.[34]

---

29 Cain, 'Introduction,' 17.
30 Cain, 'Introduction,' 17-18.
31 Jerome, *Comm. Gal.* 2.4.15-16, as cited by Cain, 'Introduction,' 20n.65.
32 Simonetti, *Biblical Interpretation*, 99, as cited by Cain, 'Introduction,' 29n.110.
33 Jerome, *Pref.* Bk. 1, as cited by Cain, 'Introduction,' 29.
34 Cain, 'Introduction,' 29-30.

Here, Cain's highly critical judgement on Jerome as exegete raises the spectre of McGuckin's (2005) appraisal of Jerome as exegete (of his reputation as exegete being over-stressed at least if we look for originality). There remains much ambivalence about Cain's reading of Jerome in regard to the commentary on Galatians. On the one hand, he calls it 'an extraordinary learned work'.[35] Then he raises doubts over its 'compositional style' and raises a question over its originality as a piece of Pauline exegesis. Having said all that, Cain then concludes his critique by offering some final praise for the work:

> Jerome was the greatest biblical scholar of the ancient Latin Church. His *Commentary on Galatians* represents his first substantial attempt at systematic biblical interpretation. Since he articulated in it the hermeneutical methodology that would come to dominate his later exegetical work, it stands as a key witness to a formative stage in his intellectual development. When compared with the other five extant Latin commentaries on Galatians from the fourth and early fifth centuries, Jerome's *Commentary* stands out for the rigor of its biblical textual criticism, the breadth of its classical and patristic erudition, and its research-intensiveness and expository thoroughness... Its greatest achievement lies in its preservation of a treasure-trove of otherwise lost Greek exegetical wisdom. This point remains valid even despite the unfortunate fact that, due to Jerome's eclectic compositional technique, the vast majority of this content cannot be firmly assigned to any specific Greek author.[36]

Whilst Cain here extols Jerome's virtues as an exegete it also omits to mention (even disguises) Cain's earlier criticisms. The one really positive note Cain strikes—and one that we have seen earlier scholars register—is Jerome acting as a theological resource for his contemporaries and later successors (Jerome's Galatians Commentary preserving 'a treasure-trove of otherwise lost Greek exegetical wisdom').

We can now ask whether or not Scheck's translation of Jerome's Galatians commentary offers a positive or negative critique of Jerome as exegete. In his 'Introduction' to his translation, Scheck bewails the paucity of English editions of Jerome's commentaries available to scholars and notes that 'in modern Scripture scholarship, St. Jerome's commentaries are almost completely neglected, even in Catholic circles'.[37] However, there is no doubt at all that Scheck is a Jerome apologist. Scheck states:

---

[35] As does Thomas P; Scheck. See *St. Jeromes' Commentaries on Galatians, Titus, and Philemon* (tr. T.P. Scheck), 23.

[36] Cain, 'Introduction,' 49-50. Cain adds, 'It was not long after its release in late 386 that Jerome's *Commentary* began to have an impact on the exegesis of Paul in the West. It influenced the Galatians commentaries of Augustine (394-395), Pelagius (406-409). It was quoted authoritatively by many early medieval commentators on Galatians...During the Middle Ages, Robert Grosseteste and Thomas Aquinas used it as a source for their own commentaries on Galatians, as did several leading Reformation figures such as Martin Luther and John Calvin' (50).

[37] Scheck, 'Introduction,' 2.

Jerome's is the lengthiest and most learned of the ancient patristic commentaries on Galatians. His work occupies 130 columns in Migne, which compares with 43 columns for Augustine's commentary, 51 for Victorinus's, 36 for Ambrosiaster's, and 19 for Pelagius's.[38]

But, is the length of a commentary any indicator of its quality? Acknowledging Jerome's own admission in his *Preface* to Book 3 that his work lacked polish, Scheck, like Cain above, suggests that 'in spite of this we are dealing with a formidable piece of exegesis'.[39]

And, again, this is notwithstanding Scheck's reference to J.N.D. Kelly's criticism that Jerome's commentaries [Ephesians and Galatians] were poor, as a result of 'Jerome's failure to understand, much less present adequately, the profound theological issues with which those letters are concerned.'[40]

So, what are the positives and negatives in Scheck's introductory critique? Scheck writes:

> Overall Jerome's exegesis of St. Paul represents a deeply Catholic synthesis of faith and post-baptismal good works, wherein paschal grace is seen as the source of the grace that enables the merits and achievements of Christian asceticism and discipleship. He supports fundamental themes in the Catholic interpretation of St. Paul, such as the distinction between pre- and post-baptismal works; pre- and post-baptismal merit; the claim that love, as a complement to faith, is equally necessary for salvation and is intrinsic to the process of the human being's justification; that St. Paul's polemic against 'works of the law' is directed primarily at the ceremonial works of the old law, not at law or good works in general; and finally that the good works that issue from faith formed by love have meritorious value before God, as an outworking of paschal grace. These themes will retain a firm place in Catholic theology in subsequent centuries.[41]

These then are the positives. But, for Scheck, there are some important negatives as well.

> There is not complete consistency or clarity in the Jerome interpretation of the Paul/Peter conflict at Antioch. In fact Jerome's remarks under 2:6 and 2:14, for example, seem to assume that the conflict was real. Moreover, Jerome apparently did not wish to dogmatize on this subject...Jerome suggests that both Peter and Paul were behaving under a spontaneous (not planned) pretense for the sake of their respective audiences, Jewish and Gentile Christians.[42]

What is interesting is that in giving overall praise to Jerome's exegesis of Paul's Galatians commentary (e.g., it represents a deeply Catholic synthesis of faith) Scheck's critique stands in direct contrast to Cain's assessment of Jerome, that

---

[38] Scheck, 'Introduction,' 23 n.60. Here Scheck notes, 'These calculations were given in Plumer, *Augustine's Commentary on Galatians*, p. 33.' See E. Plumer, *Augustine's Commentary on Galatians* (Oxford: OUP, 2003).

[39] Scheck, 'Introduction,' 23.

[40] Kelly, *Jerome*, 147, as cited by Scheck, 'Introduction,' 24 n.64.

[41] Scheck, 'Introduction,' 30-31.

[42] Scheck, 'Introduction,' 31.

'technical scholarship was his strong suit, not theological synthesis'. Here such critical scholarly variations like a number of cases we have witnessed before, mar any attempt to objectively judge Jerome against the 'McGuckin-Freeman' thesis.

Temporarily moving away from the issue of Jerome's exegesis, scholars in 2010 were again returning to Jerome's letters. We shall consider here two examples: Hilmar M. Pabel's review of Andrew Cain's *The Letters of Jerome*,[43] and Valeria Novembri's essay 'Philosophia and Christian Culture'.[44]

Pabel's review of Cain's book begins optimistically, extolling Cain's 'intellectual sophistication and authoritative clarity'.[45] Pabel finds Cain's interpretation of Jerome's letters as 'rhetorical performances in their own right that promoted Jerome's astral career ambitions of asserting himself as a leading authority on asceticism and biblical scholarship in Latin Christianity' (as opposed to either textual artefacts or passive historical documents).[46]

Of course, a book review is a strange creature, offering as it does secondary judgements on another scholars' secondary judgements (in this case Pabel on Cain on Jerome). Despite this, Pabel manages to elicit from Cain's book some new and valuable insights, especially in answering the following question, 'Why did Jerome persistently blow his own horn even to the point of distorting historical reality?'[47]

> First, Jerome did all he could to advance his controversial hermeneutic of appealing to the original biblical languages, especially Hebrew. Second, and equally controversially, as a *novus homo* or a provincial outsider he sought to plant his flag squarely among the Christian literary elite, whose authority usually rested on episcopal dignity. Cain admirably supports the second claim, which seems to attract his attention more compellingly than the first. He believes that in documenting Jerome's constant effort to assert his tenuous authority he has pursued 'a more neutral line' than the 'reductive' cynicism of the scholars who view Jerome's 'apparent bravado' as a product 'of a character defect or of rhetoric gone awry' (198). That may be his intention, but cynics might yet take comfort in Cain's exposition of the rhetorical strategies of Jerome, who comes out more as an egotistical 'rogue priest' (141) than an exegete to be pitied for crying in the wilderness. His book is by no means a hagiography, but the parenthetical reference to 'Jerome's sincere sense of Christian charity' (152) in the analysis of ep. 125 is surprising, given the relentless and riveting scrutiny of Jerome's 'triumphalist rhetoric' (198).[48]

---

[43] H.M. Pabel, review of A. Cain, *The Letters of Jerome: Asceticism, Biblical Exegesis, and the Construction of Christian Authority in Late Antiquity* (Oxford: OUP, 2009); *Church History* 79.3 (Sept. 2010), 683-745

[44] V. Novembri, '*Philosophia* and Christian Culture: An Antidote for Female Weakness in Jerome's Letters,' *StP* 44 (2010), 471-85.

[45] Pabel, review of Cain, 683.

[46] Pabel, review of Cain, 684.

[47] Pabel, review of Cain, 684.

[48] Pabel, review of Cain, 684.

Here Cain's interpretation of Jerome's early letter (through Pabel's critique) clearly seeks to temper those traditional portraits of Jerome we have too often become accustomed.[49]

Pabel concludes his review of Cain's book with further praise for its salutary contribution to modern Jerome scholarship:

Cain completes his study with three appendices. They propose a new taxonomy for Jerome's letters, identify lost letters, and review the early manuscript tradition of epistolary collections. Sixty years ago Paul Antin dismissed the effort to classify the letters as 'arbitrary', a critique that obviously did not deter Cain... Rhetoric, not taxonomy, is Cain's focus, of course. He admirably succeeds not only in revealing the deliberate, rhetorical performances that Jerome's letters are but also in reviving interest in a collection of fascinating documents of ancient Christianity. Cain has emerged as an indispensable Hieronymist for his colleagues as well as for a wider readership.[50]

In Novembri's essay '*Philosophia* and Christian Culture' we find another scholar who, like Cain, is keen to help retrieve Jerome from his somewhat ubiquitous image as a flawed character. In this case, it is Jerome's opinion on women which comes under the spotlight. Novembri states:

As anyone of his readers knows, Jerome's opinion on women is truly dualistic, and with no doubt the implacable Christian polemist inherited this double evaluation from the two-sided judgement on women elaborated in the classical world, but he substantiated it, holding up with a variety of assessments firmly rooted in the Christian thought since its very beginning, through the influence of the Jewish culture.[51]

Noting how 'Jerome's dualistic thought... was perfectly in line with these traditions: the classical and the Biblical one,' and how, 'in his writings we notice a constant mingling of elements taken from both the pagan philosophers and from the Holy Scriptures, even on this matter he relies on the two different sources, both in praise and in blame of female beings,'[52] Novembri, wisely, perhaps on this topic (a notoriously controversial one) adopts a balanced stance, recording both Jerome's negative evaluations of women with those times when Jerome wrote commendations (often in his letters) of positive female models.

Novembri makes make one judgement on Jerome's treatment of women that is particularly telling: 'as for his caustic attitude towards women, Jerome appears as Juvenal's most direct heir: no one, with the exception of Tertullian maybe, had depicted such pitiless female portraits as Jerome did'.[53] She then describes how

---

[49] For example, as found in Murphy et al, *A Monuments to St. Jerome*.

[50] Pabel, review of Cain, 685.

[51] Novembri, '*Philosophia*,' 471.

[52] Novembri, '*Philosophia*,' 472. Here Novembri states, 'To express the double perspective on women Jerome often uses the long-established Christian contrast between the two opposite figures of Eve, cause of death and perdition, and Mary, donor of a new life: *Mors per Evam, vita per Mariam*, he writes to Eustochium [*Ep.* 22-21].'

[53] Novembri, '*Philosophia*,' 473.

in his writings Jerome regarded 'weakness as a distinctive feature of the female sex,' and 'to the human infirmity, women have to add the one typical of their sex, and they have to overcome this one at first, in order to reach an equal position with men'.[54]

Novembri gives further illustration of what she deems to be Jerome's caustic attitude towards women:

The other attribute constantly used by Jerome to characterize women is *fragilitas*… When the brilliant satirist has to praise a woman, he says she is *oblita sexus* and *fragilitatis immemor*, that is to say she forgave her sex and overlooked her weakness, like Fabiola [*Ep.* 77.9], who consecrated herself to the ascetic life and sought for loneliness, or like Paula [*Ep.* 108.14], who craved for living with her young companions among the Egyptian monks.[55]

As to the possible genesis of Jerome's sometimes negative attitude towards women Novembri is careful to remind us that 'in fact, Jerome shares the classical opinion according to which women were unreliable, inconsistent, always changeable in their minds: [*Feminarum*] *mutabilis fluctuansque sententia, si suo arbitrio reliquantur* (Ep. 130.17)'.[56] But, is this a sufficient defence for Jerome's apparent 'antifeminism'? Novembri offers a further explanation for the possible foundation for Jerome's sometimes disparaging remarks about women.

It is a matter of evidence that the passionate Bible commentator could use the same negative evaluation of women also as an interpretative category in his exegetical works, in contexts that were already deeply influenced by the Jewish 'antifeminism'. In a passage taken from the *Commentarium in Isaiam* warning to escape any occasion for arrogance, we read that people who will exhibit their own success, then will enervate all their virtues and 'loosing their male strength, will be led in female weakness'.[57]

Novembri adds a final qualification to Jerome's negative attitude towards women, stating that Jerome believed that 'women reveal the frailty of their gender by the weakness of their soul'.[58]

---

54 Novembri, '*Philosophia*,' 474.
55 Novembri, '*Philosophia*,' 474.
56 Novembri, '*Philosophia*,' 475.
57 Jerome, *Comm in Esaiam* 11 39. 3-8, as cited by Novembri, '*Philosophia*,' 475n.26. Novembri finds similar evidence of Jerome's Jewish-inspired 'antifeminism' in his *Comm. In Amos* 3 6:12-15, where he 'interprets the horses of the prophet (being manly strong souls free of the powers of evil…fortified by God's might)', who, when they find an effeminate mind, weakened by perfumes and pleasures, and turned to female weakness,' are unable 'to stop up, are driven insane and act as they want' (475n.27).
58 It is surprising (and unhelpful) that Novembri does not reference the source of Jerome's words here. However, Novembri does observe that 'In his allegorical analysis of some passages of the Holy Scriptures, Jerome associates any reference to women and the weaker sex also with the matter (*materia*), explaining that 'women are next to material things.' Jerome, *Comm. In Eccl.* 2.8, as cited by Novembri.

Finally, what of Jerome's positive comments about women? Here Novembri cites Jerome's recognition of 'female prophets in the Bible (e.g. Deborah, Huldah and Hanna)'[59] and his declarations that 'in the service of Christ differences of sex are not worth, but of mind' [*Comm. In Esaiam* XII, *prol.*],[60] and 'among proselytes there is no difference, but men and women are equally called to salvation' [*Comm. In Esaiam* XV 56.3].[61] Novembri states:

> Therefore, we may conclude that, in spite of all the attacks against female weakness, Jerome is surely less misogynistic than he can appear...if we have a look to his whole work, we notice that a large number of writings is addressed to women, and this was not common indeed at his time.[62]

Jerome could recognise women's equality with men on a spiritual level and their importance in certain passages of the Holy Scriptures (e.g., the great female characters of the OT). This latter point—that Jerome acknowledged how the Bible exalted women's life[63]—is significant, for Jerome felt that he was compelled to address so much of his letter correspondence to women because they (and not men) longed for the Scriptures.[64]

Novembri concludes her essay by considering Jerome's 'ultimate female model,' described by Jerome in his portrayal of Marcella, where he 'commends not only her "virtue and ability," her "holiness and purity," and her longing for the Christian knowledge and the ability in learning... and the reading method to apply to the Scriptures'.[65] Thus, for Jerome it was to be, 'the Christian education (the authentic *philosophia*)'—emphasizing 'the virtues acquainted through the Christian way of life (moderation and modesty)'—that would allow women 'to overcome the weakness and the vices connatural to their sex.'[66]

In 2010 Andrew Cain published the first of what would be two studies examining the importance of Jerome's patron, Paula, for Jerome's corpus.[67] Paula's support for Jerome in Bethlehem was crucial for 'Jerome believed that his work as a biblical scholar thrived in the Holy Land, as it could in no other place on earth.[68] Cain observes:

---

59 Novembri, '*Philosophia*,' **476.**
60 Novembri, '*Philosophia*,' **477**n.32.
61 Novembri, '*Philosophia*,' **477**n.33.
62 Novembri, '*Philosophia*,' **477.**
63 Novembri, '*Philosophia*,' **479.**
64 Jerome, *Ep.* 65.1, as cited by Novembri, '*Philosophia*,' **478**n.37.
65 Jerome, *Ep.* 127.7, as cited by Novembri, '*Philosophia*,' **483.**
66 Novembri, '*Philosophia*,' **484**-85.
67 A. Cain, 'Jerome's Epitaphium Paulae: Hagiography, Pilgrimage, and the Cult of Saint Paula,' *JECS* 18.1 (2010), 105-39. Cain writes 'Paula was the chaste widow, benefactress of the poor, monastic foundress, and most famously patron of Jerome' (105). In 2013 Cain (as editor) published a fuller account of Jerome's Epitaph on Paula. See A. Cain (ed.), *Jerome's Epitaph on Paula: A Commentary on the Epitaphium Sanctae Paulae* (Oxford: OUP, 2013).
68 Cain, 'Jerome's Epitaphium,' 113.

About two years after moving to Bethlehem he wrote that the one who has studied Judea with his own eyes has a clearer comprehension of Scripture. In several letters sent to Western Christians from the middle 380s on, Jerome tried to persuade correspondents that being in the Holy Land, as either a pilgrim or a permanent resident, provided a unique spatial context within which to authenticate their faith.[69]

Cain cites as of special significance Jerome's *Ep*. 108, which was 'intended to be circulated broadly throughout the Christian world,'[70] and it offered Paula 'to contemporary aristocratic Christians…as the embodiment of his teachings about sacred geography and the Christian's duty to deepen his or her faith by going on pilgrimage'.[71]

Cain's reception of *Ep*. 108 is measured and balanced, and particular reference is made to the epistle's value in presenting Paula 'as the epitome of Jerome's ascetic, theological and scholarly special interests… having an unwavering commitment to orthodoxy and a disgust of Origenism.[72] *Ep*. 108 is also an important 'cultic document'.[73] On the question of 'whether Jerome conceived *Ep*. 108 to be the textual underpinning of a cult of St. Paula,'[74] Cain writes, 'After capturing the essence of Paula's eternal victory in a triptyoh of scriptural allusions, Jerome goes on to characterize her as a martyr——a powerfully suggestive way to claim that she belongs, in death as in life, to the spiritual elite of Christianity.'[75] Cain concludes:

In life she [Paula] made much of his scholarship possible in the first place through her patronage and had given it a degree of legitimacy by virtue of her endorsement. In death, she continued to validate his labours by lending a retroactive seal of saintly approval to them.[76]

And, again,

He [Jerome] promoted Bethlehem as a major Christian cult center and even more ambitiously as the spiritual (and scholarly) center of gravity of the universal church.[77]

---

[69] Cain, 'Jerome's Epitaphium,' 113.

[70] Cain, 'Jerome's Epitaphium,' 117.

[71] Cain, 'Jerome's Epitaphium,' 120.

[72] Cain, 'Jerome's Epitaphium,' 122.

[73] Cain, 'Jerome's Epitaphium,' 124.

[74] Cain, 'Jerome's Epitaphium,' 125.

[75] Cain, 'Jerome's Epitaphium,' 126. Cain notes: Paula, even prior to her death, had been the object of something approximating cultic devotion throughout the Christian world' (132).

[76] Cain, 'Jerome's Epitaphium,' 138.

[77] Cain, 'Jerome's Epitaphium,' 138. Cain adds: 'Paula did become officially recognized as a saint by the Latin church, possibly as early as within a generation of her death, and her canonization is directly attributable to the literary activity of Jerome' (139).

In Stark's monumental study, *The Triumph of Christianity*,[78] following upon his earlier *The Rise of Christianity*,[79] Stark considers Jerome very briefly (with minimum coverage) in the context of 'The Church of Power' (i.e., the Church during the period of Emperor Constantine (306-337) and after, to 400).[80] After 341 (Council of Sardica) 'the Church had faced increasing tensions within the ranks of bishops and clergy which had resulted in dissolute, corrupt, lax and insincere persons gaining high positions'.[81] It is here that Stark notes the following observation made of Jerome: 'St. Jerome attacked many clerics of his era for having entered the church mainly in order "to have access to beautiful women".'[82]

Is it not perhaps ironic that of all the aspects of Jerome's work(s) that Stark might have made acknowledgment to, he merely chooses Jerome's invective against assumed imposter clerics motivated by assumed thoughts of sexual gratification? Here, of course, is the double irony that it was Jerome himself who, having become a priest, was then sent away from Rome (in 385) following accusations of sexual impropriety. Stark's failure to offer fresh judgement (assessment) on Jerome's *oeuvre* and his dependence on a sole secondary-source citation (itself leaning heavily towards the 'jeromanesque') is, to say the least, disappointing.

Also in 2011 scholars renewed their interest first, in Jerome's views of divine-inspired dreams and their relation to the doctrine of God and Christology,[83] and second, in reassessing Jerome's commentary on Isaiah.[84]

Wei's essay describes how 'Divine-inspired dreams in patristic texts were a unique locus where epiphany took place, and humanity could encounter the divine "visually and tangibly".'[85] Wei states:

> Almost all of the patristic dream texts which narrate or discuss dream epiphany appear in the context or treatises that aim to demonstrate the doctrine of God or Christology by representing the divine images and attributes. When many church fathers encountered the dreams in which epiphany manifests, they not only interpreted them but doctrinalized them, just as what they did to all other phenomena or

---

[78] R. Stark, *The Triumph of Christianity: How the Jesus Movement became the World's Largest Religion* (New York: Harper One, 2011).

[79] R. Stark, *The Rise of Christianity: How the Obscure, Marginal Jesus Movement Became the Dominant Religious Force* (San Francisco: Harper San Franscisco, 1997).

[80] Stark, *Triumph*, 300-301. 'The Church of Power' was the main body of the Church as it evolved in response to the immense status and wealth bestowed on the clergy by Constantine (300).

[81] Stark, *Triumph*, 300-301.

[82] N. Cheetham, *Keeper of the Keys: A History of Popes from St. Peter to John Paul I* (New York: Scribner, 1983), 23, as cited by Stark, *Triumph*, 308.

[83] S.L. Wei, 'Doctrinizing Dreams: Patristic Views of Divine-inspired Dreams and their Relation to the Doctrine of God and Christology,' *StP* 50 (2011), 73-86.

[84] M.R. Crawford, 'Scripture as "One Book": Origen, Jerome, and Cyril of Alexandria on Isaiah 29:11,' *JTS* 64.1 (April, 2011), 137-53.

[85] Wei, 'Doctrinalizing Dreams,' 73.

aspects of human life. At the same time, they melted the two doctrines into their explications of the dreams.[86]

On Jerome's reference to, and use of, divine-inspired dreams, Wei focuses upon two writings in particular: *Epistola* 22 and *Apologia contra Rufinum* 1.30, in both of which Jerome described his dream in which he met the Lord who stood before him as the Judge.[87] This famous encounter whereby Jerome was accused by the Judge of being a follower of Cicero (and not of Christ) and then duly flogged for his sin, revealed to Jerome that the Lord judges in the present time and not only at the Last Judgement. Wei considers this event (Jerome's 'Cicero' dream) was seen by Jerome as 'a holy place where the Lord appeared, and his divine court was held'.[88] But is Wei correct in his interpretation? We shall look now at Jerome's own recording of the event.

In *Ep.* 22.30 Jerome writes:

> Suddenly I was caught up in the spirit and dragged before the judgment seat of the Judge...amid the strokes of the lash... I was tortured more severely still by the fire of conscience, considering with myself that verse, 'In the grave who shall give thee thanks?' [Ps. 6.5]... Accordingly I made an oath and called upon His name, saying: 'Lord, if ever again I possess worldly books, or if ever again I read such, I have denied Thee...' And that this was no sleep nor idle dream, such as those by which we are often mocked, I call to witness the tribunal before which I lay, and the terrible judgment which I feared. May it never, hereafter, be my lot to fall under such an inquisition! I profess that my shoulders were black and blue, that I felt the bruises long after I awoke from my sleep, and that thenceforth I read the books of God with a zeal greater than I had previously given to the books of men.[89]

Whilst Jerome does suggest in *Ep.* 22.30 that his 'Cicero' dream-encounter was sited in a 'holy place' ('Suddenly I was caught up in the spirit and dragged before the judgement seat of the Judge'), he does not actually describe that he found himself before a 'divine court'. Rather he describes the setting as a 'tribunal', akin to an 'inquisition'. It would seem then, that Jerome's use of such 'hard' adjectives suggests he did not feel he was in the presence of a 'divine court' (ie., a court of law).

---

86 Wei, Doctrinalizing Dreams,' 73-74. Wei is careful to note that it was not only church fathers like Tertullian, Jerome and Augustine, who made reference to divine-inspired dreams but also other early Christians such as Constantine and Martin of Tours (79, 83).
87 Doctrinalizing Dreams,' 81.
88 Doctrinalizing Dreams,' 81.
89 Jerome, *Ep.* 22.30, NPNF[2] 6:35-36. Elsewhere, Stefan Rebenich has noted: 'His [Jerome's] conversion was followed by the radical negation of his former conduct and implied the revocation of his classical (i.e., 'gentile') education and the subsequent study of the Bible and Christian authors...We may conclude that this [Jerome's 'Cicero' dream account] magnificent piece of showmanship refers to Jerome's decision to serve God taken in Trier in about 370.' See, Rebenich, *Jerome*, 9.

The value of Crawford's essay 'Scripture As "One Book",' lies in its clear demonstration of a Jerome-Origen linkage in the exegesis of Isaiah 29:11. Crawford states:

> Jerome's exegesis [of Isaiah 29:11] is indebted to Origen's argument, found in book 5 of his *Commentary on the Gospel of John*, that the numerous individual books of Scripture are 'one book' in the divine Word who unites them. Thus, Origen's exegetical labours continued to have influence beyond the outbreak of the Origenist controversy, even among those authors who otherwise took issue with his legacy. This instance highlights one way the patristic exegetical tradition developed, as later authors mined and redeployed the exegesis of their predecessors to meet new challenges in their own day.[90]

However, Crawford's example of Isaiah 29:11, where he finds Cyril of Alexandria's exegesis of the '"sealed book" discussed in the passage as Scripture which is spoken by one "Holy Spirit" and so "is called one book,"'[91] closely paralleling Jerome's interpretation, must be treated with caution. The suggestion that Jerome may have influenced Cyril of Alexandria is extremely implausible. Cyril did not, and could not, read works in Latin. Crawford's error is compounded further by his statement 'it seems likely that Cyril had recourse to Jerome's commentary'.[92]

An interesting example of Jerome acting as a 'theological resource' for others was identified by James Papandrea in his study of the third-century priest of Rome, Novatian.[93] Here the Jerome-Novatian linkage is of particular interest in that both were (at different times) priests of Rome and both held steadfast to their Christian faith whilst, at the same time, creating enemies amongst their contemporaries.[94] On Jerome's contribution to our knowledge of Novatian, Papandrea refers to Jerome's citations in *On Illustratious Men*, 70, the *Apology in Answer to Rufinus* 2.19, and *Ep.* 10.2, 42.1.[95] However, Papandrea offers a word of caution regarding the total reliability of Jerome's writings about Novatian. For example, though Jerome was aware of 'the true authorship of [Novatian's] *On the Trinity*, he confused Novatian with Novatus'.[96] And yet, somewhat ironically, given Papandrea's censure of Jerome, we find Papandrea's own study—extolling Novatian as a 'brilliant character of the early church'[97] whose exposition of Christology [in *On the Trinity*] showed him to be 'both the spokesperson for the

---

90 Crawford, 'Scripture as "One Book",' 137.

91 Crawford, 'Scripture as "One Book",' 137.

92 Crawford, 'Scripture as "One Book",' 140.

93 J.L. Papandrea, *Novatian of Rome and the Culmination of Pre-Nicene Orthodoxy* (Eugene: Pickwick, 2011).

94 See Papandrea, *Novatian*, xi. Novatian has been described as a 'schismatic Christian author'. See R.M. Grant, *Greek Apologists of the Second Century* (London: SCM, 1988), 189.

95 Papandrea, *Novatian*, x.

96 Papandrea, *Novatian*, 122n.4.

97 Papandrea, *Novatian*, ix.

church of Rome in the mid-third century and ahead of his time,'[98]—to be perhaps not entirely as historically and theologically reliable as he would have wished. Whilst acknowledging that there have been some doubts raised over the authorship of *On the Trinity*,[99] Papandrea somewhat irritatingly consistently refers to the work as 'his' [Novatian's].[100] However, Robert Grant has disagreed and his reading of Novatian's theological importance is very different from that of Papandrea.

> Novatian was certainly not a creative or original theologian, and we are not surprised to see him make use of a conventional discussion from Theophilus. A rhetorical passage on God in the second chapter of Novatian's *On the Trinity* is certainly based on Theophilus' earlier discussion, 'If you call him Light you speak of his creature more than himself; if you call him majesty you describe his honor more than himself. And why should I make a long story by passing through individual items?'[101]

It is significant that in contrast to Grant, Papandrea omits any mention of Theophilus of Antioch's direct influence upon Novatian's work, though he does go so far as to state that: 'Novatians language is not precise, and at times he falls back on the language of earlier *Logos* Christology. However, even if he inherited some terminology from Theophilus, he does not mean what Theophilus meant. The proof of this is in Novatian's [*On the Trinity* 31.3] definition of the generation of the Son as an eternal state of being, rather than an event.'[102]

We shall now focus upon two studies[103] both of which demonstrate the continuing scholarly debate on, and interest in, Jerome's contribution to the development of Christian doctrine and asceticism during the fourth and fifth centuries.

In his *Retrieving Nicaea*, Khaled Anatolios traced Jerome's response to the conflict over the differentiation of *ousia and hypostasis* between pro-Nicene and anti-Nicene forces which had continued despite the council held at Alexandria

---

[98] Papandrea, *Novatian*, xii.

[99] Papandrea, *Novatian*, 122. Papandrea records: 'Eventually, *On the Trinity* continued to be read under other names, including Tertullian and Cyprian.'

[100] Papandrea, *Novatian*, 122.

[101] Grant, *Greek Apologists*, 189-90. Here, Grant notes that 'much of the surrounding context also comes from Theophilus' first book' (190), and Theophilus' 'Book 1 belongs to deliberate oratory' and 'He begins the book with a denunciation of false rhetorical language' (143-44).

[102] Papandrea, *Novatian*, 87n.48. Papandrea further explains the distinction between Novatian and Theophilus: 'Theophilus had described the generation of the Logos as a movement from *in* the Father to *with* the Father, which implies an inherent change from a lack of distinction to a diminished connection. Novatian [*On the Trinity* 31.3] departed from Theophilus's meaning by maintaining both the external distinction between the Father and the Son, as well as the eternal connection.' See Papandrea, *Novatian*, 149n.17.

[103] K. Anatolios, *Retrieving Nicaea: The Development and Meaning of Trinitarian Doctrine* (Grand Rapids: Baker Academic, 2011); A. Nightingale, *Once Out of Nature: Augustine on Time and the Body* (Chicago: University of Chicago Press, 2011).

(362), headed by Athanasius, to resolve the matter and to finally determine a pro-Nicene consensus.[104] Anatolios looks at one of Jerome's letters (*Ep.* 15) for evidence of Jerome's posturings over, and involvement in, the development of the effort to constitute that agreement. Anatolios writes:

> Jerome became embroiled in the controversy, expressing his shocked disapproval of the language of the three *hypostaseis* to Pope Damasus and articulating the tri-unity as 'one substance, three persons' (*una substantia, tres personae*).[105] Jerome's discomfort with the three-*hypostaseis* language of Basil [of Caesarea] and Melitius is readily explicable since the Greek term *hypostasis* can be literally transcribed into Latin as *substantia*. It was under such pressures that Basil came to insist on a distinction between the signification of the terms *ousia* and *hypostasis*. As Jerome had protested, such a distinction was rather novel as inasmuch as the two terms were regularly employed as synonyms. Nevertheless, the construction of such a distinction became invaluable inasmuch as the affirmation of being that underlies both terms ensured that both the unity and the distinction within the Trinity were confessed as having equally radical ontological status.[106]

This is as far as Anatolios goes and his utilization of Jerome's *Ep.* 15 is disappointingly brief, not fully exploring either the complexity of the letter nor Jerome's display of confusion within it and his hesitancy in fully stating his own position on the 'three hypostaseis' issue.

We need to look more closely now at *Ep.* 15 (one of Jerome's early letters written in 376 or 377). The letter illustrates Jerome's attitude towards the see of Rome held by Damasus, afterwards his warm friend and admirer. In the letter he asks Damasus which is the correct terminology, to speak of three 'hypostases' in the Godhead, or of one? Jerome is appealing here for guidance.

> My words are spoken to the successor of the fisherman, to the disciple of the cross. As I follow no leader save Christ, so I communicate with none but your blessedness, that is with the chair of Peter... I reject Meletius... Just now, I'm sorry to say, those Arians, the Campenses, are trying to extort from me, a Roman Christian, their unheard of formula of three hypostases. And this, too, after the definition of Nicaea and the decree of Alexandria, in which the West has joined... If you think fit enact a decree; and then I shall not hesitate to speak of three hypostases. Order a new creed to supersede the Nicene; and then, whether we are Arians or orthodox, one confession will do for us all... And can anyone, I ask be so profane as to speak of three essences or substances in the Godhead? There is one nature of God and one only... whosoever in the name of religion declares that there is in the Godhead three elements, three hypostases, that is, or essences, is striving really to predicate three natures of God...may the faith of Rome never come to such a pass! ... Let us be satisfied to speak of one substance and of three subsisting persons—perfect, equal, coeternal.[107]

---

104 Anatolios, *Retrieving*, 22-23.
105 Jerome, *Ep.* 15.4, as cited by Anatolios, *Retrieving*, 23n.27.
106 Anatolios, *Retrieving*, 23-24.
107 Jerome, *Ep.* 15, NPNF² 6:18-19.

Here Jerome appears strident in his pro-Nicene faith but at the end of his letter confusion and hesitancy become apparent.

> I implore your blessedness, therefore, by the crucified Saviour of the world, and by the consubstantial trinity, to authorize me by letter, either to use or to refuse this formula of three hypostases.[108]

Jerome's plea for direction from Damasus was surely unnecessary since the Nicene Creed had declared the Son to be 'of one substance with the Father'. What it does show—admittedly at the stage in Jerome's life when he was yet to develop fully his career and reputation as a bible scholar—is some evidence for Freeman's (2009) stricture that Jerome was prone to cling to Nicene orthodoxy, failing to think creatively beyond it, and lacked the self-confidence to develop his own theology.

In our second study—Andrea Nightingale's *Once Out of Nature*—a renowned Stanford classicist reconsidered the Jerome-Augustine asceticism axis.[109] However, there are problems with her account. Nightingale finds Jerome's three hagiographic *Lives*[110] particularly important as key examples of Christian asceticism, and that whilst Jerome was interested in describing early ascetic practices, Augustine (unlike Jerome) 'had no interest in the counterworld of the desert'?[111] But, Nightingale's statement here is seemingly contradicted by the following:

> Augustine himself praises the desert hermits and admonishes people who believe that they have restricted humanity altogether: 'I will say nothing of those who, in complete solitude—far from the eyes of men—inhabit completely deserted regions, living on water and basic bread, which is brought to them periodically. There, they enjoy a communion with God, to whom they cleave with pure minds... Many think that they have deserted human life more than is fitting, without considering how much these hermits (whose bodies we are permitted to see) benefit us by their prayers and their exemplary lives.'[112]

---

[108] Jerome, *Ep.* 15, NPNF² 6:20. It is important to note here that the Neo-Nicenes (and later theology) spoke of one substance/essence and three hypostases in the Trinity. But 'substance' and 'hypostasis' had previously been used virtually as synonyms – hence Jerome's reluctance to accept three hypostases. In asking for Damasus' advice Jerome is not saying he can't deal with the problem himself, but is treating a pope with deference.

[109] Nightingale, *Once Out of Nature*, 141-44.

[110] Jerome, *Life of Paul the First Hermit*, *Life of Hilarion*, and *Life of Malchus*. Of these first two *Lives*, Nightingale writes: 'Jerome offers a new kind of monk-hermit as a model for educated man in the Christianized empire.' See Nightingale, *Once Out of Nature*, 19.

[111] Nightingale, *Once Out of Nature*, 141. Here Nightingale observes, 'Of course, the life of the desert hermit inspired more enthusiasm among Christians in the Greek East than in the Latin West.'

[112] Nightingale, *Once Out of Nature*, 142.

Nightingale then adds: 'But, in spite of this praise of these "unseen" hermits, Augustine chose the city over the desert, the church over the cave.'[113] Certainly this delineates the nature of the Jerome-Augustine ascetic axis in a clearer and more satisfactory way. But, equally, there was a special union within the Jerome-Augustine ascetic axis, to be found in their mutual agreement on 'the body'. Thus, 'Augustine joined Ambrose, Jerome, and others who adopted a two-tier model [of the body], in which the ascetic "athletes of Christ" were considered holier than ordinary Christians.'[114]

In contrast, Vermes, in his *Christian Beginnings*, makes four value-judgements on Jerome. First, Jerome was one of the most important sources (together with Irenaeus, Origen and Eusebius) from within patristic literature in respect of the Jesus image of the Acts of the Apostles.[115]

However, this claim has been challenged by Bart Ehrman,[116] illustrating, yet again, how scholarly contradictions surround Jerome. Second, Vermes considers Jerome to have played a significant part in the fate of the Epistle of Barnabas. Vermes records:

> The Epistle of Barnabas... came close to being accepted as part of the NT, possibly because of its fictional attribution to Barnabas, senior colleague of St. Paul in Antioch according to the Acts of the Apostles. The epistle was acknowledged as belonging to the canon of sacred Christian literature by the great third-century Alexandrian authorities, Clement and Origen, and as such was included in the oldest Greek Bible, the fourth-century Codex Sinaiticus. Subsequently, however, it was firmly downgraded by the church and relegated to the category by the church and relegated to the category of the extra-canonical writings, as we learn from Eusebius (EH 3.25, 4) and from St. Jerome (*De viris illustribus* 6).[117]

Here, Vermes holds Jerome to be a useful source of information about one particular community in the nascent church.

---

[113] Augustine, *De Mor.* 66, as cited by Nightingale, *Once Out of Nature*, 142. Nightingale notes: '*In The Catholic and Manichaean Ways of Life*, Augustine also praises the life of monks (67-68), which he seems to prefer to that of hermits.'
[114] Nightingale, *Once Out of Nature*, 181.
[115] G. Vermes, *Christian Beginnings: From Nazareth to Nicaea, A.D. 30-325* (London: Allen Lane, 2012), 85. According to Vermes, other important information 'may be obtained from traditions stemming from the Judaeo-Christians called Ebionites (the Poor) or Nazarenes (followers of Jesus of Nazareth) and preserved in patristic literature' (85).
[116] B.D. Ehrman, *Did Jesus Exist? The Historical Argument for Jesus of Nazareth* (New York: Harper One, 2012), 106-13.
[117] Vermes, *Christian Beginnings*, 135-36. Vermes notes, The Ep. Of Barnabas furnishes 'a valuable insight, independent from the NT, into the life and ideas of the early followers of Jesus' and 'the home ground of the Epistle... is supposed to be in Egypt, most likely Alexandria, as its characteristic use of allegorical OT interpretation would suggest' (136).

Thirdly, Vermes cites Jerome's importance as a source for our information about Origen—the third century 'philosopher, theologian and biblical expert all in one'.[118] Vermes states:

> [Origen] was the most versatile, exciting and influential Church Father in the early centuries of Greek Christianity. His life story was recorded by Eusebius (*EH* 6. 1-8, 15-39). Origen was an extremely productive writer. St. Jerome credits him with two thousand books (*Ad Rufinum* 2.22). He is arguably the most outstanding witness of the development of Christological ideas in the pre-Nicene church.[119]

And, fourthly, Vermes upholds the views of earlier scholars regarding Jerome's importance in the post-Nicene Christological debate.

> Despite the decision obtained by the victorious *pro-homoousios* [i.e., the Son was cosubstantial with God] party, the Christological struggle continued for over half a century. At times the Arian opposition triumphed, as may be deduced from Jerome's ironical remark after the Council of Ariminum (Rimini) in 359, 'The whole world groaned and was surprised to find itself Arian.' (*ingemuit totus orbis at Arianum se esse miratus est* '*Altercatio Luciferiani et orthodoxi* 19 in Migna, PL 23, 181B).[120]

Perhaps, this might suggest that contrary to Freeman's (2009) dismissal of Jerome's theological powers (Jerome failed to think creatively beyond Nicene orthodoxy), Jerome was at least an important contributory, and outspoken polemicist on the debate on Nicene orthodoxy and its opponents.

We will now consider Christopher Beeley's *The Unity of Christ*. In this major text Beeley (like Vermes) considers Jerome to be a significant source for our understanding and knowledge of Origen.

> Origen towered above all earlier theologians of record as the great master—or, in some cases, the persistent nemesis—of those who undertook to do serious theology for several centuries... Origen synthesized much of the theology that others had produced before him, and by the end of his life he had become the most highly regarded Christian authority of international scope since the apostles... Jerome tells

---

[118] Vermes, *Christian Beginnings*, 213.

[119] Vermes, *Christian Beginnings*, 213.

[120] Vermes, *Christian Beginnings*, 233. Vermes notes: Arius introduced the adjective homoousios into the Christological debate only to discard it straightaway as unsuitable for expressing the orthodox doctrine' (231). And 'the end came in 381 when Emperor Theodosius I made the profession of Arianism illegal. Thereafter cosubstantiality carried the day and went on to feel the kind of philosophically based dogmatic evolution that was launched at Nicene...The comment of Ephesus (431) specified that Christ's divinity and humanity were rooted in one single divine person, and the Council of Chalcedon (451) condemned the monophysite heresy, and proclaimed that the single divine person of the *Logos* made flesh harboured two separate natures, one divine, the other human' (234).

us that Origen's mother taught him to recite the Psalms at a young age (*Ep.* 39-22).[121]

Despite this reference to Jerome, Beeley shows an ambivalent attitude to Jerome's achievements and corpus. For example, whilst Beeley readily cites the important attributions to patristic tradition and development of Christianity in late antiquity (200-800 CE) of Origen, Eusebius, Athanasius, Augustine, Cyril of Alexandria, Marcellus of Ancyra, Hilary of Poitiers, Ambrose of Milan and Leo of Rome—he does not acknowledge Jerome.[122]

Whilst unwilling to include Jerome amongst his list of fourth century authorities (he only reviews Eusebius, Athanasius, Gregory of Nazianzus, Gregory of Nyssa and Emperor Constantine I),[123] he does not mention Jerome as a contributor to the construction of orthodoxy.[124]

This downgrading of Jerome by Beeley—a feature also of Stark's (2011) study—is surprising to say the least. Where Beeley identifies a significant role for Jerome—chronicling certain theological developments in the fourth century—it is still limited to the carrying forward of Origen's theological legacy.

> In his Origenist phase, Jerome landed both Pamphilius [a priest who studied under the Origenist teacher Pierius]. Jerome himself boasted of owning twenty-five volumes of Origen's *Commentary on the Twelve Minor Prophets copied by Pamphilius,* which is regarded with such joy as if he possessed the riches of Croesus (*Vir. ic.* 75. 1-2)... Jerome held Pierius in high esteem and dubbed him 'Origen junior' (Jerome, vir. Iii. 76).[125]

Beeley states that the theological legacy of Origen carried forward by Jerome (until Jerome's break with Origen in 393) was the 'emphasis on the divinity and distinctness of Christ against radical subordinationism, monarchian modalism, and Gnosticism, and a defense (or correction) of Origen against accusations of holding heretical views on the soul and the resurrection.'[126]

Finally, Beeley credits Jerome (alongside Hilary, Ambrose and, above all, Augustine) with helping Latin theology come 'into its own in the late fourth and early fifth centuries.'[127]

> The formal tradition of Latin Christology got a late start in comparison with the Greeks... The tradition of pro-Nicene Latin theology gained new momentum in reaction the Council of Sirmium in 357 and the homoian Western synods of Constantius in the late 350s and when several theologians who have traveled East later

---

[121] C.A. Beeley, *The Unity of Christ: Continuity and Conflict in Patristic Tradition* (New Haven: Yale University Press, 2012), 5.

[122] Beeley, *Unity,* xi.

[123] Beeley, *Unity,* 49-221.

[124] Beeley, *Unity,* 225. Beeley comments: 'By the end of the [patristic] era, the catholic or orthodox faith was solidly rooted in the Roman empire and its successors' (ix).

[125] Beeley, *Unity,* 50.

[126] Beeley, *Unity,* 106.

[127] Beeley, *Unity,* 205.

returned to the West, in particular, Hilary of Poitiers, Eusebius of Vercelli, and Lucifer of Cagliari.[128]

Whilst Beeley's critique of Jerome does not easily fit the 'McGuckin-Freeman' thesis, what we can say is that Beeley's views on Jerome's work and legacy, critically his acknowledgement that Jerome was indeed an important contributor to 'the full flowering of Latin Christology' that followed on from 'the lines of Christological thought found in the major fourth century Greek theologians,'[129] surely acts as testimony to the recognition by some scholars of Jerome's influence over the theology and theologies of the patristic era.

2012-2013

During 2012, some significant scholarly judgements on Jerome and his selected writings were made in the following areas: biblical interpretation in Jerome's *Vita Hilarionis*; Jerome's use of the first Christian library at Caesarea; Jerome's contribution to establishing the origins and authority of the NT books and the canon of Scripture; and Jerome's contribution to the debate on the importance of spirituality for church/Christian leadership in the early church.

We shall look first at Thomas Hunt's essay on Jerome's *Vita Hilarionis*.[130] Hunt argued that 'Comparing *Vita Hilarionis* with some statements contained within Jerome's own, near contemporary commentary on *Ephesians*, Jerome's hagiography presents its readers with the unification of exegesis and ascetic propaganda typical of the monk from Stridon,' and that 'both Jerome's exegesis and his asceticism depend on reflexive contemplation'.[131] At the time of its composition (sometime between 389 and 392) Jerome was a fervent advocate of the ascetic life[132] and Hunt considers the *Vita Hilarionis* to have been 'an expression of his [Jerome's] extended project to shape a definition of the Christian life with asceticism at its core'.[133] We saw in chapter 2 the role played by Jerome in the quest for a Christian identity. So the *Vita Hilarionis* (a work largely devoted to the promotion of an ascetic Christianity) might be viewed as an example of where

---

[128] Beeley, *Unity*, 225. Jerome, of course, was one of those who travelled East (to Rome) and later returned West (to Bethlehem). The term *homoian* relates to those theologians (e.g., Basil of Ancyra) who affirmed that the Son is like the Father in *ousia*. See Beeley, *Unity*, 160, 225.

[129] Beeley, *Unity*, 225.

[130] T. Hunt, 'Biblical Interpretation in Jerome of Stridon's *Vita Hilarionis*,' *StP* 52 (2012), 247-55.

[131] Hunt, 'Biblical Interpretation,' 247. *Vita Hilarionis* narrates the life of an itinerant Christian holy man and in it Jerome sought to demonstrate 'the particular vitures of the dead man' (247). *VH* is part legendary but some statements attach to its history.

[132] Stefan Rebenich argues that Jerome's *Life of Paul the Hermit* (Jerome's response to the 'lack of an authentic Latin monk's biography') the *Vita Hilarionis* and the *Vita Malchi*, 'all helped to establish Jerome's fame as a writer of the ascetic movement'. See Rebenich, *Jerome*, 26.

[133] Hunt, '*Biblical Interpretation*,' 248.

Jerome did show (contrary to Freeman's 2009 claim) the ability to display genuine intellectual creativity, even if at times he was influenced by a clear biblical narrative, as in the following:

> The first person bold enough to break into the presence of the blessed Hilarion was a certain woman of Eleutheropolis who found that she was despised by her husband on account of her sterility. He had no expectation of her coming when she suddenly threw herself at his feet. 'Forgive my boldness,' she said: 'take pity on my necessity. Why do you turn away your eyes? Why shun my entreaties? Do not think of me a woman, but as an object of compassion. It was my sex that bore the Saviour. They that are whole have no need of a physician, but they that are sick.' At length, after a long time he no longer turned away, but looked at the woman and asked the cause of her coming and of her tears. On learning this he raised his eyes to heaven and bade her have faith, then wept over her as she departed. Within a year he saw her with her son.[134]

Here, of course, the parallels with the ministry of Christ and Christ's miracles are obvious. Hilarionis performed other miracles too including restoring to life the three dead sons of a mother and the sight of a blind woman.

In the remainder of his account of the life of Hilarionis, Jerome's own creative capacity for storytelling is much more evident with Jerome all the while stressing that the 'true life is that which is purchased by suffering in the present'.[135] For example, at a vineyard where a monk tells his fellow monks (because it was the Lord's Day) to relieve their toil by a repast of grapes, Hilarion admonishes them declaring 'Cursed be he who looks for the refreshment of the body before that of the soul. Let us pray, let us sing, let us do our duty to God, and then we will hasten to the vineyard.'[136] Jerome further tells us that Hilarion 'abhorred such monks as were led by their lack of faith to hoard for the future and were careful about expense, or raiment [clothing], or some other of those things which pass away with the world'.[137] These two examples of Hilarionis' admonishments surely reflect, first, Jerome's own ascetic life in the Chalcis desert and, second, Jerome's polemics against corruption amongst some monastic communities.[138]

However, one scholar, Stefan Rebenich, has cast some doubt upon the historical authenticity of Jerome's *Vita Hilarionis*.

---

[134] Jerome, *The Life of S. Hilarion*, NPNF² 6:305.

[135] Jerome, *The Life of S. Hilarion*, NPNF² 6:309. According to Hunt, the *Vita Hilarionis* 'entwines Biblical interpretation with ethical instruction, both of which were rooted in self-reflection' (255).

[136] Jerome, *The Life of S. Hilarion*, NPNF² 6:309.

[137] Jerome, *The Life of S. Hilarion*, NPNF² 6:310.

[138] Rebenich, *Jerome*, 42, observes that Hilarion was 'a native of Thabata near Gaza and son of pagan parents, who allegedly founded the first, monastic community in Palestine' who 'was said by Jerome to have been known for his biblical learning and his literary education and mirrored Jerome's perception of himself as the ideal monk-scholar'.

The Saints' lives of Jerome—the *Life of Paul the First Hermit*, the *Life of Malchus*, and the *Life of Hilarion*—are masterpieces of monastic romance. They were immensely popular and drew contemporary and later readers under their spell, although some questioned the author's reliability (cf. *Vita Hilarionis* 1 [PL 23, 30B]). Jerome adopted literary forms and narrative elements of pagan provenance, borrowed from the mythological lore of classical authors, and integrated many features that were meant to entertain an educated audience... We are still in need of a modern critical edition of the lives.[139]

The year 2012 also saw scholars returning to the significance of Jerome's use of the first Christian library at Caesarea. This aspect of Jerome's work had (as we saw earlier in chapter 2) been fully documented by Grafton and Williams (2006). Two other scholars[140] offered some further interesting perspectives on Jerome's utilization of the library at Caesarea and how this signed the crucial role books played in the rise of Christianity.

Robert Wilken informs us of the history of the library at Caesarea and how Jerome's use of it contributed an important legacy.

> Begun during Origen's day, it was expanded after his death by a wealthy patron who wished to preserve Origen's writings. Over time it became a large collection of pagan, Jewish and Christian writings, and a scholarly center for the copying of books was established. One of the beneficiaries of the library in Caesarea was Jerome... Jerome was unusual in that he knew Latin, Greek, and Hebrew, and by drawing on the books collected in Caesarea he bequeathed to later generations an ideal of 'trilingual scholarship' (Hebrew, Greek, Latin) that lives on to this day among learned Christians.[141]

Whereas we have seen on a number of occasions Jerome acting as a 'theological resource' for other patristic writers, Wilken identifies here how Jerome made another major contribution—that of a new 'model' of biblical scholarship.

Like Wilken, Peter Brown finds Jerome's use of the library at Caesarea to have been a reflection of an already well-developed era of book-scholarship and testimony to just how far 'the age of Origen and the age of Jerome... were ages of the book.'[142] Brown writes:

> The libraries owned by some Christian scholars were overwhelming. The library created in the 240s by Origen at Caesarea Maritima in Palestine (and later preserved

---

[139] Rebenich, *Jerome*, 85. Rebenich's request for a modern critical edition of the lives has, in part, been met by the recent publication of a new critical version of Jerome's *Vita Malachi*. See C. Gray, Jerome, *Vita Malachi: Introduction, Text, Translation, and Commentary* (Oxford: OUP, 2015).

[140] R.L. Wilken, *The First Thousand Years: A Global History of Christianity* (New Haven: Yale University Press, 2012); P. Brown, *Through the Eye of a Needle: Wealth the Fall of Rome, and the Making of Christianity in the West, 350-550 AD* (Princeton: Princeton University Press, 2012).

[141] Wilken, *The First*, 60.

[142] Brown, *Through the Eye*, 275.

by the bishops of Caesarea) was 'one of the greatest single monuments of Roman scholarship.[143]

Furthermore, for Brown, Jerome's access to the library at Caesarea took place during that period of greater biblical reading that was emerging both in Rome and in Palestine.

In the age of Jerome, we are dealing with men and women for whom the search for nobility included the cultivation of a true nobility of the mind... Like Origen, Jerome moved in circles that expected women to be as intellectually engaged as men. What he offered them was a study of he Scriptures that was as endlessly thrilling as the mystical quest for the One had been in Neo-Platonic circles.[144]

During the years 385-412 perhaps Jerome can be credited with playing a pivotal **role in the development of a bible reading 'intellectualism' amongst women.** In 2012 there was also a return to re-assessing Jerome's role in establishing the origins and authority of the NT books and the canon of Scripture. Jerome and the canon of Scripture has been a long-standing focus for modern Jerome scholarship. Now Michael J. Kruger proffered a number of comments on Jerome and the biblical canon to stimulate the debate even further.[145] First, Kruger sets out **the historical context for Jerome's contribution:**

Early councils such as Laodicea (363), Hippo (393), and Carthage (397) produced canonical lists, but these were regional councils, and there were disagreements among them, as well as scattered disagreements even after the councils were over. E.g., Augustine was more favourable to the books of the Apocrypha (*Civ.* 18.36), but also admitted that they were not accepted by the Jews into their canon (*civ.* 19.36-38). In contrast, Jerome was decidedly against them (see prologue to *Expl. Dan.*).[146]

On Jerome's assessment of the authority of particular canonical books, Kruger observes:

We read in the prologue to Jerome's commentary on Philemon that he defended the epistle on the grounds that it is 'a document which has in it so much of the beauty of the Gospel,' which is the 'mark of its inspiration'.[147]

Thus, we can **see here how Jerome was apt to attribute a biblical texts' scriptural** authority according to the way in which it reflected the beauty of the Gospel-story (divinely inspired by Christ).[148] **Indeed, Paul's prison letter to Philemon (a**

---

[143] Grafton and Williams, *Christianity*, 131, cited by Brown, *Through the Eye*, 275n.9.

[144] Brown, *Through the Eye*, 273-274.

[145] M.J. Kruger, *Canon Revisited: Establishing the Origins and Authority of the New Testament Books* (Wheaton: Crossway, 2012).

[146] Kruger, *Canon*, 45n.**72. Jerome's commentary on Daniel was dedicated to Pamachius** and Marcella in the year 407.

[147] Jerome, Prologue to *Comm. Phlm*, as cited by Kruger, *Canon*, 128n.15.

[148] **Jerome's commentary on Philemon was written for Paula and Eustochium i**n 387. The Preface is a defence of the genuineness of the Epistle against those who thought its subject [i.e., reconciliation and relationships between Christians] beneath the dignity

Christian believer in Colossae), though a very brief document, talks of Paul being imprisoned for the gospel and of Paul calling upon Philemon to 'Refresh my heart in Christ' (Phil. 13, 20). Such statements from Paul, a 'prisoner in Christ Jesus' (Phil. 23), were clearly seen by Jerome as symbols of the beauty of Scripture and, thus, a condition (at least as far as Jerome was concerned) of Philemon's canonical acceptance. Equally significant is Jerome's prologue defence of Philemon suggesting that Jerome was calling for a deeper reading and understanding of this particular book of the Bible.

Kruger also reflects upon Jerome's views on the canonicity of the books of James, Jude, and 2 Peter (none of which Jerome provided commentaries on), as well as the role of John the Elder. First, on the book of James, Kruger writes:

> Traditionally the epistle has been given a first-century date (ranging from AD 40-62) and attributed to James, the Lord's brother, who was intimately involved with the apostolic circle and retained authority over the Jerusalem church (Acts 15; 1 Cor. 15:7). If this is correct, then there are good grounds for thinking it would have possessed reliable apostolic teaching. James clearly did not enjoy the same popularity in the early church as the core NT books like Paul's episstles), as is evidenced by the paucity of explicit Patristic citations of the book... James is cited by Irenaeus, Clement of Alexandria wrote a commentary on it which is now lost, and it was recognized as canonical Scripture by Origen... Eusebius acknowledges that some had doubts about it, but counts it among the canonical books [*Hist. eccl.* 3.25.3],[149] and the letter is fully received by Jerome, Augustine, and the councils of Hippo and Carthage.[150]

Of interest here is that whilst there was no obvious meeting of like-minds between Jerome and Augustine over the canonicity of the Apocrypha, there was a shared agreement over the canonical status of the epistle of James. This, of course, could well be explained by the subject of James which (like Philemon) centres upon practically and faithfully reminding Christians how to live. And, perhaps, nothing was more central to Jerome and Augustine than perseverance to true faith. On Jerome on Jude, Kruger suggests:

> We have good reason to think that this letter stems from apostolic circles and would therefore contain apostolic teaching. Like the book of James, Jude was largely overlooked by many Patristic authors... according to Jerome, Jude's use of Enoch may explain why some had doubts about it.[151]

The attribution to Jerome's positive reception of James, and Jerome's recognition of some contemporary (patristic) concerns over Jude, raises a number of issues. For example, P.H. Davids' assertion that Jerome fully received the letter of James

---

of inspiration. 'There are many degrees of inspiration' Jerome says, 'though in Christ alone it is seen in its fullness,' NPNF² 6:498.

[149] Kruger, *Canon*, 269-70.

[150] P.H. Davids, *The Epistle of James* (Grand Rapids: Eerdmans, 1982), 7, as cited by Kruger *Canon*, 270n.51.

[151] Jerome, *Vir. ill.* 4, as cited by Kruger, *Canon*, 270n.55.

seems remarkable given that in Jerome's day there was no unanimity on the question of the epistle's authenticity (authenticity being something that Jerome himself would surely have examined thoroughly and not too readily assumed).[152] In addition, there has been the debate (on-going ever since the time of one of Jerome's associates, Ephiphanius of Salamis) over whether or not James and Jude were in fact blood-brothers of Jesus.[153] Kruger writes:

> Jerome advanced [the position] that James and Jude were merely cousins to Jesus...[154] Richard Bauckham rightly calls this view 'the least plausible'...[155] Jerome's position also does not seem to take adequate account of the difficulties of harmonizing the picture of which women were present at the crucifixion in Mark 15.40 and John 19.25, if harmonization is truly the best way to proceed... James, Jude, Simon and Joses were the natural children of Mary and Joseph, born subsequent to Jesus, whose biological father was not Joseph.[156]

In his *The Jewish Teachers*, de Silva's position on Jerome—that Jerome asserted that James and Jude 'were merely cousins to Jesus'—is, sadly, given no Jerome reference citation. However, de Silva does, believe that James and Jude were Jesus' half-brothers,[157] and that the letters of James and Jude are authentic, with Jerome affirming Jude's authority as Scripture (*Lives of Illustrious Men*, 4).[158] On Jerome on 2 Peter, Kruger opines:

---

[152] See, for example, the discussion by deSilva, in D.A. deSilva, *The Jewish Teachers of Jesus, James and Jude: What Earliest Christianity Learned from the Apocrypha and Pseudepigrapha* (Oxford: OUP, 2012), 45-54. However, Kruger asserts the authenticity of James, stating, 'We possess several early manuscripts of James: P20, P23, P100 are all third century and suggest that the book was known and used by the early Christians. While James's canonical path was not as smooth as that of other books, these factors give no reason to doubt its place in the canon.' See Kruger, *Canon*, 270.

[153] deSilva, *The Jewish Teachers*, 32-33.

[154] deSilva, *The Jewish Teachers*, 33.

[155] R.J. Bauckham, *Jude and the Relatives of Jesus in the Early Church* (Edinburgh: T&T Clark, 1990), 20, as cited by deSilva, *The Jewish Teachers*, 33.

[156] deSilva, *The Jewish Teachers*, 33-34.

[157] deSilva, *The Jewish Teachers*, 45.

[158] deSilva, *The Jewish Teachers*, 54, 110, respectively. For Jerome's acknowledgment of the wider (patristic) uncertainty surrounding the acceptance of Jude, see M. Green, *2 Peter and Jude* (Nottingham: IVP, 1987), 58. Green writes: 'It [Jude] finds a place in the second-century muratorion Canon, Tertullian recognised it as an authoritative Christian document, so did Clement of Alexandria, who wrote a commentary on it. Origen hints that there were doubts in his day... but quotes Jude with enthusiasm... Eusebius classes it among disputed books, and it was not admitted into the Syrian canon...He [Jerome] explains the cause of the doubts about Jude as "because he appealed to the apocryphal book of Enoch as an authority it is rejected by some" (*De vir. ill.* iv). By 200 AD it was accepted in the main areas of the ancient church... only in Syria were there objections, and even there these could hardly have been in unison, because Jude was accepted into the Philoxenian and Harklean recensions of the New Testament.'

Perhaps no book has had a more difficult journey into the canon than 2 Peter. It is widely regarded as pseudonymous by modern scholars and often dated to the early second century…[159] Origen cited it six times and clearly received it as canonical Scripture,[160] and Eusebius considered it to be part of the "disputed books" in the canon that were nevertheless known to most of the church.[161] Despite some initial hesitancy toward 2 Peter from some quarters of the church, in the end it was widely received by such figures as Jerome, Athanasius, Gregory of Nazianzus, and Augustine.[162]

Interestingly, Kruger's preferred citation of Michael Green's *2 Peter Reconsidered* for confirmation of Jerome's eventual, positive reception of the epistle, tells us one story only. However, Green's later work, 2 Peter and Jude,[163] makes no mention of Jerome of as an example of the ancient church's acceptance of 2 Peter as canonical (i.e., confirming authentic Petrine authorship). In fact quite the contrary. In the following extract from the author's Preface to the book's second edition we can see how Green's change of opinion may have come about:

> This Commentary, first published in 1968, and based on the *AV*, is here reissued, based on the text of the New International Version of the Bible. While adhering to the broad positions adopted in the first edition, I have taken the opportunity afforded by this revision to make a thorough reappraisal of the text of the Epistles and the commentary in the light of modern writing. There is a resurgence of interest in this long-neglected corner of the New Testament, and a willingness to consider fresh possibilities.[164]

Therefore, whilst Kruger argues that 2 Peter was accepted by Jerome, Green, perhaps as a result of this willingness to consider fresh possibilities(?), and his exclusion of Jerome from his list of those early ancient Christian writers who accepted 2 Peter as canonical, appears to have had some doubt.[165]

We now turn to Jerome's contribution to the debate on the importance of spirituality for church/Christian leadership. Here, a leading voice has been that of Christopher Beeley, the eminent Yale Divinity School patristic scholar, who, apart from examining how various patristic theologians and church councils developed the idea of an authoritative theological tradition,[166] has also authored a

---

[159] Kruger, *Canon*, 271.

[160] Origen, *Hom. Num* 2.676; *Hom. Jos.* 7.1, as cited by Kruger, Canon, 271n.69.

[161] Eusebius, *Hist. eccl.* 3.25.3, as cited by Kruger, *Canon*, 271n.70.

[162] M.E. Green, *2 Peter Reconsidered* (London: Tyndale, 1960), 6, as cited by Kruger, Canon, 271n.71.

[163] M.E. Green, *2 Peter and Jude* (Nottingham, IVP, 2009).

[164] Green, *2 Peter and Jude*, 11.

[165] Green's list only includes two names, Origen and Clement of Alexandria. See Green, *2 Peter and Jude*, 20.

[166] See C. Beeley, *The Unity of Christ: Continuity and Conflict in Patristic Tradition* (New Haven: Yale University Press, 2012.)

study of the key principles of church leadership as these were taught by the great pastor—theologians of the early church (including Jerome).[167]

Beeley (unlike some other modern scholars such as Rebenich and Freeman) views Jerome as having been one of the great early theologians.[168]

It is extremely significant that all of the great early theologians speak strongly against relying on institutional power for one's pastoral authority. Their cautions are all the more striking when we recognize that most of them were heavily invested in formal leadership structures, and in some cases they even welcomed the patronage of the church by the Roman state. Jerome, for example—who was no mild lamb when it came to asserting himself—states very clearly that 'the blessedness of a bishop, priest or deacon does not lie in the fact that they are bishops, priests, or deacons, but in their having the virtues that their names and offices imply'.[169] Jerome's belief that those whom God appoints to lead his people must be distinguished above all by their virtue (an idea also held by Gregory Nazianzen[170]) is clearly expressed by Jerome in his *Letter* 52 (To Nepotian):

It is the glory of a bishop to make provision for the wants of the poor; but it is the shame of all priests to amass private fortunes... In a priest of Christ, mouth, mind, and hand should be at one... Be obedient to your bishop and welcome him as the parent of your soul...This also I say that the bishops should know themselves to be priests not lords. Let them render to the clergy the honour which is their due that the clergy may offer to them the respect which belongs to bishops.[171]

Here Jerome's reference to welcoming a bishop as 'the parent of your soul' reflects Jerome's spiritual priority for Christians, namely the cure of souls. And in the following extract from *Letter* 52 we can see Jerome (Beeley's 'one of the great early theologians') combining his scriptural knowledge with praxis on what the correct clerical conduct should be.

As there is but one Lord and one Temple; so also should there be but one ministry. Let us ever bear in mind the charge which the apostle Peter gives to priests: 'Feed the flock of God which is among you, taking the oversight thereof not by constraint but willingly as God would have you; not for filthy lucre but of a ready mind; neither as being lords over God's heritage but being examples to the flock,' and that gladly; that 'when the chief-shepherd shall appear ye may receive a crown of glory that fadeth not away'. It is a bad custom which prevails in certain churches for presbyters to be silent when bishops are present on the ground that they would be jealous or impatient hearers. 'If anything,' writes the apostle Paul, 'be revealed to another that sitteth by, let the first hold his peace. For ye may all prophesy one by

---

[167] See C. Beeley, *Leading God's People: Wisdom from the Early Church for Today* (Grand Rapids: Eerdmans, 2012).

[168] Beeley, *Leading*, 44.

[169] Jerome, *Ep.* 14.9, as cited by Beeley, *Leading*, 44n.42.

[170] Beeley, *Leading*, 43.

[171] Jerome, *Ep.* 52, NPNF² 6:92-93. Nepotian, the nephew of Heliodorus, had, like his uncle, abandoned the military for the clerical calling, and was now a presbyter at Altinum, where Heliodorus was bishop. *Ep.* 52 is a systematic treatise on the duties of the clergy and on the rule of life which they ought to adopt. In *Ep.* 52 Jerome refers to Gregory Nazianzen as 'My teacher'.

one that all may learn and all may be comforted; and the spirits of the prophets are subject to the prophets. For God is not the author of confusion but of peace. A wise son maketh a glad father; and a bishop should rejoice in the discrimination which had led him to choose such for the priests of Christ.'[172]

Thus we can see here how Jerome uses his scriptural knowledge of 1 Peter 1:4 ('to an inheritance that is imperishable, underfiled, and unfading, kept in heaven for you'), 1 Corinthians 14: 1-33 ('If a revelation is made to another sitting there, let the first be silent. For you can all prophesy one by one, so that all may learn and all be encouraged, and the spirits of prophets are subject to spirits. For God is not a God of confusion but of peace') and Proverbs 10:1 ('a wise son makes a glad father but a foolish son is a sorrow to his mother') to underpin his theology of proper clerical conduct. There is clear evidence here of Jerome acting as a theologian and as such it seriously contests Freeman's (2009) claim that Jerome never showed any genuine intellectual creativity or had the self-confidence to develop his own theology.

Finally, Beeley asserts that 'The great pastoral theologians of the early church are unanimous in their insistence on the importance of spiritual study for church leadership.'[173] And citing from Jerome's *Ep.* 52 (to Nepotian) Beeley notes how Jerome counsels Nepotian, 'Read the divine scriptures constantly; indeed never let the sacred volume be out of your hand. Learn what you have to teach.'[174]

During 2012, despite little negative critical reception, Jerome's view of Irenaeus' *Adversus Haereses* did attract the concern of one particular scholar. In his essay 'Tracing the Irenaean Legacy,'[175] Irenaeus Steenberg made the following observation:

> Augustine may be the most important reader of Latin Irenaeus, but he was not the only...Jerome, who is single-handedly responsible for our ascription of the title 'martyr' to Irenaeus,[176] was familiar enough with his Latin text to refer to it as a work of 'most learned and eloquent style'[177]—an interesting comment, given the Latin translator's slavish literality in rendering the Greek, his frequent inconsistencies and in general a style characterized by Unger as 'barbaric Latin'.[178]

Here, of course, it should be noted that Steenberg is not commenting on Jerome as a translator but on the anonymous Latin translator of Irenaeus.

---

[172] Jerome, *Ep.* 52, NPNF² 6:93. Jerome believed it important for the clergy to display 'prudence, justice, temperance, fortitude' (Wis. 8:7), the cardinal virtues of Greek philosophy. See Jerome, *Ep.* 52, NPNF² 6:95.

[173] Beeley, *Leading*, 103.

[174] Jerome, *Ep.* 52, NPNF² 6:92, as cited by Beeley, *Leading*, 103n.63.

[175] I.M.C. Steenberg, 'Tracing the Irenaean Legacy,' in P. Foster and S. Parris (eds), *Irenaeus: Life, Scripture, Legacy* (Minneapolis: Fortress, 2012), 199-211.

[176] Jerome, *Comm. on Isaiah*, ch. 64, as cited by Steenberg, 'Tracing,' 207n.44.

[177] Jerome, *Ep.* 75.3, as cited by Steenberg, 'Tracing,' 207n.45.

[178] D. Unger and J. Dillon, *St. Irenaeus of Lyons, Against Heresies* (New York: Paulist, 1992), 1.14, as cited by Steenbertg, 'Tracing,' 207n.46.

During 2013 scholars contributed case-studies of, amongst others, Jerome and Augustine's later correspondence on the Antioch incident (Gal. 2:11-14); Comedy in Jerome's *Vita Malchi;* Jerome's use of biblical models; Jerome's *Prologus Galeatus* and the OT Canon of North Africa; and, Jerome's spiritual and intellectual greatness.

Augustine's dispute with Jerome over the latter's exegesis of the Peter/Paul Antioch incident (Gal. 2:11-14) had occupied scholars for many years. In his article 'Law, Lies and Letter Writing'[179] Myers makes no acknowledgment of the fact that for Jerome too biblical exegesis had to bear reliable, honest and truthful testimony to the scriptures. In this particular instance Myers' lack of a positive view of Jerome is troubling, as is his contention that the Jerome-Augustine dispute over the biblical interpretation of Galatians 2:11-14 was 'one of the fiercest exchanges between two church fathers'. Some of the letter evidence suggests another view is possible. For example at the height of their 'conflict-correspondence' Jerome penned *Ep.* 115, 'a short but most friendly letter, in which Jerome excuses himself for the freedom with which he has dealt with Augustine's questions (the allusion is to Letter CXII[180]) and hopes that henceforth they may be able to avoid controversy and to labour like brothers in the field of scripture'.[181] This is hardly the sentiment of a vengeful foe.

Whilst Myers is quite correct to view the eleven letters constituting the conflict-correspondence, and exchanged between Augustine and Jerome between 394 and 405, as illustrative of the 'tenacity of the argument between the two church fathers,'[182] there appears to be no scholarly consensus and much continued debate on Jerome's case that Paul perpetuated a 'useful lie' at the Antioch incident.[183] One aspect of Jerome's corpus—namely, Jerome's work as a biographer/story-teller—has long been neglected by modern scholars. One such work sadly overlooked has been *Vita Malchi (The Life of Malchus the Captive Monk)* and whilst Freeman (2009) has asserted that Jerome never showed any genuine

---

[179] J.A. Myers, 'Law, Lies and Letter Writing: An Analysis of Jerome and Augustine on the Antioch Incident (Gal 2:11-14),' *SJT*, 66.2 (2013), 127-39.

[180] Jerome's *Ep.* 112 (written to Augustine in 404) deals at great length with the dispute between Paul and Peter: 'His language throughout is kind but rather patronizing: indeed in this whole correspondence Jerome seldom sufficiently recognizes the greatness of Augustine,' NPNF[2] 6:214.

[181] Jerome's *Ep.* 115, NPNF[2] 6:215.

[182] Myers, 'Law,' 128.

[183] See, for example the discussion in M. Graves, *The Inspiration and Interpretation of Scripture: What the Early Church can Teach us* (Grand Rapids: Eerdmans, 2014), 112-16. Graves states: 'In his commentary on Gal. 2, Jerome argued that Paul did not genuinely rebuke Peter for separating himself from the Gentiles but did so only in pretense, privately knowing Peter's noble intention to win the Jews for salvation. According to Jerome, Paul's public 'rebuke' of Peter was a kind of deception along the lines of acting, aimed at bringing harmony to the Jewish and Gentile believers. Augustine counters Jerome with strong affirmation that Scripture cannot deceive' (112).

intellectual creativity, Rebenich has described *Vita Malchi* as a 'masterpiece of monastic romance'.[184]

In her article 'The Monk and the Ridiculous,'[185] Christa Gray offers a positive critical reception to *Vita* and finds 'the moral message of the *Vita* especially note-worthy'.[186] The *Vita* (written c. 391) was Jerome's 'shortest and most novelistic saint's life,' and Brady suggests that 'the language of this work echoes all sorts of genres, including epic, history, scholastic oratory and comedy'.[187] To illustrate Jerome's capacity for creativity, humour and comedy as well as for narrating a moral, edifying tale of some substance, Gray notes:

> As in other narrative prose genres, comic stock characters and plot elements are exploited to create expectations. Examples of the dour and inflexible versus the loving idealised father figure; the impetuous youth; the unscrupulous adulteress; and the officious, self-important fellow slave. These familiar stereotypes provide a measure of orientation in a new and as yet experimental fusion of genres.[188]

The following extract from Jerome's text relating the experiences of Malchus (a monk abducted by nomadic Saracens on the Eastern fringe of the fourth century Roman Empire) may suffice:

> After a long time as I sat one day by myself in the desert with nothing in sight save earth and sky, I began quickly to turn things over in my thoughts, and amongst others called to mind my friends the monks, and specially the look of the father who had instructed me, kept me, and lost me. While I was thus musing I saw a crowd of ants swarming over a narrow path. The loads they carried were clearly larger than their own bodies. Some with their forceps were dragging along the seeds of herbs; others were excavating the earth from pits and banking it up to keep out the water. One party, in view of approaching winter, and wishing to prevent their store from being converted into grass through the dampness of the ground, were cutting off the tips of the grains they had carried in; another with solemn lamentation were remov-ing the dead. And, what is stranger still in such a host, those coming out did not hinder those going in; nay, rather, if they saw one fall beneath his burden they would put their shoulders to the load and give him assistance. In short that day afforded me a delightful entertainment. So, remembering how Solomon sends us to the shrewdness of the ant and quickens our sluggish faculties by setting before us such an example, I began to tire of captivity, and to regret the monk's cell, and long to imitate those ants and their doings, where toil is for the community, and, since noth-ing belongs to anyone all things belong to all.[189]

---

[184] Rebenich, *Jerome*, 85.

[185] C. Gray, '*The Monk and the Ridiculous: Comedy in Jerome's Vita Malchi*,' *StP* 69 (2013), 115-21. See, also, Gray's published monograph, *Jerome, "Vita Malchi": Introduction, Text, Translation, and Commentary* (Oxford: OUP, 2015).

[186] Gray, 'The Monk,' 115.

[187] Gray, 'The Monk,' 115.

[188] Gray, 'The Monk,' 115.

[189] Jerome, *The Life of Malchus, The Captive Monk*, NPNF[2] 6:317.

In the above extract we can clearly identify Jerome's pursuit of a Christian narrative ('another with solemn lamentation') using Christian discourse ('So, remembering how Solomon').

A similar mechanism can be seen at work in some of Jerome's letters. Christine McCann has made a particular study of Jerome's spiritual mentoring letters, where 'Jerome the spiritual mentor utilized biblical figures as positive role models, that is, as "incentives to virtue" that the recipients should imitate.'[190] Of particular interest to McCann are *Ep.* 22 (to the consecrated virgin Eustochium) and *Ep.* 130 (to the consecrated virgin Demetrias). McCann opines:

> Jerome had assumed the persona of an experienced Desert *abba* to give himself the authority to act as a spiritual mentor.[191] His surviving letters provide us the best insight into how he practiced spiritual mentoring, as he adapted the ideals of the Eastern mothers and fathers for a Latin, cultured audience.[192]

Arguing that 'Jerome intended *Ep.* 22 to be a major statement of his ascetic program,' McGann notes how 'Jerome called on Eustochium to compare herself with and to strive to emulate the Prophets Elisha and Elijah, King David, the patriarch Jacob, Mary the sister of Lazarus, the Apostle Paul, the Bride in the *Song of Songs*, and the Virgin Mary.'[193] In *Ep.* 130 'Jerome referred to the following biblical figures as exemplars: Elijah, Esther, the Bride of the *Song of Solomon*, Anna the daughter of Phanuel, John the Baptist, and Christ.'[194]

Thus, Jerome's spiritual mentoring letters set out the 'reader/disciple' configuration and, as such, they exemplify Jerome's importance as an inspirational author both to and for his spiritual disciples.

Returning to Jerome as biblical scholar, a study of Jerome's relation to the 22-book OT canon by Edmon Gallagher[195] offered some interesting insights into Jerome's position on the deuterocanonical books. Gallagher states:

> Jerome and the Council of Hippo almost simultaneously took opposite stances on the deuterocanonical books. While Jerome assigned *Wisdom of Solomon, Sirach, Judith, Tobit, and 1 and 2 Maccabees* to the apocrypha, the North African council included these same six books as fully canonical within the OT. Both positions were innovative; earlier patristic lists restrict the OT canon to the books accepted by the

---

[190] C. McCann, 'Incentives to Virtue: Jerome's Use of Biblical Models,' *StP* 69 (2013), 107-13 (107).

[191] Cain, *The Letters of Jerome*, 146, as cited by McCann, 'Incentives,' 108n.4.

[192] McCann, 'Incentives,' 108. McCann observes: 'Scriptural references do abound in Jerome's letters, yet only fourteen of the twenty-five letters that I classify as spiritual mentoring letters include the use of biblical persons as models that the letter recipients should or indeed had emulated' (109).

[193] McCann, 'Incentives,' 109.

[194] McCann, 'Incentives,' 110.

[195] E.L. Gallagher, 'Jerome's *Prologus Galeatus* and the OT Canon of North Africa,' *StP* 69 (2013), 99-106. For a more extended analysis of Jerome's relation to the OT canon, See E.L. Gallagher, *Hebrew Scripture in Patristic Biblical Theory* (Leiden: Brill, 2012).

Jews, though Athanasius and others maintained a middle category of useful books that were neither canonical nor apocryphal...the six books excluded by Jerome and accepted by Hippo had established themselves in the late fourth-century Latin church as the definitive collection of such 'ecclesiastical' books (to use Rufinus' terminology, *Symb.* 36) and that Jerome's unusually harsh statement about their position in the apocrypha ought to be seen as a reaction against the opposite sentiments emanating from North Africa.[196]

Gallagher's paper refers to Jerome's *Prologus Galeatus* (i.e., the 'Helmeted Preface' to his Latin translation of the Hebrew books of *Samuel* and *Kings*) in which Jerome stated the six particular OT books (see above) to be declared apocrypha. Gallagher's enquiry specifically focuses upon the triumvirate of Jerome's declared six apocryphal books—Rufinus' same six 'ecclesiastical' books – and the same six books accepted as canon by Hippo. The exact declaration of Jerome's six apocryphal OT books reads:

> This preface to the Scriptures may serve as a 'helmeted' introduction to all the books which we turn from Hebrew into Latin, so that we may be assured that what is not found in our list must be placed amongst the Apocryphal writings. Wisdom, therefore, which generally bears the name of Solomon, and the book of Jesus, the son of Sirach, and Judith, and Tobias, and the Shepherd are not in the canon. The first book of Maccabees I have found to be Hebrew, the second is Greek, as can be proved from the very style. Seeing that all this is so, I beseech you, my reader, not to think that my labours are in any sense intended to disparage the old translators. For the service of the tabernacle of God each one offers what he can.[197]

Bearing this in mind it is quite wrong for Gallagher to say that 'Jerome's expulsion of the deuterocanonicals into the apocrypha in this preface is unusually harsh,'[198] for, as we can readily see from the above, Jerome was moderate in explaining and defending his aprocryphal selection. Gallagher defends his position thus:

> I suggest that Jerome's unusually strict stance against the deuterocanonicals...represents his attempt to affirm strongly the normative status of the *Hebraica Veritas* in the face of those who would confer canonical status on any book read as divine scripture in church.[199]

---

[196] Gallagher, 'Jerome's *Prologus*,' 99. Gallagher's source reference to Rufinus should be treated with some caution. As Bart D. Ehrman has noted: 'No one was more famously connected with the alteration of inherited theological writings than Rufinus,' though he acknowledges 'Rufinus did admit that "orthodox" books could contain statements that do not toe the theological line.' See Enrman, *Forgery*, 65, 142.

[197] Jerome, *Preface* to the Books of *Samuel* and *Kings*, NPF, 6.490. The author(s) of the books of Samuel and Kings are anonymous. Jerome's *Preface* was written c. 393 and 'was set forth as an exposition of the principles adopted by Jerome in all his translations from the Hebrew—the 'Helmated Preface,' as he calls it with which he was prepared to do battle against all who impugn his design and methods,' NPNF[2] 6:489.

[198] Gallagher, Jerome's *Prologus*, 105.

[199] Gallagher, Jerome's *Prologus*, 106.

Here Gallagher's guesswork is credible if perhaps not fully explanatory. Could it rather be the case that Jerome was rejecting his six apocryphal books (demonstrating Jerome's independence of mind) due to an uncertainty about their actual authorship and not just their Hebrew provenance?

In our final case-study Andrew Lenox-Conyngham offered an apologia for Jerome's spiritual and intellectual greatness.[200] Lenox-Conyngham states:

> There is greater interest in him [Jerome] today than probably at any time in the past. The 2006 International Colloquy on Jerome held at Cardiff University, consisting of eighteen published papers,[201] is just one sign of the current recognition of the importance of this intellectual and, I would argue, spiritual giant.[202]

However, Lenox-Conyngham also notes how, despite 'increasingly international and economical recognition of his importance,' there has been (paradoxically) 'a liturgical downgrading of him in the Church of England'.[203] This downgrading of Jerome has, according to Lenox-Conyngham, been the result of a 'general, and distorted view of him' taken by the Church of England because 'Jerome does not satisfy the Anglican criterion of "niceness".'[204] (Jerome being seen as, in some way, an unpleasant character). All of this, claims Lenox-Conyngham, together with 'Jerome's present lowly place in the Church of England calendar of saints gives a false impression of his true spiritual and intellectual greatness.'[205]

On what grounds does Lenox-Conyngham claim Jerome's 'spiritual and intellectual greatness'? Lenox-Conyngham lists Jerome's 'epoch-making methods of much of his scholarship (e.g., the first theologian, according to von Campenhausen, to emphasize the scientific importance of archaeology and of the personal inspection of sites of scriptural importance); Jerome's revision of the Eusebian *Onomasticon* and his assimilation of pagan culture; and, Jerome's work as a spiritual counsellor and confidant.'[206] What is most striking here is how Lenox-Conyngham's list contains materials that would directly challenge the 'McGuckin-Freeman' thesis regarding the calibre (i.e., originality) of Jerome's scholarly work and Jerome's capacity for intellectual creativity. However, whilst Lenox-Conyngham opines 'Purely as a scholar Jerome was unequalled,'[207] he fails to qualify this statement with any supporting evidence of his own.

---

[200] A, Lenox-Conyngham, 'In Praise of St. Jerome and Against the Anglican cult of "Niceness",' *StP* 69 (2013), 435-40.

[201] See Cain and Lössl (eds), *Jerome of Stridon*.

[202] Lenox-Conyngham, 'In Praise,' 435.

[203] Lenox-Conyngham, 'In Praise,' 435. Lenox-Conyngham notes: 'This is clearly shown by the fat that his Feast Day on 30 September is no longer on the same level (that of Lesser Festival) as such saints as his contemporaries, Ambrose and Augustine, but has been lowered to the third, and lowest, level (that of a mere Commemoration).'

[204] Lenox-Conyngham, 'In Praise,' 435.

[205] Lenox-Conyngham, 'In Praise,' 435.

[206] Lenox-Conyngham, 'In Praise,' 438.

[207] Lenox-Conyngham, 'In Praise,' 438.

We will now conclude this section by considering eight books[208] each of which provided information on some familiar Jeromean themes as well as on some of Jerome's lesser-known corpus interests, writings and influences.

In his study of ascetic pneumatology, Thomas L. Humphries found some interesting links between John Cassian's and Jerome's understanding and interpretation of pneumatology (e.g., the ways in which the Holy Spirit brings about human transformation and self-transcendence) to explain Christian asceticism.[209] Both Cassian and Jerome were monks and Catholic theologians and both believed asceticism could enrich the spirituality of the monks' life. This is demonstrated by Cassian's and Jerome's view of the importance of the personal indwelling of the Holy Spirit as a precursor to the self-achieving ascetic virtue. Humphries writes:

> Cassian not only makes the indwelling of the Holy Spirit the goal of ascetic endeavour, but he also adds a personal experiential dimension to his theology. Obedience, patience, gentleness, and the perfection of love are not simply names for virtues; they are ways of life that are essentially responses to other monks. The novice monk cultivates obedience to his elders. All monks must be patient with each other.[210]

This was also familiar territory for Jerome as the following extract from Letter 14 shows:

> Where there is no honor there is contempt; and where there is contempt there is frequent rudeness; and where there is rudeness there is vexation; and where there is vexation there is no rest; and where there is no rest the mind is apt to be diverted from its purpose... not to aim at perfection is itself a sin.[211]

Andrew Hofer's study *Christ in the Life and Teaching of Gregory of Nazianzus* drew attention to Jerome's relation to his erstwhile early mentor and especially to Gregory's theology of the Word and Gregory's Christomorphic ministry. One similarity between Jerome and Gregory was that each talked about themselves in

---

[208] T.L. Humphries, Jr., *Ascetic Pneumatology from John Cassian to Gregory the Great* (Oxford: OUP, 2013); A. Hofer (O.P.), *Christ in the Life and Teaching of Gregory of Nazianzus* (Oxford: OUP, 2013); F. Young, **God's Presence: A Contemporary Recapitulation of Early Christianity** (Cambridge: CUP, 2013); D. Gibson and J. Gibson (eds), *From Heaven he Came and Sought her: Definite Atonement in Historical, Biblical, Theological, and Pastoral Perspective* (Wheaton: Crossway, 2013); M. Edwards, *Image, Word and God in the Early Christian Centuries* (Farnham: Ashgate, 2013); T.D. Still and D.E. Wilhite (eds), *Tertullian and Paul* (London: Bloomsbury T&T Clark, 2013); A. Cain (ed.), **Jerome's Epitaph on Paula: A Commentary on the Epitaphium Sactae Paulae with an Introduction, Text, and Translation** (Oxford: OUP, 2013); J.C. Paget and J. Schaper (eds), *The New Cambridge History of the Bible: From the Beginnings to 600* (Cambridge: CUP, 2013).

[209] Humphries, *Ascetic*, xiv, 22-25.

[210] Humphries, *Ascetic*, 24.

[211] Jerome, *Ep.* 14, NPNF[2] 6:16. *Ep. 14* was written c. 373/374 and is an early example of Jerome's ascetic letter-counselling.

some considerable detail. Of the latter, Hofer remarks 'Gregory undertook a continual literary reflection on his life.'[212] And, of course, Jerome's self-promotion through his letters and polemics knew no limits.

So, how did Jerome share Gregory's notion of the *logos* (Word)? According to Hofer, Gregory held the Word to be a mystery to be experienced in life.[213] Jerome's and Gregory's understanding of the Word was similar in that each appreciated how the logos (as revealed through the Bible) could guide the Christian's way of life; though in Jerome's case it is clear that he did not always readily receive or appreciate Gregory's teachings.

> When teaching in church seek to call forth plaudits but groans. Let the tears of your hearers be your glory. A presbyter's words ought to be seasoned by his reading of scripture. Be not a declaimer or a ranter, one who gabbles without rhyme or reason, but shew yourself skilled in the deep things and versed in the mysteries of God. To mouth your words and by your quickness of utterance astonish the unlettered crowd is a mark of ignorance... My teacher, Gregory of Nazianzus, when I once asked him to explain Luke's phrase 'the second-first Sabbath' [Lk. 6:1], playfully evaded my request saying: 'I will tell you about it in church, and there, when all the people applaud me, you will be forced against your will to know what you do not know at all. For, if you alone remain silent, everyone will put you down for a fool.'[214]

Here Jerome's reference to the *logos* as the 'deep things' and 'the mysteries of God' are important but it is Gregory's remarks that are especially revealing and which might perhaps be seen as an acerbic put-down to Jerome. However, there is no evidence whatsoever in Jerome's Letter 52.8 (as Hofer claims) to suggest that Gregory's interpretation of 'an abstruse biblical matter' (the 'Second-First Sabbath' in Lk. 6:1) left Jerome 'scratching his head'.[215]

We now move on to consider Jerome's relation to Gregory's Christomorphic ministry (i.e., Gregory's particular articulation of his relationship with Christ for a pastoral purpose).[216] Here the similarities between the Latin Jerome and the Greek Gregory are quite striking. Of Gregory, Hofer writes:

> Gregory's doctrinal formulations are embedded in a pervasive blending of Christ with his own life. To abstract Gregory's Christology, and leave behind his rhetorical aims, risks distorting his authentic teaching. Thus, *pace* those who consider Gregory to be a popularizer of a theological or Christological system previously worked out, his writings exude a highly sophisticated and profoundly personal insight into the mystery of Christ. He crafts his presentation to persuade others to be purified and, with Gregory himself as their model, to become like Christ in deification. In this way, Gregory articulates his relationship with Christ for a pastoral purpose.

[212] Hofer, *Christ*, 4.
[213] Hofer, *Christ*, 14.
[214] Jerome, *Ep.*, 52.8 NPNF² 6:93.
[215] Hofer, *Christ*, 17.
[216] Hofer, *Christ*, 195.

Indeed, this exemplifies how all of Gregory's writing, which so frequently appears self-referential, could be read as expressing Gregory's ministry to others.[217]

Of course, Jerome (like his mentor Gregory) was adept in his impressive and expressive use of language as well as in his use of forceful writing. In this regard, as we have previously seen both in his letters and in his homilies, Jerome sought to popularize his Christology for a pastoral purpose. Thus, it is significant that Jerome's respect for Gregory's teachings and writings eventually found expression in Jerome's *On Illustrious Men*.[218] Amongst British scholars the work of Frances Young has won a particular high regard for its contribution to patristic scholarship. In her book *God's Presence: A Contemporary Recapitulation of early Christianity*,[219] Young 'offered a systematic theology with contemporary coherence by engaging in conversation with the fathers of the church—those who laid down the parameters of Christian theology and enshrined key concepts in the creeds—and exploring how their teachings can be applied today, despite the differences in our intellectual and ecclesial environments'.[220]

Discussing methods of biblical interpretation, Young (like Graves, 2007) notes how:

> The philological method has always lain at the heart of commentary, which began as *scholia* explaining problem words, identifying figures of speech or constructing unclear sentence-structures. Here the historico-critical method is in direct continuity with the fathers, especially those like Jerome who went behind translated versions to the original Hebrew and Greek.[221]

Here Young is highlighting one of the principal achievements of Jerome as an exegete in which Jerome's exegetical style can be seen as symbolic of his whole character, personality and theological approach. And Jerome's fervour for getting behind translated versions to the original Hebrew and Greek' certainly marks Jerome as an exegetical innovator and calls into question McGuckin's (2005) judgement that Jerome's reputation as exegete is over-stressed (at least if we look for originality).

On the question of sanctification—as achieved through the ascetic ideals of 'virginity' and *apatheia* (passionlessness)—Young finds Jerome to have been on less sure ground. We have already seen a number of instances where Jerome's stress on virginity or celibacy caused conflict and rifts between his contemporaries and associates. Contrasting the unease within today's Church over issues relating to sexuality with that seen in the fourth century, Young states:

---

[217] Hofer, *Christ*, 195.
[218] See Hofer, *Christ*, 216n.110. Hofer notes: 'For the fourth-century prominence of this poem [*In praise of virginity*] among Gregory's works, see Jerome's recognition in *On Illustrious Men*' (117).
[219] F. Young, *God's Presence: A Contemporary Recapitulation of early Christianity* (Cambridge: CUP, 2013).
[220] Young, *God's* (from inside cover publishers' résumé).
[221] Young, *God's*, 30.

Stress on virginity, or celibacy, is particularly alien to our culture, and in today's world this ancient tradition poses problems. For a few celibacy may be chosen, but emerging scandals indicate the difficulties for those of whom it is expected, while sexuality is a dividing issue in church life. For many people a loving and supportive relationship is the temple-like place within which the presence and love of God are mediated, and the sexual act a sacrament—a material sign of a spiritual reality. The fathers understood this at least spiritually, through the image of Christ as bridegroom and the church as bride, metaphors reinforced by their exegesis of the Song of Songs. But ancient society, being hierarchical and patriarchal, had little conception of mutual attraction between notional equals except between male friends. So the fathers were unable to take their affirmation of the body, or indeed of marriage, far enough to find holiness outside renunciation.[222]

Young's contextualization of what we might term today as 'Jerome's dilemma' helps us to better understand Jerome's occasional invective against his opponents on the issue of sanctification through living the ascetic virtues of virginity/celibacy to attain 'purity of heart' (*apatheia*). She illustrates this with the example of Jerome's conflict with Evagrius.

> The Origenist monk Evagrius is especially associated with suppression of the 'passions' and analysis of those inner 'demons' that threaten the ascetics' contemplation and peace of mind. Jerome accused him of teaching 'insensibility, like that of a stone,' but Evagrius himself wrote, 'Love is the offspring of impassibility, and impassibility is the blossom of the practical life'—by 'practical life' he meant the cultivation of detachment by challenging the desires of body and soul, but love was its aim.[223]

Certainly, *Ep.* 133 (written to Ctesiphon in 415) is one of Jerome's most forceful letters but if we look closely at the exact text his reference to Evagrius is more of a direct criticism rather than an accusation as suggested by Young. Jerome writes:

> Evagrius... has published a book of maxims on apathy, or, as we should say, impassivity or imperturbability, a state in which the mind ceases to be agitated and—to speak simply—becomes either a stone or a God.[224]

This view (i.e., a criticism against Evagrius rather than an accusation) has been supported by Augustine Casiday who has noted not only Evagrius' 'negative reputation' by the 390s but perhaps more importantly how Jerome's *Ep.* 133 was 'merely suggestive'[225] of a complaint. Of Jerome's *Letter* 133 Casiday opines:

---

[222] Young, *God's*, 290. Jerome's translation of the Song of Songs (with Proverbs and Ecclesiastes) was completed in 393 and dedicated to Chromatius and Heliodorus.
[223] Young, *God's*, 290-291, quoting Jerome, *Ep.* 133 and Evagrius *Praktikos*, 81, 84
[224] Jerome, *Ep.* 133, NPNF[2] 6:274.
[225] A. Casiday, *Reconstructing the Theology of Evagrius Ponticus: Beyond Heresy* (Cambridge: CUP,2013), 54. Elsewhere, Casiday observes: 'There is no direct evidence that he [Evagrius] knew Jerome, but they certainly had friends (or, as if ever the case with Jerome, erstwhile friends) in common' (4).

In his breathless genealogy of heresies that support the idea that Christians can be sinless, Jerome focuses on the relationship between the passions and sins and on the necessity of grace—and, though Christ merits a mention, that mention is poles apart from the high-level speculative Christology that was condemned by the sixth-century anti-Origenists (and, in any event, it has nothing to do with Evagrius, who has receded into the background by that point in Jerome's letter.[226]

With Casiday's interpretation of *Letter* 133 we are presented with Evagrius as an innocent 'victim' of Jerome, countering Young's claim that Evagrius was a target of Jerome's 'accusing' invective. No scholarly consensus here then.

During 2013, scholarly interest in both Jerome as a theologian and Jerome's theology resumed. For example, Michael Haykin's essay 'We Trust in the Saving Blood'[227] considered (in part) Jerome's understanding of the doctrine of definite atonement (the saving work of Christ). In Haykin's view Jerome (together with Hilary of Poitiers and Ambrose) was a 'significant theologian from the fourth century'.[228] This statement clearly does not match with Freeman's (2009) assertion that Jerome both failed to think creatively beyond Nicene orthodoxy and failed to develop his own theology.

Again, describing Jerome as one of 'the most influential occidental theologians,' Haykin cites a comment made by Jerome on Christ's words in Matthew 20: 28 ('and to give his life as ransom for many'). Jerome wrote:

This took place when he took the form of a slave that he might pour out his blood. And he did not say 'to give his life as a redemption for all,' but for 'many,' that is for those who wanted to believe.[229]

Haykin observes:

Here Jerome defines the 'many' as 'those who wanted to believe'. While there may be some ambiguity here in Jerome's statement, the words at least hint that Jerome saw Christ's death to be for a particular group of people—believers.[230]

There is evidence here of Jerome acting as a theologian and, as Haykin remarks, 'While the fathers of the ancient church did not espouse a full-orbed doctrine of definite atonement...there was still a "particular and defined purpose of God in salvation" present in their writings.'[231]

---

[226] Casiday, *Reconstructing*, 70.

[227] M.A.G. Haykin, '"We Trust in the Saving Blood": Definite Atonement in the Ancient Church,' in D. Gibson and J. Gibson (eds.), *From Heaven He Came and Sought Her*, 57-74.

[228] Haykin, 'We Trust,' 59.

[229] Jerome, *Commentary on Matthew* 3.20, in *St. Jerome: Commentary on Matthew* (tr. T.P. Scheck) FOTC (Washington: Catholic University Press of America, 2008), 117, 228-29, as cited by Haykin, 'We Trust,' 70n.65.

[230] Haykin, 'We Trust,' 70.

[231] Haykin, 'We Trust,' 74n.85, citing R.A. Blacketer, 'Definite Atonement in Historical Perspective,' in C.E. Hill and Frank A. James III (eds), *The Glory of the Atonement: Biblical, Historical and Practical Perspectives* (Downers Grove: IVP, 2004), 313.

In his examination of how the early fathers saw the relationship between the scriptural and incarnate Word of God and understood the notion of a divine image in early Christianity, Mark Edwards[232] highlighted Jerome's (as well as Origen's) importance for our understanding of how some early Christians were restricted in their reading of the OT by 'the rabbis of their time' who 'forbade the young to study either the prologue or the conclusion [of Ezekiel].'[233] Thus, this restriction limited some early Christian readers in seeing and hearing God as told in particular OT writings.[234]

Throughout this study we have observed instances of Jerome acting as a 'theological resource' both for certain of his contemporaries as well as for much later theologians and scholars. In this regard one of Jerome's major works *On Illustrious Men* (*De viris illustribus*) (completed 393) has long fascinated patristic specialists despite divided opinion as to its historical/theological merits. For example, Allen Brent finds *De viris illustribus* valuable for its insights into Tertullian's 'Catholic and Montanist phase,' commenting 'Tertullian clearly always remained within the Catholic Church where Cyprian located him with his description of him as his master or teacher (*magister*).'[235]

Whilst Brent is positive here about how Jerome's work has offered up important historical/theological information abount one early Christian writer he finds *De viris illustribus* not a wholly reliable text. Jerome, it appears, was sometimes apt to error, as far example, when he mistakenly described Tertullian as a presbyter.[236]

De viris illustribus was a catalogue of the great (mostly Christian) authors past and present (up to 393) and their writings. As to its merits both Andrew Cain, and Mark Vessey have contested its importance as a historical/theological resource. Cain has remarked, 'The *De viris illustribus* is remarkable because it represents Jerome's attempt to fix a canon of Christian literature and, more to the point, to write himself into that canon,'[237] whilst Vessey has admired its influence over the composition of other 'galleries' of famous Christian men of letters (e.g., that of Eucherius of Lyon).[238] However, Vessey also has some reservations including the way in which, in compiling his catalogue of Christian writers, Je-

---

[232] M. Edwards, *Image, Word and God in the Early Christian Centuries* (Farnham: Ashgate, 2013).

[233] Edwards, *Image*, 21.

[234] Such a restriction was earlier recorded in Origen's *Homilies on the Song of Songs*, preserved now only in Jerome's Latin translation. See Edwards, *Image*, 21, 103.

[235] Jerome, *Vir. ill.* 53, as cited by A. Brent, 'Tertullian on the Role of the Bishop,' in *Tertullian and Paul*, 165-85 (184-85n.43).

[236] Jerome, *Vir. ill.* 53, as cited by A. Brent, 'Tertullian,' 261.

[237] A. Cain, 'Introduction' to St. Jerome, *Commentary on Galatians* (tr. A. Cain; Washington: CUPA, 2010), 10.

[238] M. Vessey, '*The Epistula Rustici ad Eucherium*: From the Library of Imperial Classics to the Library of the Fathers,' in M. Vessey (ed.), *Latin Christian Writers*, 278-97 (286).

rome's 'only principle of authenticity used with any regularity is that of consistency of style'.[239] This leads Vessey on to critically question both the originality and the reliability of *De viris illustribus.*

> The scattered remarks in that work on problems of attribution contain little if anything that would have struck an Alexandrian critic of an earlier age as methodologically new and nothing for which precedent cannot be found in Eusebius' *Ecclesiastical History.* The *De viris illustribus* is not a particularly rigorous instance of the efforts of Christians 'to authenticate the texts in [their] possession'. Indeed Jerome seems more intent on possessing than authenticating. His criteria for inclusion are elastic. Josephus finds a place among the *ecclesiastici scriptores*, as does the philosopher Seneca (*saepe noster*) on the strength of a spurious correspondence with Saint Paul. So too do a considerable number of Christian writers whose theological opinions could no longer pass for catholic or orthodox in the 'fourteenth year of the Emperor Theodosius' (*vir.* 135). A few years later Augustine would complain of this inconvenience and ask Jerome to add an heresiological appendix or gloss...[240] *De viris illustribus* is neither the acme of early Christian literary-critical method nor the reflection of any foundational consensus.[241]

Whilst Vessey's negative criticism of Jerome's work is clearly visible here the juxtaposition of the secondary judgements of Brent, Cain and Vessey demonstrate how the modern reception-history of the *De viris illustribus* has been extremely mixed.

One more example will illustrate this diversity of scholarly opinion regarding *On Illustrious Men.* Rebenich observes:

> The work is less a literary history than a catalogue of Christian authors... The motive of the work was apologetic, as Jerome reveals in the preface. Since the great enemies of Christianity—Celsus, Porphyry, and Julian—had always regarded the new religion as vulgar and plebeian, Jerome wanted to exhibit the intellectual, literary, and philosophical qualities of Christian authors... Although Jerome introduced a new and successful genre his work was far from being original.[242]

---

[239] M. Vessey, 'The Forging of Orthodoxy in Latin Christian Literature: A Case Study', in M. Vessey, *Latin Christian Writers*, 495-513 (507).

[240] Augustine, *Ep.* 40.6.9 (written c. 397-399), as cited by Vessey, 'Forging,' 508n.33. Vessey adds: 'By then... the scholar of Bethlehem had been forced to take a more circumspect view of the criteria for determining Christian authorship' (508-09).

[241] Vessey, 'Forging,' 509. Jerome had intended his *De viris illustribus* 'to follow the example of Tranquillus in giving a systematic account of ecclesiastical writers, and to do for our writers what he did for the illustrious men of letters among the Gentiles, namely, to briefly set before you [Dexter] all those who have published any memorable writing on the Holy Scriptures, from the time of our Lord's passion until the fourteenth year of the Emperor Theodosius,' NPNF[2] 3:359.

[242] Rebenich, *Jerome*, 97.

Rebenich's criticism of non-originality is hardly appropriate since, in his work, Jerome admits to his indebtedness to an important earlier source (Eusebius Pamphilus' ten-book *Church History*)[243] which Rebenich himself acknowledges.[244] However, what Rebenich does criticize is Jerome's 'bias, inaccuracies and inconsistencies in copying earlier texts' which 'have deformed some of the entries'.[245]

Furthermore, in selecting and writing his entries, 'Jerome did not hesitate to canonize his understanding of orthodox stauchness, ascetic championship, and literary brilliance,' and he 'either omitted or chastised contemporaries he disliked.'[246] Such criticisms are particularly damning bearing in mind Jerome's declared aim of providing a 'systematic account of ecclesiastical writers.'

We will now focus upon Andrew Cain's Commentary on *Jerome's Epitaph on Paula*.[247] Cain writes in the book's Preface:

> This volume provides the first full-scale commentary, in any language, on one of Jerome's most celebrated writings, the *Epitaph on St. Paula (Epitaphium Sanctae Paulae)*, an elaborate eulogy, composed in 404, commemorating the life of Paula, his long-time monastic collaborator and literary patron. The *Epitaphium*, which is presented here in a newly revised Latin edition accompanied by a facing-page English translation, is one of the core primary texts on female spirituality (both real and idealized) in Late Antiquity, yet until now it has not received the depth of scholarly analysis that only a proper commentary can afford.[248]

How does Cain view this particular work of Jerome, which 'by editorial convention is printed as *Epistula* 108 in modern editions of his correspondence'.[249]

Jerome's eulogy (tracing Paula's life, particularly her own version and subsequent vocation as a Christian ascetic) is one of his largest letters was written to console Eustochium for the loss of her mother who had recently died. Cain describes it as 'this remarkable specimen of early Christian literature,' being 'the principal primary source from which the biography of the historical Paula is reconstituted'.[250] This work can be seen then as another example of Jerome acting

---

[243] Jerome, *Lives of Illustrious Men*, NPNF², 3:359. Jerome writes: 'As for me, what shall I do, who, having no predecessor, have, as the saying is, the worst possible master, namely myself, and yet I must acknowledge that Eusebius Pamphilus in the ten books of his Church History has been of the utmost assistance.'

[244] Rebenich, *Jerome*, 97.

[245] Rebenich, *Jerome*, 98.

[246] Rebenich, *Jerome*, 98.

[247] A. Cain (ed.), *Jerome's Epitaph on Paula: A Commentary on the Epitaphium Sanctae Paulae* (ed. with an Introduction and Translation by A. Cain; Oxford: OUP, 2013). Although he does not list it here in his bibliography, Cain had already made an earlier excursion into analysing this work. See A. Cain, 'Jerome's Epitaphium Paulae', *JECS* 18.1 (2010), 105-39.

[248] Cain notes, 'By contrast with the works of other major canonical Latin authors, Jerome's have received less attention in this regard than is their due' (ix).

[249] Jerome, *Ep.* 108, NPNF² 6:195-212.

[250] Cain, *Jerome's Epitaph*, 5.

as a theological/historical resource. The framework for Cain's apologia for *Ep.* 108 is set thus:

> For all the scholarly attention that the *Epitaphium* has received, its key literary, propagandistic, and cultic dimensions—the very ones that define the true brilliance of the Hieronymain tour de force—have been overlooked by previous scholarly studies... Far from being the essentially extemporaneous outpouring that Jerome implies it to be, the *Epitaphium* is the product of considerable advance planning, as is evident form the very high quality of literary craftsmanship underlying it.[251]

Cain proceeds, 'The *Epitaphium* indisputably is one of Jerome's finest and most ambitious compositions,'[252] a work in which he 'extolled a very dear friend and long-time monastic compatriot who in his view approximated evangelical perfection more closely than any senatorial Christian of his time'.[253] According to Cain, 'The historical Paula, as soon as she was refracted by the lens of his narrative, became an icon for Jerome's ascetic theology.'[254]

There is some hint in the following citation that Cain is approving of Jerome's tactics is using *Ep.* 108 and Paula's death for his own (theological) self-promotion:

> The suggestion is that her outstanding spiritual successes were the direct result of his mentoring and evidently profound personal influence upon her. She therefore became a credible spokesperson, albeit from beyond the grave, for his controversial brand of ascetic spirituality, and as such she was in a position to bring a measure of credibility to his cause among western Christians by showing the legion of critics that his teachings had eternally salvific effects.[255]

Cain then gives a further illustration Jerome's use of *Ep.* 108 and Paula's death for his own theological self-promotion:

> We are told that Paula voraciously read and studied the Bible in Hebrew and Greek (under Jerome's watchful eye, no less), and we are given the impression that even her everyday language was steeped in the words of Scripture. Thus circumscribed, she stands as an enduring standard-bearer for Hieronymian-style *lectio divina* and biblical scholarship... In life, she had made much of his scholarship possible in the first place through her patronage and had given it a degree of legitimacy by virtue of her endorsement. In death, she continued to validate his labors by stamping them with a retroactive seal of saintly approval.[256]

What, then, can be said about the ethics and validity of *Ep.* 108 as a vehicle for Jerome's self-promotion of his teachings and scholarship? Cain remains mute on

---

[251] Cain, *Jerome's Epitaph*, 6-7. Cain particularly observes 'the nuances of Jerome's Latinity and the traditional rhetorical techniques that he profusely deploys in the *Epitaphium* in order to increase the potency of his prose' (6n.39).

[252] Cain, *Jerome's Epitaph*, 33.

[253] Cain, *Jerome's Epitaph*, 34.

[254] Cain, *Jerome's Epitaph*, 34.

[255] Cain, *Jerome's Epitaph*, 34.

[256] Cain, *Jerome's Epitaph*, 34-35.

this point preferring instead to give one other example of Jerome getting Paula to endorse his work and theology.

On Jerome's recruitment of Paul for his anti-Origenist cause, Cain writes:

> The fact that such a holy woman is said to have applauded and also actively supported him in his campaign against 'heresy' not only presupposes that she herself was irreproachably orthodox but it also lends a certain credence to Jerome's efforts above and beyond the perceived theological merits of his argumentation.[257]

Cain's reception of Jerome's *Ep.* 108 is carefully balanced throughout and he avoids (quite rightly) any modern, critical idioms to describe Jerome's self-promotion strategies. For example, whilst we might perhaps be tempted to think of Jerome (in the modern sense) as having 'groomed' Paula for his own devices, Cain prefers to think of Jerome as having 'fashioned' his holy women disciples.[258]

At the end of 2013 *The New Cambridge History of the Bible: From the Beginnings to 600* appeared containing an important essay by Adam Kamesar,[259] directly addressing Jerome's contribution to biblical scholarship. Kamesar deems Jerome's work on the OT to have been of a 'radical nature', culminating in 'his substitution of the Hebrew text for the Greek Septuagint as the basis for a new Latin version'[260] (i.e., for his Vulgate Latin edition of the Bible). Kamesar comments:

> This change is more profound than we might think, because the Hebrew text and the Septuagint had been evolving separately for five or six hundred years, and represented quite different textual traditions by 400 CE. Even variations that might appear to us to be minor were felt quite acutely by ancient interpreters of the Bible, because they read the text very closely, attributing significance to the smallest details in wording. Corresponding to Jerome's use of the Hebrew as the base text of the Latin OT was his advocacy of the Hebrew canon. In this initiative he was perhaps carrying certain tendencies in the Eastern Church to their logical conclusion, although, as far as the final form of the Vulgate is concerned, he did not completely succeed in imposing his position.[261]

What we clearly see here are elements of both success (his use of the Hebrew as the base text of the Latin OT) and failure (his advocacy of the Hebrew canon) for Jerome's Latin Vulgate version of the OT.

---

[257] Cain, *Jerome's Epitaph*, 35.

[258] Cain, *Jerome's Epitaph*, 36n.171.

[259] A. Kamesar, 'Jerome,' in Paget and Schaper (eds.), *New Cambridge History*, vol. 1, 653-75.

[260] Kamesar, 'Jerome,' 659.

[261] Kamesar, 'Jerome,' 659. For another recent assessment of Jerome and the OT canon, see Gallagher, *Hebrew Scripture*, 50-53. Here Gallagher neatly describes Jerome's OT conceptual framework: 'Just as he advocated the Hebrew text as the correct textual base for the Christian OT, so also Jerome advocated the Jewish canon for the Church' (53).

Kamesar offers a more positive reception to Jerome's appreciation of the literary quality of the scriptures,[262] observing how Jerome was 'a born *philologus* and a master stylist'.[263] Kamesar offers the following example:

His sensitivity in matters of literary appreciation emerges in an early discussion of biblical translation, which appears in the preface to his Latin edition of Eusebius' *Chronicle*, from around 380. He points out that the translation of the seventy does not preserve the same 'flavour' (*sapor*) of the original and goes on to discuss what is 'lost in translation,' not in regards to content but in regards to style and literary appeal. This approach stands in contrast to what had been handed down about translation in the biblical tradition.[264]

Kamesar highlights the context for one of Jerome's contributions to biblical scholarship, and one which we might interpret as one of Jerome's greatest achievements:

There had developed over time especially among the more educated classes, the perception that the Bible was lacking in literary quality. This perception is not surprising, because the biblical corpus was a foreign entity in the Graeco-Latin literary context. The genres represented among the biblical writings often did not neatly correspond with those employed by classical authors, and the language of the Bible, in Greek and Latin, was felt to be well below the standards of Sophocles, Plato or Cicero. This problem came to be particularly acute in the fourth century…However, he [Jerome] was able to express more forcefully than anyone before him the idea that the scriptures, if read in the original Hebrew, had great literary appeal. And more importantly, he was able to bring practical application to this idea, and understand its implications in order to advance appreciation and criticism of scripture.[265] His evaluation of the style of the Prophets is a most creative application of Graeco-Latin scholarship to the biblical corpus.[266]

Here Kamesar's critique shows Jerome's contribution to biblical scholarship to have been especially noteworthy thus raising serious doubts about the 'McGuckin-Freeman' thesis regarding Jerome's lack of originality and creativity. There remains, however, one caveat. Kamesar states:

While not a theologian of significance, his achievements as editor, translator and scholar are perhaps unparalleled in Antiquity… His philological/literary sensitivities and his own ability are what confer distinction on his role in the creation of a new Latin Bible, the Vulgate, as editor and as translator. As a commentator, although perhaps not prolific, in original insights, his erudition and appreciation of the Hebrew and Greek traditions allowed him to produce works of lasting importance for the interpretation of the scriptures.[267]

---

[262] Kamesar, 'Jerome,' 664-66.

[263] Kamesar, 'Jerome,' 664.

[264] Kamesar, 'Jerome,' 664-65. In his preface, Jerome wrote: 'It is hard to follow another man's lines and everywhere keep within bounds. It is an arduous task to preserve felicity and grace unimpaired in a translation,' NPNF[2] 6:483.

[265] Kamesar, 'Jerome,' 666.

[266] Kamesar, 'Jerome,' 667.

[267] Kamesar, 'Jerome,' 674-75.

2014

During this last year of our study no major book studies solely devoted to Jerome appeared. However, a number of citations of Jerome in books relating to other allied subjects, as well as to Jerome's possible influence over the patristic interpretation of the Gospel of John, were published and are worthy of our attention.

First, Matthew Crawford's study of Cyril of Alexandria's Trinitarian Theology of Scripture[268] again argued the view that Jerome was a source for Cyril.[269] Here, two examples will suffice. Noting how Jerome 'often provides parallels for Cyril's exegesis of the prophets,'[270] Crawford writes:

> The fact that both Cyril and Jerome give John 14:27 as a cross-reference in their exposition of Isaiah 9:6 could be evidence that the Alexandrian archbishop relied to some degree upon the Latin exegete in this instance.[271]

And, again:

> Cyril undoubtedly had access to Jerome's works, and so would have known of his objections to the Montanists[272]… there are other passages in Cyril's corpus in which he describes prophetic inspiration as a vision of future events… This is an idea that he could have picked up from Jerome given that it is clear he had access to at least some of Jerome's works.[273]

However, this is very disappointing and suggests, as we saw earlier, that Crawford's proposition that Jerome's exegesis may have influenced Cyril is highly improbable, given that Cyril did not read works in Latin.

Also in 2014, a newly published festschrift for Gillian Clark[274] spotlighted Jerome's literary oeuvre and its place in the developing tradition of, what Mark Vessey describes as, 'Christian Ways with Books'.[275] Focusing in particular upon Jerome's Latin translation and updating of the Christian world-chronicle of Eusebius of Caesarea, Vessey proffers a positive reception to Jerome's 'bold venture'.[276] Vessey states:

> Apart from extending Eusebius' coverage into recent decades and supplying what he saw as his deficiencies in the matter of Roman political history, he added two main types of material: a set of notices on building works in the city of Rome, and

---

[268] M.R. Crawford, *Cyril of Alexandria's Trinitarian Theology of Scripture* (Oxford: OUP, 2014).

[269] Crawford, *Cyril*, 29, 30n.60, 112, 122-24, 164-65.

[270] Crawford, *Cyril*, 29.

[271] Crawford, *Cyril*, 30n.60.

[272] Crawford, *Cyril*, 81.

[273] Crawford, *Cyril*, 91.

[274] C. Harrison, C. Humfress, and I. Sandwell (eds), *Being Christian in Late Antiquity* (Oxford: OUP, 2014).

[275] M. Vessy, 'Fashions for Varro in Late Antiquity and Christian Ways with Books,' in *Being Christian*, 253-77.

[276] Vessey, 'Fashions', 261n.32, citing Rebenich, *Hieronymus und sein Kreis* (Stuttgart: Franz Steiner Verlag, 1992), 115-39.

another on Latin writers and orators… Jerome, it appears, was intent on creating a monumental setting for his initiatives as a Christian Latin.[277]

Here in Vessey's critique we can see clear indications of Jerome being innovative thus inviting a retort to Freeman's judgement that Jerome's writings lack creativity.[278]

Further interesting insights into Jerome's principles and practice of exegesis were provided by Chris Keith[279] and Michael Graves.[280] Keith mentions Jerome in relation to the patristic interpretation of the Gospel of John, specifically how Jerome (and Ambrose and Augustine) read and interpreted John 7.53-8.11 (the earliest demonstrable location for *pericope adulterae*).[281]

> Comments by Ambrose and Jerome reveal that these writers read *PA* in G John, though they do not reveal exactly where in that narrative the story appeared. *PA*'s precise location, however, is revealed by contemporaneous Greek and Old Latin manuscripts, Jerome's placement of *PA* in the Vulgate, and the running commentaries by Augustine… There is widespread agreement based on the Vulgate manuscript tradition that *PA* was at John 7.53-8.11 in those manuscripts, but none from this period have survived.[282] Therefore, both the manuscript evidence and patristic evidence confirm that *PA*'s earliest demonstrable location in John is at John 7.53-8.11. The Vulgate, Codex D, and the Old Latin tradition offer textual evidence for this location from the 380's on. Comments from Ambrose, Jerome and Augustine corroborate this evidence.[283]

Therefore, according to Keith's reading of Jerome on John 7.53-8.11, Jerome was an important contributor to the early location of *PA* in this particular bible passage. This, then, would clearly contest McGuckin's (2005) claim that Jerome's reputation as an exegete is over-stressed (at least if we look for originality).

In contrast to Keith, Michael Graves considered Jerome's role in, and contribution to, 'ways of seeing the Bible as great literature.'[284] Graves observes 'As

---

[277] Vessey, 'Fashions,' 262.

[278] Vessey offers a further example of Jerome's capacity for innovation: 'Instead of an *imago* or portable portrait of Origen [in his Latin translation/updating of Eusebius' *Chronicle*], Jerome would publish an *index* or Landlist of the Alexandrian's writings' (264).

[279] Keith, *The Pericope Adulterae*.

[280] Graves, *Inspiration and Interpretation*.

[281] Keith, *The Pericope Adulterae*, 122-30. Here, the *PA* denotes a particular 'story' interpreted from a particular biblical passage, in this case how Jesus twice 'bent down and began to write on the earth'.

[282] Keith, *The Pericope Adulterae*, 122-23.

[283] Keith, *The Pericope Adulterae*, 130. Keith adds: 'The evidence concerning Ambrose and Jerome being the first Christian authors to comment upon Jesus' acts of writing *PA* may suggest that *PA*'s insertion is closer to the context of these fathers in the fourth century than, e.g., Papias in the early second century. Ambrose and Jerome know *PA* in John *and* find Jesus' writing to be significant' (252).

[284] Graves, *Inspiration and Interpretation*, 72-80.

Christian Scripture took on the status of a major cultural symbol, it was necessary to explore what literary merit it might possess. Two figures in particular, Jerome and Augustine, made significant observations about the potential literary quality of Scripture.'[285] Specifically on Jerome, Graves argues:

> Jerome loved pointing out figures of speech in the Hebrew text [of the OT], and he had a good eye for wordplay in Hebrew... In spite of natural imperfections in his knowledge given his time and circumstances, Jerome attained strong competency in Hebrew and represents the high point of Hebrew scholarship in the early church. His appreciation of the literary merits of the OT in Hebrew was a significant contribution to early Christian thought.[286]

Here Graves accords Jerome a high-rank both as an exegete and as a philologist, and his assessment of Jerome again clearly counters McGuckin's (2005) claim that Jerome's reputation as exegete is over-stressed (at least if we look for originality).

It is appropriate that we now conclude this final chapter of our study by looking at some secondary judgements on Jerome contained in the second volume of the *Cambridge History of Christianity*.[287] First, Bronwen Neil's reflections upon Jerome and literary culture:

> Jerome's early life exemplifies what good use a Christian convert could make of his pagan rhetorical training... he became one of the most prolific writers and translators of Christian literature in the West...perhaps the best example of early Christian biography is Jerome's *De viris Illustribus*... Jerome was unusual in applying... a modern standard of literary criticism to his contemporaries. Most Christian writers, in keeping with the Grace-Roman tradition, sought not originality but continuity with their Christian forebears.[288]

Again, with this assessment by Neil, Freeman's (2009) remark that Jerome's writings lack creativity appears to be seriously mis-judged.

And, finally, Paul Blowers on Jerome's interpretation of Scripture:

> The 'literal' sense... could indicate the coherence of biblical narratives, a major concern of exegetes like Jerome [and Theodoret]... Narrative coherence, for early Christian interpreters, ultimately concerned the 'realism' of the whole biblical drama, according to which individual stories could be judged 'literally' true in their 'figural' relation to the larger narrative...[289]

---

[285] Graves, Inspiration and Interpretation, 78.
[286] Graves, Inspiration and Interpretation, 78.
[287] A. Casiday and F.W. Norris (eds), *The Cambridge History of Christianity*, vol. 2: *Constantine to c. 600* (Cambridge: CUP, 2014).
[288] B. Neil, 'Towards defining a Christian culture: The Christian transformation of classical literature,' in Casiday and Norris (eds), *Cambridge History of Christianity*, 317-42 (322, 334-35).
[289] P.M. Blowers, 'Interpreting Scripture,' in Casiday and Norris (eds), *Cambridge History of Christianity*, 618-36 (631). For one of the best recent critical overviews of the

But, of course, for Jerome, narrative coherence could only be achieved by the interpreter of Scripture (here Jerome) embellishing the text (via exegesis) with scriptural eloquence to enable the reader to clearly understand what the text teaches about God. That was Jerome's great task as a Bible scholar and, also, perhaps his greatest achievement.

---

interpretation of scriptural texts, see M. Bird and M. Pahl (eds) *The Sacred Text: Excavating the Texts, Exploring the Interpretations, and Engaging the Theologies of the Christian Scriptures* (Piscataway: Gorgias, 2010), chapters 5-8.

Chapter 7

Conclusion

This study of *Jerome and his Modern Interpreters* has shown how, due to the sometimes complex nature of Jerome's writings and thoughts, Jerome's corpus has very often puzzled modern scholars. The investigation has shed light on the origins and development of Jerome's exegetical principles and practice (including his hermeneutic), the composition of his commentaries, homilies, letters and polemics as well as how these affected his relations with his associates and contemporaries. Having looked at these aspects of Jerome's work through the lens of modern Jerome scholarship, the study has illuminated the changing directions and perspectives of Jerome studies between 1880 and 2014 and offered a unique account of the modern scholarly representation of Jerome's oeuvre.

In asking whether or not modern scholars have read Jerome's ancient works anew, more critically and with greater objectivity (for example, by trying to avoid the 'jeromeanesque'), than previous, the various secondary reassessments were, for the most part, critiqued using a particular theoretical model constructed by the present author, namely, the 'McGuckin-Freeman' thesis. This model argued (in part) that Jerome's reputation as an exegete is over-stressed (at least if we look for originality) and that his writings display a failure to think creatively beyond Nicene orthodoxy. The enquiry has found that Jerome's exegesis is a prime example of patristic commentating both at its best and at its most problematic. Jerome's theological/hermeneutical formula *Hebraica Veritas*, as well as his sometimes dubious interpretative tactics, caused much controversy and opposition. Yet despite these faults Jerome's oeuvre holds many important insights into the development of the nascent early Christian Church, including the formation of Christian identity and Christian orthodoxy (e.g., the debate over the small 's' nature of sin, the fall of man, the Trinity and transfiguration).

This study has sought to identify and address a number of key questions and issues (described in chapter 1) regarding the critical reception given by modern scholars (writing in English/ or in English translation) to selected texts/writings drawn from Jerome's corpus a particular attempt has been made to explore in some detail modern scholarly opinion on the variety of Jerome's *oeuvre*, how it was constructed and how it was transmitted to readers during the fourth and fifth centuries.

Whilst this critique has had two main aims: first, to describe and explain many of the arguments that have been advanced by scholars critical of Jerome's corpus, and, secondly, to outline the changing scholarly directions taken and perspectives offered by historians and theologians on selected Jerome texts/writings, both before and since J.N.D. Kelly's influential study, *Jerome* (1975). These dual aims were set in order that a systematic explanation of Jerome's principles and practice might be revealed. The research contributes to our knowledge and understanding of the modern scholarly critical reception given to selected Jerome texts/writings, by providing a chronological survey and appraisal of past and current scholarly thinking about Jerome—the exegete, the theologian (scholars have differed on whether or not we should label Jerome as a 'theologian'), the ascetic and the polemical controversialist—and establishing how, in the aftermath of the histor-ical-literary revolution of the nineteenth century, the search for the real Jerome still continues to fascinate scholars. The research further confirms that the schol-arly understanding of the principles and practice of Jerome remains one of the most challenging and enduring of problems.

For Jerome the correct interpretation of the Bible was the 'literal', or histori-cal-grammatical, interpretation although, as we have seen, Jerome did not always keep to 'literal-historical' exegesis alone. He had just as much typology—inter-preting OT texts to relate to Christ or the Church as other patristic commentators. And yet, despite all of this, modern scholars have disagreed on the issue of how this complex but important patristic writer should be read and interpreted. We have seen (chapters 2-6) how many of these scholars have been divided about the best way to approach Jerome's works and the degree of originality/creativity to be found within them. What this particular study has demonstrated is that even today there is no case for closure on the 'Jerome debate'.

Modern Jerome scholarship has clearly established Jerome as a pioneer figure in the interpretation and uses of Scripture. This scholarship has further identified and confirmed how Jerome's linguistic philosophy (the correct contextual use of language in bible translation/commentary) and scripture hermeneutic (*Hebraica a Veritas*) lay at the root of his ideas that sometimes offended the early church. It has also often challenged some of the familiar assumptions made about Jerome (e.g., that Jerome was a borrower of others' exegesis and may even have plagia-rized some of the materials for his biblical commentaries). However, some recent Jerome scholars, notably those after 2000 (e.g., Rebenich, Hale Williams, Cain and Lössl), have not succeeded in arguing a case for Jerome as the pre-eminent Doctor of the Church (that accolade is generally given to Augustine who contin-ues to dominate scholarly research, debate and publications in the field of patris-tics).

It has been against the 'McGuckin-Freeman' (*M-F*) thesis, namely, that 'whilst Jerome was one of the most important argumentative ascetics of the fourth century and perhaps the most important biblical scholar of the early West-ern church, his reputation as exegete is over-stressed (at least if we look for orig-inality)' (McGuckin, 2005), and that Jerome 'proved too pedantic a thinker ever to engage fully with the intricacies of Greek philosophy' and that 'one can see from his writings how he clung to Nicene orthodoxy but failed to think creatively beyond it and never showed any genuine intellectual creativity or had the self-confidence to develop his own theology' (Freeman, 2009), that many of the se-lected scholarly reassessments of Jerome were evaluated in order to assess the degree (if any) of a modern scholarly consensus on the value (or otherwise) of aspects of Jerome's *oeuvre*.

Since Jerome's works exhibit his intertwined methodological, hermeneutical and theological development, these mixed but joined features of Jerome's principles of textual criticism and practice of translation have not always been easy for scholars to discern and interpret. Consequently, it is no surprise to find that modern scholars' secondary judgements on selected aspects of Jerome's corpus do not reach a consensus when viewed against the *M-F* thesis. Whilst not offering a corrective to the *M-F* proposition, modern Jerome scholarship has shown certain features of Jerome's canon (e.g., the *Vulgate* translation of the Bible) to have been of major importance for the understanding of the Church in the Catholic tradition of the West, as well as the Orthodox traditions of the East.

It is hoped that this study has contributed to the accumulation of modern scholarly interpretative thought on some selective texts/writings drawn from Jerome's corpus. Using already known material but with a fresh interpretation (the 'M-F' thesis), we have seen how Jerome's principles and practice (despite each of these displaying a profound continuity) were far from simple and straightforward. Even where scholars have agreed on the meaning of a particular text/writing, they have not always found it easy to see how this literature fits into the history of the early Church (e.g., what community nurtured and venerated it?) While such questions and issues will continue to arouse scholarly debate, the value of Jerome's corpus to our knowledge and understanding of the growing Christian Church in the fourth and fifth centuries must not be obscured.

With regard to Jerome's rules of scriptural interpretation scholars have analysed and affirmed their unity, disclosing Jerome's intention to give his early readers a clearer understanding of Scripture. As a critical survey and analysis of the scholarly landscape of modern research into particular aspects of Jerome's *oeuvre* this study has situated Jerome within the socio-historical background of Graeco-Roman society of the fourth and fifth centuries. Looking at the views of a number of modern interpreters of Jerome and his work, this enquiry has revealed a man deeply indebted to the Jewish, Greek and Roman past and yet distinctly Christian.

This study has particularly highlighted the manner in which Jerome used his writings to express his theological vision and infused those works with theological content. As such, the study offers a comprehensive critique of readings by modern scholars of some of Jerome's works—particularly his use of syntax when engaged in exegesis—and provides an accessible point of entry into Jerome's literary output and thought. In making their reassessments of particular parts of Jerome's oeuvre, scholars have differed markedly not only in their interpretive choices but also in their evaluations and judgments. Whilst many scholars accept that Jerome's corpus underscores his ability as a chronicler of the transition from paganism to Christianity (i.e., the development and maintenance of a Christian identity in the pluralistic ancient world) and the changing views on Christian orthodoxy, others have questioned just how far Jerome's works were original.

The figure of Jerome has been viewed by modern scholars in the context of his position as one of our ancient ancestors of the faith, where he worked as an exegete describing and interpreting the Scriptural vistas as he saw them. Thus, it was important for scholars to examine Jerome's interpretive principles and contributions in the intellectual context of his time (i.e., principally the exegetical Alexandrian Tradition, which began at the beginning of the third century when Alexandra was the intellectual capital of the Roman Empire in late antiquity and lasted until Cyril of Alexandria in c. 378-444).

This critique of the critical reception by modern scholars of selected texts/writings drawn from Jerome's corpus *Jerome and his Modern Interpreters* takes Jerome studies further than some previous accounts, both in method and in scope. Whereas other scholarly examinations of Jerome's work have largely focused upon individual case-studies (e.g., studies of Jerome's commentaries and homilies and letters), the present analysis has offered a wider treatment of features of Jerome's oeuvre. Whilst no scholarly consensus has been reached on the issue of the quality of Jerome's corpus and Jerome's celebrity as an exegete, there has been general agreement that Jerome's work reflected its basis in traditional, orthodox Christianity.

First, we have seen the contributions made by Jerome's exegetical and other writings to the development of Christian identity during the fourth and fifth centuries, most especially in the context of a more powerful Church which evolved during the age of Emperor Constantine (306-337) and after, to 400. Second, fresh reassessments on aspects of Jerome's oeuvre have confirmed Jerome's position as one of the most important sources of information from within patristic literature about the early Church, as well as about Origen (i.e., Jerome acting as a theological resource). Thirdly, we have noted, how scholars have judged Jerome's importance in the post-Nicene Christological controversy. Whilst some scholars have suggested that Jerome may have had an initial aversion to Nicene orthodoxy, seemingly unwilling to fully support the notion of *homoousios* (i.e., that the Son was consubstantial with God) he eventually came to accept it. It must be said, however, that there is no general scholarly consensus surrounding these points. For example, Professor Richard Price has stated: 'Surely Jerome never questioned the homoousion as defined at Nicaea. What he criticized were eastern developments in Nicene theology (nowadays often called 'neo-Nicene') which seemed to him excessively narrow. Jerome was always a loyal Nicene.'[1]

What can be said here is that contrary to Freeman's (2009) criticism of Jerome's theological powers (namely, that Jerome failed to think creatively beyond Nicene orthodoxy) Jerome was at least a significant contributor, and outspoken polemicist, on the debate over Nicene orthodoxy and its opponents. We have further seen how scholars have shown a sometimes ambivalent attitude to Jerome's corpus and achievements. For example, not all scholars are persuaded of the importance of Jerome's works as contributions to the patristic tradition and development of Christianity in late antiquity, unlike say the works of Origen,

---

[1] Letter to author, 8 April, 2014.

Eusebius, Athanasius, Augustine, Ambrose of Milan, Gregory of Nazianzus and Gregory of Nyssa.

In their quest for the real (historical) Jerome, this study has shown how modern scholars have confirmed, refined and extended various features of Jerome's widely debated positions on some of the great and formative questions of the Christian faith, such as the Trinity, the incarnation, the Transfiguration and the nature of the Church. Jerome has been a controversial figure throughout history and, as we have seen, the polarization of scholarly opinion and judgement on this "*master of the faith*" has not abated. The sometimes complex nature of his thought and writings largely accounts for this polarization. Rather than finding balanced scholarly critiques, we have, in this study, too often encountered extremes with, on the one hand, those scholars keen to advance Jerome's skills as exegete, translator and history chronicler, and, on the other, those scholars critical of Jerome's works for their evidence of self-promotion and plagiarism.

The period of modern Jerome scholarship covered by this study (1880-2014) has presented us with a variety of secondary judgments on Jerome, notably portraits of Jerome the 'Vir Trilinguis' and systematic exegete, and of Jerome the ascetic and theological controversialist, each claiming equal validity. Scholarly opinion during our period of enquiry has generally agreed the Jewish provenance of much of Jerome's corpus (ie., just as Jerome favoured the Hebrew text as the true textual base for the Christian Old Testament, so he also favoured the Jewish canon for the Church). Although in recent years (since 2000) the sharp polarized positions of scholars studying Jerome's oeuvre have become more measured, certain aspects of his literary output have not been sufficiently researched and clarified (e.g., his letters of reply to Bishops Cromasius and Heliodorus regarding the later Gospel of Pseudo-Matthew to further the support for the Davidic descent of the Virgin Mary and the veneration of the Virgin Mary). We have also seen how, in seeking to reassess the nature of Jerome's hermeneutic, some scholars have charged Jerome with being guilty of imposing a doctrinal system on his hearers and compromising the truth of the gospel for the sake of personal strategic victories.

What of the future for Jerome studies? There seems to be abundant room now for scholars to examine a number of outstanding questions and issues. First, the question of whether or not Jerome went beyond borrowing others' exegetical methods and willingly plagiarized some materials for his own advancement as an exegete. Second, whether or not Jerome's reputation as an authoritative defender of Scripture and the orthodox Christian faith depended largely upon Jerome's own zeal for self-promotion rather than upon the critical acclaim won from his contemporaries in the fourth and fifth centuries. Third, there needs to be a greater focus upon the storyline of Jerome and more investigation into the factors which helped shape the making of this important biblical scholar (e.g., Jerome's early and later education and Jerome's relations to his associates and contemporaries). Future Jerome scholarship also needs to further address the

J.N.D. Kelly/Gribmont dichotomy we identified in chapter 4 as well as the psychology of Jerome (e.g., his 'sexual awakening' in the Desert of Chalcis, his attitudes towards women and reasons for his sometimes violent invective against his opponents).

Scholarly interest in Jerome will undoubtedly continue because within him is found the faith of the Latin West and of the Christian Church, which has motivated and still motivates oncoming generations of scholars into pursuing both biblical and patristic scholarship. Simply put, there is already, and will continue to be, within the academy of historical theology, an ever-growing debate about St. Jerome's legacy to patristic biblical exegesis, asceticism and the development of early Christianity. Whilst there still continues to be no consensus amongst scholars on the 'McGuckin-Freeman' thesis, there is some acknowledgement of Jerome's important influence over the theology and theologies of the patristic era.

Bibliography

Primary sources employed in the monograph include the following:

Ambrose, *Letters*

Athanasius, *First Epistle to Serapion*

Augustine, *Adv. Marc. Cont.*; *De civitate Dei*; *De fide et op*; *De doctrina Christiana*; *De mor*; *De sancta virginitate*; *The Catholic and Manichaean Ways of Life*; *The City of God*; *The Homilies of St John*; *On the Good of Marriage*; *On the Trinity*; *Paedag*; *Sermon* 269.2

Basil of Caesarea, *Eph.* 54

Chrysostom, John, *On the Priesthood*

Clement of Alexandria, *Paedag*; *On Virginity*

Didymus the Blind, *The Holy Spirit* 57

Eusebius, *Ecclesiastical History*

Gregory of Nyssa, *Against Eunomius* 3.5

Irenaeus, *Contra Haer*

Jerome, *Adv. Jov*; *Against the Pelagians*; *Adv. Rufuius*; *Alercatio* (*Altercatio Lucieriani et Orthodox*); *Apology* 1; *Chronicle of Eusebius*; *Commentary on Amos*; *Commentary on Daniel*; *Commentary on Ecclesiastes*; *Commentary on Ephesians*; *Commentary on Esa*; *Commentary on Galatians*; *Commentary on Isaiah*; *Commentary on Jeremiah*; *Commentary on Kings*; *Commentary on the Psalms*; *Commentary on Philemon*; *Commentary on Samuel*; *Commentary on Titus*; *Commentary on Zechariah*; *Dialogue against the Luciferians*; *Gospel according to the Hebrews*; *Homily for Epiphany*; *Homily on Mark*; *Homilies on Psalms*; *Letters*; *Liber conta Helvidium de perpetua virginitate Marie*; *Liber Hebraicorum Quastionum in Genesion*; *Liber de Nominibus Hebraicis*; *Liber de Viginitate Servanda* (letter 22); *Liber de Situ et Nominibus Locorum Hebraicorum*; *Life of Chariton*; *Life of Hilarion*; *Life of Malchus*; *Life of Papias*; *Life of Paul the Hermit*; *Lives of Illustrious Men* (*De Vir. IU*); *On First Principles* (trans *Of Origen*); *Prologus Galeatus* ('Helmeted Preface' to Latin translation of the Hebrew books of Samuel and Kings); *Vita Hilarionis*; *Vita Malchi* (*De monacho capituo*); *The Vulgate Bible*; *Commentary on Romans*; *On First Principles*; *Homily on Leviticus*; *Homilies on Numbers*

Justin Martyr, *Dialogue* 56-62

Novatian, *On the Trinity*

Origen, *Homily on Numbers*; *Homily on Joshua*; *Against Celsus* (*Contra Celsum*)

Palladius, *Lausiac History* (*The Paradise or Garden of the Holy Fathers*)

Rufinus, *Apol. Adv. Hier*, 2.6-7

Tertullian, *Adversus Marcenonian*; *Adv. Prax* 5.1; *Exhortation to Chastity and on Monogamy*

Secondary Sources

Ackroyd, P.R., and C.F. Evans (eds), *The Cambridge History of the Bible*, vol. 1: *From The Beginnings to Jerome* (Cambridge: CUP, 1970).

Adkin, N., 'Ambrose and Jerome: The Opening Shot,' *Mnemosyne* 4.46 (1993), 364-76.

—. 'Jerome, Ambrose and Gregory Nazianzen (Jerome, Epist. 52, 7-8),' *Vichiana*, 4 (1993), 294-300.

—. *Jerome on Virginity: A Commentary on the Libellus de Virginitate Servanda* (Letter 22) (Cambridge: CUP, 2004).

Alexander, D.C., **Augustine's Early Theology** *of the Church: Emergence and Implications* (New York: Peter Lang, 2008).

Allen, P.S. (ed.), *Erasmi Epistolde* (Oxford, 1910).

Anatolios, K., *Retrieving Nicaea: The Development and Meaning of Trinitarian Doctrine* (Grand Rapids: Baker, 2011).

Andreopulous, A., A. Casiday and C. Harrison (eds), *Meditations of the Heart: The Psalms in Early Christian Thought and Practice* (Turnhout, Brepols, 2011).

Anson, P.F., *The Call of the Desert: The Solitary Life in the Christian Church* (London: SPCK, 1964).

Augustine, *Confessions* (rev. T. Gill; Alachua: Bridge Logos, 2003).

—. *De Doctrina Christiana* (ed. and tr. R.P.H. Green; Oxford: Clarendon, 1995).

—. *Essential Sermons* (Introduction and notes by D.E. Doyle, tr. E.H.K, ed. B. Ramsey; New York: New City Press, 2007).

—. *On Faith and Works,* Ancient Christian Writer Series vol.48 (tr. and annotated by G.J. Lombardo; New York: Newman, 1988).

Ayres, L., *Augustine and the Trinity* (New York: CUP, 2013).

—. *Nicaea and its Legacy: An Approach to Fourth-Century Trinitarian Theology* (Oxford: OUP, 2004).

Barrett, M., *Salvation by Grace: The Case for Effectual Calling and Regeneration* (Phillipsburg: P&R, 2013).

Bartholomew, C.B., *Ecclesiastes* (Grand Rapids: Baker, 2009).

Batas, M., *The Hermeneutics of the Apostolic Proclamation: The Center of* **Paul's Method of Scriptural Interpretation** (WACS: Baylor University Press, 2012).

Bauckham, R.J., *Jude and the Relatives of Jesus in the Early Church* (Edinburgh: T&T Clark, 1990).

Béchard, D.P. (ed.), *The Scripture Documents: An Anthology of Official Catholic Teachings* (Collegeville: Liturgical, 2002).

Beckwith, C., 'Athanasius' in B.G. Green (ed.), *Shapers of Christian Orthodoxy: Engaging with early and medieval theologians* (Nottingham: Apollos, 2010), 153-89.

Bede the Venerable, *Homilies on the Gospels I: Advent to Lent*, Cistercian Fathers Series 110 (tr. L.T. Martin and D. Hurst; Kalamazoo: Cistercian, 1990).

BeDuhn, J.D., *Augustine's Manichaean Dilemma, 1: Conversion and Apostasy, 373-388 C.E.* (Pennsylvania: University of Pennsylvania Press, 2010).

—. *Augustine's Manichaean Dilemma, 2: Making a 'Catholic' Self, 388-401 C.E.* (Pennsylvania: University of Pennsylvania Press, 2013).

—. *The First New Testament: Marcion's Scriptural Canon* (Salem: Polebridge, 2013).

—. *The Manichaean Body: In Discipline and Ritual* (Baltimore: John Hopkins University Press, 2000).

Beeley, C.A., *Gregory of Nazianzus on the Trinity and the Knowledge of God: In Your Light We Shall See Light* (New York: OUP, 2008).

—. *Leading God's People: Wisdom from the Early Church for Today* (Grand Rapids: Eerdmans, 2012).

—. (ed.), *Re-Reading Gregory of Nazianzus: Essays on History, Theology, and Culture* (Washington: CUAP 2012).

—. *The Unity of Christ: Continuity and Conflict in Patristic Tradition* (New Haven: Yale University Press, 2012).

Benedict XVI, Pope, *The Fathers of the Church: From Clement of Rome to Augustine of Hippo* (Grand Rapids: Eerdmans, 2009).

Benstead, J.B., (ed.), *The Birth of Philosophic Christianity: Studies in Early Christian and Medieval Thought: Ernest Fortin — Collected Essays*, vol. 1 (Lanham: Rowman and Littlefield, 1996).

Bettenson, H (ed. and tr.) *The Early Christian Fathers: A Selection from the Writings of the Fathers from St. Clement of Rome to St. Athanasius* (Oxford: OUP, 1956).

Bird, M.F., *The Gospel of the Lord: How the Early Church Wrote the Story of Jesus* (Grand Rapids, Eerdmans, 2014).

Blowers, P., 'Doctrine of Creation', in Harvey and Hunter/eds), *The Oxford Handbook of Early Christian Studies*, 906-931.

Blowers P., A.R. Christman, D.G. Hunter and R.D. Young (eds), *In Dominceo Eloquio — In Lordly Eloquence* (Grand Rapids: Eerdmans, 2002).

Bock, D.L. and M. Glaser (eds), *To the Jew First: The Case for Jewish Evangelism in Scripture and History* (Grand Rapids: Kregel, 2008).

Bockmuehl, M. and G.E. Stroumsa (eds), *Paradise in Antiquity: Jewish and Christian Views* (Cambridge: CUP, 2010).

Bray, G., *Biblical Interpretation: Past and Present* (Downers Grove: IVP, 1996).

—. *Creeds, Councils and Christ: Did the early Christians Misrepresent Jesus?* (2nd edn; Fearn, Ross-shire: Mentor/Christian Focus, 2009).

Bredero, A.H., *Christendom and Christianity in the Middle Ages* (Grand Rapids: Eerdmans, 1994).

Brown, D, '**Jerome** and the Vulgate: in Hauser and Watson (eds), *A History of Biblical Interpretation*, vol. 1, *The Ancient Period*, 355-378.

—. *Vir Trilinguis: A Study in the Biblical Exegesis of St. Jerome* (Kampen: Kok Pharos, 1992).

—. '*Vir Trilinguis — A Study in the Biblical Exegesis of St. Jerome* (M. Litt thesis, University of Oxford, 1989).

Brown, P., *Augustine of Hippo: A Biography* (London: Faber, 1967).

—. *Society and the Holy in Late Antiquity* (London: Faber and Faber, 1982).

—. *The Rise of Western Christendom: Triumph and Diversity, A.D. 200-1000* (2nd edn; Oxford: Blackwell, 2003).

—. *Through the Eye of a Needle: Wealth, the Fall of Rome, and the Making of Christianity in the West, 350-550 AD* (Princeton: Princeton University Press, 2012).

Brown, S.F., 'The Theological Role of the Fathers,' in M. Dauphineis and M. Lavering (eds), *Reading John with St. Thomas Aquinas: Theological Exegesis and Speculative Theology* (Washington: CUA, 2005), 9-20.

Bryan, C., *Listening to the Bible: The Art of Faithful Biblical Interpretation* (New York: OUP, 2014).

Burke, A.J., *John the Baptist: Prophet and Disciple* (Cincinnati: St. Anthony Messenger, 2006).

Burnett, C.C., 'The Interpretation of the Bible before the Modern Period', in M. Gorman (ed.), *Scripture: An Ecumenical Introduction to the Bible and its Interpretation* (Peabody: Hendrickson, 2005), 133-45.

Butterworth, G.W., 'Translator's Introduction,' in *Origen: On First Principles* (Foreword by J.C. Cavadini and Introduction by Henri de Lubac; Notre Dame: Ave Maria, 2013), xxxiii-lxxvi.

Cain, A., 'An Unidentified Patristic Quotation in Jerome's *Commentary on Galatians* (3.6.11)', *JTS* 61.1 (April 2010), 216-25.

—. 'Jerome's Epataphium Paulae: Hagiography, Pilgrimage, and the Cult of Saint Paula,' *JECS* 18.1 (2010), 105-39.

—. (ed), *Jerome's Epitaph on Paula: A Commentary on the Epitaphium Sanctae Paulae with an Introduction, Text, and Translation* (Oxford: OUP, 2013).

—. 'Origen, Jerome and the *Senatus Pharisaeorum*,' *Latomus*, 65 (2006), 727-34.

—. 'Rethinking Jerome's Portraits of Holy Women,' in A. Cain and J. Lössl (eds), *Jerome of Stridon*, 47-57.

—. *The Letters of Jerome: Asceticism, Biblical Exegesis, and the Construction of Christian Authority in Late Antiquity* (Oxford: OUP, 2009).

—. and J. Lössl (eds), *Jerome of Stridon: His Life, Writings and Legacy* (Farnham: Ashgate, 2009).

Campenhausen, von H., *The Fathers of the Latin Church* (London: Adam and Charles Black, 1964).

—. *The Formation of the Christian Bible* (tr. J.A. Baker; London: Adam and Charles Black, 1972).

—. *Tradition and Life in the Church: Essays and Lectures on Church History* (London: Collins, 1968).

Casiday, A.M., *Evagrius Ponticus. The Early Church Fathers* (London: Routledge, 2006).

—. *Reconstructing the Theology of Evagrius Ponticus: Beyond Heresy* (Cambridge, CUP, 2013).

—. and F. Norris (eds), *The Cambridge History of Christianity*, vol. 2: *Constantine to c. 600* (Cambridge: CUP, 2014).

Cavallera, *Saint Jerome — Sa vie et son oeuvre*, 2 vols (Louvain/Paris, 1922).

Chadwick, H., *Augustine* (Oxford: OUP, 1986).

—. *East and West: The Making of a Rift in the Church — From Apostolic Times until the Council of Florence* (Oxford: OUP, 2003).

—. *History and Thought of the Early Church* (London: Variorum, 1982).

—. *Origen: Contra Celsum* (tr., introduction and notes by H. Chadwick; Cambridge: CUP, 1953, reprinted 1986).

—. 'Pachomios and the Idea of Sanctity,' in H. Chadwick, *History and Thought of the Early Church*, 14.11-24.

—. 'St. Peter and St. Paul in Rome: The Problem of the Memoria Apostolorum ad Catacumbas,' *JTS* 8 (1957), 31-52.

—. *The Church in Ancient Society: From Galilee to Gregory the Great* (New York: OUP, 2001).

—. *The Early Church: The Story of Emergent Christianity from the Apostolic Age to the Dividing of the Ways between the Greek East and the Latin West* (London: Pelican, 1967).

Chapman, J., 'St. Jerome and the Vulgate New Testament,' *JTS* 24 (1923), 33-51, 113-25, 282-99.

Cheetham, N., *Keeper of the Keys: A History of Popes from St. Peter to John Paul I* (New York: Scribner, 1983).

Christie-Burton, D., *The Word in the Desert: Scripture and the Quest for Holiness in Early Christian Monasticism* (Oxford: OUP, 1993).

Clark, E.A., *The Origenist Controversy: The Cultural Construction of an Early Christian Debate* (Princeton: Princeton University Press, 1992).

—. 'The Place of Jerome's Commentary on Ephesians in the Origenist Controversy: The Apokatastasis and Ascetic Ideals,' *VC* 41.2 (1987), 154-71.

—. *Women in the Early Church*. Message of the Fathers of the Church 13 (Wilmington: Michael Glazier, 1983).

Clark, M., *Augustine* (Washington: Georgetown University Press, 2007).

Conyham — Lenox, A., 'In Praise of St. Jerome and Against the Anglican Cult of "Niceness",' StP 69 (2013), 435-40.

Crawford, M., *Cyril of Alexandria's Trinitarian Theology of Scripture*. OECS (Oxford: OUP, 2014).

Crawford, R., 'Scripture as "One Book": Origen, Jerome and Cyril of Alexandria on Isaiah 29:11,' *JTS* 64.1 (April 2013), 137-53.

Cristaudo, Wayne and Heung Wah Wong (eds) *Augustine: His Legacy and Relevance* (Hindmarsh: ATF, 2010).

Cross, F.L., *The Early Christian Fathers*. Studies in Theology (London: Gerald Duckworth, 1960).

Crouzel, H., *Origen: The Life and Thought of the First Great Theologian* (tr. A.S. Worall; San Francisco: Harper and Row, 1989).

Cummings, J.T., 'St. Jerome as Translator and as Exegete,' *StP* 7 (1975), 279-82.

Cunningham, M.B., and E. Theokritoff (eds), *The Cambridge Companion to Orthodox Christian Theology* (Cambridge: CUP, 2008).

Daley, B., *'Origen's De Principiis:* A Guide to the Principles of Christian **Spiritual Interpretation,'** in J. Petruccione (ed.), *Nova et Vetera: Patristic Studies in Honor of Thomas Patrick Halton* (Washington: Catholic University of America Press, 1998), 3-21.

Dauphinais and M. Levering (eds), *Reading John with St. Thomas Aquinas: Theological Exegesis and Speculative Theology* (Washington: Catholic University of America Press, 2005).

Davids, P.H., *The Epistle of James* (Grand Rapids: Eerdmans, 1982).

Deakle, D.W., 'The Fathers against Marcionism: A Study of the Methods and Motives in the Developing Patristic Anti-Marcionite Polemic (PhD thesis, Saint Louis University, 1991) (Ann Arbor, MI: UMI Dissertation Services, No. 9130991).

de Silva, D.A., *The Jewish Teachers of Jesus, James, and Jude: What Earliest Christianity Learned from the Apocrypha and Pseudopigrapha* (Oxford: OUP, 2012).

Douglas, S. and M. Ludlow (eds), *Reading the Church Fathers* (London: T&T Clark, 2011).

Drever, M., *Image, Identity and the Forming of the Augustinian Soul* (Oxford: OUP, 2013).

Driver, S., 'The Development of Jerome's Views on the Ascetic Life,' *Rec. Th* 62 (1995), 44-70.

Dungan, D.L., *Constantine's Bible: Politics and the Making of the New Testament* (Minneapolis: Fortress, 2007).

Edwards, M., (ed.), *Ancient Christian Commentary on Scripture, New Testament VIII, Galatians, Ephesians and Philippians* (Downers Grove: IVP, 1999).

—. *Catholicity and Heresy in the Early Church* (Farnham: Ashgate, 2009).

—. *Christians, Gnostics and Philosophers in Late Antiquity* (Farnham: Ashgate, 2012).

—. *Image, Word and God in the Early Christian Centuries* (Farnham: Ashgate, 2013).

—. 'Pagan and Christian Monotheism in the age of Constantine,' in S.R.C. Swain., and M.J. Edwards (eds), *Approaching Late Antiquity* (Oxford: OUP, 2004), 211-34.

Elliott, C.J., 'Hebrew Learning Among The Fathers,' *DCB* 2 (1880) 851-72.

Enos, R.L. and R. Thompson et al. (eds), *The Rhetoric of St. Augustine of Hippo: De Doctrine Christiana and the Search for a Distinctly Christian Rhetoric* (Waco: Baylor University Press, 2008).

Erasmus, D., *Erasmus' Jerome: Life and Letters, 1516 and 1524* vol. 61, *The Collected Works of Erasmus* (ed. R.D. Sider; Toronto: University of Toronto Press, 1974).

—. *Patristic Scholarship: The Edition St. Jerome* (ed. J. Brady and J. Olin; Toronto: University of Toronto Press, 1992).

Erhman, B.D., *Forgery and Counter-forgery: The use of Literary Deceit in Early Christian Polemics* (Oxford: OUP, 2013).

Evans, G.R., 'Jerome' in G.R. Evans (ed.), *The First Christian Theologians* (Oxford: Blackwell, 2004), 234-37.

—. *Old Arts and New Theology: The Beginnings of Theology as an Academic Discipline* (Oxford: Clarendon, 1980).

—. 'The Early Church in the World' in G.R. Evans (ed.), *The First Christian Theologians*, 58-64.

—. (ed.), *The First Christian Theologians: An Introduction to Theology in the Early Church* (Oxford: Blackwell, 2004).

Farkasfalvy, D., *Inspiration and Interpretation: A Theological Introduction to Sacred Scripture* (Washington: Catholic University of America Press, 2010).

Farrar, F.W., *History of Interpretation (1896)* (Grand Rapids: Baker, 1961).

Fear, A., J. Fernandez Ubina and M. Marcos (eds), *The Role of The Bishop in Late Antiquity: Conflict and Compromise* (London: Bloomsbury, 2014).

Ferguson, E., *Church History*, vol.1, *From Christ to Pre-Reformation: The Rise and Growth of the Church in its Cultural, Intellectual and Political Context* (Grand Rapids: Zondervan, 2005).

—. 'Creeds, Councils and Canons' in Harvey and Hunter (eds), *The Oxford Handbook of Early Christian Studies*, 427-45.

—. 'Tertullian, Scripture, Rule of Faith, and Paul' in T. Stial and D.E. Wilhite (eds), *Tertullian and Paul* (London: Bloomsbury, 2013), 22-33.

Fontaine, J., *Isidore de Seville et la culture classique dans l'Espagne wisigothique* (2nd edn, Paris, 1983).

Fortin, E.F., 'Augustine and the Problem of Christian Rhetoric (1974)' in R.L. Enos and R. Thompson et al (eds), *The Rhetoric of St. Augustine: De Doctrina Christiana and the Search for a Distinctly Christian Rhetoric* (Waco: Baylor University Press, 2008), 219-33.

Foster, P. (ed.), *Early Christian Thinkers* (Minneapolis: Fortress, 2012).

—. and S. Parvis (eds.), *Irenaeus: Life, Scripture, Legacy: The lives and legacies of twelve key figures* (London: SPCK, 2010).

—. and S. Parvis (eds.), *Irenaeus: Life, Scripture, Legacy* (Minneapolis: Fortress, 2012).

Fowl, S., *Engaging Scripture: A Model for Theological Interpretation* (Oxford: Blackwell, 1998).

Fowl, S.E (ed.), *The Theological Interpretation of Scripture: Classic and Contemporary Readings* (Oxford: Blackwell, 1997).

Fox, R.L., *Pagans and Christians in the Mediterranean World from the Second Century AD to the Conversion of Constantine* (London: Penguin, 2006).

Freeman, C., *The Closing of the Western Mind: The Rise of Faith and the Fall of Reason* (London: Heinemann, 2002).

Frend, W.H., *The Early Church: From the Beginnings to 461* (2nd imp; London: SCM, 1982).

Fritz, A.X.J., *To the Jew First or to the Jew at Last? Romans 1:16c and Jewish Missional Priority in Dialogue with Jews for Jesus* (Eugene: Pickwick, 2013).

Froelich, K., *Biblical Interpretation in the Early Church* (Philadelphia, Fortress, 1984).

Freeman, C., *A New History of Early Christianity* (New Haven: Yale University Press, 2009).

Fürst, A., 'Jerome Keeping Silent: Origen and his Exegesis of Isaiah' in A. Cain and J. Lössl (eds.), *Jerome of Stridon*, 141-52.

Gallagher, E.L., *Hebrew Scripture in Patristic Biblical Theory* (Leiden: Brill, 2012).

—. 'Jerome's Prologus Galeatus and the OT Canon of North African' *STP* 69 (2013), 99-106.

Gavrilynk, P.L. *The Dialectics of Patristic Thought* (Oxford: OUP, 2004).

Geisler, N.L. and W.C. Roach, *Defending Inerrancy: Affirming the Accuracy of Scripture for a New Generation* (Grand Rapids: Baker, 2011).

George, T (ed.), *Evangelicals and the Nicene Faith* (Grand Rapids: Baker, 2011).

Gibson, D. and J. Gibson (eds), *From Heaven he Came and Sought her: Definite Atonement in Historical, Biblical, Theological and Pastoral Perspective* (Wheaton: Crossway, 2013).

Gioia, L., 'Augustine on the Triune God' in C.C. Pecknold and T. Toom (eds), *T&T Clark Companion to Augustine and Modern Theology* (London and New York: Bloomsbury T&T Clark, 2013), 3-19.

González, J.L., *The Story of Christianity*, vol 1. *The Early Church to the Dawn of the Reformation* (New York: Harper One, 2010).

Gorman, M.J., (ed.), *Scripture: An Ecumenical Introduction to the Bible and its Interpretation* (Peabody: Hendrickson, 2005).

Gräbe, P.J., *New Covenant, New Community: The Significance of Biblical and Patristic Covenant Theology for Contemporary Understanding* (Milton Keynes: Paternoster, 2006).

Grafton, A. and M. Williams, *Christianity and the Transformation of the Book: Origen, Eusebius, and the Library of Caesarea* (Cambridge: The Belknap Press of Harvard University Press, 2008).

Grant, R.M., *Irenaeus of Lyons* (Abingdon: Routledge, 1997).

Graves, M., *Jerome's Hebrew Philology: A Study Based on his Commentary on Jeremiah* (Leiden: Brill, 2007).

—. *The Inspiration and Interpretation of Scripture: What the Early Church can Teach us* (Grand Rapids: Eerdmans, 2014).

—. 'The Literary Quality of Scripture as Seen by the Early Church,' *Tyndale Bulletin* 61.2 (2010), 161-82.

Gray, C., *Jerome, 'Vita Malchi': Introduction, Text, Translation, and Commentary* (Oxford: OUP, 2015).

—. 'The Monk and the Ridiculous: Comedy in Jerome's *Vita Malchi*,' *StP* 69 (2013), 115-21.

Green, B., *Christianity in Ancient Rome: The First Three Centuries* (London: T&T Clark, 2010).

Green, B.G. (ed.), *Shapers of Christian Orthodoxy: Engaging with early and medieval theologians* (Nottingham: Apollos, 2010).

Green, M., *2 Peter and Jude: An Introduction and Commentary* (1st edn, 1968; 2nd edn, 1985; repr. 2009: Nottingham, 2009).

—. *2 Peter Reconsidered* (London: Tyndale, 1961).

Gregg, R,C, (ed.), *Arianism: Historical and Theological Reassessments* (Philadelphia: Patristic Foundation, 1985).

—. and D.E. Groh, *Early Arianism: A View of Salvation* (London, SCM, 1981).

Greenslade, S.L. (ed), *Early Latin Theology: Selections from Tertullian, Cyprian, Ambrose and Jerome* (Louisville: WJK, 2006).

—. (ed.), *The Cambridge History of the Bible: The West from the Reformation to the Present Day* (Cambridge: CUP, 1963).

Greenspan, L., 'Hebrew into Greek: Interpretation in, by and of the Septuagint' in A.J. Hauser and D.F. Watson (eds), *A History of Biblical Interpretation*, vol. 1, *The Ancient Period* (Grand Rapids: Eerdmans, 2003).

Gribmont, J., 'Jerome' in J. Quaston, *Patrology*, vol 4: *The Golden Age of Latin Patristic Literature: From the Council of Nicaea to the Council of Chalcedon* (Westminster: Christian Classics, 1986), 195-246.

Grillmeier, A., *Christ in Christian Tradition*, vol. 1: *From the Apostolic Age to Chalcedon* (AD 451) (2nd rev. edn; Oxford: Mowbray, 1975).

Grützmacher, G., *Hieronymus, Eine biographische Studie zur alten Kirchengeschichte* (Leipzig/Berlin, 1901-1908).

Hadrill-**Wallace, D.S., 'A Fourth Century View of the Origins of Christianity,'** *ExpT* 67 (1955-1956), 53-56.

Hagendal, H., 'Jerome and the Latin Classics,' *VC* 28.3 (1974), 216-27.

—. *Latin Fathers and the Classics: A study on the apologists, Jerome, and other Christian writers* (Göteborgs universitets årsskrift 64, Göteborgs, 1958).

Hahn, S.W., *Covenant and Communion: The Biblical Theology of Pope Benedict XVI* (London: DLT, 2008).

—. *Kinship by Covenant: A Biblical Theological Study of Covenant Types and Texts in the Old and New Testament* (New Haven: Yale University Press, 2005).

Hahnenberg, E.G., *Bible Maker: Jerome* (Bloomington: Author House, 2005).

Hall, C.A., *Learning Theology with the Church Fathers* (Downers Grove: IVP, 2002).

—. *Reading Scripture with the Church Fathers* (Downers Grove: IVP, 1998).

Hall, S.G., *Doctrine and Practice in the Early Church* (2nd ed; London: SPCK, 2006).

Hand, T.A., *Augustine on Prayer* (New York: Catholic Publishing, 1986).

Hanson, R.P.C., *The Search for the Christian Doctrine of God: The Arian Controversy 318-381* (Edinburgh: T&T Clarke, 1988).

Harmless, J.W., 'Monasticism' in S.A. Harvey and D.G. Hunter (eds), *The Oxford Handbook of Early Christian Studies*, 493-517.

Harmon, S.R., *Every Knee Should Bow: Biblical Rationales for Universal Salvation in Early Christian Thought* (Lanham: University Press of America, 2003).

Harnack, A., *Der kirchengeschichtliche Ertrag der exegetischen Arbeiten des Origenes* (1919).

Harries, J., 'Patristic Historiography' in I. Hazlett (ed.), *Early Christianity*, 269-79.

Harrison, C., *Beauty and Revelation in the Thought of Saint Augustine* (Oxford: Clarendon, 1992).

—. and C. Humfress and I. Sandwell (eds), *Being Christian in Late Antiquity: A Festschrift for Gillian Clark* (Oxford: OUP, 2014).

—. *Rethinking Augustine's Early Theology: An Argument for Continuity* (Oxford: OUP, 2006).

Harrison, N.V., 'Gregory of Nazianzen Homily on the Nativity of Christ' in R. Valantasis (ed.), *Religions of Late Antiquity in Practice* (Princeton: Princeton University Press, 2000), 443-53.

Hartmann, L.N., 'St. Jerome as an Exegete' in F.X. Murphy (ed.), *A Monument to Saint Jerome* (New York: Sheed and Ward, 1952), 37-81.

Harvey, P., 'Saints and Satyrs: Jerome the Scholar at Work', *Athenaeum* 86 (1998), 35-56.

Harvey, S.A., and D.G. Hunter (eds), *The Oxford Handbook of Early Christian Studies* (Oxford: OUP, 2008).

Hauser A.J. and D.F. Watson (eds), *A History of Biblical Interpretation*, vol.1. *The Ancient Period* (Grand Rapids: Eerdmans, 2003), 80-113.

—. 'Introduction and Overview' in Hauser A.J. and D.F. Watson (eds), *A History of Biblical Interpretation*, vol.1. *The Ancient Period* (Grand Rapids: Eerdmans, 2003), 1-54.

Haykin, M.A.G., '"We Trust in the Saving Blood": Definite Atonement in the Ancient Church' in D. Gibson and J. Gibson (eds), *From Heaven He Came and Sought Her: Definite Atonement in Historical, Biblical, Theological and Pastoral Perspective* (Wheaton: Crossway, 2013), 57-74.

Hayward, C.T.R., 'Jewish Traditions in Jerome's Commentary on Jeremiah and the Targum of Jeremiah,' *PIBA* 9 (1985), 100-120.

Hayward, R., 'Saint Jerome, Jewish Learning, and the Symbolism of the Number Eight,' in A. Andreopoulous, A. Casiday and C. Harrison (eds), *Meditations of the Heart: The Psalms in Early Christian Thought and Practice* (Turnhout, Belgium: Brepols, 2011), 141-59.

—. 'Some Observations on St. Jerome's Hebrew Questions on Genesis' *PIBA* 13 (1990), 58-76.

Hazlett, I., (ed.), *Early Christianity: Origins and Evolution to A.D. 600* (London: SPCK, 1991).

Helm, R., (ed.) *Eusebius Werke, Siebenter Band: Die Chronik des Hieronymus* (Berlin: Verlag, 1956).

Heimann, D.F., 'The Polemical Application of Scripture in St. Jerome,' *StP* 12 (1975), 309-16.

Hill, R.C., *Theodoret of Cyrus: Commentary on the Letters of St. Paul*, vol. 1 (tr. With an introduction by R.C. Hill; Brookline: Holy Cross Orthodox, 2001).

Hofer (O.P.), A., *Christ in the Life and Teaching of Gregory of Nazianzus* (Oxford: OUP, 2013).

Hoffmann, R.J., *Marcion: On the Restitution of Christianity – An Essay on the Development of Radical Paulinist Theology in the Second Century* (Chico: Scholars, 1984).

Hollingsworth, M., *Saint Augustine of Hippo: An Intellectual Biography* (London: Bloomsbury, 2013).

Holmes, W.M., '*The Biblical Canon*' in Harvey, S.A. and D.G. Hunter (eds), *The Oxford Handbook of Early Christian Studies* (Oxford: OUP, 2008), 406-26.

Horton, M.S., *Covenant and Eschatology: The Divine Drama* (Louisville: WJK, 2002).

Hulley, K., 'Principles of Textual Criticism Known to St. Jerome,' *HSCP* 55 (1944), 87-109.

Humphries, Jr. T.L. *Ascetic Pneumatology from John Cassian to Gregory the Great* (Oxford: OUP, 2013).

Hunt, T. 'Biblical Interpretation in Jerome of Stridon's *Vita Hilarionis*', *StP* 52 (2012), 247-55.

Hunter, D.G., *Marriage, Celibacy and Heresy in Ancient Christianity: The Jovinianist Controversy* (Oxford: OUP, 2007).

—. 'Rethinking the Jovinianist Controversy: Asceticism and Clerical Authority in Late Ancient Christianity,' *JMEMS* 33.3 (2003), 453-70.

Insley, M., 'Aspects of Pagan/Christian Relations in the First Four Centuries of the Christian Era with Special Reference to Origen' (MPhil thesis, University of Nottingham, 1985).

Jardine, L., *Erasmus, Man of Letters: The Construction of Charisma in Print* (Princeton: Princeton University Press, 1993).

Jeanrond, W.G., *A Theology of Love* (London: T&T Clark, 2010).

Jensen, A., 'Women in the Christianization of the West' in A. Kreider (ed.), *The Origins of Christendom in the West* (Edinburgh: T&T Clark, 2001), 205-26.

Jerome, *Commentary on Ecclesiastes* (tr. and ed. with a Commentary by R.J. Goodrich and D.J.D. Miller; New York: Newman, 2012).

—. *Commentary on Galatians* FOTC. vol. 121 (tr. A. Cain. Washington: Catholic University of America Press, 2008).

—. *St. Jerome's Commentaries on Galatians, Titus and Philemon* (tr. T. Scheck; Notre Dame: University of Notre Dame Press, 2010).

—. *Commentary on Matthew* (FOTC, tr. T.P. Scheck; Washington: Catholic University of America Press, 2008).

—. *Homily 80* in Saint Jerome, *The Homilies of St. Jerome*, vol.2 (Homilies 60-96) FOTC Series 57 (tr. Sister M.L. Ewald; Washington: Catholic University of America Press, 1965), 159-68.

—. 'Jerome's Commentary in Ezek.,' *PL* 25, 231 C.

—. Jerome's *Hebrew Questions on Genesis* OECS (tr. with an introduction and commentary by C.T.R. Hayward; Oxford: Clarendon, 1995).

—. *Letters of St. Jerome*, vol.1. *Letters 1-22* (tr. C.C. Mierow with introduction and notes by T.C. Lawler; New York: Newman, 1963).

—. 'Life of Paul of Thebes,' in C. White (ed.), *Early Christian Lives* (London: Penguin, 1998), 71-84.

—. *On Illustrious Men* FOTC. vol. 100 (trans. T.P. Halton, Washington: Catholic University of America Press, 1999).

—. *Select Letters* (tr. F.A. Wright; Cambridge: Loeb Classical Library/Harvard University Press, 1933).

—. *Select Letters of Saint Jerome* (tr. F.A. Wright; Cambridge: Harvard University Press, 1954).

—. *The Homilies of St. Jerome*, vol. 2 (*Homilies 60-96*) FOTC Series 57 (tr. Sister M.L. Ewald; Washington: Catholic University of America Press, 1965).

Johnson, L.T., and W.S. Kurz., *The Future of Catholic Biblical Scholarship: A Constructive Conversation* (Grand Rapids: Eerdmans, 2002).

Johnson, P., *A History of Christianity* (New York: Simon and Schuster, 1995).

Jones, C.P., *Between Pagan and Christian* (Cambridge: Harvard University Press, 2014).

Kamesar, A., *Jerome, Greek Scholarship and the Hebrew Bible: A Study of the Quaestiones hebraicae in Genesion* (Oxford: Clarendon, 1993).

Kannengiesser, C., 'Biblical Interpretation in the Early Church' in D.K. McKim (ed.), *Dictionary of Major Biblical Interpreters* (Downers Grove: IVP, 2007), 1-13.

Karamanolis, G., *The Philosophy of Early Christianity* (Durham: Acumen, 2013).

Kedar-Kopfstein, B., 'The Vulgate as a Translation: Some Semantic and Syntactical Aspects of Jerome's Version of the Hebrew' (PhD thesis, Hebrew University, 1968).

Keith, C., *Jesus' Literacy: Scribal Culture and the Teacher from Galilee: Library of Historical Jesus Studies 8* (London: T&T Clark, 2011).

—. The *'Pericope Adulterae,' The Gospel of John, and the Literacy of Jesus* (Leiden: Brill, 2014).

Kelhoffer, J.A., *The Diet of John the Baptist: 'Locusts and Wild Honey' in Synoptic and Patristic Interpretation* (Tubingen: Mohr Siebeck, 2005).

Kelly, J.F., 'Pelagius' in D.K. McKim (ed.), *Dictionary of Major Biblical Interpreters* (Downers Grove: IVP, 2007).

—. *The Concise Dictionary of Early Christianity* (Collegeville: Liturgical, 1992).

Kelly, J.N.D., *Early Christian Creeds* (3rd edn; London: Continuum, 2006).

—. *Early Christian Doctrines* (5th rev. edn; London: A&C Black, 1977).

—. *Jerome: His Life, Writings and Controversies* (London: Duckworth, 1975).

Kelly, M.J., 'Life and Times as Revealed in the Writings of St. Jerome Exclusive of his Letters' (PhD thesis, Washington, 1944).

Knight, C.K., 'Jerome and his Interpreters: A Critique of Modern Jerome Scholarship (In English), with Particular Reference to the Critical Reception

Given by Scholars to Selected Texts/Writings Drawn from St. Jerome's Patristic Corpus' (MTh thesis, London School of Theology, 2014).

Kolbert, P.R., *Augustine and the Care of Souls: Revising a Classical Ideal* (Notre Dame: University of Notre Dame, 2010).

Komoszewski, J.E., M.J. Sawyer and D.B. Wallace, *Reinventing Jesus: How Contemporary Skeptics Miss the Real Jesus and Mislead Popular Culture* (Grand Rapids: Kregel, 2006).

Köstenberger, A.J. and M.J. Kruger (eds.), *The Heresy of Orthodoxy: How Contemporary Culture's Fascination with Diversity has Reshaped our Understanding of Early Christianity* (Nottingham: Apollos, 2010).

Kreider, A., (ed.), *The Origins of Christendom in the West* (Edinburgh: T&T Clark, 2001).

P. Leithart, 'Semiosis and Social Salvation (mostly) in *De Doctrina Christiana*' in W. Cristaudo and Henry Who Wong (eds), *Augustine: His Legacy and Relevance* (Hindimarsh: ATF, 2010), 1-36.

Kruger, M.J., *Canon Revisited: Establishing the Origins and Authority of the New Testament Books* (Wheaton: Crossway, 2012).

—. *The Gospel of the Savior: An Analysis of P. OXY. 840 and its place in the Gospel Traditions of Early Christianity* (Leiden: Brill, 2005).

Kugel, J. and R. Greer, *Early Biblical Interpretation* (Philadelphia: Westminster, 1986).

Lampe, G.W.H. (ed.), *The Cambridge History of The Bible*, vol. 2: *The West from the Fathers to the Reformation* (Cambridge: CUP, 1969).

Lane, A.N.S., 'Scripture, Tradition and Church: An Historical Survey,' *Vox Ev* 9 (1975), 37-55.

Lauro, E.D., *The Soul and Spirit of Scripture within Origen's Exegesis.* The Bible in Ancient Christianity 3 (Boston: Brill, 2005).

Layton, R.A., 'From "Holy Passion" to Sinful Emotion: Jerome and the Doctrine of Propassion' in P.M., Blowers, A.R. Christman, D.G. Hunter and R.D. Young (eds), *In Dominico Eloquio — In Lordly Eloquence*, 280-293.

Leclercq, J., *The Love of Learning and the Desire for God* (tr. C. Misrahi; New York, 1961).

Letham, R., 'The Three Cappadocians' in B.G. Green (ed.), *Shapers of Christian Orthodoxy*, 190-234.

—. *Through Western Eyes — Eastern Orthodoxy: A Reformed Perspective* (Fern: Mentor/Christian Focus, 2007).

Lieu, S.N.C. (ed), *The Emperor Julian* (Liverpool: Liverpool University Press, 1986).

Liften, B., 'Origen' in B.G. Green (ed.), *Shapers of Christian Orthodoxy: Engaging with early and medieval theologians* (Nottingham, Apollos, 2010).

Lightfoot, J.B., *The Epistle of St. Paul to the Galatians* (1st edn. London: Macmillan, repr. 1890).

Lister, R., *God is Impassible and Impassioned: Toward a Theology of Divine Emotion* (Nottingham: IVP, 2012).

Loewe, R., 'The Jewish Midrashin and Patristic and Scholastic Exegesis of the Bible,' *StP* 1 (1957), 492-514.

Logan, A., 'Rehabilitating Jephthah,' *JBL* 128.4 (2009), 665-85.

Lossky, A., *The Mystical Theology of the Eastern Church* (London: James Clarke, 1957).

Lössl, J., 'Martin Luther's Jerome: New Evidence for a Changing Attitude' in A. Cain and J. Lössl (eds), *Jerome of Stridon*, 237-51.

—. *The Early Church: History and Memory* (London: T&T Clark, 2010).

Louth, A., *St. John Damascene: Tradition and Originality in Byzantine Theology* (Oxford: OUP, 2002).

—. 'The Cappadocians' in F.M. Young, L. Ayres and A. Louth (eds), *The Cambridge History of Early Christian Literature* (Cambridge: CUP, 2004), 289-01.

—. 'The Literature of the monastic movement' in F.M. Young., L. Ayres and A. Louth (eds), *The Cambridge History of Early Christian Literature* (Cambridge: CUP, 2004), 373-81.

Ludlow, M., 'Anatomy: Investigating the Body of Texts in Origen and Gregory of Nyssa' in S. Douglas and M. Ludlow (eds), *Reading the Church Fathers*, 132-53.

—. *The Early Church* (London: Tauris, 2009).

—. *Universal Salvation: Eschatology in the Thought of Gregory of Nyssa and Karl Rahner* (Oxford: OUP, 2009).

Lyman, J.R., 'Arins and Arians' in S.A. Harvey and D.G. Hunter (eds), *The Oxford Handbook of Early Christian Studies* (Oxford: OUP 2008), 237-57.

Lynch, J.H., *Early Christianity: A Brief History* (Oxford: OUP, 2010).

MacDonald, S., 'Primal Sin' in G.B. Matthews (eds), *The Augustinian Tradition* (Berkeley: University of California Press, 1999), 110-39.

Macmillan, R., *Christianity and Paganism in the Fourth to Eighth Centuries* (New Haven: Yale University Press, 1997).

Malherbe, A.J., F.W. Norris and J.W. Thompson (eds), *The Early Church in its Context* (Leiden: Brill, 1998), 74-91.

Matthews, G.B. (ed.), *The Augustinian Tradition* (Berkeley: University of California Press, 1999).

Markus, R.A., *Christianity in the Roman World* (London: Thames Hudson, 1974).

—. *The End of Ancient Christianity* (Cambridge: CUP, 1998).

Martens, P.W., *Origen and Scripture: The Contours of the Exegetical Life* (Oxford: OUP, 2014).

Matera, F.J., *God's Saving Grace: A Pauline Theology* (Grand Rapids: Eerdmans, 2012).

Mathisen, 'The Use and Misuse of Jerome in Gaul during Late Antiquity' in A. Cain and J. Lössl (eds.), *Jerome of Stridon*, 191-208.

McCann, C., 'Incentives to Virtue: Jerome's use of Biblical Models,' *StP* 69 (2013), 107-13.

McGowan, A.T.B., (ed.), *Always Reforming: Explorations in Systematic Theology* (Leicester: Apollos, 2006).

McGrath, A.E., *The Making of Modern German Christology, 1750-1990* (2nd edn; Leicester: Apollos, 1994).

McGuckin, J., *Saint Gregory of Nazianzus: An Intellectual Biography* (Crestwood: St. Vladimir's Seminary Press, 2001).

McLynn, N.B., *Ambrose of Milan: Church and Court in a Christian Capital* (Berkeley: University of California Press, 1994).

McMahon, R., **Augustine's Prayerful Ascent:** *An Essay on the Literary Form of the 'Confessions'* (Athens: University of Georgia Press, 1989).

McWilliam, J., (ed.), *Augustine: From Rhetor to Theologian* (Waterloo: Wilfrid Lauvier University Press, 1992).

Meinardus, O.F.A., *Monks and Monasteries of the Egyptian Deserts* (Rev. edn; Cairo: American University in Cairo Press, 1992).

Metzger, B.M., 'The Practice of Textual Criticism among the Church Fathers,' *StP* 12 (1975), 340-49.

Mierow, C.C., 'An Early Christian Scholar,' *TCJ* 33.1 (Oct, 1937), 3-17.

—. *Saint Jerome: The Sage of Bethlehem* (Milwaukee: Bruce, 1959).

Monceaux, P., *St. Jerome: The Early Years* (London: Sheed and Ward, 1933).

Mohr, A., 'Jerome, Virgil, and the Captive Maiden: the attitude of Jerome to classical literature' in J.H.D. Scourfield (ed.), *Texts and Culture in Late Antiquity: Inheritance, Authority, and Change* (Swansea: Classical Press of Wales, 2007), 299-322.

Moorhead, J., *Gregory the Great* (Abingdon: Routledge, 2005).

Murphy, J.J., 'St. Augustine and the Debate about a Christian Rhetoric' in R.L. Enos and R. Thompson et al (eds), *The Rhetoric of St. Augustine*, 205-18.

Myers, J., 'Law, Lies and Letter Writing: An Analysis of Jerome and Augustine on the Antioch Incident (Galatians 2:11-14)', *Scottish Journal of Theology* 66.2 (2013), 127-39.

Neeley, S.D., D.B. Magee and L.M. Thomas, 'Synoptic Outline of Saint Augustine's *De Doctrina Christiana*' in R.L. Enos and Thompson et al (eds), *The Rhetoric of St. Augustine: De Doctrina Christiana and the Search for a Distinctly Christian Rhetoric*, 11-32.

Neinhuis, D.R. and R.W. Wall, *Reading the Epistles of James, Peter, John, and Jude as Scripture* (Grand Rapids: Eerdmans, 2013).

Norris, R.A., *God and World in Early Christian Theology: A Study in Justin Martyr, Irenaeus, Tertullian, and Origen* (London: Adam and Charles Black, 1966).

—. 'Irenaeus' in D.K. McKim (ed.), *Dictionary of Major Biblical Interpreters*, 558-60.

Novembri, V. 'Philosophia and Christian Culture: An Antidote for Female Weakness in Jerome's Letters,' *StP* 44 (2010), 471-85.

Nugent, P., 'Patristics and Pedagogy: Jerome and Augustine,' *StP* 49 (2010), 3-7.

O'Connell, R.O., *St. Augustine's* Confessions*: The Odyssey of Soul* (Cambridge: Belknap / Harvard University Press, 1969).

—. *St. Augustine's Early Theory of Man, A.D. 386-391* (Cambridge: Belknap / Harvard University Press, 1968).

—. *The Eschatology of St. Jerome* (Mundelein: Pontificia Facultus Theologica Seminarii Sanctae Mariae ad Lacum, 1948).

—. *The Origin of the Soul in St. Augustine's Later Works* (New York: Fordham University Press, 1987).

Oden, T.C., 'The Faith Once Delivered: Nicaea and Evangelical Confession' in T. George (ed.), *Evangelicals and Nicene Faith: Reclaiming the Apostolic Witness* (Grand Rapids: Baker, 2011), 3-19.

O'Donnell, J.J., *Augustine: A New Biography* (New York: Harper Collins, 2005).

Ogg, G., *The Chronology of the Life of Paul* (London: Epworth, 1968).

O'Keefe and R. Reno, *Sanctified Vision: An Introduction to Early Christian Interpretation of the Bible* (Baltimore: Johns Hopkins University Press, 2005).

Old, H.O., *The Reading and Preaching of the Scriptures in the Worship of the Christian Church* vol. 2. *The Patristic Age* (Grand Rapids: Eerdmans, 1998).

Oldfather W.A. (ed.), *Studies in the Text Tradition of St. Jerome's 'Vitae Patrum'* (Urbana: The University of Illinois Press, 1943).

Olin, J.C. and J.F. Brady, *Patristic Scholarship: The Edition of St. Jerome* (Toronto: University of Toronto Press, 1992).

O'Meara, J.J., 'Augustine's *Confessions*: Elements of Fiction' in J. McWilliam (ed.), *Augustine: From Rhetor to Theologian*, 77-95.

Origen, *On First Principles* (intro Henri de Lubac and tr. G. Butterworth, Foreword by J.C. Cavadini: Notre Dame: Ave Maria, 2013).

Orlinsky, H.M., *Essays in Biblical Culture and Bible Translation* (New York, 1974).

Pabel, H.M., Book review of A. Cain, *The Letters of Jerome: Asceticism, Biblical Exegesis, and the Construction of Christian Authority in Late Antiquity* (Oxford: OUP, 2009), *Church History* 79.3 (2010), 683-85.

Paget, J.C. and J. Schaper (eds), *The New Cambridge History of the Bible: From the Beginnings to 600* (Cambridge: CUP, 2013).

Palladius., Lausiac, *History – The Paradise or Garden of the Holy Fathers being Histories of the Anchorites, Recluses, Monks, Cenobites and Ascetic Fathers of the Deserts of Egypt between 250 and 400 AD*. Circiter compiled by Athanasius Archbishop of Alexandria: Palladius Bishop of Helenopolis, St. Jerome and others (tr. E.A. Budge; London, 1907).

Papandrea, J.L., *Novation of Rome and the Culmination of Pre-Nicene Orthodoxy* (Eugene: Pickwick, 2011).

—. *Reading the Early Church Fathers: From the Didache to Nicaea* (Mahwak: Paulist, 2012).

Parvis, S. and P. Foster (eds), *Justin Martyr and his Worlds* (Minneapolis: Fortress, 2007).

Paton, C., 'Selections from Nicholas of Lyra's *Commentary on Exodus*' in S.E. Fowl (ed.), *The Theological Interpretation of Scripture*, 114-28.

Payton, Jr., J.R., *Irenaeus on the Christian Faith: A Condensation of Against Heresies* (Cambridge: James Clarke, 2012).

Pease, A.S., 'The Attitude of Jerome towards Pagan Literature,' *Transactions and Proceedings of the American Philological Association* 50 (1919), 150-67.

Pecknold, C.C. and T. Toom (eds), *T&T Clark Companion to Augustine and Modern Theology* (London: T&T Clark, 2013).

Pelikan, J., *The Christian Tradition 1: A History of the Development of Doctrine – The Emergence of the Catholic Tradition* (100-600) (Chicago: University of Chicago Press, 1971).

—. 'The Two Sees of Peter' in E.P. Sanders (ed.), *Jewish and Christian Self-Definition*, 57-73.

Pence, M.A., 'Satire in St. Jerome,' *CJ* 36 (1941), 322-36.

Penna, A., 'The Vow of Jephthah in the Interpretation of St. Jerome,' *StP* 4 (1961), 162-70.

Piper, J.K., *The Legacy of Sovereign Joy: God's Triumphant Grace in the Lives of Augustine, Luther and Calvin* (Wheaton: Crossway, 2000).

Plantinga, R.J., T.R. Thompson and M.D. Lundberg, *An Introduction to Christian Theology* (Cambridge: CUP, 2010).

Plumer, E., *Augustine's Commentary on Galatians* (OUP, 2003).

Pope, H., 'St. Jerome's Latin Text of St. Paul's Epistles,' *ITQ* 9 (1914), 413-45.

Prestige, G.L., *God in Patristic Thought* (2nd edn; London: SPCK, 1969).

Preus, J.E.O., 'St. Jerome's translation Terminology' (PhD thesis, Minnesota, 1951).

Price, R., *Augustine* (London: Fount, 1996).

—. 'Martyrdom and the Cult of the Saints' in S.A. Harvey and D.G. Hunter (eds), *The Oxford Handbook of Early Christian Studies*, 808-25.

Quasten, J., *Patrology*, vol. 3, *The Golden Age of Greek Patristic Literature: From the Council of Nicaea to the Council of Chalcedon* (ed. A.D. Beradino; Intro. J. Quasten; Westminster: Newman / Antwerp: Spectrum, 1960).

—. *Patrology*, vol. 4: *The Golden Age of Latin Patristic Literature from the Council of Nicaea to the Council of Chalcedon* (Westminster: Christian Classics, 1986).

Ramsey, B., *Ambrose* (Abingdon: Routledge, 1997).

—. *Beginning to Read the Fathers* (London, DLT, 1986).

Rapp, C., *Holy Bishops in Late Antiquity: The Nature of Christian Leadership in an Age of Transition* (Berkeley: University of California Press, 2005).

Raspanti, G., 'The Significance of Jerome's Commentary on Galatians in his Exegetical Production' in A. Cain and J. Lössl (eds), *Jerome of Stridon*, 163-71.

Rebenich, S., *Jerome* (Abingdon: Routledge, 2002).

—. 'Jerome: The "Vir Trilinguis" and the "Hebrew Veritas",' *VC* 47.1 (1993), 50-77.

Rengers, C., *The 33 Doctors of the Church* (Rockford: Tan, 2000).

Retif, A., *John the Baptist: Missionary of Christ* (Westminster: Newman, 1953).

Reymond, R., 'Classical Christology's Future in Systematic Theology' in McGowan, A.T.B. (ed.), *Always Reforming*, 67-124.

Reynods, P.L., *Marriage in the Western Church: The Christianization of Marriage during the Patristic and Early Medieval Periods* (Leiden: Brill, 2001).

Rich, A.D., *Discernment in the Desert Fathers: Diakrisis in the Life and Thought of Early Egyptian Monasticism* (Milton Keynes: Paternoster, 2007).

Richards, J., *Consul of God: The Life and Times of Gregory the Great* (London: Routledge, 1980).

Richardson, A., 'The Rise of Modern Biblical Scholarship and Recent Discussion of the Authority of the Bible' in Greenslade, S.L. (ed.), *The Cambridge History of the Bible* (Cambridge: CUP, 1963), 294-338.

Rombs, R.J., 'Augustine on Christ' in C.C. Pecknold, and T. Toom (eds), *T&T Clark Companion to Augustine and Modern Theology*, 36-53.

—. and A. Hwang (eds.), *Tradition and the Rule of Faith in the Early Church* (Washington: Catholic University of America Press, 2010).

Rosenberg, H., 'Jovinian' in Ferguson, E. (ed.), *Encyclopaedia of Early Christianity* (London: St. James, 1990).

Rottelle, J.E. (ed.), *The Works of Saint Augustine: Answer to the Pelagians*. (intro. tr. R.J. Teske; Augustinian Heritage Institution; New York: New City Press, 1997).

Rousseau, P., *Ascetics, Authority, and the Church in the Age of Jerome and Cassian* (Oxford: OUP, 1978).

—. *Pachomius: The Making of a Community in Fourth-Century Egypt* (Berkeley: University of California Press, 1985).

Rutherford, W., '*Altercatio Jasonis et Papisci* as Testimony for Justin's "Second God"' (Notre Dame: University of Notre Dame Press, 2008).

Salzman, M.R., 'Pagans and Christians' in Harvey and Hunter (eds), *Oxford Handbook of Early Christian Studies*, 186-2002.

Sanders, E.P. (ed.), *Jewish and Christian Self-Definition*, vol. 1. *The Shaping of Christianity in the Second and Third Centuries* (London: SCM, 1980).

Schaff, P. and H. Wace (eds), *Nicene and Post-Nicene Fathers*, vol. 3 *Theodoret, Jerome, Gennadius Rufinus: Historical Writings, Etc.* (Grand Rapids: Eerdmans, Repr. 1979); vol. 6 *St. Jerome: Letters and Select Works* (Grand Rapids: Eerdmans, 1996).

Schatkin, M.A. 'The influence of Origen upon St. Jerome's Commentary on Galatians,' *VC* 24.1 (1970), 49-58.

Schmemann, Alexander, *The Historical Road of Eastern Orthodoxy* (London: Harvill, 1963).

Schwab, G.M., *Right in Their own Eyes: The Gospel According to Judges* (Phillipsburg: P&R, 2011).

—. *Commentary on Romans* (Notre Dame: University of Notre Dame Press, 2009).

Schwarz, W., *Principles and Problems of Biblical Translation: Some Reformation Controversies and their Background* (Cambridge: CUP, 1955).

Scourfield, J.H.D. (ed.), *Texts and Culture in Late Antiquity: Inheritances, Authority, and Change* (Swansea: Classical Press of Wales, 2007).

Semple, W.H., 'St. Jerome as a Biblical Translator,' *BJRL* 48 (1965-1966), 227-43.

Sheppard, G.T., and A.C. Thiselton, 'Biblical Interpretation in the Eighteenth and Nineteenth Centuries' in D.K. McKim (ed.), *Dictionary of Major Biblical Interpreters*, 45-66.

Simonetti, M., *Matthew 1a* (ACC; Downers Grove: IVP, 2001).

Skehan, P.W., 'St. Jerome and the Canon of the Holy Scriptures' in F.X. Murphy (ed.), *A Monument to Saint Jerome*, 259-87.

Souter, A., 'Notes on Incidental Gospel Quotations,' *JTS* 42 (1941), 12-18.

—. *The Text and Canon of the New Testament* (London: Gerald Duckworth, 1913; repr, 1965).

—. 'The Type or Types of Gospel Text Used by St. Jerome as the Basis of his Revision, with Special Reference to St. Luke's Gospel and *Codex Vercellensis*,' *JTS* 12 (1911), 583-92.

Sparks, K., *God's Word in Human Words* (Grand Rapids: Baker, 2008).

Stander, H.F., 'Fourth – and Fifth – century Homilists on the Ascension of Christ' in A.J. Malherbe, F.W. Norris and J.W. Thompson (eds), *The Early Church in its Context* (Leiden: Brill), 268-86.

Stark, R., *The Rise of Christianity: How The Obscure, Marginal Jesus Movement Became the Dominant Religious Force* (San Francisco: Harper San Francisco, 1997).

—. *The Triumph of Christianity: How the Jesus Movement Became the World's Largest Religion* (New York: Harper One, 2011).

Steenberg, I.M.C., 'Tracing the Irenaean Legacy' in P. Foster and S. Parvis (eds), *Irenaeus: Life, Scripture, Legacy* (Minneapolis: Fortress, 2012), 199-211.

Steinhauser, K.B., 'The Literary Unity of the *Confessions*' in J. McWilliam (ed.), *Augustine: From Rhetor to Theologian*, 15-30.

Steinmann, J., *Saint Jerome and his Times* (tr. R. Matthews; Notre Dame: Fides, 1959).

Stevenson, J. (ed.), *A New Eusebius: Documents illustrative of the history of the Church to A.D. 337* (London: SPCK, 1957).

Stevenson, K., *Rooted in Detachment: Living the Transfiguration* (London: DLT, 2007).

Stewart, C., *Cassian the Monk* (Oxford: OUP, 1998).

—. 'Evagrius Ponticus on Prayer and Anger' in R. Valantasis (ed.), *Religions of Late Antiquity in Practice* (Princeton: Princeton University Press, 2000), 65-81.

Still, T.D. and D.E. White (eds), *Tertullian and Paul, Pauline and Patristic Scholars in Debate* (London: Bloomsbury T&T Clark, 2013).

Stroumsa, G.G., 'Introduction: the paradise chronotype' in M. Bockmuahl and G.G. Stroumsa (eds), *Paradise in Antiquity: Jewish and Christian Views* (Cambridge: CUP, 2010), 1-14.

Stylianopoulos, T.V.G., 'Scripture and tradition in the Church' in M.B. Cunningham and E. Theokritoff (eds), *The Cambridge Companion to Orthodox Christian Theology* (Cambridge: CUP, 2008), 63-77.

—. *The New Testament — An Orthodox Perspective*, vol. 1: *Scripture, Tradition, Hermeneutics* (Brookline: Holy Cross Orthodox, 1997).

Sutcliffe, F.W., 'Jerome' in G.W.H. Lampe (ed.), *The Cambridge History of the Bible*, vol. 2: *The West From the Fathers to the Reformation* (Cambridge: CUP, 1969), 80-101.

Swain, S.C.R. and M.J. Edwards (eds), *Approaching Late Antiquity* (Oxford: OUP, 2004).

Swidler, L., *Jesus was a Feminist: What the Gospels Reveal about his Revolutionary Perspective* (Lanham: Sheed and Ward, 2007).

Tallaferro C. and C. Meister (eds), *The Cambridge Companion to Christian Philosophical Theology* (Cambridge: CUP, 2010).

Teske, R.J., 'Augustine's Appeal to Tradition' in Rombs and Hwang (eds), *Tradition and the Rule of Faith in the Early Church*, 153-172.

Testa, R.L., 'Christianization and Conversion in Northern Italy' in A. Kreider (ed.), *The Origins of Christendom in the West*, 47-95.

Toom, T. 'Augustine on Scripture' in C.C. Pecknold and T. Toom (eds), *T&T Clark Companion to Augustine and Modern Theology* (London: Bloomsbury T&T Clark, 2013), 75-90.

Trigg, J., *Biblical Interpretation* (Collegeville: Michael Glazier, 1988).

—. *Origen: The Bible and Philosophy in the Third-century Church* (London: SCM, 1985).

Turner, H.E.W., *The Pattern of Christian Truth: A Study in the Relations between Orthodoxy and Heresy in the Early Church* (London: Mowbray, 1954).

Unger, D. and J. Dillon, *St. Irenaeus of Lyons, Against the Heresies*, Book I. (New York: Paulist, 1992).

Valantasis, R., 'Introduction' in R. Valantasis (ed.), *Religions of Late Antiquity in Practice* (Princeton: Princeton University Press, 2000), 3-15.

—. (ed.), *Religions of Late Antiquity in Practice* (Princeton: Princeton University Press, 2000).

Vermes, G., *Christian Beginnings: From Nazareth to Nicaea, A.D. 30-325* (London: Allen Lane, 2012).

Vessey, M., 'Erasmus' Jerome: The Publishing of a Christian Author,' *Erasmus of Rotterdam Society Yearbook* 14 (1994), 62-99.

—. 'Jerome and the Jeromanesque' in A. Cain and J. Lössl (eds), *Jerome of Stridon*, 225-35.

—. 'Jerome's Origen: The Making of a Christian Literary *persona*,' *StP* 28 (1993), 135-45.

—. *Latin Christian Writers in Late Antiquity and their Texts* (Aldershot: Ashgate 2005).

—. 'Literature, Patristics, Early Christian Writing' in S.A. Harvey and D.G. Hunter (eds), *The Oxford Handbook of Early Christian Studies* (Oxford: OUP, 2008), 42-65.

Veyne, P., *When our World Became Christian* (tr. J. Lloyd; Cambridge: Polity, 2010).

Walker, W., *History of the Christian Church* (New York: Scribner's Sons, 1918, repr. Edinburgh: T&T Clark, 1949).

Walsh, L.G., *The Sacrament of Initiation* (London: Geoffrey Chapman, 1998).

Walters, P., (ed.), *From Judaism to Christianity: Tradition and Transition* (Leiden: Brill, 2010)

Ward, A., 'Jerome's Work on the Psalter,' *ExpT* 44 (1932), 87-92.

Watkin, E.L., 'The Mysticism of St. Augustine' in M.C. D'Arcy et al, *A Monument to St. Augustine*, 105-19.

Weston, A., 'Latin Satirical Writing Subsequent to Juvenal' (PhD thesis, Yale University, 1915).

White, C. (ed.), *Early Christian Lives* (London: Penguin, 1998).

Widdecombe, P., *The Fatherhood of God from Origen to Athanasius* (Rev. edn; Oxford: OUP, 2004).

Wiesen, D.S., *St. Jerome as a Satirist: A Study in Christian Latin Thought and Letters* (Ithaca: Cornell University Press, 1964).

Wilcox, P., 'John Calvin's Interpretation of Lamentations' in R.A. Parry and H.A. Thomas (eds), *Great Is Thy Faithfulness*, 125-30.

Wiles, M., *Archetypal Heresy: Arianism through the Centuries* (Oxford: Clarendon, 1996).

Wiles, M.F., *The Divine Apostle: The Interpretation of St. Paul's Epistles in the Early Church* (Cambridge: CUP, 1967).

—. *The Making of Christian Doctrine: A Study in the Principles of Early Doctrinal Development* (Cambridge: CUP, 1967).

Williams, D.H., *Evangelicals and Tradition: The Formative Influences of the Early Church* (Milton Keynes: Paternoster, 2005).

Williams, R., 'Origen' in G. Evans (ed.), *The First Christian Theologians* (Oxford: Blackwell, 2004), 132-42.

Wright, D. 'The Latin Fathers' in I. Hazlett (ed.), *Early Christianity: Origins and Evolution to A.D. 600* (London: SPCK, 1991), 148-62.

Wright T., *Scripture and the Authority of God* (2nd rev. edn; London, SPCK, 2013).

Young, F.M., *Biblical Exegesis and the Formation of Christian Culture* (Cambridge: CUP, 1997).

—. 'Interpretation of Scripture' in S.A. Harvey and D.G. Hunter (eds), *The Oxford Handbook of Early Christian Studies* (Oxford: OUP, 2008), 845-63.

—. and L. Ayres, A. Louth (eds), *The Cambridge History of Early Christian Literature* (Cambridge: CUP, 2004).

Adkin, N., 33, 107-108
Alexander, D.C., 28
Anatolios, K., 167, 168
Anson, P.F., 23, 64-65
Antin, P., 160
Arnheim, M.T.W., 149
Ayres, L., 19, 28

Barrett, M., 34
Bartholomew, C., 29
Bates, M., 17
Bauckham, R., 178
Béchard, D.P., 6
Beckwith, C., 9
BeDuhn, J.D., 30, 85
Beeley, C., 107, 108, 171-173, 173, 179-180, 181
Bettenson, H., 53-54
Bickerman, E., 55
Bird, M., 200
Blacketer, R.A., 191
Blackman, E.C., 85
Blowers, P.M., 27, 200
Bock, D.L., 26, 42
Bray, G., 18, 101
Bredero, A.H., 97, 110
Brent, A., 192, 193
Brown, D., 2, 7, 8, 16, 25, 50, 51, 98, 99, 104
Brown, P., 31, 36, 37, 86, 97, 102-104, 106, 114, 121, 122, 175-176
Brown, S.F., 56
Budge, E.A.W., 41
Burke, A.J., 23, 24
Burnett, C.C. jr., 8
Burton-Christie, D., 23
Butterworth, G.W., 80

Cain, A., 3, 18, 133, 138, 139, 142, 144-147, 149, 154-155, 156-157,

158, 159-160, 162-163, 186, 187, 192, 193, 194-196, 203
Cameron, J., 139, 140
Campenhausen, H. von, 23
Casiday, A., 13, 87, 112, 190-191, 200
Chadwick, H., 17, 35, 71, 72, 76, 84, 87, 98, 115, 121
Chapman, J., 46
Cheetham, N., 164
Childs, B.S., 51
Chrisope, T.A., 84
Clark, G., 198
Clark, M., 32
Clarke, E.A., 19, 33, 101
Crawford, M.R., 164, 166, 198
Cross, F.L., 56-57, 62
Crouzel, H., 12
Cummings, J.T., 90, 92, 93

Daley, B.E., 16, 151-152
Davids, P.H., 177-178
Deakle, D.W., 85
Den Boer, W., 49, 50
de Silva, D.A., 178
Dillon, J., 181
Drever, M., 26, 32
Driver, S., 110, 111
Dungan, D.L., 129

Edwards, M., 22, 25, 28, 43, 74, 83, 187, 191
Ehrman, B.D., 88, 170, 185
Elliott, C.J., 44, 54
Emory, G., 56
Ernest, J.D., 33
Evans, G.R., 12, 37, 96
Ewald, M.L., 69-70

Farkasfalvy, D., 49, 50, 153
Farrar, F., 42
Ferguson, E., 19, 27, 28, 37, 54, 74

Fontaine, J., 122
Fortin, E.F., 8
Foster, P., 74
Fowl, S., 29
Freeman, C., 2, 9, 25, 55, 56, 65,
    71, 72, 77, 80, 84, 93, 100, 101,
    104, 111, 118, 128, 131-132, 135,
    136, 137, 153, 155, 169, 171, 174,
    180, 181, 182, 191, 199, 200, 203
Frend, W.H., 18, 19
Fritz, A.X.J., 26, 42
Froehlich, K., 99
Fulford, B., 79
Fürst, A., 17

Gallagher, E.L., 76, 184-186, 196
Gamble, H.Y., 35
Geisler, N.L., 43
George, T., 28
Gibson, D., 187
Gibson, J., 187
Glaser, M., 26, 42
González, J.L., 6
Gräbe, P.J., 84
Grafton, A., 2, 15, 16, 175
Grant, R.M., 74, 166, 167
Graves, M., 76, 129-130, 152-153,
    182, 189, 199-200
Gray, C., 175, 183
Green, B.G., 36, 37, 85
Green, M.E., 178-179
Greenslade, S.L., 28
Greer, R., 29
Gregg, R.C., 18
Gribomont, J., 100, 101
Grillmeier, A., 93-94, 95
Groh, D.E., 18
Grützmacher, G., 83, 113

Hagendahl, H., 83, 84, 131
Hahn, S.W., 6, 84
Hahnenberg, E.J., 5, 122, 133
Hall, C.A., 13, 17, 19
Hall, S.G., 13, 15

Hanson, R.P.C., 9
Harmon, S.R., 119, 120
Harnack, A., 72
Harries, J., 37
Harrison, C., 15, 32, 198
Harrison, N.V., 91
Hartmann, L.N., 50, 51
Hauser, A.J., 3
Harvey, P., 111, 112
Haykin, M.A.G., 191
Hayward, C.T.R., 99
Hayward, R., 104-105, 108
Heimann, D.F., 90, 92, 93
Hilderbrand, S.M., 21
Helm, R., 152
Hill, C.E., 85
Hill, R.C., 64, 91
Hofer, A., 187, 188, 189
Hoffmann, R.J., 84, 85
Hollingsworth, M., 28, 30
Holmes, M., 29
Horton, M.S., 29
Hulley, K., 48-49, 91
Humfress, C., 198
Humphries, Jr., T.L., 187
Hunt, T., 173, 174
Hunter, D.G., 33, 120, 121, 122,
    133
Hwang, A., 28

Insley, M., 20

Jardine, L., 109
Jeanrond, W.G., 35
Jensen, 114
Johnson, P., 113
Jones, C.P., 21

Kamesar, A., 137, 196-197
Kannengiesser, C., 10
Karamanolis, G., 15, 20
Keddar-Kopfstein, B., 75-76, 89,
    140
Keith, C., 199

Kelhoffer, J.A.,　24
Kelly, J.F.,　31, 33
Kelly, J.N.D.,　2, 21, 22, 23, 24, 39,
　70, 88-90, 91, 92, 93, 94, 95, 96,
　100, 101, 104, 132, 158, 202, 207
Kelly, M.J.,　43
Kolben, P.R.,　32
Komoszewski, J.E.,　51
Köstenberger, A.J.,　7
Kreider, A.,　114
Kruger, M.J.,　7, 85, 122, 123, 176-
　177, 177, 179
Kugel, J.,　29

Lampe, G.W.H.,　77
Lane, A.N.S.,　17
Lauro, E.D.,　16
Lawler, T.C.,　63-64, 66
Layton, R.,　116
Leclercg, J.,　64
Leithart, P.J.,　35
Lennox-Conyngham, A.,　186
Letham, R.,　2, 17, 21, 31, 32
Lieu, S.N.C.,　33
Lightfoot, J.B.,　8, 83
Lister, R.,　13
Litfin, B.,　18, 20
Loewe, R.,　54-55
Logan, A.,　63
Lossky, A.,　13
Lössl, J.,　2, 3, 15, 18, 138, 139,
　143-144, 186, 203
Louth, A.,　21, 66, 135
Ludlow, M.,　2, 6, 16, 101
Lundberg, M.D.,　12
Lyman, J.R.,　19
Lynch, J.H.,　2

MacDonald, S.,　32
Macmullen, R.,　43
Magee, D.B.,　29
Marcus, R.A.,　113, 114, 130
Mathisen, R.,　139, 141-142
McCann, C.,　184

McGrath, E.A.,　40
McGuckin, J.,　1, 9, 25, 27, 45, 46,
　47, 54, 55, 56, 60, 65, 67, 72, 73,
　77, 80, 89, 95, 98, 100, 107, 111,
　112, 123, 130, 133, 135, 136, 157,
　189, 203
McLynn, N.B.,　30, 36
McMahon, R.,　31
Meinardus, O.F.A.,　41, 87
Meredith, A.,　21
Metzger, B.M.,　90-91
Mierow, C.,　48, 55, 56
Mohr, A.,　130-131, 132, 133
Monceaux, P.,　23
Moorhead, J.,　54
Murphy, J.J.,　42, 50
Murphy, F.X.,　5
Myers, J.A.,　182

Neeley, S.D.,　29, 35
Neil, B.,　200
Nightingale, A.,　167, 169, 170
Norris, F.W.,　200
Norris, R.A.,　27, 28
Novembri, V.,　159-160, 162
Nugent, P.,　154

O'Connell, J.P.,　135
O'Connell, R.,　32
O'Donnell, J.,　127-128, 129
O'Keefe, J.J.,　14
Old, H.O.,　3
Oldfather, W.A.,　49
O'Meara, J.J.,　31
Orlinsky, H.M.,　140

Pabel, H.M.,　159-160
Paget, J.C.,　187
Pahl, M.,　200
Papadogiannakis, Y.,　52
Papandrea, J.L.,　71, 101, 166-167
Parvis, S.,　74
Patton, C.,　26
Payton, Jr., J.R.,　27

Peake, A.S.,   46
Pecknold, C.C.,   28
Pelikan, J.,   84-85, 86, 121
Pence, M.A.,   66
Penna, A.,   63
Piper, J.,   33
Plantinga, R.J.,   12, 32
Plumer, E.,   158
Pope Benedict XVI,   2
Pope, H.,   45
Price, R.,   33, 35, 36, 97, 205

Quasten, J.,   62-63, 89, 100

Ramsey, B.,   34, 111
Rapp, C.,   123-126
Raspanti, G.,   139
Raymond, R.,   70
Rebenich, S.,   3, 5, 6, 14, 21, 22, 23,
   24, 26, 27, 27, 37, 41, 45, 50, 62,
   65, 71, 76, 86, 99, 103, 104, 106,
   107, 108, 113, 115, 126, 132, 139,
   146, 147, 149, 165, 173, 174-175,
   180, 183, 193-194, 198, 203
Rengers, C.,   2
Reno, R.R.,   14
Rétif, A.,   23
Reynolds, P.L.,   33
Rich, A.D.,   66, 87
Richards, J.,   54
Richardson, A.,   39
Roach, W.C.,   43
Rombs, R.,   28, 93
Rosenberg, H.,   120, 121
Rotelle, J.E.,   31
Rutherford, W.,   133-134
Rousseau, P.,   5, 52, 87

Salzman, M.R.,   21
Sandwell, I.,   198
Sawyer, M.J.,   51
Schaper, J.,   187
Schatkin, M.A.,   83, 99

Scheck, T.P.,   14, 135, 136-138,
   154, 157
Schemann, A.,   13
Schwab, G.,   63
Schwarz, W.,   55
Semple, W.H.,   67-68
Sheppard, G.T.,   40-41
Simon, R.,   136
Simonetti, M.,   138, 156
Skehan, P.W.,   51
Soulen, R.N.,   16
Souter, A.,   44, 45, 46, 136
Sparks, H.F.D.,   42, 57, 58, 62
Sparks, K.,   33
Stander, H.F.,   70
Stark, R.,   164, 172
Steenberg, I.M.C.,   181
Steinhauser, K.B.,   31
Steinmann, J.,   55, 56, 88
Stevenson, J.,   55
Stevenson, K.,   134, 135
Stewart, C.,   91, 114
Still, T.D.,   187
Stroumsa, G.G.,   124
Stylianopoulos, T.G.,   14, 15, 17
Sutcliffe, E.F.,   77-79, 80, 81, 82
Swidler, L.,   6

Teske, R.,   28
Testa, R.L.,   115
Theokritoff, E.,   19, 20
Thiselton, A.C.,   40-41
Thomas, L.M.,   29
Thompson, T.R.,   12
Toom, T.,   28, 43
Trigg, J.W.,   14, 36
Turner, H.E.W,   12, 52

Unger, D.,   181

Valantasis, R.,   91
Vermes, G.,   170, 171

Vessey, M.,   2, 5, 109, 120, 129,
    133, 139, 142, 143, 146, 192, 193,
    193, 198-199
Veyne, P.,   75
von Campenhausen, H.,   65, 67, 71,
    87, 88

Walker, W.,   41, 42, 143
Wallace, D.B.,   51
Wallace-Hadrill, S.,   43
Walsh, L.G.,   33
Ward, A.,   47
Watkin, E.L.,   32
Watson, D.F.,   3
Wei, S.L.,   164, 165
Weston, A.,   66
Whidden III, D.L.,   56
Widdicombe, P.,   22
Wiesen, D.S.,   65, 66-67
Wiles, M.,   5, 8, 28, 70, 72, 73, 74,
    75, 130
Wilhite, D.E.,   187
Wilken, R.,   175
Williams, D.H.,   17, 19, 25, 26, 175
Williams, H.,   203
Williams, M.H.,   2, 3, 5, 145, 146,
    148
Williams, R.,   15, 16
Wright, D.,   30, 115
Wright, F.A.,   47-48
Wright, N.T.,   8
Young, F.M.,   7, 31, 187, 189-190

Ageruchia, 117-118

Ambrose, 13n.8, 13n.9, 23n.61, 43, 55, 63, 107, 108, 111, 115, 115n.63, 119, 119n.83, 120, 120n.88, 121, 124n.115, 128, 129, 135n.176, 146, 147, 170, 172, 186n.203, 191, 199, 199n.283, 206

Ambrosiaster, 129, 140n.210, 155n.25, 158

Amphilochius, 108n.11

Antony, 112n.40

Appollinaris of Laodicea, 106n.5, 140n.210, 154n.22

Aquinas, Thomas, 8, 56n.94, 118, 157n.36

Aristotle, 118

Arius, 18, 19, 22, 22n.54, 70, 171

Artemia, 116

Asella, 139, 139n.202

Athanasius, 13n.7, 13n.9, 17n.24, 70, 91n.138, 152n.3, 168, 172, 179, 185, 206

Athenagoras, 12

Augustine, 3, 7, 8, 8n.24, 10, 11, 12n.1, 12n.3, 13n.7, 13n.8, 13n.9, 14n.11, 17n.24, 20, 22, 23n.61, 26, 26n.82, 27-38, 43, 47, 51n.71, 55, 56n.94, 69, 70, 72, 73, 73n.24, 75, 76, 83, 85n.98, 86, 91n.138, 93n.153, 94, 95, 96, 98, 106, 107, 113, 114, 116, 120n.88, 121, 122, 126, 128, 128n.138, 129, 129n.138, 131n.150, 135, 135n.176, 136, 141n.218, 142, 143, 143n.233, 146, 147, 151, 152, 152n.3, 154, 155, 157n.36, 158, 165n.86, 169-170, 170n.113, 172, 176, 177, 177, 179, 181, 182, 182n.183,

186n.203, 190, 193, 199, 200, 203, 206

Barrabanus, 44

Basil of Ancrya, 173n.128

Basil of Caesarea, 42, 108n.11, 124n.115, 168

Basil the Great, 13n.9, 21, 23n.61

Bernard of Clairvaux, 13n.14

Calvin, John, 8, 157n.36

Cassian, John, 64, 114, 114n.57, 129, 187

Celsus, 193

Chromatius, 70

Chrysostom, John, 13n.9, 23n.61, 56n.94, 73n.26, 124, 125

Cicero, 47n.45, 48, 55, 83, 165, 197

Claudianus of Gaul, 142n.223

Clement of Alexandria, 12, 49, 50, 95n.175, 119n.83, 124, 124n.115, 125, 170, 177, 178n.158, 179n.165

Clement of Rome, 12

Commodion, 57n.101

Constantine, Emperor, 164, 165n.86, 172, 205

Cromasius, Bishop, 206

Ctesiphon, 190

Cyprian, 126, 167n.99, 192

Cyril of Alexandria, 13n.7, 151, 166, 172, 198, 205

Cyril of Jerusalem, 95

Cyril of Scythopolis, 64n.153

Damasus, Pope, 78, 93n.154, 98, 168, 169, 169n.108

Demetrias, 148-149, 184

Didymus the Blind, 17n.24, 56n.94, 62, 89, 89n.123, 106n.5, 115, 119n.80, 119n.83, 140n.210, 154n.22

Eleutheropolis, 174
Epiphanius of Salamis, 106n.5, 178
Erasmus, 106, 109, 143, 143n.228, 143n.229
Evagrius, 107n.10, 112n.40, 119n.83, 190, 190n.225, 191
Eucherius of Lyon, 192
Eusebius, 53, 70
Eusebius of Caesarea, 81, 106n.5, 170, 171, 172, 178n.158, 179, 193, 198-199, 206
Eusebius of Cremona, 56, 136, 137
Eusebius of Emesa, 106n.5, 140n.210, 154n.22, 155
Eustochium, Julia, 120, 131, 160n.52, 176n.148, 184, 194

Fabiola, 125n.118, 161
Faustus of Gaul, 142n.223
Fortunctus, Venantius, 122
Furia, 147

Gratian, 86
Gregory of Nazianzus, 13n.7, 13n.9, 23n.61, 107, 107n.11, 108, 119n.83, 172, 179, 180, 180n.171, 187-189, 206
Gregory of Nyssa, 13n.7, 13n.9, 23n.61, 107n.10, 108n.11, 119n.83, 172, 206
Gregory of Thammaturgus, 57n.101
Gregory the Great, 13n.9, 15n.14, 23n.61, 49n.59, 54n.86, 121, 135n.176
Grosseteste, Robert, 157n.36

Heliodorus, 124, 125, 125n.117, 180, 206
Hilarionis, 173-175
Hilary of Poitiers, 93, 96, 129, 134, 172, 191
Hippolytus, Sextus Julius Africanus, 57n.101, 106n.5
Hume, David, 75n.34

Ignatius of Antioch, 12, 53
Irenaeus, 12, 27, 27n.83, 29, 74, 87, 90n.136, 152n.3, 170, 177, 181

John of Jerusalem, 126
John of Lycopolis, 112n.40
Josephus, 55, 58, 137
Jovinian, 114, 120, 121n.97, 146
Julian of Eclanum, 32, 193
Justin Martyr, 12, 134

Leo of Rome, 172
Luther, Martin, 8, 106, 143-144, 157n.36

Malchus, 183
Marcella, 133, 139, 139n.202, 146, 150, 156, 162
Marcellus, 172, 176n.146
Marcion of Sinope, 84n.94, 85
Martin of Tours, 165n.86
Maximus, 116
Melania, 65
Melitius, 168
Melito of Sardis, 57n.101
Methodies of Olympus, 57n.101
Minncius, Felix, 57n.101

Nepotian, 108, 180n.171, 181
Nicholas of Lyra, 25
Novatian, 57n.101, 166-167

Origen, 3, 7, 7n.21, 8, 8n.24, 10, 11, 12, 12n.3, 13, 14-27, 37, 49,

49n.59, 52, 53, 54, 56n.94, 57, 59, 62n.136, 69, 71n.8, 72, 73, 73n.20, 74, 75, 79, 79n.61, 83, 84, 89, 90, 93, 94, 99, 101, 103, 104, 106, 119n.83, 120n.92, 124n.115, 125, 126, 128, 133, 137, 140n.210, 146, 153n.11, 154n.22, 156, 163, 166, 170, 171-172, 175, 176, 177, 179, 179n.165, 192, 205

Pachomius, 87n.108
Palladius, 41, 86
Pammachius, 80, 127n.131, 150, 176n.146
Pamphilius, 172
Pantaenus, 57n.101
Papius, 58, 199n.283
Paula, 162-163, 162n.67, 163n.75, 163n.77, 176n.148, 194-196
Paulinus of Nola, 86, 113n.52, 122, 150
Pelagius, 31, 31n.99, 32, 33, 33n.111, 86, 91n.139, 95, 146, 147, 157n.36, 158
Peter of Alexandria, 71
Pierius, 57n.101, 172
Plato, 197
Pliny, 47n.45
Polycorp, 57n.101, 58
Porphyry, 193
Praetextatus, 131-132
Principia, 147
Prudentius, 129
Pseudo-Dionysius, 56n.94

Quadratus, Aristo of Pella, 57n.101
Quintilian, 84

Rufinus of Aquilea, 53-54, 71n.8, 89, 132n.160, 147, 185, 185n.196

Rusticus, 116-117

Sallust, 83
Salvina, 147
Seneca, 47n.45, 193
Siricius, 120n.88, 127n.131
Sophocles, 197
Spinoza, 75n.34
Syrus, Ephraem, 54

Tatian, 87n.110
Terence, 83, 156
Tertullian, 12, 53, 66n.165, 73n.26, 74, 85, 88, 97, 102, 102n.214, 106n.5, 121n.96, 124, 124n.115, 126, 134, 160, 165n.86, 167n.99, 178n.158, 192
Theodoret of Cyprus, 64n.149, 200
Theodore of Mopsuestia, 52
Theodorus of Heraclea, 106n.5, 154n.22
Theodosius, Emperor, 43, 71, 145, 193, 193n.241
Theophilus of Antioch, 57n.101, 167, 167n.101, 167n.102
Tranquillus, 193n.241

Vergil, 83
Victorinus, Marius, 36n.126, 57n.101, 106n.5, 129, 140n.210, 155n.25, 158
Vigilantius, 86n.103, 98

ambition,   78

asceticism,   3, 6n.16, 23, 36, 39, 47, 65, 86, 110-111, 114n.54, 123, 169-170, 173

biblical interpretation,   12

biblical scholar,   5, 9, 46, 47, 51, 53, 58-59, 104, 133-134, 146, 154, 156, 162, 169, 175, 184, 195, 196-197, 201

bishops, on,   180-181

character,   2, 78

churchmanship,   39

comedy, and,   183

conflicts,   3, 4

cosmology,   48

creativity,   56, 135, 137, 169, 183, 197, 199

divergence from Origen,   18-27

education,   47, 154, 162

emotions, and,   116-117

eschatology,   95, 119-120, 135

exegete (exegesis),   1, 3, 4, 6, 7n.21, 9, 10, 11, 15, 24, 27, 36, 39, 46, 50, 54, 56, 61, 63, 67, 68, 71, 74, 76, 77, 78-80, 83, 89, 92, 95, 100, 104, 106-107, 109, 110, 123, 130, 133, 143, 153, 156-157, 203

Hebraica Veritas,   1, 42, 42n.12, 49-50, 60, 185, 202, 203

Hebrew, and,   39, 44, 111, 129, 138, 140, 152-153, 159, 175, 206

Hebrew Psalter,   47

humanism,   39

inconsistency,   52

invective, and,   39, 48, 164

legacy,   39

misogyny,   161-162

monastic ideals,   3

monastic vocation,   25, 47, 64

Old Testament, and the,   152-153

originality,   1, 9, 10, 11, 21, 25, 45, 53, 56, 59, 107

orthodoxy,   37, 71, 71n.8, 96, 168, 169

patronage,   3, 104, 112n.40, 148, 162-163, 180

philosophy,   39, 155

polemics,   2, 25

propaganda,   144-147

reputation,   1

rhetoric,   124, 125

scholar, as,   30, 37. 44, 67, 71, 73, 108, 111-112

sexual awkwardness,   6n.16

sexuality,   33, 35, 47

theology (theologian),   4, 8, 11, 21

union with Origen,   14-18

universalism,   120

virginity,   47, 48, 114n.54

works
Against Helvidius,   35
Against Jovian,   85n.100, 92, 103, 120, 121n.94
Against Rufinus,   154, 165, 171
Against Vigilantius,   86n.103, 98
commentaries,   2, 7, 46, 46n.38, 56, 57, 61, 72, 78, 81, 91, 98-99, 119, 123, 136, 146, 153; Commentary on Amos, 161n.57, Commentary on Daniel, 176n.146, Commentary on Ecclesiastes, 90, Commentary o Ephesians, 62, 89, 90, 94, 101, 103, 104, 158, 173, Commentary on Galatians, 16, 62, 72n.17, 73, 74, 83, 90, 126-127, 140, 154-158,

Commentary on Isaiah, 94, 112, 120, 161, 162, 164,
Commentary on Matthew, 56, 94, 136-138, *Commentary on Obadiah*, 24, *Commentary on Philemon*, 73, 94, 176-177, 176n.148, *Commentary on Romans*, 74n.30, *Commentary on the Gospel of John*, 166, *Commentary on Zachariah*, 119n.80
Epitaph on Paula, 194-195
Hebrew Questions, 104, 105
homilies, 2, 69-70, 135n.178; *Homily* 75, 70, *Homily* 76, 69, *Homily* 80, 70
letters, 2, 18, 20, 23, 24, 32-33, 33n.109, 39, 45, 47-48, 63-64, 66, 75, 82n.76, 83, 84, 86, 109, 135n.178, 139, 141-142, 144-147, 148-149, 150, 159-160, 162, 168, 182, 184, 188, 206; *Letter* 2, 145, *Letter* 4, 23, *Letter* 10, 166, *Letter* 14, 124, 125, 187, 187n.211, *Letter* 15, 21-22, 70-71, 168, *Letter* 21, 45, *Letter* 22, 64, 85n.100, 102n.218, 103, 108, 120, 131, 132, 160n.52, 165, 184, *Letter* 24, 139, *Letter* 42, 166, *Letter* 46 114, *Letter* 52, 180, 180n.171, 181, 188, *Letter* 53, 52, *Letter* 54, 147, *Letter* 56, 94, *Letter* 57, 80, 81, 81n.72, *Letter* 60, 84, *Letter* 65, 147, *Letter* 70, 131, *Letter* 75, 104, *Letter* 77, 161, *Letter* 79, 147, *Letter* 102, 94, *Letter* 106, 94, *Letter* 108, 161, 163, 194-196, *Letter* 112, 55n.88, 94, 182n.180, *Letter* 115, 94, 182, *Letter* 120, 94n.160, *Letter* 122, 116-117, *Letter* 123, 102n.216, 117-118, *Letter* 125, 82, 159,

Letter 127, 139, *Letter* 128, 154, *Letter* 130, 115, 148-149, 161, 184, *Letter* 133, 112n.40, 191
Letter to Pammachius, 127
Life of Hilarionis, 173, 173n.131, 173n.132, 174, 175
Life of Hilary, 151
Life of Malchus, 175, 182-183
Life of Paul, the, 112n.40, 175
On Illustrious Men, 109, 166, 178, 189, 192, 193, 193n.241, 200
Pachomian Rule, 62, 87
Prologus Galeatus, 151, 182, 185
translations, 2, 3, 26, 39, 41, 43, 45, 53-54, 55, 57, 58, 59, 67-68, 77, 80-81, 88, 89, 100, 119, 126, 140, 152, 155, 189
treatises, 39
Vulgate, the, 2, 7, 39, 45, 46, 48-49, 51, 51n.71, 56, 58, 68, 76, 82n.76, 129n.140, 136, 139-140, 196, 197, 200, 204

Scripture Index

Genesis
1:1   134
4:10   110
31:47   81

Deuteronomy
18:21   81
21:23   141

Psalms
1   54
2:9   81
6:5   165
22:1   81
71:12   81

Proverbs
10:1   181
22:20   79, 79n.61

Isaiah   112
3:7   34
5:1-7   110
6   17
8:14   123
9:6   198
9:14   123
22:6   153
23:4   153
29:11   166
37:21-22   121

Jeremiah   112
6:2-3   153
27:1   129-130

Ezekiel   112
1:3   54n.86

Amos
6:12-15   161

Matthew
3:15   138
5:48   32
18:8-9   73
19:12   73
19:15   110
20:28   191
21:33-43   110

Mark
1:1-12   70
1:13-31   69
4:30-43   134-135
15:40   178

Luke
6:1   188

John
7:53–8:11   199
14:27   198
19:25   178

Acts
15   177

Romans
1:16   42n.12
11:25-26   120

1 Corinthians
9:19   73
14:1-33   181
15:17   177

Galatians
1:16   74
2   182n.183
2:6   158

2:11-14   36n.124,
    37, 126, 140,
    151, 182
2:14   158
3:13   95n.172
3:13-14   141
4:29   73
5:4-12   73
5:12   73
6:11   155

Ephesians
4:31   110

1 Timothy
3   124n.115

Titus
1:5-9   123

1 Peter
1:4   181

Subject Index

Alexandrian School, the, 7, 7n.21, 49, 51, 62

Antiochene School, the, 7, 7n.21, 49, 51, 100

apatheia, 189, 190

Apocrypha, the, 176, 177, 184, 185

Apostle's Creed, the, 27n.83

Arianism, 18, 20, 70, 108, 168

ascetic movement, the, (asceticism), 2, 29, 30, 66n.167, 85, 86, 103, 149, 169-170, 187

atonement, the, 191

baptism, 95-96, 95n.175

Bible, the, 14, 18, 42-43, 76, 92, 94, 153, 196, 203; inerrancy of, 94, 95

biblical interpretation, 35

catholicism, 85

Catholic theology, 6

celibacy, 35, 86, 102, 103, 120, 190

chastity, 116-117, 149

Christ, 6, 7n.21, 9, 20, 22n.55, 23n.58, 32, 34, 49, 50, 54, 56, 93, 103, 125, 143n.233, 152, 174, 188-189; deity of, 9, 18-19, 22n.55, 153, holy, 85, humanity of, 93-94, incarnation, and, 206, *logos* (Word), 70, 188, 192, '**our Preacher**', 29n.93, Saviour, 70, sonship, 17, 19, 70-71, 93, suffering, 93

Christian literacy, 2

Christian identity, 1, 12, 19, 106, 113, 173

Christian orthodoxy, 1, 12, 13, 17, 17n.27, 19

Christology, 188-189, 191, 205

Church, 7n.21, 18, 35

Church Fathers, the, 5

Constantinople Creed, the, 121

cosmological doctrine, 20

Council of Alexandria, the, 22n.54

Council of Carthage, the, 176, 177

Council of Chalcedon, the, 171

Council of Constantinople, the, 9, 13, 19

Council of Hippo, the, 176, 177, 184

Council of Laodicea, the, 176

Council of Nicaea, the, 9, 19, 19n.37, 22n.54, 70, 93, 101

Council of Rimini, the, 171, 172

Council of Sardica, the, 164

Council of Trent, the, 136

cult of the saints, the, 97

Dated Creed, the, 19

devil, the, 17, 65, 116

divine truth, 8

Donatists (ism), 28, 36

Ebionites, 170n.115

Epistle of Barnabas, the, 170

faith, 72, 94, 95, 143n.233, 147, 158

Fall, the, 1, 20, 35, 95, 202

filioque, 121

Gnosticism, 27n.83, 30

God, eternal, 22, Father, 9, grace of, 24, 31, 31n.99, 32, 34, 72, 95, 143, 158, Judge, 165, mercy of, 95, impassivity, 190-191, incomprehensible, 21, unapproachable, 21

gospel, the, 70

Greek philosophy, 15

heaven, 70

hell, 70

Hexapla, the, 15-16, 18, 70

240

Holy Spirit, the,   17, 62, 69, 70, 73, 75, 82, 95, 121, 121n.96, 166, 187
homoousios,   9, 19, 19n.37, 22n.54, 171
human freedom,   31, 32, 34
hypostasis,   7, 22, 22n.54, 167-168

Jewish traditions,   3
John the Baptist,   23-24, 23n.61

law of God, the,   52, 70

Manichees,   28, 30, 36, 37
marriage,   35, 85, 86
McGuckin-Freeman thesis,   1, 9, 10, 66, 69, 74, 88, 100, 108, 115, 135, 159, 186, 197, 202, 203, 204, 207
mission,   14, 49
monasticism,   66n.167, 86

Neoplatonists,   29-30, 31, 37
nepotism,   126
Nicene Creed, the,   9, 13, 21, 27n.83, 169
Nicene orthodoxy,   1, 9, 13, 21, 22, 69, 71, 76, 77, 89, 101, 191, 202, 205

Origenism,   20
original sin,   24, 31, 32, 32n.106, 95, 96
ousia,   9, 19, 167-168

paganism,   3, 43, 46, 86, 113
Pelagians (ism),   28, 31, 31n.99, 36, 95, 143
piety,   13, 20, 22
Platonism,   20
predestination,   31, 34
propassio,   116-117

repentance,   116-117
resurrection,   13, 17, 102n.214

rhetoric,   106
rule of faith, the,   27, 29, 49, 138

salvation,   20, 31, 32, 34, 35, 95, 101-102, 148n.267
sanctification,   190
self-restraint,   117
Septuagint, the,   14, 16, 55, 67, 70, 140, 141, 196
scripture,   6-7, 12, 34, 50, 82, 176,
scriptural authority,   2
sexuality,   6, 102
sin,   1, 72, 95n.175, 96, 101, 187, 202

transfiguration, the,   1, 134, 202, 206
Trinity, the,   1, 19, 21, 70, 71n.7, 135, 168, 202, 206

virgin birth,   85
virginity,   85, 86, 102, 111, 120, 189, 190

widowhood,   117
Word, the,   20, 22, 43, 166, 187, 192

ND - #0082 - 090625 - C0 - 229/152/14 - PB - 9781780781785 - Gloss Lamination